AF412474

Revolution in the House

Revolution in the House

FAMILY, CLASS, AND
INHERITANCE IN SOUTHERN
FRANCE, 1775–1825

Margaret H. Darrow

PRINCETON UNIVERSITY PRESS
PRINCETON, NEW JERSEY

Copyright © 1989 by Princeton University Press
Published by Princeton University Press, 41 William Street,
Princeton, New Jersey 08540
In the United Kingdom: Princeton University Press, Oxford

Darrow, Margaret H., 1950–
Revolution in the house : family, class, and inheritance in Southern France, 1775–1825 /
    Margaret H. Darrow.
p.   cm.
Bibliography: p.
Includes index.
ISBN 0-691-05562-9 (alk. paper)
1. Montauban (Tarn-et-Garonne, France)—History.   2. France—History—Revolution,
    1789–1799—Influence.   3. Family—France—Montauban (Tarn-et-Garonne)—
    History.   4. Inheritance and succession—France—Montauban (Tarn-et-Garonne)—
    History.
I. Title.
DC801.M76D37   1989
944'.75—dc20   89-4028
                                                                                              CIP

This book has been composed in Linotron Galliard

Printed in the United States of America by Princeton University Press
Princeton, New Jersey

TO MARION G. DARROW

In loving memory

Contents

Illustrations

Tables

Acknowledgments

THIS PROJECT has been a long one, beginning in Philip Greven's graduate seminar on family history at Rutgers University in 1974, growing into a doctoral dissertation, branching off into an article and several papers, and finally reaching maturity in this book. Much of the development was delightful, some of it painful, and all of it challenging; I am glad it is finished. But I would never have reached this point without the generous support, encouragement, and inspiration of many institutions and individuals. Thanks to a French government grant awarded through the Fulbright-Hayes Program, a grant from the American Council of Learned Societies, and a Dartmouth Faculty Fellowship, I was able to spend the better part of two years in France, working in Montauban's lovely archives. A Rutgers University Fellowship and Dartmouth Faculty Research Grants allowed me to learn to use the computer, hire research assistance, and prepare the final manuscript.

But financial assistance is only one type of support. I have also incurred numerous debts of a different sort to my advisers, professors, colleagues, students, and friends first in the Rutgers History Department, where I was a graduate student, and then in the Dartmouth History Department, where I have taught for the past eight years. Special thanks go to Larry Levine for his unfailing comprehension of my computer problems, his helpful advice, and his prompt and efficient solutions; to my research assistant, Mariken Straub, for her virtually flawless coding of notary documents; to Wendy Sussman and Daniel Baudin, who have cheerfully (and repeatedly) provided me with bed and board in Paris; to Jim Wright for the long-term loan of his microfilm reader; to cartographer, Tim Burdick; and to Gail Patten for her unflagging all-around assistance. My colleagues in the Dartmouth History Department, including three department chairs, Jere Daniel, Marysa Navarro, and Ken Shewmaker, and especially my fellow Europeanists David Roberts, Charlie Wood, Michael Ermarth, David Lagomarsino, and Heide Whelan, have supported my work in innumerable ways, even to the extent of rearranging their own research and teaching plans to facilitate mine. The staff of Baker Library has been another fountain of assistance, especially Patricia Carter, Genevieve Williamson, William McEwen, and John Crane. Teaching French history and social history and discussing ideas with students and reading their work have nourished my own intellectual growth. Among the many Dartmouth students whose ideas have fed my own are Beth Johnson, Daniel Katzir, Marilyn Gisser, and Robert Shen.

I was fortunate in my choice of French departmental archives. The archives of the Department of the Tarn-et-Garonne, under the direction of Mlle La Forgue, is small, personal, and superbly organized and catalogued. I owe special thanks to Mme Badou for her friendly assistance and to M. Balanzar, who microfilmed hundreds of documents for me. I also enjoyed the collegiality of the Amis des Archives du Tarn-et-Garonne, especially Mme Anne Katz.

I was also fortunate in my choice of a press. The editors at Princeton, Joanna Hitchcock, Deborah Tegarden, Janet Stern, and Dalia Lipkin, have been unfailingly helpful and efficient. I am especially grateful to Joanna Hitchcock, whose encouraging letters came at just the right times to boost my flagging energies.

Collegial groups have been an important source of inspiration and support, challenging me and helping me refine my approach and my conclusions. I am grateful for the sustaining professional and sisterly support of the Berkshire Conference of Women Historians, the Dartmouth Feminist Inquiry Seminar, and the Bishop House Women's Conspiracy, now, alas, defunct. Special thanks to Suzanne Lebsock, Ellen Mappen, Amy Richlin, and Bea Gottlieb, to my fellow Dartmouth *dix-huitièmistes* Virginia Swain and Susanne Zantop, and to my library corridor-mate, Dan Goldstein.

Then there are people without whose friendship scholarship would be a barren and joyless enterprise: Judy Stern Anderson and Margot Leah Anderson, Joan Hummel, Suzanne Brown, Kevin Reinhart, Deborah King, Janice and Chuck Hardy, Bruce and Donna Nelson, and Kathleen Higgins. My dissertation advisers, Mary Hartman and John R. Gillis, deserve special thanks for their repeated investments of time, energy, and ideas and for their long-term friendship and support. Finally, behind every book, there is a family. Mine includes my aunt Elizabeth Fouchaux and especially my sister Sarah T. Darrow, who edits my manuscripts as well as listens to my problems. It is to my mother, however, that I owe the most; this book is dedicated to her memory.

Revolution in the House

CHAPTER ONE

The Revolution in French Inheritance Law

I do not know, Gentlemen, how one can reconcile the new French constitution, which in all aspects follows from the great principles of political equality, with a law which permits a father, a mother to forget these sacred principles of natural equality with regard to their own children. . . . There are no longer eldest sons, no longer privileged persons in the great national family; there must be none in the small families of which it is composed.[1]

So wrote Mirabeau, the great politician and legislator of the French Revolution's early years. In the spring of 1791 he was to introduce a bill into the National Assembly that would change French civil law to provide for the equal inheritance rights of all children. Although not Mirabeau's best effort, the speech bore the mark of the master orator, lucidly stripping the question to its essentials and forcefully applying Enlightenment doctrines to answer it. To the equality of individuals in the family as in the state, he fused a second theme: the family as the school of virtue and citizenship.

A system of perfect equality within families [would produce] uncountable domestic advantages . . . the natural bonds which would unite fathers to their children, children to their fathers, . . . the tender and sincere expressions of that natural penchant for love, respect and gratitude.

Equal inheritance, he argued, would reform the family and thereby reform the individual and the state.

Mirabeau's speech resolved two currents of Enlightenment thought

---

[1] *Moniteur Universel* (Paris), April 5, 1791. Although Talleyrand, who gave the speech, attributed it to Mirabeau, like most of Mirabeau's productions it was probably a joint effort. In the spring of 1791 Mirabeau was on his deathbed. In his memoirs, Dumont, one of Mirabeau's speechwriters, speculated that Reybaz had actually written the speech and moralized over Mirabeau's willingness to clothe himself in "borrowed glory" even to the last. It seems likely that, despite his painful illness, Mirabeau had followed his standard practice of outlining the main points he wanted to make and then reworking the draft his writers produced. According to Talleyrand, Mirabeau was lucid and working almost until his death. After one particularly bad spasm, he gave Talleyrand the text of the speech, calling it his "testament." Probably Talleyrand edited it further since he had acted as Mirabeau's editor in the past. See Etienne Dumont, *Souvenirs sur Mirabeau et sur les deux premières assemblées législatives* (Paris: Librairie de Charles Gosselin, 1832), pp. 308–310; Oliver J. G. Welch, *Mirabeau; A Study of a Democratic Monarchist* (London: Cape, 1951), pp. 144, 211–212.

about the family into a single, sweeping reform. One was a critique of hierarchical relationships in the family on the bases of natural law and individual rights, and the other was an attack on authority from the perspective of love and personal happiness. According to Mirabeau's argument, equal inheritance would promote the growth of equality and of mutual affection within families.[2]

Historians have identified the eighteenth century as a period of transition in Western European familial relationships. Although the nuclear family, consisting of the married couple and their unmarried children, dates from at least the Middle Ages, the dynamics of this durable institution have changed over time. In early modern Europe, most families were hierarchical and authoritarian. All power rested with the husband/father and duty regulated relationships. Love was supposed to reinforce duty, to make it joyful rather than grudging, but duty, not love, was the glue that held families together. In the eighteenth century, the priorities of duty and love shifted. The family was to be a place where love was not dutiful but passionate and demonstrative, and marriage was to create a lifetime companionship welded by esteem, tenderness, and sexual attraction. Children were accorded rights as well as duties so that fathers were no longer to rule but only to persuade with affection, reason, and good example. Between individuals united by affection and mutual respect, duties became labors of love. With all its psychological benefits and costs, the romantic, egalitarian family was born.[3]

Yet for Mirabeau, the main purpose of equal inheritance was not to assail patriarchal families or to strengthen egalitarian ones; it was to regenerate the body politic. Historian Lawrence Stone has identified three successive philosophies of family in Western Europe since the Middle Ages: the lineage, the patriarchal family, and finally the modern nuclear family.[4] Mirabeau's speech explicitly equated each of these notions of family with a particular political regime. He attacked lineage in the institution of primogeniture as a vestige of feudalism and condemned patriarchy as a form of absolute monarchy. According to his view, a constitutional regime founded on popular sovereignty required a new sort of family, one in

---

[2] Traer, *Marriage and the Family*, pp. 48–78. Also see Mauzi, *L'Idée du bonheur*; Mary Lyndon Shanley and Peter G. Stillman, "Political and Marital Despotism: Montesquieu's *Persian Letters*," in Elshtain, ed., *The Family in Political Thought*, pp. 66–79; Joan B. Landes, "Hegel's Conception of the Family," in the same volume, pp. 125–144; and Dianne Lynn Alstad, "The Ideology of the Family in Eighteenth Century France" (Ph.D. diss., Yale University, 1971).

[3] Ozment, *When Fathers Ruled*; Trumbach, *The Rise of the Egalitarian Family*; Stone, *The Family, Sex and Marriage*; Flandrin, *Families in Former Times*; Mitterauer and Sieder, *The European Family*.

[4] Stone, *The Family, Sex and Marriage*.

which equality took the place of hierarchy and affection replaced authority. Equal inheritance was the means to effect this transformation.[5]

Mirabeau's conviction rested on three assumptions: social structure replicated family structure, family structure was defined by inheritance, and inheritance was governed by law. Linked together, these assumptions appeared to form a chain of necessary causality so that to change inheritance law would inevitably result in social change. In this chain, inheritance law was the first link, the state's entrée into the family and the lever with which the rock of society could be moved.

Despite Mirabeau's exclusive focus on it, inheritance was only one of many instruments of the strategies with which families hoped to maintain and reproduce themselves. Family strategies are the implicit rules and principles that inform and direct familial decisions and the behavior of individuals in families.[6] Some may be common to the culture as a whole, encoded in proverbs, law, or religious tenets—for example, that a younger sister may not marry before the elder, that landed property must pass in the male line, and that the marital bond is indissoluble. Some may be unique to a particular family—for example, the need to provide for a blind child or to marry a cousin to join family land. Many strategies fall between these extremes, being common but not universal, conventional but not dictated by law or custom. Historians have studied family decisions about marriage, about having children, about their education, and about retirement.[7] Central to all of these studies is the perception that, having limited resources, families decide how best to make use of them, how to distribute them, and to whom. Family history, to a large degree, is an effort to understand what these decisions were in the past and how they came to change.

---

[5] This argument was also made during the American Revolution. See Katz, "Republicanism and the Law of Inheritance," pp. 11–29.

[6] Louise A. Tilly, "Individual Lives and Family Strategies in the French Proletariat," in Wheaton and Hareven, eds., *Family and Sexuality in French History*, pp. 202–203; Bourdieu, "Les Stratégies matrimoniales," p. 1105.

[7] See, for example, Gillis, *For Better, For Worse*, and McFarlane, *Marriage and Love in England*, for two very different studies of marital decisions; J. A. Banks and Olive Banks, *Feminism and Family Planning in Victorian England* (New York: Schocken Books, 1964), for a classic and controversial study of the decision to have children. On education, see, for example, William H. Pease and Jane H. Pease, "Paternal Dilemmas: Education, Property and Patrician Persistence in Jacksonian Boston," *New England Quarterly* 53, no. 2 (June 1980): 147–167, and Tilly, "Individual Lives and Family Strategies." See Held, "Rural Retirement Arrangements in Seventeenth to Nineteenth Century Austria," for a recent study of peasant retirement. Another decision that has received attention is migration. See Leslie Page Moch and Louise A. Tilly, "Joining the Urban World: Occupation, Family and Migration in Three French Cities," *Comparative Studies in Society and History* 27 (January 1985): 33–56, and Virginia Dejohn Anderson, "Migrants and Motives: Religion and the Settlement of New England, 1630–1640," *New England Quarterly* 58, no. 3 (September 1985): 339–383.

Social scientists have agreed with Mirabeau that inheritance laws and customs are a fundamental part of family strategies. Jack Goody has written:

> Yet transmission *mortes causa* is not only the means by which the reproduction of the social system is carried out (in so far as that system is linked to property, including the ownership of the means by which man obtains his livelihood); it is also the way in which interpersonal relationships are structured. . . . Consequently a different quality of relationships, varying family structures and alternative social arrangements . . . will be linked to differing modes of transmission.[8]

According to Emmanuel LeRoy Ladurie, French inheritance custom furnishes the historian with a kind of grid of Old Regime society, which simultaneously organizes and brings to the light of analysis the "underpinnings of family life."[9]

Within the spectrum of decisions facing French families in the eighteenth and nineteenth centuries, inheritance emerged for many as the definitive distribution of resources and the ultimate instrument of decision-making power. Decisions about inheritance reveal much about the structure of families: who was reckoned to be "family" and who was a "stranger," who had power and who did not, and what were the relative strengths of various claims, all neatly measured in *livres* and *sous*.[10] Apparent as well are familial dynamics—how power was used, transmitted, balanced, and challenged. In short, inheritance was a main terrain of family governance.

In his speech, Mirabeau linked family governance to national governance and thus inheritance law to national law. Until his speech, the Revolutionaries had not perceived inheritance law as a constitutional issue. There had been no previous ground swell of criticism of Old Regime family law. A few *cahiers de doléances* and petitions to the National Assembly had condemned primogeniture as an abusive privilege but had not questioned the *faculté de tester*, the right of the individual to leave his property as he chose by written testament.[11] The issue of inheritance was first raised in the National Assembly in November 1790 in a joint report by the Constitution Committee and the Committee on the Alienation of National Lands. The following month, two articles in the *Moniteur Uni-*

---

[8] Goody, introduction to Goody, Thirsk, and Thompson, eds., *Family and Inheritance*, p. 1.

[9] LeRoy Ladurie, "Système de la coutume," p. 825.

[10] These Old Regime currencies appear so frequently in this work that they will rapidly become familiar to the reader and thus require no further italicizing.

[11] Aron, "Etudes sur les lois successorales," pp. 460–467; Godechot, *Les Institutions de la France*, pp. 205–207; Traer, *Marriage and the Family*, pp. 82–84.

versel linked "a truly free constitution" with equal inheritance.[12] The National Assembly ordered its Constitution Committee to investigate the question in more detail; Mirabeau was to be their spokesman. His response, presented posthumously to the Assembly by Talleyrand, placed inheritance law at the center of the Revolutionary task and there it remained. Each constitutional revision—1793, 1795, 1799, 1804, 1815—led to a reexamination of inheritance law. April 4, 1791, was only the first of many occasions on which successive legislatures hotly debated the rights of the individual, the role of the family, and the prerogatives of the state in inheritance.[13]

In the debates, first Mirabeau, then Robespierre and others argued in favor of equal inheritance on the basis of natural right, individual liberty, and equality. Other delegates replied with arguments based on a view of the family as a naturally hierarchical unit and of the patriarch as its natural head. They defended the right of the patriarch to do what he chose with his property and to bequeath it in whatever way he willed. To restrict this right, they argued, was to prevent the patriarch from exercising his authority to reward virtue and punish vice. Saint Martin, one of the first speakers against equal inheritance in April 1791, stated that it was necessary to maintain testators' rights in the interests of social justice. Suppose, he argued, there is "a child who has stayed in the paternal home in order to farm his invalid father's land and thus support his family; wouldn't it be an injustice to divide the fruits of this virtuous son's labors among his brothers who never shared his toil?"[14]

Opponents in the National Assembly conjured up two competing models of familial relations, one supposedly typical of the north and one typical of the south and each representing an ideal form of government. The family from northern France, where equal inheritance was customary, was a republic in miniature, whereas the southern family, in which Roman law established the faculté de tester, doubled as a benevolent monarchy.

[12] Traer, *Marriage and the Family*, p. 158. *Moniteur Universel*, December 11, 1790, and December 19, 1790.

[13] For an overview of French inheritance law during the Old Regime, see Yver, *Egalité entre heritiers et exclusion des enfants dotés*, and Imbert, *Histoire de droit privé*. For the changes in family and inheritance law during the Revolution, see Aron, "Etudes sur les lois successorales," pp. 444–489, 585–620; Lefebvre, "Le Droit successoral"; Dejace, *Les Règles de la dévolution successorale*; and Godechot, *Les Institutions de la France*, pp. 208–215, 373–377. For Napoleonic Code see Bloch, "L'Institution d'heritier et le legs universel," and Traer, *Marriage and the Family*, pp. 166–191.

[14] *Moniteur Universel*, April 6, 1791. This argument remained a favorite of conservatives into the present century. In 1939 the Daladier Law revised the Napoleonic Code to permit such recognition. See Richard Tomlinson, Marie-Monique Huss, and Philip E. Ogden, " 'France en Péril': The French Fear of Dénatalié," *History Today* 35 (April 1985): 24–31.

Cazalès, a monarchist delegate from Rivière-Verdun, a country town near Toulouse, and son of a magistrate in the Toulouse Parlement, described the social benefits of the right to make a will.

> The faculté de tester given by Roman law to patriarchs is a necessary consequence of paternal authority. . . . It is by this right that they govern their families and obtain respect from them. This is essentially a system of education, and it is by education, says J-J Rousseau, that the Athenians did such great things. Each house was a school and the patriarch was more feared in his family than the magistrate. If anyone doubts the happy influence of this education, he should come to those happy southern provinces where the patriarch never dies. He who succeeds him succeeds to his affectionate attachments as well as to his rights. There is not one case where the house of the eldest son is not the common house of the whole family, and, if there were one, it would be viewed with horror. Compare these customs with those of this region [Paris had a legal custom of equal inheritance] whose courts resound with scandalous disputes between fathers and children; these latter have neither respect nor regard for their parents. . . . The arrogance of a foolish independence has destroyed the most tender of natural sentiments between them.[15]

Although their views of the family differed markedly, both Mirabeau and Cazalès asserted that the family, as the cradle of citizenship, must reproduce the organization of the state. Because their views of ideal family organization differed, so did their views of the ideal state. In 1791 the National Assembly was in a deep struggle over the constitution of the New Regime. The royal veto and other such issues were revealing unbridgeable gulfs between men all of whom considered themselves revolutionaries. Therefore, it is not surprising that the debate over inheritance law ended in a deadlock. The vote on April 8 sidestepped the issue by providing for equal inheritance only for intestate cases and left individuals free to make wills as they liked.

But Cazalès's benevolent monarchy proved treacherous. Louis XVI was first removed from the constitutional throne and then executed. The choice was made; the New Regime would be a republic. With the end of the constitutional monarchy, the campaign for a revolutionary inheritance law resumed, stronger than before. Equal inheritance came to be seen as a necessary foundation for the Republic of Virtue.

The campaign opened in March 1793, six weeks after the execution of the king. Mailhe, the spokesman for the Committee on Legislation, branded the faculté de tester a privilege and an aristocratic device, invariably used to disinherit worthy patriots.

---

[15] *Moniteur Universel*, April 8, 1791. Cazalès published a longer version of this argument in *Opinion de M. de Cazalès sur les successions. Prononcée dans l'Assemblée nationale le 5 avril 1791* (Paris: n.p., 1791).

It is certain that, since the beginning of the Revolution, an infinite number of fathers have shown their hatred of the Revolution in the manner they treat their children who are its partisans.[16]

In response and almost without debate, the Convention passed the law of March 7, 1793, which forbade a parent to favor one child over another. In the fall, the Convention extended equal succession to collateral heirs—brothers, sisters, cousins—in the law of 5 *brumaire* Year 2 (October 26, 1793).[17] The law of 12 *nivôse* Year 2 (January 1, 1794) plugged the remaining loopholes. Heirs had to return all dowries and other gifts to the succession. Only a small portion of the estate, known as the *portion disponible,* was left free to be assigned by will, and it could be left only to nonheirs—to charity, for example. Finally, equal inheritance was made retroactive to July 14, 1789, the date on which the New Regime was supposed to have begun.

From January 1794 until March 1800, equal inheritance was the law of the land. Efforts to write a new constitution in 1795 reopened the debate but led to no new conclusions. Although not aspiring to be a Republic of Virtue, the Directory was nonetheless to be a republic and the legislators continued to regard equal inheritance as fundamental to republican government. It was Napoleon's coup that brought the first abridgment; the law of 4 *germinal* Year 8 (March 25, 1800) permitted the testator to assign the portion disponible to an heir, thereby increasing his or her share. This was the first step toward the final revision of inheritance law, Napoleon's Civil Code.

Promulgated in 1804, the Napoleonic Code endorsed the ideal of equal inheritance in intestate cases. However, the Code also retained and enlarged the portion disponible, which, as in the law of 4 *germinal* Year 8, a person could leave to anyone he or she chose by written will. The portion disponible was an equal share in the succession. If its recipient were not among the legal heirs, he or she shared in the estate equally with them. If an heir, he or she received a double portion (see table 1–1).

Napoleon's Civil Code also reconciled marital settlements with inheritance law, which Revolutionary laws had not attempted. Although the Code defined three alternative marital regimes—community, dowry, and separate property—it restricted the transfer of property between husband and wife. In each regime, the husband administered his wife's property during the marriage and then returned it to her upon his death. A husband could make further provision for his widow only by leaving her the portion disponible or by assigning her the use, but not the property, of his

[16] *Moniteur Universel,* March 9–10, 1793.

[17] In France, a law is generally called by the date it was passed, hence the Law of 5 *brumaire* Year 2, and so on. I have given the Gregorian date here as well so that readers unfamiliar with the Revolutionary calendar may follow the chronology.

estate. If the couple had no children, the Code permitted a testator to leave the surviving spouse the use of the entire estate. If they had children, the Code reduced the usufruct to one half of the estate. If the spouse was also to receive the portion disponible, usufruct was further reduced to one quarter of the estate. In the absence of such express provisions, the Code recognized no widow's or widower's rights. Only if a person had no kin to the seventh degree and no illegitimate children did the surviving spouse count as an heir.[18]

The provisions of the Napoleonic Code regarding inheritance and marital property remained virtually unchanged until the end of the nineteenth century. After a decade and more of debate, a clear winner had finally emerged whose victory was reconfirmed in 1826. In that year the marquis de Maleville introduced a bill in the Chamber of Peers to reestablish primogeniture in intestate successions of substantial worth. In his words, the object of the measure was to "ensure the preservation of families and their fortunes," "to provide every family with a head, a representative, a bulwark to exercise for the family those political rights which are founded upon property," and to prevent "those losses, those social extinctions, so frequent of late, which cause such grave damage to a State, especially to a Monarchy."[19] However, it was clear even to Maleville that the public was vociferously opposed to his bill. He was inundated with letters and petitions demanding that he drop the project. This antipathy, he explained, was the result of "thirty-five years of error and popular prejudice." His fellow peer, the comte de Molé, had a different interpretation. "It was," he argued, "in order to achieve equality, to abolish privileges, that the Revolution was made," and Frenchmen were justly disturbed by this bill, born of that spirit "of bitterness and defiance which has engendered so many vain efforts to lead us back to an order of things abolished long since."[20] The majority of his colleagues agreed and the bill was roundly defeated in the House of Peers.[21]

Judging by this debate, the French Revolution was as significant to the history of French families as it was to the history of French politics al-

---

[18] Napoleonic Code, articles 1094–1099. The Napoleonic Code assigned degrees of kinship by the Roman law system, counting back to the common ancestor and then forward to the kin in question. For example, a niece is kin in the third degree counting one degree back to the parents, two degrees forward to the sibling, and a third degree to the sibling's child. An example of a seventh-degree kinsman is a third cousin once removed.

[19] *Moniteur Universel*, March 16, 1826.

[20] Ibid., March 30–31, 1826.

[21] The debate ceased to trouble the legislature but was not entirely closed. In the first half of the nineteenth century, peasants continued to petition for a return to testamentary freedom. See Theodore Zeldin, *France, 1848–1945*, vol. 1, *Ambition, Love and Politics* (Oxford: Clarendon Press, 1973), pp. 143–145.

though political revolutions have not always been so viewed by historians of the family.[22] But the French Revolution went far beyond politics; it was intended to re-form society itself. A Revolution that transformed time with a new calendar, space with new measurements, social identity with a new form of address (*citoyen*), and even personal identity with a host of new names like Gracchus and Egalité could hardly leave the family unchanged. For the Revolutionaries (and their opponents) as for historians (equally on both ends of the political spectrum), the Revolution was an end and a beginning, France's birth into the modern world.[23]

And there is certainly enough evidence of family upheaval to lend verisimilitude to the assumption that the French family was reborn in the Revolution as well. There was, for example, the secularization of marriage and the institution of divorce, the creation of legal adoption and the recognition of the rights of illegitimate children.[24] Most of all there was equal inheritance. The Revolution, it seems, must mark the end of the Old Regime family in which authoritarianism and primogeniture held sway and the birth of the modern family based on affection and equality.[25]

Throughout the nineteenth century, equal inheritance remained as controversial in some circles as it had been in 1791 and for many of the same reasons. In most arguments, inheritance law remained firmly ensconced in the role of fundamental governor of society. For some, as for Molé, equal inheritance was a cause of progress, of liberation and equality, a landmark on the road to social justice and harmony. Michelet, for example, declared that equal inheritance had not destroyed the nobility but rather created "thirty-four millions of nobles"; peasants, each with their own plots of land, became free and ennobled.[26] The Republican League of Small Property, headed by Paul Deschanel, propagated the notion that equal inheritance promoted small-property holding, which in turn promoted republicanism.[27]

For others, equal inheritance was one of the Revolution's most deadly legacies. Frédéric Le Play, the pioneering sociologist, made the strongest

---

[22] Laslett, *The World We Have Lost*, pp. 150–161.

[23] François Furet, *Interpreting the French Revolution*, trans. Elborg Forster (Cambridge: Cambridge University Press, 1981), pp. 1–17.

[24] Phillips, *Family Breakdown*; Brinton, *French Revolutionary Legislation on Illegitimacy*; on adoption see Traer, *Marriage and the Family*, pp. 152–154.

[25] Roland Mousnier has written that France in the eighteenth century was "still a society of lineage" moving toward the society of "houses" and "households" in the nineteenth century, a transition that was sealed, apparently, by the Revolution. *Les Institutions de la France sous la monarchie absolue*, vol. 1, *Société et état* (Paris: Presses universitaires de France, 1974), pp. 47, 82.

[26] Jules Michelet, *The People*, trans. G. H. Smith (New York: Appleton, 1846), p. 39.

[27] Zeldin, *France, 1848–1945: Ambition, Love and Politics*, p. 143.

and most persuasive case. His studies of workers' and peasants' work and family life persuaded him that equal inheritance had destroyed social cohesion by destroying family cohesion. It had led, he believed, to social atomization and the worst evils of modern life—selfishness, alienation, and rootlessness. Equal inheritance was the cause, he concluded, of France's social and political instability.[28] After 1870, economists and demographers saddled equal inheritance with the opposite charge: it had made France, especially rural France, pot-bound. In the eighteenth century, France had had a vigorous economy that had rivaled England's. Why had France not experienced the Industrial Revolution and why, even as industrialization arrived, did it penetrate France so slowly and painfully? (Why had France lost the Franco-Prussian war so decisively and disastrously?) Equal inheritance, they said, was one culprit. Because every peasant could expect to inherit a tiny plot of land, few were willing to leave their villages to work in factories, and because every peasant wanted to leave his children enough land to survive on, peasants had fewer children, causing the relative decline in French population, overheating the market in land, and drawing capital away from industry.[29] In these theories, inheritance figured as the leading, sometimes the only, component of family strategy, and inheritance law was its effective governor.

Despite the role that Revolutionary inheritance law has been called upon to play in social, political, and economic theories, there have been few empirical studies of its effect on French families.[30] One reason for this neglect is undoubtedly the compartmentalization of the historical profession in the French academy, where the study of the Old Regime, the Revolution, and the nineteenth century are separate specialties. This has led to studies of the Old Regime family that stop at 1789 and studies of the family in the nineteenth century that begin around 1815 although their authors do not claim that such a chronological division is meaning-

[28] Le Play, *L'Organisation de la famille*, introduction. See Joseph L. Spengler, *France Faces Depopulation (Postlude ed. 1936–1976)* (Durham, N.C.: Duke University Press, 1979), pp. 146–156, and Assier-Andrieu, "Le Play et la famille-souche des Pyrénées."

[29] Spengler, *France Faces Depopulation*, pp. 121–134; Gordon Wright, *France in Modern Times*, 4th ed. (New York: Norton, 1987), pp. 271–273; Theodore Zeldin, *France, 1848–1945*, vol. 3, *Anxiety and Hypocrisy* (Oxford: Oxford University Press, 1981), pp. 184–204. As examples, see Alexander von Brandt, *Droit et coutumes des populations rurales de la France en matière successorale* (Paris: L. Larose, 1901); Michel Augé-Laribé, *L'Evolution de la France agricole* (Paris: Armand Colin, 1912); Jacques Bertillon, *La Dépopulation en France* (Paris: Alcan, 1911); and especially the books and pamphlets by Fernand Auburtin such as *Une Législation qui tue: Le Régime successoral du Code Civil*, published in 1922 by the Alliance nationale pour l'accroissement de la population française. Such alarmist arguments did not carry all before them. See René Worms, *Natalité et régime successoral* (Paris: Payot, 1917), which casts doubt on the connection between equal inheritance and "Malthusianism."

[30] A notable exception is Shaffer, *Family and Farm*.

ful.[31] In some areas of study, to bridge the Revolution poses almost insurmountable problems because wholesale changes in institutions and in documentation make useful before-and-after comparisons difficult if not impossible. Yet this is not the case for a study of families, in either theoretic or practical terms. Families, marriage, and inheritance continued to exist throughout the Revolution, and the public records of these institutions continued to be kept as well.

This is a study of the impact of the revolution in inheritance law on families in Montauban, a southwestern city where in the Old Regime the faculté de tester had applied. Only thirty miles north of Toulouse, Montauban was securely in Roman France. The Custom of Montauban, a pastiche of Roman statutes drawn up in the twelfth century, followed Roman law in its regulation of inheritance.[32] When a person died intestate, that is, without having made a will, the law divided his or her estate equally among the heirs, first direct descendants, then direct ancestors, and then collateral kin of the closest degree. For example, if a man had children, his estate was divided among them; if he had no children (or grandchildren), it went to his parents. If his parents were dead, it went to his siblings, and so on. The group of relatives who inherited abintestate were his legal heirs. However, Montaubaners could exercise the faculté de tester, the right to leave their property in whatever way they chose by written will. The Custom reserved only a small portion of the estate, called the *légitime*, for the legal heirs. A Montaubaner could leave the rest of the estate to whomever he or she appointed, to one heir or to several, to a "stranger," that is, a person outside the pool of legal heirs, to the church, or to charity. And a testator could disinherit an heir of the légitime for cause—for example, if a son married without his parents' consent or if a daughter joined a religious order, thereby "abandoning" her family. Thus patriarchs could reward, punish, and name a successor. As for inheritance law, in the eighteenth century Montauban families could operate as the little monarchies that Cazalès described.

The Custom of Montauban also defined the spouse's rights in the estate and the property arrangements between husband and wife. Following the Roman system, the Custom created a dowry for the bride that was inalienable while the marriage lasted. The husband administered it and was

---

[31] Flandrin, *Families in Former Times*; Lebrun, *La Vie conjugale sous l'ancien régime*; Collomp, *La Maison du père*; Segalen, *Love and Power in the Peasant Family*. An exception is a delightful and idiosyncratic book by two ethnologists, Elisabeth Claverie and Pierre Lamaison, *L'Impossible mariage: Violence et parenté en Gévaudan, XVIIe, XVIIIe et XIXe siècles*. However, it has virtually no chronology at all.

[32] When it required clarification, magistrates cited Roman law as the ultimate authority. See Ourliac, "Le Droit privé," p. 131, and Maillet, "De l'exclusion coutumière des filles dotées," p. 519.

Table 1–1
Percentage of the Estate Guaranteed to Each Heir

Number of Heirs	Custom of Montauban (legitime)	Civil Code	Law of 12 Nivôse (Equal Inheritance)
1	33%	50%	100%
2	16	33	50
3	11	25	33
4	8	19	25
5	10	15	20
6	8	12	17

entitled to its income "to defray the costs of marriage," as the standard phrase went. However, he could not dispose of the capital even with his wife's consent. If the wife died first, the dowry went to her children, and if she had none, to her husband. If the husband died first, his widow reclaimed her dowry; if there were no children, she also received "nuptial gains" from the husband's estate equal to one half of her dowry. Any of the bride's property not placed in the dowry was called paraphernalia and was hers alone to employ as she chose. If the couple married without a contract their property remained separate. Thus, under the Custom of Montauban, marriage was a strange sort of limited corporation; if it failed, that is, produced no children, the survivor had a claim upon the partner's estate based on the size of the initial investment, the dowry.

Beginning with the law of March 7, 1793, national inheritance law contravened the Custom of Montauban. Between March 1793 and January 1794, the faculté de tester was reduced until little occasion remained for writing a will. The Civil Code restored some choice with the increase of the portion disponible, but in no way did it revive the faculté de tester. Whereas under the Old Regime Custom, Montaubaners had been free to dispose of the bulk of their property as they wished with only a small portion reserved for their legal heirs, under the Civil Code the ratio was reversed. Montaubaners could leave only a small portion by will; the distribution of the rest was determined by law.

Revolutionary inheritance law also invalidated Montauban's customary marital settlement because it denied the surviving spouse any claim on the estate. The Napoleonic Code then further widened the gap between local custom and national law. Not only did the Code specifically outlaw "nuptial gains," it severely restricted a wife's control over her property. Any of her property not placed in a dowry went into a marital community administered by her husband. The Custom of Montauban had made the dowry inalienable and had left the paraphernalia in the wife's hands; the

Napoleonic Code gave control of both to the husband exclusively. Under the Custom of Montauban a marriage had been a limited partnership; under the Civil Code it became a corporate takeover.

Montauban, therefore, constitutes a test case for the inheritance debate. In the eighteenth century, Montaubaners were free to use and abuse the freedom of Roman law in the prerogative of the faculté de tester. Did they then adhere to "aristocratic" notions of lineage and primogeniture as the advocates of equal inheritance claimed? Or were the defenders of the faculté de tester correct in saying that patriarchal power was exercised in the interests of equity, justice, and family stability? And what of equal inheritance? We may, I think, discount the claims of its supporters that it turned families into mini-republics of virtue. Nonetheless, it is reasonable to ask whether equal inheritance led to more egalitarian families.

More important, Montauban is a good subject for an investigation of the effects of inheritance law reform on family strategies. Between 1793 and 1804, the grid that supposedly had shaped family structure and behavior there since the Middle Ages was suddenly reversed. How did this affect Montauban families? Were family hierarchies overthrown? Which families and which family members were most affected? Did the restriction of the faculté de tester curtail patriarchal power? Did equal inheritance empower younger sons and daughters? In short, did the revolution in inheritance law produce a revolution in family relations?

To study the impact of the Revolutionary laws of equal inheritance on Montaubaners' family strategies requires first an examination of several of the assumptions on which Mirabeau and subsequent theorists built their arguments. Mirabeau assumed that inheritance law shaped practice, that inheritance practice shaped families, and that families shaped society. The last assertion in particular is both obvious and interminably debatable. Society is composed of families, but not of families alone; it is also composed of work groups, peer groups, neighborhoods, religious affiliations, social classes, and many other institutions. Families may be a more fundamental form of social organization, but their influence on society is nonetheless mediated by these other institutions. Historians of the family have repeatedly shown that there has been no simple cause-and-effect relationship between family organization and social change.[33]

A second issue to consider is the relationship between inheritance law and inheritance practice. There are numerous studies of French inheritance law and customs, but that is not the same as a study of inheritance. Rules of inheritance may have been a grid imposed on families, constraining strategies within certain predetermined lines; nonetheless, there was considerable room for distinctive if not unique choices both under Old

---

[33] Hareven, "Family History at the Crossroads," pp. xvi–xx.

Regime legal custom and under Napoleon's Civil Code. Even under the strictest rule of equal inheritance during the Revolution it is possible that some families did not adhere to either the spirit or the letter of the law. Inheritance was governed by civil law, and like all civil practice, was consensual as well as juridical. With his heirs' agreement, for instance, a property owner might continue to practice primogeniture despite its illegality, and no one but his heirs (and in due course, their heirs) was empowered to prevent him. In fact, Le Play discovered that this was the case in his model stem-family (*famille-souche*) the Mélougas, who, by 1856, had weathered two successions since 1793 without succumbing to the rule of equal inheritance.[34]

The enforcement of a law also depends on the cooperation of the courts and of the legal profession. In the eighteenth century, there were judges who did not enforce inheritance laws they found grossly unfair. For example, the Parlement of Toulouse refused to sanction the disinheritance of Protestants to the advantage of their Catholic relatives. And, of course, there were always lawyers capable of discovering enough loopholes in inheritance laws to enable their clients to slip through the grid if they so desired.[35] Therefore, it cannot be a foregone conclusion that Revolutionary inheritance law had any impact on inheritance practice, let alone the one desired by its authors.

The third issue is the extent to which inheritance shaped family strategies. A wealthy patriarch could use the lure of succession to govern his family, but in the hands of the poor man this incentive was less powerful. And in the eighteenth and nineteenth centuries, the majority of the French population was without property. Adeline Daumard has found that more than half of the adults who died in four French cities in the first half of the nineteenth century left no estate at all and three quarters left less than one hundred francs.[36] To their families, equal inheritance, the faculté de tester, and primogeniture were equally irrelevant. Inheritance could be only a minor theme in their family strategies.

Mirabeau and his successors assumed that inheritance played the same role in all families and that changes in inheritance law would have comparable effects regardless of social class or gender. The familial drama evoked

[34] However, when his disciple Emile Cheysson returned to the Pyrenees to interview the family in 1869, he found that a descendant of an heir excluded from the succession in 1835 had brought suit against them. Land was sold in 1874 to ward off a complete partition, which finally occurred in 1882. See the appendix to the third edition (1884) of *L'Organisation de la famille*.

[35] Bien, "Catholic Magistrates and Protestant Marriage," Giesey, "Rules of Inheritance and Strategies of Mobility."

[36] Daumard, ed. *Les Fortunes françaises au XIXᵉ siècle*, p. 122. This situation had not changed much since the eighteenth century. See Roche, *Le Peuple de Paris*, pp. 66–97; and Aboucaya, *Le Testament lyonnais*, p. 144.

in the legislative debates over inheritance law, whether it was acted out between aristocratic tyrants and their patriotic progeny or between benign patriarchs and unfilial ingrates, always starred fathers and sons. That it would treat daughters and sons equally, a truly revolutionary aspect of the law, rarely raised comment. Also the rule of primogeniture had applied only to feudal properties, although it was assumed by Revolutionary debaters and their nineteenth-century successors to have been widely practiced among the landowning peasantry as well. In these debates, no one speculated about the inheritance practices of artisans, shopkeepers, and merchants. Yet most of these families also had strategies that included inheritance.

The literature of family history raises another question: is it appropriate to speak of the family as an entity and to use familial decisions rather than individual decisions as units of analysis? The notion of family strategies appears to presume that the family operated as a single organism so that the good of the whole was also the good of each member, as a healthy body implies the good health of the arms and legs and vice versa.[37] The Revolutionary legislators had no such illusions about familial solidarity; they were quite willing to concede, for example, that equal inheritance would diminish paternal power because many believed that such a reduction was necessary to the good of the whole family. It is well to keep in mind Louise Tilly's caveat about family strategies, that they are both "problematic and contingent" and the product of "both negotiation and struggle."[38] Changes in inheritance law affected different members of families in different ways. Because inheritance had to do with family dynamics as well as with family structure, changes in inheritance entailed changes in the distribution and use of power. Family strategies might change because the rules governing them changed; they might also change because of the varying impact different family members had on familial decisions.

The main sources for this study are the notary records conserved in the archives of the department of the Tarn-et-Garonne in Montauban. At the end of the eighteenth century, Montauban possessed eight notaries licensed by the king to record the civil contracts of his subjects. Notary clients came from all over the city and the surrounding countryside and from all walks of life, particularly from the ranks of property owners because most contracts involved some kind of property transaction and the services of a notary cost money—two sous per page.[39] The most common occasions for employing a notary's services were to record a loan or the

---

[37] Hareven, "Family History at the Crossroads," pp. xv–xvi; Berkner, "The Use and Misuse of Census Data."

[38] Louise A. Tilly, "Rich and Poor in a French Textile City," in Moch and Stark, eds., *Essays on the Family and Historical Change*, p. 67.

[39] Magnon, *Le Notariat et la révolution française*, pp. 14–15.

repayment of a debt and to buy or sell property. Montaubaners also used notaries to record once-in-a-lifetime events—apprenticeship contracts, marriage contracts, wills—and to settle civil suits out of court. Most of Montaubaners' major decisions were recorded in a notary clerk's round, even hand, witnessed by four respectable citizens and bound into large volumes that make up the departmental archive series 5E. Many historians have been grateful for the French legal-mindedness.[40]

Samples of marriage contracts and wills notarized between 1775 and 1825 generated the statistics that are the skeleton of this book. Supplementing them are smaller samples of the records of debts, property sales, and powers of attorney.[41] Other archival material, such as police and judicial records, a census, the minutes of town council meetings, guild records, and private family papers, furnished incident and example—flesh and blood. From notary and parish records I was able to construct mini-histories of a number of families in order to understand better how particular decisions and documents had fitted into family experiences and strategies. As a result, the reader will become familiar with the Garrisson merchants, the Mouméja clan of bricklayers and gardeners, and the Ruelle family of peasant proprietors, among others. These families were in no way extraordinary, or, rather, were only as unique as every family is. Their circumstances and decisions illustrate problems and solutions shared by many Montauban families in this period.

Readers will not find in this book the sort of demographic statistics, such as age at marriage, average number of children per marriage, and so on, with which they may be familiar from village studies. Historians assemble such data by reconstructing all the families of a parish from the birth, marriage, and death records kept by the parish priest. Such a project is impossible for a city like Montauban because of the size of the population and the inhabitants' propensity for moving in and out of the city. As a result of the technique of family reconstitution, we know a good deal about the changing family patterns of European village life but little about urban families.[42] This book begins to redress the balance.

[40] See, for example, Roche, *Le Peuple de Paris*, and Sewell, *Structure and Mobility*.

[41] The departmental archives of the Tarn-et-Garonne possess the complete (and fully catalogued) series of Montauban's notarial records for this period. However, the selection of a true random sample of documents would have been inconceivably tedious and time consuming and would probably have driven the archivists to justified rebellion. Instead, I randomly selected two notary registers per year and then sampled the appropriate documents within each volume to achieve the desired number—seventeen per year of the wills and marriage contracts, ten per year of the powers of attorney, and five per year of the debts, quittances, and sales. For a few years, notably during the Terror, when notary business fell off dramatically, especially in the writing of wills (see chapter 3), I had to select three volumes to find enough documents.

[42] For an explanation and discussion of family reconstitution as a demographic technique, see E. A. Wrigley, ed., *An Introduction to English Historical Demography* (London: Weidenfeld

To understand the history of Montauban families during the Revolution, it is important first to understand Montauban's history, both its somewhat unusual political history and its more common economic trajectory. This is the subject of the next chapter. Chapter 3 begins the analysis of inheritance patterns to identify those factors which most influenced the decisions Montaubaners made regarding their families and property. Of these, socioeconomic status is particularly important in understanding Montaubaners' choice of heirs and the reasons that their choices changed during the Revolution. The succeeding four chapters look at the family strategies of each of the town's important social groups, beginning with the elite of merchants, professionals, and landowners in chapter 4, the artisans and retailers in chapter 5, the working poor in chapter 6, and concluding with the peasantry in chapter 7. For all of these families, the Revolution created new conditions, problems, and alternatives. Neither Montauban nor Montauban's families were in 1825 what they had been in 1775.

---

and Nicolson, 1966), and Louis Henry, *Manuel de démographie historique* (Geneva: Droz, 1967). See Smith, "Family and Class," Segalen, "The Family Cycle and Household Structure," Berkner, "The Stem Family and the Development Cycle," and Bourdieu, "Les Stratégies matrimoniales," as examples of village studies based on family reconstitution.

CHAPTER TWO

Montauban in Revolution

EVERY YEAR on August 15, Montauban's cafés fill with observers of the great summer event, the annual traffic jam that ties up all of southwestern France as half the population tries to go to Spain while the other half tries to come home. The Montaubaners on the terrace of the Café du Quai admire the latest styles in campers, count the out-of-town license plates, and hope for a minor accident to add drama to the spectacle. Any local resident going to Spain, of course, has left long since; living less than one hundred miles from the border, the Montaubaner seeking a cheap vacation can easily beat the tidal wave from the north. The café sitters are observers rather than participants in the national migration. With chairs angled to take advantage of the deep shade cast by a high wall, *pastis* and cigarettes in easy reach, they contemplate an agreeable view: red brick, blue sky, lazy blue-gray river winding between gray-green trees, and the three bridges packed with crazy Parisians sweltering in their cars, one line crawling slowly south, the other crawling no less slowly north.

In the 1780s, the view that would have struck the idle observer was significantly different. The setting was similar; the river, the wharves, and even the buildings have changed little in the intervening two centuries. In the eighteenth century, however, there was only one bridge, the one now called the Old Bridge, which joins the center of town on the right bank of the Tarn with the district of Villebourbon on the left bank. The bridge once had guard towers similar to the Valenté Bridge in Cahors, but by the mid-eighteenth century the picturesque had given way to the needs of commerce; in 1758 the town had torn down the towers and widened the bridge. Then, of course, no cars had choked its approaches, but wagons, hand trucks, horses—which occasionally bolted and ended up in the river—and pedestrians amply filled their place.

To an observer, the major difference between the scene in the 1780s and the one in the 1980s is the activity on the river and the wharves. Whereas on a contemporary summer day the river sports only a few speed boats and the wharves host lethargic games of *boules*, some stray dogs, and a few nodding fishermen, in the 1780s the river and wharves were the center of Montauban's activity. Although February and October were high season on the Tarn as merchants sent their goods down the river to exhibit at the semiannual fairs in Bordeaux, in August river traffic was less feverish but no less businesslike. Along the wharves barges and sailboats lined up waiting for their loads of goods while others, already loaded and low in the water, maneuvered with sails and sweep-oars to begin the eight-day journey to Bordeaux and the sea. On the wharves, stevedores unloaded wagons, hoisting bundles of tanned hides, barrels of flour, and rolls of cloth to their shoulders to stow them aboard ship under the supervision of merchants and their scurrying clerks, who kept careful notes of what was dispatched to whom. Dodging among the scaffolding jutting from the warehouses and dye shops, Bruté, the inspector of manufactures, checked the bolts of fabric to make sure they were labeled correctly. Only first-quality cloth was marked with the name of the manufacturer and only cloth made by Vialètes d'Aignan or by Serres carried the royal manufacturer's lead seal. Above his head, silks, flannels, serges, cheesecloth, and the famous *cadis de Montauban*, in white, black, sky blue, green, peasant gray, and brilliant scarlet, fluttered in the breeze. Below the bridge, lines of draft horses, urged on by small stable boys, waited their turn at the municipal watering trough. Across the river and farther up lay moored the laundry barges where laundresses washed and rinsed the town's linens in the flowing water of the Tarn.[1]

In the contemporary scene at the bridge, the action takes place on the roads and Montaubaners are mostly observers, but in the 1780s the action was on the river and wharves and the populace was actively involved. Between 1775 and 1825 one scene was transformed into the other, as Montauban withered from a bustling urban center into a dying shell of a city. Loss of commerce, loss of industry, loss of population, stagnation, decline—these are the salient features of Montauban's entry into the contemporary era.

Eighteenth-century descriptions of Quercy, the province in which Montauban was located, emphasized that the area was ill defined and lacked coherence. The *Atlas Moderne*, which was published in 1771, depicted each province separately and marked every *pays* in a different color, but it divided Quercy between two maps, half in Guyenne and half in Languedoc.[2] Arthur Young's description of his trip through the province

---

[1] See Gausseran, "L'Evolution social de la bourgeoisie montalbanaise," pp. 94–97; Archives Nationales (hereafter AN) F¹² 559 Report de l'Etat général et précis des manufactures et du commerce de la ville et généralité de Montauban, 1783. In 1779 the royal government abolished regulations on textile manufacture. In 1781 Montauban's Manufacturers' Association established its own regulatory system, but even Bruté, "an inspector who bothers us on the least pretext and interrupts our operations," could not enforce compliance. By the time of the Revolution, all pretense of regulation had disappeared. Forestié, *Fabrication des draps*, pp. 29–31, and Archives Departmentales de Tarn-et-Garonne (hereafter AD T-et-G) 12-J-7 Lettres missives; Lagravère à Airolles 6–2–1783.

[2] Bourchenin, *La Géographie du Tarn et Garonne*, p. 4.

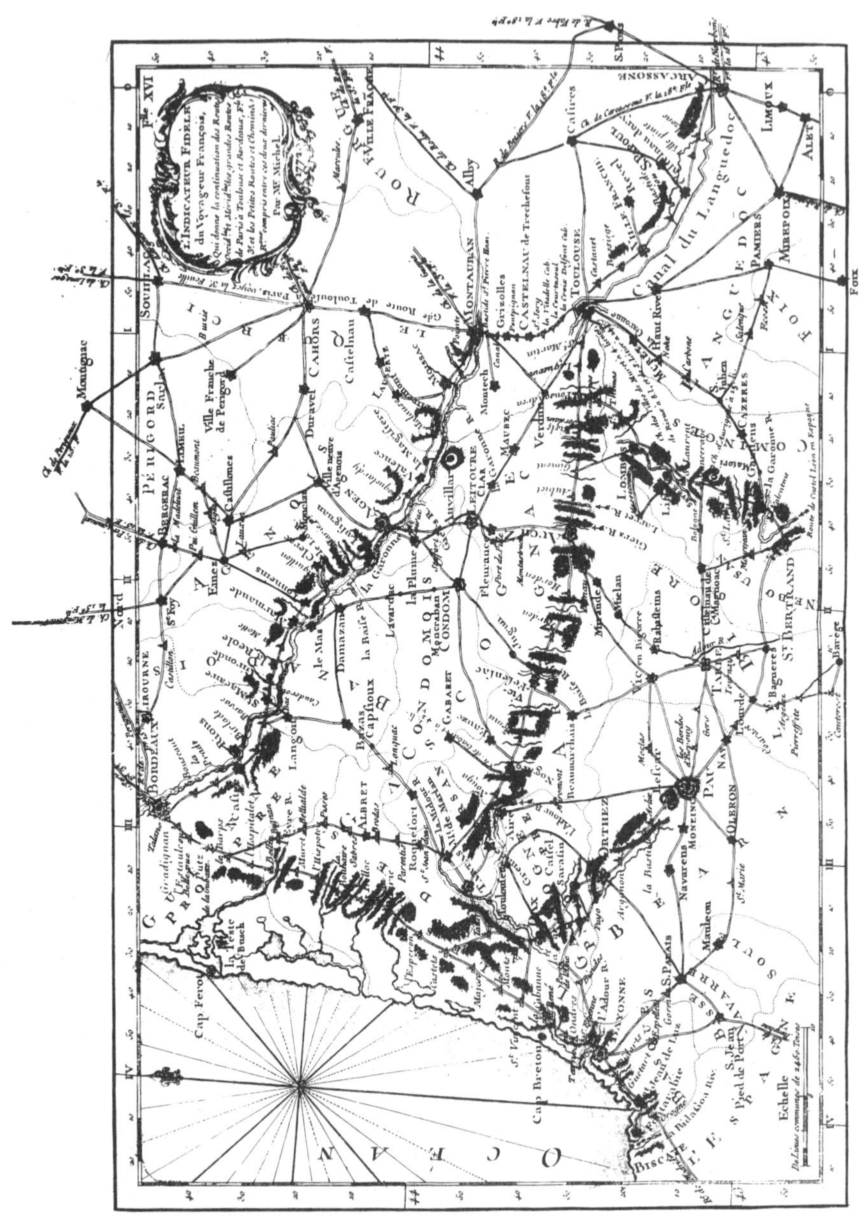

Map 2–1. Southwestern France in 1772. (From Michel, *L'Indicateur fidèle du voyageur françois*. Paris, 1772. Reproduced with the permission of the Map Division of the New York Public Library, Astor, Lenox, and Tilden Foundations.)

emphasizes another division, between the mountainous north of "black" Quercy and southern Quercy, which was "dead level."[3]

Again and again authors used the word *carrefour*, crossroads, to describe both the province and the town. Quercy was a province in which jurisdictions met and competed. Having no parlement of its own, it was claimed by both Toulouse and Bordeaux.[4] Northern Quercy had its center in Cahors and southern Quercy in Montauban. The rivalry between the two abated only in 1808, when, to give Montauban its own department, Napoleon created the Tarn-et-Garonne.

Montauban was a crossroads in a more literal sense. Possessing the only bridge over the Tarn, it commanded the road that, even this far south, was known as the Paris road, the main artery between Paris, the southern provinces, and Spain. The "road" that crossed the Paris-Spain road at Montauban was the river Tarn. This highway was open all year round, which could hardly be said of the overland routes. Navigable from Albi, the Tarn emptied into the Garonne about sixteen miles west of Montauban, and the Garonne went down to Bordeaux, the Atlantic Ocean, and the world.[5]

Montauban was a meeting point of commercial, administrative, and agricultural worlds. Along the north-south road tax collectors, soldiers, and officials traveled to and from Paris, Toulouse, and Spain. It was also a regional administrative center of some importance. Quercy, however, was, in Arthur Young's words, "an oceanic vastness" of cultivation crisscrossed with peasant tracks.[6] These different spheres impinged on one another— Quercy peasants, for example, grew wheat that fed slaves in Saint Domingue and paid taxes that supported court life in Versailles—but the connections were tenuous. Montauban's bridge seems symbolic of their separation; there these various worlds crossed each other but did not merge.

Montauban was an administrative seat, a market town, and a commercial and industrial center. Although these aspects intermingled, each was somewhat distinct, with its own participants, hierarchy, and clientele; without too much distortion, it is possible to associate each sphere with its own section of town.

Administrative Montauban was the oldest section of town, situated on the right bank of the Tarn between two tributary streams, the Tescou and

[3] Young, *Travels* 1: 39–40.

[4] Sol, *La Révolution* 1: 13.

[5] In February 1815, the prefect wrote that the roads, although sufficient in summer, were very bad in winter and that the Garonne was so changeable that it was unusable and the Aveyron was not navigable. Consequently the Tarn was "precious to the commerce of the department." AD T-et-G M182.

[6] Young, *Travels* 1: 40.

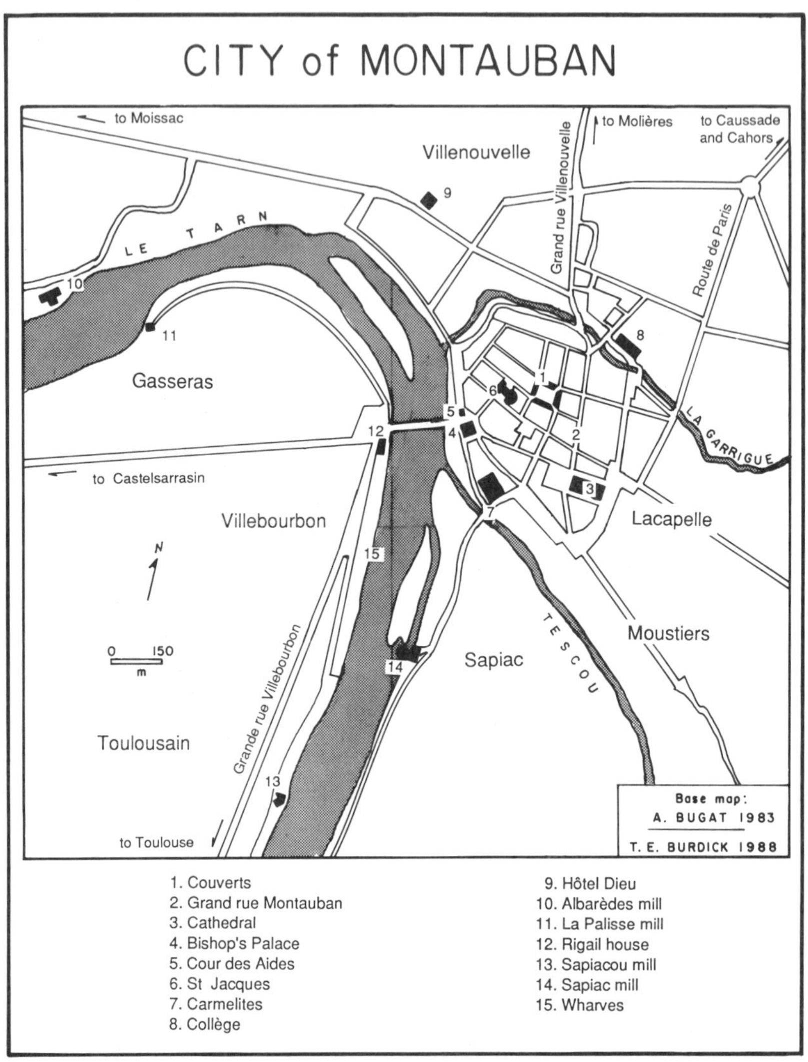

Map 2–2. The City of Montauban, circa 1775.

the Garrigue. Within a few blocks of one another were located the séné-chal, the intendance, the cathedral, the bishop's palace, and the various courts headed by the Cour des Aides. Here the streets were regular but narrow, shaded from the southern sun by an unbroken façade of brick, rising three or four stories high. These ample but outwardly unpretentious buildings housed a cross section of urban dwellers.

In this part of the city, the ground floor fronting the street was usually

Clients' Occupation		Residence of Notary Client Montauban and Surrounding District				
	Center City	Villebourbon	Villenouvelle	Semirural Faubourgs	Rural Environs	Other
Bourgeois	30%	2%	1%	2%	8%	22%
Commerce	20	34	14	5	2	15
Artisans						
Nontextile	24	20	19	27	9	20
Textile	6	33	14	15	4	7
Poor workers	19	11	31	21	2	7
Peasants						
Landowners	0	0	4	0	31	16
Farm workers	1	0	17	30	44	10
N	313	55	90	84	361	164

Note: Significance level = .01, contingency coefficient = .621.

an arcade of vaulted boutiques and workshops. Behind these was a courtyard in which the ground floor once again was given over to workshops and warehouses and to living quarters for the artisans and shopkeepers. For the main street the *capitation* roll of 1731 shows a great variety of artisans and shopkeepers—tailors, bakers, locksmiths, wig makers, chandlers, saddlers, butchers, shoemakers, *charcutiers*, and tavern keepers.[7]

These petty merchants served a wealthy, or at least a comfortable, clientele who inhabited the first- and second-floor apartments. Although from the street these apartments looked scarcely more prestigious than the ground-floor shops, the courtyard façades were often more elaborate. Staircases of wood or brick with decorative wrought-iron banisters wound upward to arcaded galleries. Plaster or stone medallions embellished doorways, and windows sported balconies. Their inhabitants are easy to spot on the tax lists; among the many artisans assessed five or six livres, they stand out, assessed twenty or thirty livres or more. On the main street in 1731, for example, lived four lawyers, six bourgeois, an officer of the Cour des Aides, a painter, a merchant, an apothecary, a doctor, and a "M de . . ." (presumably a nobleman), plus one wealthy commercial family, the Delons, whose head, Delon nephew, paid 165 livres in tax. But the Delon family was an exception; the wealthy residents of the center city were of

[7] Archives Municipales de Montauban (hereafter AM Mont) 5 CC 8 capitation 1731.

the noble, legal, and administrative classes, not commercial. A census of the wealthiest residents probably taken in 1775 shows that in this section of town only 5 percent of the wealthy were in commerce, whereas 35 percent were connected with the courts or the royal administration. A further 32 percent were large landowners and military officers and 23 percent were clergy, mostly belonging to the cathedral chapter.[8]

Besides shopkeepers and artisans unconnected with textiles and the elite of lawyers, officials, nobles, and bourgeois, the city center housed a considerable number of poor people (see table 2–1). In the third- and fourth-floor attics lived servants, day laborers, porters, water carriers, seamstresses, peddlers, dealers in old clothes, street sweepers, and beggars. The poor also found homes in the section of town northwest of the center known as Villenouvelle. Here the buildings were smaller and lower because they included no bourgeois apartments. Montauban's Terrorist, Jeanbon Saint-André, was born in one of these undistinguished houses.

Commercial Montauban, the textile city, the flour exporter, the city of the river and the Atlantic trade, was located on the left bank of the Tarn in the section of town named Villebourbon (in honor of Henri de Navarre, who had made Montauban a base of operations during the Wars of Religion). Its major edifice was not a church or a court but the long wharf lined with commercial entrepôts, dye shops, and warehouses and flanked by the imposing mills of Sapiacou and La Palisse. In 1774, the largest buildings on the wharf were *hôtels particuliers* inhabited by the Rigail merchant family; by Dumas, a large dealer in flour; by Bergis, merchant-dyers; and by the Lacostes, also merchants and related to the Bergis clan by marriage. Farther along the wharf lived Mariette, the largest dealer in grain and flour and the major shareholder in the Palisse mill; the Garrisson merchant clan; and several more dyers and merchants. Here the ground-floor rooms also contained shops, but these were less abundant and less varied than those in the center of town. Thirty-three percent of notary clients from Villebourbon were textile artisans.

Behind the imposing premises of the merchants ran streets inhabited by wool carders, combers, spinners, shearers and finishers, small-scale manufacturers, and the ubiquitous *sargeurs*, the local term for textile workers. Here also lived clerks, foremen, bargemen, stevedores, coopers—flour was shipped in barrels—and ships' carpenters. At the very ends of the streets near the mills lived the mill clerks and the millers. Shopkeepers and artisans not directly involved in textiles or the flour trade were few. The urban elite so prominent in the center city was also absent; the 1775 listing of the

8 Ibid.; AM Mont 10 HH 1 dénombrement sd (ca. 1775).

wealthiest residents shows eighteen merchants but only one military officer, one noble, one bourgeois, three clergymen, and one banker.[9]

Outside the foundations of the old city walls, the agricultural world pressed in. Buildings in the peripheral neighborhoods were smaller—only one or two stories with a garret below the roof—and farther apart. Courtyards became kitchen gardens and gardens blended into fields. Behind the urban façade of Lacapelle's main street were gardeners' plots, producing vegetables and fruits for bourgeois tables. Sapiac appeared to be a small village, each house having its pigs, garden, vines, and tiny fields, all grouped around the parish church. Except for the street running along the wharf to the mills, the districts of Toulousain and Gasseras could hardly be distinguished from the adjoining rural parishes. Thirty percent of the notary clients from these neighborhoods were gardeners and farm workers, sometimes serving also as part-time porters, stevedores, and construction workers. The fringes of town, with their numerous taverns and inns and their enclaves of teamsters and boatmen, also housed many farm workers who commuted to the fields beyond.[10]

Montauban attempted to dominate the surrounding countryside or at least to draw its resources to the city, in part through a program of road building. In the seventeenth century, official reports repeatedly stressed the inadequacy of the roads in the southwest and their deplorable condition. They were narrow and often impassable, but worse still, they were circuitous, wandering miles out of the way to reach every remote hamlet. In the early eighteenth century, the intendant began a massive project of improvements, spending twelve hundred thousand livres annually on road construction between 1725 and 1728. Construction and repair continued throughout the century, although at a more moderate rate. The Paris road was completed only in 1780 by a bridge over the Aveyron at Albias. Other construction improved and straightened the roads to Toulouse and to Moissac. An entirely new road was built between 1740 and 1756 from the Paris road at Caussade east to Caylus, Villefranche, and Rodez, connecting the Rouergue to the Montauban system.[11]

These new roads were heavily traveled. The routes of the Great Fear, the panic of the summer of 1789, attest to the success of the new roads in linking the region. Rumors of approaching brigands swept through southern Quercy by two different routes. One came slowly by secondary roads from the northeast to Tournon d'Agenais on July 30 and from there down to Lauzerte and Lafrançaise, reaching Montauban on July 31 or

---

[9] AM Mont 10 HH 1 dénombrement 1775.
[10] Ligou, *Montauban*, p. 96.
[11] Frêche, *Toulouse*, pp. 643–645.

August 1. The second wave came directly down the Paris road from Cahors, reaching Montauban in only one day. From Caussade, the news was transmitted along the new road to the Aveyron and the Rouergue, quickly penetrating these once isolated regions.[12]

The main beneficiary of the new roads was Montauban. Its merchants could now travel more easily within the region, and a regional market centered on Montauban began to develop.[13] Some of these merchants were little more than peddlers, hawking a variety of cheap wares from market to market. Others, however, were agents for textile and grain dealers, buyers rather than sellers, bringing once isolated regions into Montauban's commercial sphere. By moving into the Rouergue, Montauban displaced Albi as the market for this region. Albi's role in the flour trade declined drastically as Montauban began to mill the Rouergue grain. Moissac, another local milling town, suffered a similar fate, and Toulouse never developed a major milling business because Montauban grain dealers early established connections in northern Languedoc.[14]

Montauban's growing commercial network, although impinging on other urban centers, changed little for the peasant producer. Rarely did he benefit from the regional competition because his produce rarely went to market directly. Usually, even before he planted the seed, the peasant owed the harvest to various middlemen—to the landlord for rent, the seigneur for dues, the tax collector, tithe collector, and moneylender. However, Montauban's growth as a regional market had some effect on rural life. Montauban's weekly market attracted people from far afield. In 1793, for instance, the inns of Villebourbon lodged peddlers from Italy and the Ariège, a dance troupe from Grenoble, and merchants from Bordeaux, Toulouse, Foix, Marseilles, and Cahors. The market also attracted less desirable people—charlatans, pickpockets, and thieves. How could the village markets hope to compete with this spectacle, which offered at once variety, entertainment, temptation, and risk? Some country towns managed to keep up their markets by specialization. Molières, for example, held the regional poultry fair. For the most part, however, it was cheaper

[12] Latouche, *La Vie en bas-quercy*, p. 311. The second wave, although provoking a fresh panic in Toulouse on August 3, appeared in Montauban as a rumor to the effect that the brigands had been captured and destroyed. See Ligou, *Montauban*, p. 210, and Georges Lefebvre, *La Grande Peur de 1789* (Paris: Librairie Armand Colin, 1932), p. 228.

[13] A passport delivered to Guilhaume Bastoul, merchant of Montauban, on 13 *floréal* Year 2 (May 2, 1794) shows these ports of call: 13 *floréal* in Toulouse, 17 *floréal* in Revel and then back to Toulouse, 5 *prairial* in Cahors, 14 *messidor* in Revel, and then back to Montauban. Another from 1796 shows a simple loop from Montauban to Villefranche to Rodez to Toulouse to Gaillac back to Montauban. AM Mont 5 i 1 passeports.

[14] Frêche, *Toulouse*, pp. 643–645; Butel, *Les Négociants bordelais*, pp. 95–99; and Paul Butel, "Marchands de Garonne entre la Mediterranée et l'Atlantique," in Garrisson-Estèbe and Ferro, eds., *Une Histoire de la Garonne*, pp. 350–351.

and more interesting to make purchases in Montauban, so in most country towns the weekly markets shrank or were discontinued, and everywhere artisanal production languished.[15]

Montauban's prominence as an administrative and judicial center augmented its place as a market and an entertainment center. Officials based in Montauban extracted taxes, recruited soldiers and public workers, and, on occasion, dispensed charity and relief. Montauban's mounted police patrolled the highways and its magistrates sat in judgment. Given the abundance of overlapping claims, confused titles, and traditional rights of way, plus the vagaries of cattle, sheep, and neighbors, litigation was a constant rural pastime. Quercy peasants fought out their property disputes, suits for damages and slander in Montauban's courts. Peasants also patronized Montauban's notaries. Despite the presence of notaries in most country towns, 34 percent of the clients of Montauban's notaries were from rural parishes.

The most powerful link between Montauban and the region was the direct human interaction of frequent visits, seasonal migration, and outright emigration. Although eighteenth-century census figures were estimates at best, there can be no denying that between 1715 and 1790 Montauban's population grew enormously. An expert in the 1720s estimated the population of the city at ten thousand. By the 1790s it had topped twenty-eight thousand. Some of this extraordinary growth was due to a higher than average birth rate and a lower than average death rate, but much was due to immigration. In the last quarter of the eighteenth century, only 64 percent of Montauban's grooms in the sample of marriage contracts had been lifelong residents of the city and 22 percent had lived in Montauban for less than five years. Some of these men came from the Rouergue, Cantal, and the Pyrenees, traditional regions of migration, but more came from northern Quercy and one third were born in the countryside immediately surrounding Montauban. Migration swelled the city's population both directly and indirectly by adding to the age cohorts who had the highest fertility and the lowest mortality.[16]

In the second half of the eighteenth century, the countryside around Montauban—as in many other areas of France—faced overpopulation,

---

[15] Latouche, *La Vie en bas-quercy*, pp. 265, 309. See AM Mont 4 i 15 police générale, voyageurs de passage and 1 U 1 tribunal correctionnel, vendémiaire Year 13, for the interrogation of two couples of traveling peddlers arrested in the Montauban market as pickpockets.

[16] Gausseran, "La Population montalbanaise," p. 60; Daniel Ligou, "Montauban des lumières," in Ligou, ed., *Histoire de Montauban*, p. 168. Pinède, "La Population," pp. 51–103. A census taken at the behest of the Montauban city council in 1774 reported 24,599 inhabitants. AM Mont 2 BB 13 Délibérations du Conseil Général, 19–6–1774, pp. 276–277. Such migration was typical of the late eighteenth century. See Poussou, *Bordeaux et le Sud-Ouest*, pp. 73–78.

TABLE 2–2
Origin of Montauban Grooms, 1775–1799

All grooms resident in Montauban	$N = 237$
Montauban born	64%
Immigrants	36
Immigrant grooms born in	$N = 85$
Tarn-et-Garonne	33%
Lot (Cahors)	14
Haute Garonne (Toulouse)	12
Other neighboring departments (Gers, Tarn, Lot-et-Garonne, Aveyron)	12
Other southern departments	13
Rest of France	14
Foreign countries	2

rising prices, and intense competition for land. Peasants worked the land either as sharecroppers renting a complete farm or as owners or renters of scattered plots of land. In neither case could agriculture absorb the population growth.

Montauban's nobility and gentry owned much of the best farmland around the city and along the river valleys, which they divided into individual farms known as *métairies*. Even the largest landholdings were broken into these small units and rented out separately. The farms usually took the name of the landlords, so that Montauban's countryside was dotted with farmsteads and hamlets called Garrisson, Ponset, Scorbiac, Godoffre, Vialettes, and Debia, all names of important Montauban families.

Most landholders, however, were peasants who owned only fields or portions of fields rather than a complete farm. The average landholding was small. In the district of Montauban, well-to-do landowners owned about half of the available land. Peasant farmers owned another quarter, with an average holding of seven-and-one-half hectares. The remaining quarter of the land was divided into tiny parcels averaging only two hectares each. Most of these holdings were insufficient to support a family.[17]

These figures impose a static quality on rural landholding that is false. Peasants and landowners bought and sold land constantly. Seventy-one percent of the sample of sales and purchases registered by notaries between 1775 and 1790 were for agricultural land. While some people struggled to patch together new farms out of bits and pieces, others were forced to sell or divide existing farms. A good example is a transaction that occurred in 1803. Philibert, a tenant farmer, bought a piece of land in St Nauphary

---

[17] Ligou, *Montauban*, p. 77; Bergeon, "La Terre et le paysan," pp. 7–26.

from Antoine Bousquet. The land lay between a strip Philibert had recently purchased from Gerard Bousquet, brother of Antoine, a second strip owned by Jean Bousquet, another brother, and a vineyard owned by another party. With his purchase, Philibert reunited two thirds of the original Bousquet field, which inheritance had divided among the three brothers.[18] Much rural property was probably in such an intermediary state, neither completely fragmented nor completely consolidated.

In areas where large landholdings predominated, as in northern Quercy, the growing population could find work as farm servants, but on the small farms around Montauban it was much harder to find employment. In only the substantial *métairies* were field hands hired regularly and then only if the farmer's family was unable to supply enough labor. As a result, most young men needed their own pieces of land in order to earn a living and so entered the great land scramble. Arable land was expanded beyond its natural limits. Peasants cut down trees, plowed up roads, and impinged on common lands. The result was repeated flooding, rare in this region before the eighteenth century, and the loss of topsoil.[19] Land prices soared and landlords made new demands on sharecroppers. One of the most popular new additions—popular with landlords, that is—was the *avantage préciputaire*, a cut usually equal to the amount of seed, taken from the harvest before the traditional division was made in the first year of the lease. Like "key money," the bribe demanded by Manhattan landlords, the first cut was negotiated privately between the landowner and the tenant and rarely appeared in the rental agreement. Because of this and other practices, the portion of the harvest (excluding seed) that the sharecropper could retain fell from an average of 32 percent in the seventeenth century to 27 percent by the end of the eighteenth century.[20]

Contributing to peasants' problems was the famous "feudal reaction," which was particularly virulent in southern Quercy. Although Montauban was free of seigneurial obligations, Nègrepelisse, Corbarieu, St Nauphary, and other nearby towns and villages were not so fortunate. In 1782 the mayor of Molières expressed the fear that the town would soon be impoverished by the numerous lawsuits brought by ambitious *feudists* who sought to reimpose long-forgotten obligations.[21] In the Toulouse area, about 18 percent of the revenues of local nobles came from seigneurial dues; seigneurs in the Montauban area probably received as much if not more. Bressols, for example, paid more than two thousand livres in seigneurial dues in 1778.[22]

The weight of the feudal reaction was not confined to financial extrac-

---

[18] AD T-et-G 5E 12870 Grelleau no. 1 1–1–1781 vente Bousquet à Philibert.
[19] Latouche, *La Vie en bas-quercy*, pp. 153–154.
[20] Frêche, *Toulouse*, p. 248.
[21] Latouche, *La Vie en bas-quercy*, p. 81.
[22] Bastier, *La Féodalité*, pp. 309, 265; Ligou, *Montauban*, p. 30.

tions. Many seigneurs were equally anxious to maintain or create rituals of respect and·subservience. Often they forced their peasants to submit through lawsuits and sometimes violence. However, the peasants, too, had personal honor to maintain, which required that subservience be bestowed discriminately. They particularly resented inventions and even traditional forms of submission when commanded by seigneurs of recent or dubious nobility. Sometimes peasant resistance took the form of a court case against the seigneur—almost always a hopeless gesture—but more often peasants attacked the seigneur through acts of minor vandalism and defiance such as letting cattle into the lord's field, poaching, cutting trees, or omitting to doff the cap. Lawsuits and prosecution for such misdemeanors increased tensions. Not only did the number of rural misdemeanors escalate in the second half of the eighteenth century, but the number of crimes of violence like armed robbery and assault increased as well. Social as well as economic pressures encouraged peasants to emigrate to the city.[23]

Although by midcentury officials were aware of growing rural poverty,[24] Montaubaners did not become concerned about the migration of peasants into the city until the 1770s and 1780s. Until this time, Montauban offered extensive opportunities to young people seeking work. Expansion in textiles, flour trade, and commerce in general created a need for unskilled labor—porters, boatmen, and common laborers—as well as textile workers, both male and female.[25] The depressions during and after the Seven Years' War and in the 1780s changed Montaubaners' views of immigration. In 1783, in reply to a circular from the intendant, Montauban's parish priests complained that the influx of the poor from the countryside prevented any effective relief in the city. In 1789, Cinfraix, a town councillor, registered his disapproval of relief payments, which he believed simply drew poor people into the city. In his view, rapidly endorsed by the Charity Bureau, only work projects in the countryside would prevent Montauban from being flooded with indigent people.[26]

---

[23] Bastier, *Féodalité*, pp. 94–95, 209–211, 289–294; Castan, *Honnêteté*, pp. 21–22, 259–260; and Castan, *Criminels de Languedoc*, pp. 86–95, 103–112. Hilton Lewis Root, in "Challenging the Seigneurie," argues that in Burgundy, what peasants may have begun as resistance to seigneurs' innovations, became, through the encouragement of lawyers and royal officials, a rejection of seigneurial rights in toto. This escalation is evident around Montauban as well.

[24] For example, in 1757 the municipality of Montpezat, a country town north of Montauban, reported that at least one third of its inhabitants depended on charity. Latouche, *La Vie en bas-quercy*, p. 349.

[25] Poussou, "Recherches sur l'immigration quercynoise," pp. 407–408.

[26] Sol, "Les Bureaux de charité," pp. 260–284; AM Mont 29 GG 1–2 Bureau de charité 5–1–1789 and following. Cinfraix's ideas for work projects responded well to his image of the rural influx as a deluge; he thought the poor should be put to work repairing the riverbanks and filling the swamps!

The bustling activity of the Villebourbon wharf described earlier was of relatively recent origin in the 1780s. Since the Middle Ages there had been a textile industry in Montauban, but in the seventeenth century it had been in decline, unable to compete with English fabric, which was both cheaper and of better quality. Then late in the century several of the larger manufacturers began to experiment with different fibers and weaves. In the early eighteenth century, Vialètes d'Aignan and Serres, two brothers-in-law, perfected a new woolen fabric called *cadis*. As Abbé Expilly described it, it was "neither elegant nor costly but of good quality. . . . Its cheapness stimulates consumption."[27] Heavy and durable, the cloth found markets in Brittany and Canada, in religious orders and among sailors and peasants throughout France. By 1742, 170 manufacturers were turning out eight thousand pieces of cloth a year. Others, in an attempt to repeat Vialètes d'Aignan and Serres's success—their successors eventually became royal manufacturers—experimented with other fabrics, particularly serges, knits, and lightweight cloth for the West Indian trade. What had begun as a single-product industry was, by midcentury, so diverse and adaptable that even the loss of the Canadian market in 1763 appeared to be only a temporary setback. In the last decades of the Old Regime, Mariette, a grain dealer, and several other merchants received government backing to launch into silk manufacture, which, with the aid of the latest technical innovations, showed considerable promise of success.[28]

Throughout the second half of the eighteenth century the textile industry consolidated. Before 1750, master craftsmen, assisted by their journeymen and apprentices, had produced most of the cloth in small workshops. The average *fabrique* had less than five workers. Gradually these independent craftsmen lost out to the larger entrepreneurs, who were better able to withstand the economic crises and adapt to the changing market conditions. The loss of the Canadian market, in particular, "shook out" a number of smaller manufacturers who went bankrupt. However, as the number of *fabriques* declined, that of textile workers rose. By 1780 there were only sixty manufacturers, but these employed eight to ten thousand workers. Many of them were still small establishments, but several, like Serres, Vialètes d'Aignan, Rachou, and Debia, had developed into workshops that resembled factories. In the Serres establishment, although there was no power equipment, a team of workers did all the preparatory tasks including washing, combing, carding, twisting, and spinning, as well as the finishing processes, under one roof. Serres directly employed approxi-

[27] Expilly, *Dictionnaire géographique* 4: 805. AN F¹² 559 L'Etat général et précis des manufactures et du commerce de la ville et généralité de Montauban, 1783, described the cloth: "What they call felted *cadis* is a fabric in which the warp is combed wool and the weft is carded wool and which is crossed on the loom. This fabric is fulled, felted, sheared and finished like frieze."

[28] Ligou, *Montauban*, pp. 108–110.

mately four hundred people in his Montauban manufactory and probably twice as many in the countryside, where, to avoid guild regulations, most of the weaving was done. About 80 percent of the urban textile workers were without guild protection; they included many women and children.[29]

The other major industry in Montauban was the milling of grain and the transport of grain and flour. Milling was not as big a direct employer as the textile industry, at its height employing only about two thousand workers. Indirectly, however, it was extremely important. The mills in Montauban and Moissac shipped out about eighty thousand barrels of flour a year and so of course provided work to hundreds of barrel makers, teamsters, wagon builders, innkeepers, stevedores, and boatmen. Like textiles, the grain industry had expanded rapidly. In 1768 there were one dozen flour mills in Montauban; by 1788 there were forty-two. In the 1780s, the value of the flour exported from Montauban and Moissac was worth about three and a half million livres, about double that of cadis production, making the grain trade both more lucrative and more secure than textile manufacture.[30]

By the early 1780s Montauban's textile industry was in trouble due to economic difficulties and to internal disorganization. Although the industry had recovered from the depression brought by the Seven Years' War, its growth was irregular and hampered by periodic slumps. The merchants disagreed over what was the best course of action. When the government first abolished manufacturing regulations in 1779, the Merchants' Guild hailed the new freedom as a solution to the industry's doldrums, but many merchants were skeptical. When conditions did not improve, they lobbied within the guild to reimpose regulation in Montauban.

In a 1785 petition to the king, the wardens of the Merchants' Guild attempted to define a policy that would solve the problems of Montauban's textile industry. Their proposal was an unsuccessful compromise between the demand of traditional manufacturers of cadis to reimpose regulation lock, stock, and barrel and the needs of more freewheeling entrepreneurs who were experimenting with lighter-weight and lower-quality cloth and wanted the freedom to continue to innovate. The wardens asked that the size of the warp be standardized for various types of cloth and that frauds be prosecuted, but they also concluded that dyers should be exempt from most regulation and that cottage industry must be exempt from any at all. The petition concluded with an attack on the

[29] Ibid., p. 105, 128; Ombret et al., *Montauban, cité drapière*; Forestié, *Fabrication des draps*; and AN F12 559 L'Etat général et précis des manufactures 1783.

[30] Frêche, *Toulouse*, p. 779; Jean-Pierre Poussou, "Une Vallée riche et peuplée," in Garrisson-Estèbe and Ferro, eds., *Histoire de la Garonne*, p. 372; and AN F[12] 559 L'Etat général et précis des manufacturers 1783.

Royal Manufacturers, Vialètes d'Aignan and Serres, requesting that the king suppress the "privileges and prerogatives" of some manufacturers or else extend them to everyone of the same importance. The petition, incoherent in itself, pleased no one and was never dispatched to Paris, but it aptly reflects the disorganization and division within the industry.[31]

The free trade treaty with Great Britain brought more problems. Signed in 1786, the Vergennes treaty opened French markets to English cloth. As in the seventeenth century, Montauban's products were found to be not competitive in an unprotected market. Particularly hard hit was the most traditional branch of the industry, the manufacture of cadis. Since the loss of Canada, cadis production had been in decline, but merchants had recently developed new markets in Brittany. Now these too were lost to Great Britain. The year 1788 was the worst that Montauban's textile industry had experienced since the Seven Years' War. As many as seven thousand people, about one quarter of the population, were unemployed. Already disorganized and of several minds about how to proceed, Montauban's manufacturers were unable to meet this new challenge.[32]

The crisis in the textile industry added fuel to conflicts between textile workers and the merchant-manufacturers which had been heating up since midcentury. The craft guilds argued for protection whereas merchant-manufacturers espoused the ideal of free trade—at least until the Vergennes treaty. Guild regulations were a constant annoyance to textile manufacturers. In 1765 cloth-shearing workers walked out when, in an effort to cut costs, manufacturers began to make cloth wider and longer than allowed by the guild's regulations and expected the workers to finish it at the same wages. The judges appointed by the Merchants' Guild, of course, found for the manufacturers, judging the workers' organization to be illegal, but they also directed the manufacturers to abide by the guild regulations in the future. To avoid oversight of the guild, many manufacturers resorted to using rural weavers and finishers even though they were often undependable.[33] In 1789, the *cahier de doléances* from Montauban expressed the point of view of merchant-manufacturers and ignored the artisans' and smaller merchants' demands for the rehabilitation of the guild system. The Carpenters' Guild protested the final version and registered a complaint to this effect.[34]

---

[31] AM Mont 8 HH 7 Manufactures 1754–1785, pp. 134–142, 174; Forestié, *Fabrication des draps*, pp. 29–31.

[32] AN F[12] 1378 Lettre de M. Bruté, inspecteur des manufactures, 14–12–1788; Ombret et al., *Montauban, cité drapière*.

[33] AM Mont 8 HH 7 Manufacture 1754–1785, pp. 87–93; AN F[12] 559 Etat général et précis des manufactures 1783.

[34] Malrieu, ed. *Cahiers de doléances de la sénéchaussée de Montauban*; Ligou, *Montauban*, p. 199.

The conflicts within the textile industry were only the most public of social tensions in Montauban on the eve of the Revolution. The landlord-tenant and the seigneur-peasant conflicts we have already discussed would explode into violence in 1790. Meanwhile, courts, assemblies, and officials squabbled over jurisdictions and precedence. The most serious was a campaign of the Cour des Aides in the 1750s to curtail the power of the royal intendant. As a result, the king ordered the exile of two magistrates but replaced the intendant. Such half-hearted attempts at reform, however, exacerbated the quarrels in the long run.[35] The writing of the cahiers also made evident a long-standing split within the clergy. After a "tumultuous" assembly, the clergy presented two cahiers, one from the upper clergy and one from the lower.[36]

An overriding cleavage in religion camouflaged these conflicts. Montauban had been a Protestant stronghold during the Wars of Religion, a designated place of refuge under the Edict of Nantes, and, after Paris and La Rochelle, the most important Protestant city in France. The campaign for re-Catholicization had been vigorous. At least six hundred people had emigrated while a whole new Catholic administration had been imported to take charge. In the early eighteenth century Montauban had become a Catholic town with a Protestant minority.[37]

Excluded by law from the legal profession and from public office and by tradition and prudence from owning land, most well-off Protestants had gone into commerce and industry. Most of Montauban's major commercial and manufacturing families, such as Mariette, Debia, Garrisson, and Rigail, were Protestant. Throughout the eighteenth century these well-off Protestants were careful to remain within the law. They avoided the wilderness assemblies, the secret open-air meetings that were popular with lower-class and rural Protestants. Even when implicit toleration permitted regular, if semiclandestine, services in Montauban itself, the Protestant beau monde did not attend.[38] Obliging priests baptized, married, and even buried wealthy Protestants in the Catholic church.[39]

---

[35] Cuillieron, *Contributions à l'étude de la rebellion des cours souverains.*

[36] Ligou, *Montauban*, p. 200. In 1779, the royal government created a number of new provincial assemblies in order to involve local notables in government by entrusting them with some powers, for instance, in apportioning taxes and directing public works. Such an assembly was created for Quercy and Rouergue, but its jurisdiction overlapped with both the intendance and the Cour des Aides. Vigorously defending their prerogatives, these officials effectively prevented the assembly from assuming any responsibility. Ibid., pp. 16–19.

[37] Bost, "Les Protestants montalbanais," pp. 42–57; Gausseran, "L'Exode des protestants," pp. 35–54; Poland, *French Protestants and the French Revolution*, p. 16.

[38] Jeannette Philippine Leclerc, daughter of a family that had fled to Germany after the Revocation, visited Montauban in 1773 and went to the local assembly. She described the congregation as "force de petit peuple, et peu de beau monde" (lots of nobodies and few notables), cited in Richard, *La Vie quotidienne des protestants*, pp. 296–298.

[39] Some priests apparently made a racket of these marriages, performing them without proper instruction and proof of baptism for a price. Castan, in *Honnêteté*, p. 430, cites one

By the 1780s, outright persecution of Protestants, or adherents of the *religion prétendu reformé* (RPR), as it was called, had abated. The elite of both faiths branded religious enthusiasm as fanaticism and embraced comfortable moderation if not fashionable deism. R. R. Palmer wrote of Montauban's Protestant minister and future Terrorist Jeanbon Saint-André: "Calvinism in him was diluted into a generalized morality. He disliked religious excitement because it interfered with public order, and he demanded toleration for Protestants, not as a right, but as a means of making Frenchmen cooperate in worldly and national concerns."[40]

The Edict of Toleration of 1787 capped the end of open religious conflict. The official view, expounded by the Protestants who had led the campaign for toleration, was that Protestants were good citizens, good Frenchmen, and that reason—as opposed to fanaticism—demanded they be treated as such.

In this climate, the exclusion of Protestants from public life began to break down and the social gulf between the Protestant commercial elite and the Catholic official elite narrowed. For example, in 1787 Marc Antoine Sartre de Salir, a barrister at the Parlement of Toulouse and the younger son of a local seigneur, married Jeanne Catherine Elizabeth Baillo, daughter of a prominent Protestant merchant.[41] Some of the wealthiest merchant-manufacturers began to dissociate themselves from the dockside activity, moved into the old town, retired to bourgeois status, and bought country homes. They began to strive to live *noblement*, in elegance and leisure, gave receptions, dinners, and balls, and entertained the common folk with spectacles and fireworks. The wealthiest Protestant merchant-manufacturers, like Lagravère and Vialètes d'Aignan, sought out appointments as municipal councillors, overseers of the hospital and other posts which had been traditional routes to ennoblement.[42] At the same time they were overcoming the old fears about investment in real estate. In 1772, Anne Mariette, daughter of one great merchant and widow of another, gave her sons a house and garden in Moustiers—the

---

priest from the Montauban diocese who was disciplined for performing about sixty of these quickie ceremonies. See AD T-et-G G 456b Procédures devant l'Officialité 1745–1749, 14–7–1746, a petition to reprimand the priest of Villedieu for marrying two wealthy Montaubaners without proper procedure or proof of Catholicism.

[40] R. R. Palmer, *Twelve Who Ruled: The Committee of Public Safety During the Terror* (Princeton: Princeton University Press, 1941), p. 11. Wemyss, in "Les Protestants du midi," pp. 307–322, gives a similar evaluation of well-off Montauban Protestants.

[41] AD T-et-G 5E 1943 Caminel no. 207 17–4–1787 contrat de mariage Sartre de Salir-Baillo.

[42] Vialètes d'Aignan, in a petition in 1776 to have his privilege as royal manufacturer maintained, claimed to be "descended from a Noble family of Rouergue where the castle still exists which gives the family its name and has their arms over the door." A Mont AA 77 Livre rouge neuf, p. 47, 5–3–1777. In fact, he was the descendant of an alliance between two manufacturing families, the Vialettes and the Daignans.

new fashionable district on the right bank of the Tarn—as well as two large farms in St Nauphary worth one hundred thousand livres.[43] In the Sartre de Salire–Baillo marriage, part of Mlle Baillo's dowry was a house and farm.

Under a patina of reason and tolerance, however, religion remained an explosive issue in Montauban on the eve of the Revolution. First, it was only some twenty-five years since religious violence had last scarred the region. In 1761 and 1762 the Rochette affair in Caussade, followed closely by the more famous Calas affair in Toulouse, had opened up a Pandora's box of mutual misunderstanding, suspicion, and hostility.

The Rochette affair, which occurred within Montauban's jurisdiction, summoned up old fears of peasant jacqueries. Rochette was a Protestant preacher arrested by a highway patrol on suspicion of being a highwayman. After a mob of local Protestants failed to obtain his release, rumors flew that an army of Protestant peasants was forming to storm the town of Caussade, where he was being held. A hastily gathered Catholic militia arrested three respectable tradesmen as the leaders of this insurrection. Montaubaners apparently believed in this tale, including the reports of six hundred marauding Protestants led by a man on horseback who charged shouting "Kill! Kill!" Even in the Protestant community, few questioned the tales and fewer still did anything to obtain the acquittal of Rochette or the three so-called ringleaders, all of whom were executed.[44]

The Calas affair, which followed hard on the heels of the Rochette trial, was more complex and aroused greater anxiety. It concerned the mysterious death of Marc-Antoine Calas, son of a Protestant merchant of Toulouse. There was evidence suggesting that young Calas had quarreled with his family and was on the verge of converting to Catholicism. The police arrested the Calas family and a Protestant merchant who was visiting them, charging them with murdering the young man to prevent him from dishonoring the family by converting. A pamphlet by Abbé de Contezat argued that Calvinist doctrine permitted or even commanded such executions[45] and rumors ran wild of secret assemblies that pronounced sentence against recanting Protestants. In these tales, Montauban played a large and sinister role as the source of the Protestant conspiracy. One of

---

[43] Gausseran, "La Bourgeoisie montalbanaise" and AD T-et-G 418 registre pour l'insinuation des donations entre vifs no. 85 18–12–1772.

[44] Bien, *The Calas Affair*, pp. 77–81. Montauban's Protestant community was upset by the Rochette affair, but their only recorded protest was woefully inadequate. Merchant Lacoste-Rigail wrote in his *livre de raison* on the day following Rochette's execution: "No one from Villebourbon [the Protestant commercial neighborhood] at yesterday's concert. M. Rochette, minister, hung in Toulouse and the three gentlemen brothers decapitated." Quoted in Ligou and Garrisson-Estèbe, "La Bourgeoisie réformée," p. 399.

[45] A. Coquerel, *Jean Calas et sa famille* (Geneva: Slatkine Reprints, 1970), p. 180.

the witnesses against Calas senior, a young seamstress and supposed ex-Calvinist, testified that Marc-Antoine had warned her against accepting employment in Montauban because it was sure to be a trap set for her by vengeful Protestants.[46] The Calas outburst was more explicitly anti-Protestant than the Rochette affair had been, but like the Rochette case it also revealed class antagonisms. Much of the anti-Protestant rhetoric was directed at the well-to-do merchant community and revealed deep misunderstanding and suspicion of commercial activities. In the popular mind, the connections of Toulouse Protestants to those of Montauban and Bordeaux were evidence of a vast and nefarious conspiracy rather than the product of normal business relationships.

In the 1780s there were five to six thousand Protestants living in Montauban, one fifth of the population. In rural towns mostly to the west of the city lived about three thousand more. In both town and country, their relative economic prominence belied their minority position. Protestant peasants tended to be landowners, and almost half of the urban Protestants were merchants, manufacturers, and bourgeois. They were vulnerable to charges of exploitation and hoarding that would be hurled at them during the Revolution. Even among the working people, there were conflicts of interest between Protestants and Catholics. Montauban's Protestants tended to be textile artisans; rarely were they shopkeepers or common laborers. Their work brought them into direct involvement with the needs of commerce such as the elimination of internal tariffs and the abolition of guild privileges. As landowners, merchants, and even textile workers, the Protestant minority threatened traditional order, not only the hegemony of the Catholic church but also the values of the moral economy.

Throughout the 1770s and 1780s minor incidents continued to occur, which indicated that the quasi-official tolerance did not penetrate Montauban society very deeply. In 1771, for example, the intendant had to forbid the production of a play that threatened to provoke a riot. The play, called *The Honest Criminal*, was a sentimental plea for religious toleration. The hero was a young Protestant who took his father's place in the galleys after the father had been arrested at a wilderness assembly. The villains, of course, were the Catholic officials.[47]

On the eve of the Revolution, Montauban's future was uncertain but hopeful. The textile industry was drifting, but recovery and growth seemed more likely than collapse. Social and religious divisions remained but integration seemed possible. In any case, Montaubaners had lived and

---

[46] Bien, *The Calas Affair*, p. 122.

[47] The play was later produced in Year 4 and did indeed cause a riot. Malrieu, " 'L'Honnête criminel,' " pp. 109–111.

even prospered with those divisions for a century or more. The Revolution tipped the balance decisively against Montauban and turned the teaming wharves of the eighteenth century into the semideserted quay of the twentieth.

The Revolution in Montauban was not particularly violent; the Terror authorized only one execution. Nevertheless, the Revolution changed the town and the lives of the inhabitants. The rivalry for municipal authority in 1790 formed political factions that dominated local politics well into the nineteenth century. The English blockade and the new market found in army contracts conspired to redirect and eventually destroy Montauban's commerce and industry. Internecine municipal politics and industrial and commercial depression, added to the city's pre-Revolutionary ills, proved fatal.

The Revolution in Montauban began with the revolt of the magistrates in 1786–1788, which captured public attention in Paris and Toulouse. Montauban's magistrates, who had familial as well as professional ties to the Parlement of Toulouse, had waged their own intermittent guerrilla war with the royal government in the person of the intendant throughout the 1750s and 1760s and supported the parlementarians' resistance to the royal government in 1771.[48] However, unlike their Parisian colleagues, these magistrates did little to popularize their cause locally. By the fall of 1788 opposition to the magistrates was already growing among the merchants. After the municipal officers responded to a royal circular about the Estates General with a spirited defense of the Cour des Aides and the Parlement of Toulouse without a single mention of the needs or rights of the Third Estate, the leading merchants took matters into their own hands. They organized a public meeting in December, which voted overwhelmingly in favor of the program identified with the Third Estate—vote by head, fiscal equality, elected local government, and so forth.[49]

The Revolution was already beginning to draw lines within the ranks of the elite, but as yet neither the officials nor the merchants had made much of an attempt to interest the general public. Even after the fall of the

[48] Cuillieron, *Contributions à l'étude de la rebellion des cours souverains*; Caston, *Criminels de Languedoc*, p. 253.

[49] The resolutions of this assembly actually went further in demanding a predominant role for the Third Estate than did Abbé Sièyes's famous pamphlet. Rather than simply calling for the doubling of the Third Estate's delegation, the Montauban meeting demanded that the deputies of the Third Estate make up three fifths of the total number of deputies and that the three orders deliberate and vote together "so that the superiority of the representation in the assembly of the Estates General not be illusory." One hundred and seventy men signed the deliberation, their names a roster of the merchant and manufacturing families as well as a sprinkling of lawyers and town councillors. The syndics of several guilds also signed—the wig makers, tanners, cabinetmakers, and bakers—and twenty men including two peasants made their mark. AM Mont 2 BB 21 Délibérations du Conseil général, May 1788–October 1789, pp. 75–85.

Bastille, the local power struggle in Montauban was more of a palace coup than a popular uprising. The Patriotic Committee, which took over the municipal government, included officials and magistrates as well as merchants. The circumstance that "revolutionized" the situation was the Great Fear.

On July 31, Montaubaners learned that brigands had pillaged Lauzerte, a town about twenty-five miles away, and were descending on Montauban. Although the next day reports arrived that the bandits had been captured, the people of the town were excited and involved as they had not been before. Merchants and artisans rushed to join the Bourgeois Militia, which the Patriotic Committee had created. In the militia, soon to be called the National Guard, the divisions present since the preceding year became clear. Although the Patriotic Committee included many of the Old Regime elite—Catholic and official but not noble—the officers of the guard were largely merchants and the majority were Protestant.[50]

As the Patriotic Committee began to build a group of supporters, opposition began to form as well. First, the abolition of the Toulouse Parlement, the Cour des Aides, and the other lesser courts ended whatever ambiguity Montauban's magistrates may have felt about the National Assembly. Second, in the partitioning of France into departments, the Patriotic Committee failed to obtain for Montauban the departmental seat that went to Cahors. Although this failure probably had little impact on the already disaffected magistrates, it was a major blow to the legal profession, which had been reconciled to the loss of the Old Regime courts only by the promise of replacement institutions. This promise was not fulfilled.[51] Equally hard hit were artisans of the luxury trades—wig makers and jewelers, for example—who had outfitted the pageantry of the Old Regime. Third, the high clergy fulminated against what they saw as policies favoring Protestants. In their *cahier*, the high clergy had demanded that the Estates General revoke the 1787 Edict of Toleration, and Verdier, the grand vicar of the cathedral, censored local priests who preached in favor of tolerance or the natural equality of man. When the National Assembly granted full civil rights to Protestants, the bishop of Montauban ordered public prayers as for a national disaster.[52]

The rural uprisings in early 1790 forged links of fear and common interest within the elite, which consolidated the core of the Catholic Aris-

[50] Arches, "Les Débuts de la garde nationale de Montauban," pp. 303–310; AM Mont 2 BB 21 Conseil général 1788–1789, pp. 190–192.

[51] The battle over departmental capitals is a minor theme of bitterness that runs through the history of the Revolution in the provinces. For example, Marseilles, slighted by the choice of Aix as the capital of the Bouches du Rhone, kidnapped the departmental administration in August 1792. See Scott, *Terror and Repression in Revolutionary Marseilles*, pp. 27–29, 35–36.

[52] Lapeyre, *Les Insurrections du Lot en 1790*, p. 42; and Galabert, "Le Club jacobin," p. 131.

tocrat party in Montauban. In January and February, bands of peasants attacked, burned, and looted a number of châteaux owned by Montauban nobles and clerics. Here, as elsewhere, the main targets were archives containing "proofs" of seigneurial obligations. Although there was little violence to persons, its threat sent many landlords and their agents to Montauban seeking protection, retribution, and revenge.[53] When the Patriotic Committee refused to use the National Guard to patrol the countryside, the vicomte de Chaunac formed a volunteer force to do the job. This company formed an organized—and armed—body of support for the opposition.

The first municipal elections held in February 1790 offered the nobility and clergy a chance to reclaim direction of local affairs. Formed in response to fear, and in particular, to unaccustomed feelings of impotence, the new party masked its defense of property and privilege with a mobilizing ideology of militant Catholicism. The leaders, nobles Caumont-Laforce and Cieurac and clerics Mulot and Verdier, whipped up popular discontent with the Patriot government, playing on both the worsening economic situation and the latent religious divisions. They ascribed the food shortages, unemployment, and the Revolution itself to a vicious Protestant plot. The Protestants, they claimed, were bent on decimating the Catholic poor and taking over France. When regarded from the local perspective, these charges were not so farfetched. Booksellers hawked pamphlets lauding the freedom of religious practice and distributed the speeches of Paul Rabaut de Saint Etienne, a Protestant minister from Nîmes serving in the National Assembly. Meanwhile, Montauban's wealthy Protestants were everywhere in evidence among the Patriots, in the Electoral Assembly, on the Patriotic Committee, and in the National Guard. These men were also textile merchants and wholesale dealers in wheat and flour. The thrust of the campaign, however, was less economic than religious; it attacked the Patriots less as hoarders or exploiters, characterizations used later by the sansculottes, than as Protestants. The religious issue proved very effective in polarizing public opinion and getting out the vote. Although the Patriots won in the merchant district of Villebourbon and in the worker district of Villenouvelle, the four center city districts, inhabited mainly by artisans and shopkeepers, elected aristocrats. The marquis de Cieurac became the mayor, and thirty of the forty-five municipal councillors were nobles, officials, and clerics. Only six were merchants and only three Protestants.[54]

Throughout the spring, Montauban's legally elected government took steps in a counter-Revolutionary direction. The vicomte de Chaunac neu-

53 Sol, *Révolution en Quercy* 1: 236–237; and Boutier, "Jacqueries en pays croquant," pp. 760–786.

54 Bibliotèque Forestié, index; Ligou, *Montauban*, pp. 218–219, 222–225; Arches, "Les Débuts de la garde nationale de Montauban," p. 310.

tralized the National Guard as a revolutionary force by adding new aristocratic companies. The town council regularly ignored orders from Paris
and set about making Montauban a stronghold of aristocracy much as it
had been a stronghold of Protestantism in the sixteenth century. It was
only a matter of time and opportunity before the central government
would lay siege as Richelieu had done a century and a half earlier.

The incident that provoked intervention by the national government
occurred on May 10. A group of National Guardsmen of the old Patriot
guard, following orders from Paris, attempted to inventory the contents of
a convent in preparation for their sale. A large rowdy crowd, which the
guardsmen claimed had been hired by the municipal government, blocked
entry. The two groups exchanged insults, blows, and perhaps shots until
the guardsmen were "rescued" by a detachment of the regiment of Languedoc, a body whose officers were in close agreement with the municipal
authorities. This rescue ended with 5 guardsmen dead, 16 wounded, and
55 imprisoned, 44 of them merchants and textile manufacturers. The
confrontation was the worst in a series of skirmishes between the municipal government and the defeated Patriotic Committee. This time, the
spilling of Patriot blood (among the dead were such notables as merchants
Louis Garrisson and Rouffio-Crampes), as well as the arrest of loyal National Guardsmen for carrying out their duties, provided the National
Assembly with a clear-cut case of counter-Revolutionary action.

Patriot merchants not directly involved in the incident quickly left town
both in fear for themselves and to solicit support for their imprisoned
colleagues. The commercial community in Bordeaux with which Montauban merchants had close ties organized a volunteer force to liberate
Montauban. Agen and Castelsarrasin, which were on the line of march
from Bordeaux to Montauban, offered to mediate the situation to prevent
more bloodshed and to resolve the affair before the Bordeaux volunteers
had a chance to wreak havoc in the countryside. Montauban's government
held out against such offers partly in response to local feelings, now thor-
oughly aroused against the Bordelais "invasion," and partly because they
expected to be supported by Toulouse. Toulouse, however, refused to
become involved. On May 29, Cieurac capitulated to the demands of the
National Assembly and released the prisoners. Throughout June and July
the National Assembly scrutinized Montauban's affairs and eventually
concluded that the municipal regime could not continue. It suspended the
town council and replaced it with an appointed commission. Although
clashes continued between the two factions, by the following winter the
leadership of the Aristocrat party had recognized that their position was
untenable. Many emigrated, and the field was left to the merchant Patriots.[55]

[55] *Extrait du livre des délibérations du conseil de l'armée patriotique bordelaise* (Bordeaux:
1790); Ligou, *Montauban*, pp. 232–244.

The rank and file that had supported the Aristocrats remained ambivalent toward the Revolution, or at least toward the local leadership. For example, one night in 1791, a sentinel on the bridge challenged two merchants returning home after a town council meeting. When they told him they were municipal officials, he replied that "the whole clique of Patriots are a pack of scoundrels and rascals and that he shat on them."[56] Artisans, shopkeepers, and boatmen made up the crowd that had fought with the guard in May, *menu peuple* who in Paris were among the sansculottes. If, in Montauban, their religious enthusiasm lent a reactionary coloring to their activities, many of their concerns were nonetheless the same as popular Revolutionary demands.[57] Of these, food, especially bread, was primary. Prices that had fallen to reasonable levels in 1790–1791 rose again thereafter in ways unexplained by the quality of the harvests, which were fairly good. The working people insisted on a controlled market, at least in grain, a program that had had the full support of the Aristocrat government.[58] The deteriorating economic situation forced the appointed commission and the elected Patriot government, which supplanted it, to continue and even expand the Old Regime policies of stockpiling, controlling the grain trade, and distributing bread to the poor. In 1793 the municipality imposed a forced loan of three hundred thousand francs on 150 of the richest inhabitants to buy grain to replenish depleted municipal stores. When this proved insufficient, the Surveillance Committee created a Revolutionary army to scour the region for grain and to arrest peasant "hoarders."[59]

Employment was also a major issue, especially for the textile workers. The slump in textiles worsened during the early years of the Revolution, and even those who could find work experienced a severe decline in real wages. Paid at traditional rates but in paper money, workers lost about one quarter of their earning power between 1790 and 1793.[60] They expressed their anger at continued unemployment, low wages, and high prices in "unpatriotic" songs, street violence, and sometimes direct action. One target was Vialètes d'Aignan, an extremely wealthy textile manufac-

[56] AM Mont 8 i 10 Juges de paix.

[57] James N. Hood and Colin Lucas make the same argument for the Midi, where bitter confessional conflict and economic grievances also often appeared to overlap. See Lucas, "The Problem of the Midi," and Hood, "Patterns of Popular Protest in the French Revolution."

[58] The Aristocrat government forbade grain shipments to Bordeaux to keep local markets well stocked, thereby at once satisfying their working-class supporters and striking at their merchant opponents. Ligou, *Montauban*, p. 376.

[59] Ibid., p. 379; Cobb, *People's Armies*, pp. 161–162, 173–174, 294–295, 297–298. Malrieu, in "Notes sur la navigation du Tarn en 1793," pp. 75–76, states that the town also curtailed traffic on the Tarn to permit the grist mills to work overtime.

[60] Ligou, *Montauban*, pp. 371–372.

turer, grain dealer (hoarder), and a major employer. On August 9, 1791, a mob invaded one of his textile enterprises, breaking windows and causing other damage. When in February of the following year he was again the object of an attack of "a crowd of evil-intentioned persons," he demanded that the municipality provide special protection for himself and his property.[61]

The draft was the other issue that caused popular demonstrations. The February 24, 1793, draft of 300,000 called for 240 recruits from Montauban. This call-up provoked resistance throughout the region; Moissac, Lafrançaise, Caylus, Bioule, and Réalville all reported problems, but resistance centered in Montauban. Recruiters managed to sign up only 18 Montaubaners, and on March 10, a large antidraft, antigovernment demonstration occurred, led, according to the authorities, by a harness maker named Claudel. The police arrested thirty-one people, almost all artisans, including several tailors, masons, bakers, shoemakers, a carpenter, a potter, a cabinetmaker, and the like. Only five were textile workers.[62] Claudel was guillotined, the only execution to occur in Montauban during the Revolution.

Officially, after July 1790, Montauban remained fairly calm and stable. There was little change in municipal personnel from one regime to the next until 1795. Several members of the original Patriotic Committee served over and over again in successive governments. These leaders weathered the Feuillant split, at first urging unity on their delegates and then siding with the Jacobins. They firmly resisted the attractions of the Federalist movement even though it was promoted by their friends in Bordeaux. Although the Terror brought stricter control of neighborhoods and the sequestration of anyone still in residence who had been implicated in the 1790 government, it brought no change of personnel, no purges comparable to those which were going on in the national government. Local Patriots were well aware that their real opposition came not from within their own ranks but from the outside. They knew that they were a minority government in power only because the opposition was in prison or in exile and that without the support of the central government they would lose their authority.[63]

---

[61] Ibid., p. 278; Sol, *Révolution en Quercy* 2: 131; and AM Mont de Mont 8 i 2 Tribunal de police municipal; plaints, extrait de jugement 1791–Year 2.

[62] Ligou, *Montauban*, p. 416.

[63] In this, Montauban's Revolution differed from the experience of Patriot municipal regimes in southern cities that became involved in Federalism. In Nîmes, for example, local patriots had dealt summarily with their Aristocrat municipal government (they massacred them and about three hundred supporters!) without outside intervention or Parisian support. In Marseilles, the Patriot's Club not only ran the town and the department and sent envoys and National Guard battalions to shore up the Revolution throughout the south, but even dispatched troops—the famous *Fédérés*—to revolutionize Paris. Their firm belief in the

R. R. Palmer wrote that Montauban's Terrorist Jeanbon Saint-André was an essentially conservative man, an administrator rather than a rebel. "Saint-André had the utmost respect for the government of the king. He looked to it to protect the Protestants from the Catholic hierarchy and from Catholic mobs. He was by temperament a government's man."[64] This assessment could apply equally well to Montauban's municipal officials. They were willing to accept the shifts in Parisian politics, the fall of the king, the Terror, even the fall of Robespierre, if the government in Paris would continue to ensure their tenuous position as Protestant merchants in a town that was becoming increasingly Catholic and noncommercial.

The Revolution had reawakened militant Catholicism. In the popular view, the battles of 1790 were part of a religious war. A woman in the crowd who had defended the convent on May 10 told investigators, "They wanted to take away the monks but we defended them against those filthy Huguenots [*bougres de huguenots*]." The merchants who took refuge in Bordeaux claimed that in Montauban all Patriots were branded as Protestants, "or at least as bad Catholics."[65] Despite Helen Maria Williams's impression that patriotic harmony reigned between Protestants and Catholics in the Montauban countryside,[66] the overtones of religious conflict continued to resonate. When the National Assembly ruled that all parish priests must swear allegiance to the Civil Constitution of the Clergy, only the priests of Sapiac and Le Fau complied. The replacement of unsworn priests provoked widespread disturbances both in the countryside and in Montauban Cathedral, where, according to Bruté, one of the few prominent Catholic Patriots, the women of the congregation met the new constitutional priest with catcalls and heckling.[67]

Against this background of stubborn Catholic resistance, de-Christianization did more to weaken Protestantism than Catholicism. Most Patriot Protestants abandoned Protestant services for the official

---

efficacy of their own commitment to the Revolution and their ability to run their own affairs led them to reject Parisian "tyranny." See Lucas, "The Problem of the Midi"; Hood, "Revival and Mutation of Old Rivalries"; and Scott, *Terror and Repression in Revolutionary Marseilles*.

[64] Palmer, *Twelve Who Ruled*, p. 11.

[65] Both cited in Galabert, "Le Club jacobin de Montauban," 1: 145–146.

[66] Helen Maria Williams reported a letter from Nègrepelisse detailing the complicated but harmonious way the town had celebrated the Feast of Federation in 1790, officiated by both a Catholic curé and a Protestant pastor; in J. M. Thompson, ed., *English Witnesses of the French Revolution* (Oxford: Basil Blackwell, 1938), pp. 85–86.

[67] Bruté maintained that the outbursts were engineered by the Aristocrat party, which planned to disrupt society and ruin Montauban's economy by manipulating the faith of women who had become "the trumpets of these dangerous intriguers." Cited in Galabert, "Le Club jacobin de Montauban," 1: 242–243. One wonders what Mme Bruté's opinion was.

ceremonies of the Cult of Reason, whose pageantry included the wives and daughters of leading merchants representing Liberty, Equality, and Victory and other Revolutionary ideals. In March 1794, the Protestant church closed completely, and although it reopened the following year, it never inspired the kind of enthusiasm that greeted the return of the Catholic church.[68] The Protestant elite became increasingly secular and anticlerical, whereas the Catholic elite remained militantly Catholic.

After the fall of Robespierre, the municipal government released suspects detained since the summer of 1790 and dismantled the local version of the Terror. Although the government did not purge itself, the Patriotic Society did, calling upon Poncet-Delpech, the former delegate to the Estates General, and other reputed moderates to take over. However, this half-step backward did not satisfy local feelings. In the election for the national government, Poncet-Delpech lost to a royalist candidate, and the municipal elections produced a government similar to the one elected in February 1790, composed mostly of *ci-devants*—nobles, magistrates of the Cour des Aides, and the two royal manufacturers, Vialètes d'Aignan and Serres. They restored Catholic worship and chopped down the Liberty Trees that their predecessors had planted, and their supporters harassed Patriots and posted royalist propaganda.[69]

However, this government, like municipal governments before it, administered only with the compliance of the national government. The coup of 18 *fructidor* Year 5 (September 4, 1797), which purged their representatives from the national legislature, appalled Montaubaners. As news of the coup arrived, threatening crowds gathered at the homes of well-known "Jacobins." When the municipal government refused to intervene, the departmental administration sent in a troop of about 150 police and soldiers to restore order. Mayor Sadoul, a former magistrate of the Cour des Aides, placed cannons to protect the entries to the city and rallied the inhabitants to the defense. At this point, the Directory suspended the municipal government and sent in fifteen thousand National Guardsmen to enforce order.[70]

The Directory installed a governing commission composed of Patriots, most of them well known from previous administrations. It kept a close

[68] Ligou, "Protestants et sans-culottes," pp. 182–185; Poland, *French Protestants and the French Revolution*, p. 204; Malrieu, *Les Fêtes civiques*, pp. 11–14; and Daniel Ligou and Philippe Joutard, "Les Deserts (1685–1800)," in Mandrou, ed., *Histoire des protestants en France*, pp. 259–260.

[69] Ligou, "Montauban des lumières," pp. 200–202.

[70] AM Mont 8 i 20 Tribunal criminel du Lot. Procès des officiers municipaux de Montauban, fructidor Year 5; 1 D 1 and 2 Délibérations, proclamations, procès-verbaux divers des officiers municipaux de Montabuan. Livre jaune 1 and 2, 31 May 1790–30 September 1817; 3 D 5 Délibérations du Conseil Général de la Commune de Montauban, 2 prairial Year 3–25 messidor Year 6.

watch on Montauban, purging six members of the town council elected in 1798 whom it thought too "anarchist." Close surveillance prevented Montauban from joining the counter-Revolutionary uprisings, which sputtered in the southwest throughout August 1799. In these revolts, as in the revolts provoked by the coup of 18 *fructidor*, religious themes continued to surface in the Montauban area. A Protestant landowner of St Etienne de Tulmon, a small town east of Montauban, complained that after the *fructidor* coup villagers had threatened him, accusing him of being a Robespierrist, a "jamboniste"[71] (Jeanbonist!), and a Terrorist who went running from house to house inciting all the Protestants to slaughter the Catholics. In the summer of 1799 in Saint Sardos, the hub of rural counter-Revolutionary activity in the Montauban region, the crowds chanted "Long Live the King! May the Protestants Perish!"[72]

Napoleon's coup brought no immediate change to Montauban's government, but in 1806 Napoleon rewarded an early supporter, Vialètes de Mortarieu, by appointing him mayor. Son of one of the city's wealthiest merchant families with distinctly aristocratic ambitions, Vialètes de Mortarieu served Montauban well. He lobbied hard to correct the slight done to the city in 1789 when it was passed over as a departmental seat. In 1808 Napoleon created the department of the Tarn-et-Garonne, mostly to redress this grievance. However, by 1813, both Vialètes and Montauban were no longer feeling grateful for the attention. Draft resistance escalated to epidemic proportions and the municipal government complained that the sacrifices the town was forced to make to supply the army in Spain were ruining the economy. As the English pushed through the Pyrenees, Vialètes de Mortarieu rallied to the Bourbon cause, and Montauban followed.[73] The Hundred Days found few of the Montauban elite willing to serve but also few people willing to defend the monarchy. The militia and the police worked efficiently to still any rebellion, but the cases that came before the Correctional Tribunal as "seditious crimes" were minor in the extreme—a fight between a group of apprentices singing Napoleonic songs and another group shouting royalist slogans, a gambler who toasted the king one evening in the tavern where he was plying his trade, and other such incidents.[74] Neither Bonaparte nor Louis XVIII attracted the public as the political and religious conflicts of the 1790s had done.

The Second Restoration was more troubled, stirring once more the

---

[71] This is a particularly delicious misnomer since St Etienne de Tulmon is known today for its country hams.

[72] AD T-et-G L 448 Tribunal civil du district de Montauban, Affaires politiques Years 5–7 and Malrieu, *L'Insurrection royaliste*, pp. 4–16.

[73] Jean Estèbe, "La Vie politique de Vialètes de Mortarieu à Irénée Bonnafous (1800–1939)," in Ligou, ed., *Histoire de Montauban*, pp. 246–251.

[74] AM Mont 1 U 3 tribunal correctionnel 1814–1815.

waters of religious conflict. Initially Montauban was quite calm. There was no massacre of Protestants as occurred in Nîmes or even a systematic purge of Bonapartists and Patriots as happened in Toulouse and Marseilles. The only victims of violence were four officers of the Imperial Guard, and most of the political arrests were for sedition similar to the ones prosecuted during the Hundred Days. However, the prefect, Villeneuve, fearing Protestant opposition, ordered a house-to-house search to seize Protestants' weapons. This action, unprecedented since the early eighteenth century, ripped through any veneer of religious reconciliation which the Napoleonic era had applied and established the political divisions of the town once more along religious lines.[75]

The Revolution's legacy to nineteenth-century municipal politics was intense factional hostility that substituted religious cleavages for social ones. During the Restoration and the July Monarchy, wealthy Catholic landowners dominated Montauban's government. Like their predecessors, the Aristocrat governments of 1790 and 1795, they mobilized the population largely with religious slogans. In the momentous elections of June 1830, artisans and workers demonstrated in favor of ultra-Rightist Vicomte de Gironde, and later that summer a group of boatmen shot down the tricolor that flew over the prefecture.[76] The Revolution of 1848 was a one-act replay of 1790. Universal suffrage produced a royalist and an outspokenly anti-Protestant municipal government led by Baron de Scorbiac and Vicomte de Gironde. The Republican government in Paris replaced it with an appointed commission including, according to a Catholic opponent, "two of the most fanatical Huguenots of the city."[77] These religious and political divisions persisted into the Third Republic. Political scientists Landrou and Landrevie argue that the elections of the 1870s reflected a bizarre "double inversion" of "legitimate" interests. "The Protestant bourgeois voted on the Left when he should have been conservative because of his economic position, and the Catholic worker, more legitimately open to social arguments, lined up on the Right. Each voted against the logical aspirations of his group; religion won out over economics."[78]

The government of the wealthy Protestant businessmen who were Montauban's Patriots had never been the choice of the majority of Montaubaners. During and after the Revolution these men lost whatever basis

---

[75] Daudet, *La Terreure Blanche*, p. 243; Resnick, *The White Terror*, p. 132; and Estèbe, "La Vie politique," p. 251.

[76] Armengaud, *Les Populations de l'est aquitain*, p. 341; Ligou, *Montauban*, p. 667.

[77] Valmary, "Une Révolution montalbanaise," pp. 18–25.

[78] Landau and Landrevie, *De l'Empire à la République*, p. 212. The Revolution had a similar effect in Nîmes. See Hood, "Revival and Mutation of Old Rivalries," pp. 83–86, and Gwynne Lewis, *The Second Vendée: The Continuity of Counter-Revolution in the Department of the Gard, 1789–1815* (Oxford: Oxford University Press, 1978).

of popular support they had possessed—the Protestant textile workers—
as Montauban's economy faltered and then abruptly collapsed. This too
was the result of the Revolution. It upset the balance that the eighteenth
century had maintained between commerce and agriculture, a balance the
region has been trying to restore ever since.

The wars and the English blockade together worked to restructure Montauban's economy. The revolt in Saint Domingue (Haiti) and the blockade
closed the colonial market to Montauban's cloth and flour. The war, however, brought government contracts for both products. In the spring of
1793, the government ordered cloth to outfit one thousand recruits. In
the following months these orders increased until the government had put
all the town's *fabriques* under requisition. The effect was technically retro-
gressive. All experimentation with popular lighter-weight fabrics, cotton
and silk, ceased. The army wanted cloth that was durable and that could be
produced quickly and cheaply. Consequently, the quality of even the traditional cadis declined drastically. When the war interrupted the supplies of
Spanish wool, manufacturers substituted inferior local fleeces. Mass conscription made skilled labor so scarce that many jobs were simplified or
eliminated. Thread was often spun of unwashed wool; in other cases the
finished cloth was not fulled properly, leaving it coarse, greasy, and lumpy.
Soldiers supplied with such unattractive foul-smelling stuff were not likely
to be impressed by Montauban's product. The repercussions in the domestic market were immediate and long lasting. Montauban never regained its
pre-Revolutionary reputation for quality.[79]

In 1802 a local subprefect, in a commentary called "Notes on Montauban's Commerce, As It Was Before the Revolution, As It Is Today,"
reported that before the Revolution there had been 12 large woolen manufactures and at least 50 smaller ones, 8 silk factories, 30 flour dealers, and
25 to 30 workshops producing barrels. Now he found only half as many
textile manufacturers, the barrel production reduced by 90 percent, and
the flour trade practically extinct. On every side he saw "a total loss of that
industry which assured the comfort of the inhabitants."[80]

His report hardly exaggerated matters. Flour, like textiles, lost its market in the West Indies. Rural upheaval, public animosity toward speculators and wholesalers, the price ceilings and market regulations, and especially the army monopoly worked to put all but the largest dealers out of
business. In the process, Montauban's merchant-manufacturers lost their
competitive edge. With market and profit entirely dependent on political
contacts, they became lobbyists rather than entrepreneurs. When the gov-

---

[79] AM Mont 4 F 2 Etat des fabriques de toute espèce fourni au district le 9 frimaire an 3;
Ombret et al., *Montauban, cité drapière*, p. G-2; Ligou, *Montauban*, pp. 590–595.
[80] AD T-et-G 152 J.

ernment withdrew the army contracts, Vialètes d'Aignan, the largest dealer of them all, went out of business in 1812. The remaining mills and *fabriques* served local needs only.[81]

The commercial and industrial depression was general in the southwest during the first decades of the nineteenth century. Agen, for example, a town on the Garonne only one hundred miles from Bordeaux, had employed almost fifteen hundred people in textiles in 1780. In 1801, only six hundred remained. Of course Bordeaux itself was drastically affected. In 1806, for example, the English sank forty of the ships that put to sea from the port. During the Restoration, Bordeaux's municipal council continued to complain of declining business and competition from Nantes and Le Havre. In 1822, the exports were only half of what they had been in 1789.[82]

By the 1830s, and especially by midcentury, the southwest was making a comeback. Although unable to recapture its markets for flour and textiles, Bordeaux found economic salvation in the expanding wine trade. In some of the inland towns, the textile industry revived. Castres and Mazamet specialized and mechanized following the English model. In fact, Castres took over the rural weavers who had once worked for Montauban's merchants. By 1845 the Castres-based cottage industry employed more than thirty thousand people in the region. St Antonin Noble Val in Aveyron and St Affrique in Rouergue, two eighteenth-century textile towns, although isolated and lacking good transportation, also retooled and reentered the market in the nineteenth century.[83]

Montauban's merchants, by contrast, rejected diversification and mechanization. One manufacturer invested in spinning machines at the height of the army's demand for cloth in 1806, but none of his competitors followed suit. "The simplest machines are always the best," they stated. Earlier, a prospectus for a charity workshop had argued that to copy the British was foolhardy: "In order to carry out such a senseless project, you

---

[81] Pierre Deffontaines, *Montauban: Étude de géographie urbaine* (Montauban: n.p., n.d.), p. 468. Thomson, in *Clermont-de-Lodève*, pp. 374–430, argues that royal privileges to the textile industry in the seventeenth century had a similarly stultifying effect. AN F^{12} 870A reports quarterly business failures from Montauban and Moissac. The year 1811 saw Garrigues and Boé, two large Montauban merchants, go bankrupt, leaving some three hundred thousand francs in debt. In 1813 flour dealer Lafont Bergis went under, as well as merchant Garrigues-Blumat. Moissac's flour trade also collapsed.

[82] Butel, *Les Négociants bordelais*, p. 98; Albert Soboul, "La Reprise économique et la stabilization social 1797–1815," in Fernand Braudel and Ernest Labrousse, eds., *Histoire économique et sociale de la France*, 3 vols. (Paris: Presses universitaires de France, 1976), vol. 3, pt. 1: 102; A. Tudesq, "La Restauration, renaissance et deceptions," in Higounet, ed., *Histoire de Bordeaux* 6: 50.

[83] P. Guillaume, "L'Economie sous le Second Empire," in Higounet, ed., *Histoire de Bordeaux* 6: 179–210; Armengaud, *Populations de l'est-aquitain*, p. 118.

would need to employ unknown workers, rely upon foreign foremen, and spend enormous amounts for machines that no one has and that no one knows how to use. . . . Should we be astonished if such a huge and complicated machine cannot operate successfully and if it breaks because its many parts cannot work together?"[84] In 1832 the Chamber of Commerce denied that Montauban's neglect of mechanization had brought about the industry's ruin. Rather, it was machines introduced elsewhere that were to blame. "Our misfortune comes from the ease with which anyone can make [cloth] now, which deprives us of a market for our product. In the past, you needed to make something well; today, all you need is to make it fast, and it's the cheap goods that take all," they complained.[85]

Montauban's efforts to revive the city's commerce were pitiful. The most decisive action was to enlarge Montauban's three annual fairs and to turn one of them into a wool fair. But, as even the Chamber of Commerce admitted, the fairs dwindled rapidly into purely local events "without sufficient interest to attract strangers away from other cities."[86] They pleaded for government support in the form of renewed army contracts as the popularity of cadis declined in the open market. The Chamber of Commerce fulminated against "the luxury that has spread through all classes of society, which has made a large portion of our consumers among the artisans replace [cadis] with broadcloth." Local peasants continued to dress in cadis de Montauban, as did Breton fishermen and priests for whom the dyers dyed it "Jesuit black." None of these markets was large to begin with and all were shrinking yearly.[87]

In general, Montauban's merchants were less interested in innovation and economic growth than they were in security and social status; like many merchant-manufacturers, they were not risk takers. In 1765 a frustrated inspector of manufactures described them thus: "Such people, rather comfortably off, always have a good opinion of themselves and do not want to give themselves the trouble or the expense to reform their operations."[88] Instead of gambling on high returns from mechanization, they had preferred the moderate profits of the putting-out industry, which effectively passed the risk to the subcontractor.[89] During the Revolution

---

[84] Cited in Forestié, *Fabrication des draps*, pp. 32, 40.

[85] Cited in François Grézes-Rueff, "Assoupissement économique et desindustrialization (1799–1940)," in Ligou, ed., *Histoire de Montauban*, p. 231.

[86] AN F[12] 1271, Foires et marchés 1790–1823.

[87] Forestié, *Fabrication des draps*, pp. 48–51; Grézes-Rueff, "Assoupissement économique," pp. 230–231; and Crouzet, "Les Origins du sous-developpement économique," p. 75.

[88] AN F[12] 1378, Draperie: Memoirs des inspecteurs; 1765 Memoir Holker à M. de Trudaine.

[89] They were not alone in this preference. Chaline concluded that Rouen's booming factory industry in the early nineteenth century depended almost entirely on immigrants from England and Alsace. Local merchant-manufacturers invested only reluctantly, infinitely

they had abandoned competition for the guaranteed profits from government contracts, and most of their efforts thereafter were to regain a secure market, through regulation, monopoly, or renewed government favor.

When these efforts failed, Montauban's merchant elite abandoned commerce and industry for the more "honorable" professions of law and public office or to live as gentlemen on the income of their land. Already in the period from 1775 to 1790, 64 percent of the purchases recorded for Montauban merchants involved rural real estate.[90] The sale of national property strengthened this trend. Between February 1791 and August 1799, the government auctioned off more than 750,000 francs' worth of confiscated property in the Montauban region. Thirty-three of the fifty-eight biggest buyers were merchant-manufacturers; most were also Patriots and Protestants. For example, Pierre Garrisson, a Protestant merchant-manufacturer, member of the Patriots' Club and of several Revolutionary governments, bought the Capuchin convent's property for more than 30,000 francs. Along with dyer Bergis, flour dealer Mariette, and textile manufacturers Rachou and Debia, he transformed his commercial fortune into real estate.[91]

Merchants' investments in land continued after the sale of national property was discontinued. From 1805 to 1825, three quarters of the sample of merchant purchases recorded by notaries were farms and fields.[92] During the same period merchants played a decreasing role in Montauban, both numerically and in political and economic importance. By midcentury, almost two thirds of Montaubaners who paid at least two hundred francs in direct taxes were lawyers, officials, and landowners whereas only 18 percent were engaged in industry or commerce. In Castres 27 percent of these major taxpayers were merchants and manufacturers, and in Toulouse, 37 percent.[93] Table 2–3 tells the story. While the other socioeconomic groups remained stable, the merchants experienced a decline and the professional and landowning group rose in prominence.

Compared with surrounding departments, the Tarn-et-Garonne was in decline. The birth rate dropped from 30 to 26 per thousand in the decade 1811 to 1820 and to 24 in the 1830s. Over the same period, the Haute-Garonne (Toulouse) had a stable birth rate of 28 and the Tarn (Albi) had a rate that approached 30. Although the death rates in all three departments

---

preferring traditional cottage industry. Chaline, *Bourgeois de Rouen*, pp. 373–374. See Reddy, *The Rise of the Market Culture*, pp. 22–23, 51–57, for a discussion of the continued attraction of the putting-out industry.

[90] Sample of 250 notarized sales. Significance level = .01, contingency coeffiecient = .451.

[91] Ligou, "Notes sur la vente des biens nationaux," pp. 361–387, and Sol, *Révolution en Quercy* 1: 341–342.

[92] Again, this was not an unusual preference. See Chaline, *Bourgeois de Rouen*, pp. 100–102.

[93] Armengaud, *Populations de l'est-aquitain*, p. 139.

Table 2–3
The Changing Population of Montauban Notary Clients,
1775–1824

Occupation of Notary Client	Period	
	1775–1790	*1805–1824*
Farm workers	18%	18%
Peasant owners	13.5	13
City workers	13	12
Artisans and retailers	28	28
Merchants	13.5	8
Bourgeois	14	21
N	1057	1306

Note: Significance level = .01, contingency coefficient = .120.

were similar, ranging from 21 to 24, the Tarn-et-Garonne was the only one in which an excess of deaths over births occurred. This happened in 1820 and again during the cholera epidemic of 1832–1834. The first half of the nineteenth century also saw the beginning of the trend of out-migration, which has predominated ever since. In the first decades of the nineteenth century, Montauban still attracted immigrants but at a much lower rate than in the eighteenth century. Whereas in the last quarter of the eighteenth century 22 percent of Montauban's grooms had lived in the city for less than five years, in the first quarter of the nineteenth century only 7 percent of grooms were new immigrants.[94] Other people, mostly artisans and merchants, began to leave the region permanently. In the 1840s, property taxes accounted for 79 percent of the direct taxes paid in the Tarn-et-Garonne; the tax on commercial and industrial assets paid only 4 percent, the lowest in the region. Although almost one quarter of the population of the Tarn-et-Garonne lived in towns with a population of at least two thousand, only 17 percent worked in commerce or industry.[95]

Abel Hugo wrote in his 1835 *France pittoresque*: "The department is one of those which, at the product exhibition of 1827, had nothing to offer of distinction. In fact the region lacks industry; lacking the capital vital to manufacturing, the inhabitants turn all their efforts toward making a profit from agricultural products."[96] In the eighteenth century, Mon-tauban had been a commercial island in a sea of agriculture; in the nine-

[94] Significance level = .01, contingency coefficient = .259.

[95] Armengaud, *Populations de l'est-aquitain*, pp. 73–75, 135–136; Pinède, "Les Migra-tions temporaires en Quercy," pp. 122–134; and Pinède, "L'Emigration dans le Sud-Ouest," pp. 237–251. Also see Grézes-Rueff, "Assoupissement économique," pp. 221–224.

[96] Hugo, *France pittoresque* 3: 200.

teenth century, the sea reclaimed it and, like Atlantis, the Montauban of clacking looms and teeming wharves sank from sight.

Montauban's change in character, from crossroads to backwater, was important to local families, to the decisions they made, the ways they organized and distributed their resources, and the ways in which they exercised authority. As Montauban moved away from commerce and industry, families that had developed strategies to profit from commercial opportunities shifted to patterns built on landholding. However, the impetus did not come from the economy alone. Changes in family organization also supported and promoted economic change. In this story, the new family law of the Revolution and the Napoleonic Code played a part at least equal to that of the British blockade and Napoleon's wars. Not only did Montaubaners move and have their being in a world of politics and production, they were also family men.

CHAPTER THREE

Inheritance in Montauban Families

ON THE MORNING of August 16, 1792, Demoiselle Françoise Valette, widow of a merchant-goldsmith, went to Maître Caminel's notary office to dictate her will.[1] Her intentions for her property were detailed and specific. Valette had six children who had survived to adulthood, five boys and one girl, but her second son had died leaving a son. Valette remembered each of the younger children with a legacy: her daughter received two thousand livres; her third son received three hundred livres besides what she had promised him in his marriage contract; and her fourth son and her dead son's son received fifteen hundred livres each. She selected her eldest son as her general heir and executor.

A decade later, on April 2, 1804, Antoine Barreau, a peasant landowner from the outskirts of Montauban, went to a notary office for the same reason.[2] The will he dictated was both as detailed and as straightforward as Valette's, but it was significantly different. He enumerated three legacies to his wife, Raimonde Sevignes. First, she was to have the sole use of a room in his house plus access to the kitchen, corridor, staircase, oven, and well, and the use of "a square of garden" behind the house. Second, she was to have the use of the wardrobe in her room and of its contents. Third, she was to receive from his heirs an annual pension in grain, flour, wine, and pork fat. He left her all this apart from "any claims the said Sevignes might have on the goods of her said husband," that is, her dowry. Finally he named as his heirs his three sons and his daughter plus the child with whom his wife was pregnant and any future children he and his wife might have. The children were to share and share alike, to pay his debts, the legacies, and the pension to their mother, and to divide the remaining property among them.

These wills reflected the legal changes in the dozen years that separated them. Valette dictated her testament under the faculté de tester of Old Regime Roman law; Barreau dictated his under the constraints of Napoleon's Civil Code. Between the two stretched the whole decade of Revolutionary inheritance law. Within seven months of when it was written, Valette's will was invalid. The law of March 7, 1793, prohibited parents from favoring one child over others and condemned her prefer-

---

[1] AD T-et-G 5E 1949 Caminel no. 338 16–8–1792 testament Valette.

[2] AD T-et-G 5E 2130 Latreille-Olivié no. 568 12 germinal Year 12, testament Barreau.

ence for her eldest son as aristocratic and counter-Revolutionary, inimical to the rule of equality on which the new society was to be built. Barreau's will reflects these egalitarian principles. All his children, his daughter as well as his sons, younger as well as eldest, were to share his estate equally.

A comparison of these two wills reveals other tracks, less obvious than the well-preserved footprints of legal change. Barreau's detailed provisions for his wife compare with Valette's carefully calibrated legacies to her children and grandson, and his legacies in usage and kind contrast with hers in cash. The change in law and official ideology focuses our attention on the choice of heir, but both testators were also concerned with appropriate provisions for nonheirs. The differences in these provisions derived only in part from the different legal systems. Marital status made an obvious difference. Widowed Valette had no spouse for whom to provide. But gender was also important; a woman would not have provided so comprehensively for a husband as Barreau did for his wife. Differences in social class were relevant, too. Valette, well-to-do widow of an urban artisan, assigned legacies measured in cash; Barreau, a comfortably off but far from wealthy peasant, measured his value in sacks of grain and barrels of wine, in rooms and garden plots.[3] And age played a role. With five adult children and a grandchild, Valette was middle-aged or elderly. Barreau, whose wife was pregnant, was probably younger and certainly in a different stage of the family cycle. Whereas Valette envisioned the ultimate dispersal of her family through the division of her property, Barreau planned the continued existence of his through the maintenance of its core, his wife.

Wills and marriage contracts are untrustworthy records of the material realities of family life. We do not know if Valette's grandson collected his fifteen hundred livres or if there was ever that much in her estate at all. Nor do we know if Sevignes's children permitted her to use the garden plot or if Barreau's daughter obtained an equal share of the inheritance. Instead, wills and marriage contracts documented beliefs about family fairness and intentions to establish or maintain particular kinds of familial order. They mediated between the abstractions of law and ideology and the realities, not to say the peculiarities, of individual experience in family life. In these legal documents, Montaubaners attempted to realize, to concretize their

---

[3] The legacies in Valette's will—5,300 livres in all—indicate she was well-to-do. If 1,500 livres—the legacy to her youngest son—equaled the légitime, her estate was worth 15,000 livres. Further indication of the social class of this testator comes from the honorary titles of D[emoise]lle and Sieur applied to her, her late husband, and her heir. One of her younger sons was a goldsmith and another a solicitor in the *Cours de Commerce*. This was an artisanal family on the brink of the bourgeoisie. Indications of Barreau's economic position come from the pension he established for his wife; it was quite adequate but included no delicacies such as eggs, poultry, or meat.

beliefs about the family through the distribution of their property. Like Barreau, they gave and withheld power; like Valette, they created or enhanced hierarchies and equalities. Their wills and marriage contracts reveal their ideals, not for the Best of All Possible Families, but for the best possible for their particular families.

In this chapter we will examine what these ideals were and how they were shaped by individual circumstances. Gender, martial status, age, and occupation all contributed to what Montaubaners intended for their families. Within this context, we will analyze the impact of the Revolution on inheritance law. To what extent did hierarchical, patriarchal intentions for the family prevail before the Revolution? To what extent did egalitarianism triumph thereafter? Did the revolution in family law mark a revolution in family relations?

To begin to answer these questions, I have drawn samples of wills and marriage contracts recorded by Montauban's notaries over a fifty-year period spanning the Revolution, from 1775 through 1824.[4] As sources of information about Montaubaners' families and concepts of family, notary records are rich but problematic. First, the population of notary clients was not entirely representative of the population as a whole. The average notary client was more prosperous and more independent than the average inhabitant. Because the services of a notary cost money and because almost all notary documents involved some form of property transaction,[5] the poor and those deprived of control of their property, like minors and married women, were consistently underrepresented among notary clients whereas property owners and male heads of households were overrepresented. Testators, in particular, were older, less mobile, and wealthier than the average Montaubaner, and married women made far fewer wills than did married men.[6] The parties to a marriage contract, the bride and groom

[4] The sample includes 847 wills and 833 marriage contracts, randomly selected to average seventeen of each type of document per year.

[5] Notaries charged by the page, two sous a page for a register entry and considerably more for a *gross*, a large fair copy admissible as evidence in court. Magnon, *Le Notariat et la révolution francaise*, pp. 14–15. The major part of a notary's business was to facilitate and record financial transactions—loans, property sales, leases, and so on. See Jean Paul Poisson, "Une Etude quantitative des actes notaires (la préenquête sur l'année 1749)," *Revue d'histoire économique et sociale* 55, nos. 1–2 (1977): 24–41. About 40 percent of the documents kept by Montauban notaries involved family affairs. Most of these were marriage contracts, wills, and codicils. Other common documents were *partages* (divisions of estates), *resilliements de mariage* (cancellation of marriage contracts), emancipations of minor children, *ouvertures verbales* (formal readings of wills), and acts and accords that recorded and resolved family disputes.

[6] Some Montaubaners were ineligible to make wills—persons in religious orders, foreigners, transients, and unemancipated minors; others were seriously underrepresented as testators, especially the poor. The majority of those with something to leave made wills, especially in the popular classes; however, people with nothing at all outnumbered them in both urban and rural society. Poor workers, who made up at least one third of Montauban's

and their parents, were much more typical inhabitants. Even poor couples who declared they had no resources beyond the daily work of their hands had their agreements to marry notarized in due form. But not everyone married, and those without property had fewer opportunities to marry than property owners.[7] Both documents underrepresented the poorest residents.

A more serious problem is the question of whose views and intentions notary documents actually recorded. The notaries who drew up the wills and marriage contracts must have influenced their contents to a greater or lesser extent.[8] This was certainly the case with marriage contracts that, especially before 1804, reflected regional custom and notarial habit more than the considered choice of the contracting parties. Eighty-three percent of the sampled contracts written before the Revolution followed the Custom of Montauban (see table 3–2). A marriage contract that Maître Latreille-Olivié, one of Montauban's busiest notaries, drew up in 1799 for a young peasant couple suggests the common practice. In this contract, one of the clauses of the Custom of Montauban was crossed out and amended in the margin, having been disputed by the parties after the clerk had read the finished contract aloud. Latreille-Olivié or his clerk had elicited the requisite information about names, residences, and dowry amounts from the parties and then cast the contract into standard form according to the Custom of Montauban without discussing the provisions of the Custom with the parties.[9] This couple was sufficiently opposed to

---

population, made only 20 percent of wills. See Aboucaya, *Le testament lyonnais*, pp. 144–152. Nineteen percent of the sample of testators were married women and 39 percent were married men (significance level = .01, contingency coefficient = .308). In part, this was because the succession of dotal property was already established by the marriage contract and in part because married women's legal capacity was under debate in the Toulouse Parlement of the eighteenth century. Timbal, "La Succession testamentaire," p. 295, and Aron, "Etude sur les lois successorales," p. 489.

[7] Almost every marriage in the southwest was preceded by a contract. See Petit, "Mariages et contrats de mariages à Agen," pp. 215–229, and Sicard, "Les Contrats de mariage à Toulouse," pp. 311–320. In Montauban, marriage contracts were a better index to the married population than were parish registers because Protestants made contracts but did not always record their marriages with the Catholic clergy. However, the poorest were disproportionately unmarried. More than one third of the urban poor who made wills were unmarried, but only 16 percent of other testators were single (significance level = .01, contingency coefficient = .191).

[8] See Briffaud, "La Famille, le notaire et le mourant," pp. 389–409.

[9] See AD T-et-G 5E 1970 Latreille-Olivié no. 36 8 pluviôse Year 7 contrat de mariage Gibert-Gineste. Lelièvre, in *La Pratique des contrats de mariage*, pp. 14–15, argues that in eighteenth-century Paris marrying couples had little idea of the variety of marital settlements available to them and usually followed the legal custom of the area without seriously considering alternative arrangements. One of the few Montauban contracts that renounced a dowry in favor of a community property arrangement was written for two recent immigrants from the north, where community property was the rule. AD T-et-G 5E 10877 Martin no. 469 8–9–1788 contrat de mariage Joli-Meunier.

the clause, when they heard it, to object and insist on substituting one of their own devising, but most Montaubaners went along with the notaries.

In this case, the wills are a better source because they were often highly individualistic in both their language and their provisions. Except during the period from 1794 to 1800, when a testator's options were strictly limited by law, Montaubaners' wills show little conformity to any standard model. The majority of wills were short and simple, but nearly one quarter named at least three legatees. Most were sons and daughters, but some testators remembered kin as distant as first cousins once removed or spouses' grandnephews, whereas others left legacies to servants, masters, co-workers, or friends. The most complicated will in the sample, drawn up for a lawyer's widow in 1801, appointed two heirs and named twenty-two legatees and three life-rights beneficiaries.[10]

Third, there is the problem of what the documents do not mention. Both wills and marriage contracts were primarily vehicles for distributing property. Property was an important family resource, and its control and distribution were central to family strategies, but it was not the only family resource, nor always the essential one. From their families individuals could also receive social status, authority, occupational training, emotional support, and many other less tangible legacies that wills and marriage contracts rarely mentioned.[11] But Montaubaners routinely used wills to demonstrate their preferences, to confirm or repay other less tangible favor. This was so much the case that the rare instances to the contrary called for comment. In 1809 Jeanne Barrière, widow of a surgeon, left her daughter a double share of her succession, as her will stated, "not as a mark

[10] AD T-et-G 5E 2349 Martin no. 206 17 pluviôse Year 9 testament Rossaldy v^e Carrié. Twenty-nine percent of the wills in the sample simply designated universal heirs with no specific legacies at all; 48 percent included one or two legacies; 23 percent included three or more legacies. In the decade 1775–1784, the 171 wills in the sample named 388 legatees. Of these, 60 percent were children of the testator, 13 percent nephews and nieces, 9 percent grandchildren, 6 percent siblings, and less than 2 percent spouses. The remaining 10 percent were divided between assorted kin and nonkin, including parents, grandparents, cousins, siblings-in-law, spouses' nephews and nieces, nephews' and nieces' spouses, first cousins once removed, grandchildren's spouses, grandnieces and grandnephews, servants, masters, friends, and godchildren.

[11] Occasionally a will documented such support. For example, in AD T-et-G 5E 2356 Martin no. 40 18–1–1809 testament Albouy, a seamstress appointed as heir her great-aunt "who has taken the place of a mother." In 5E 2008 Garrigues no. 606 19–8–1788 testament Lacassaigne, a goldsmith's daughter remembered her brother and sister-in-law's "fraternal generosity." Other wills recalled support the testator had provided to the heir: for example, in 5E 2008 Garrigues no. 256 24–3–1788 testament Border, a farm worker specified that the sums expended on his sons' apprenticeships be deducted from their portions, and in 5E 1944 Caminel no. 116 14–2–1788 testament Capelle, a woodcutter left to his younger son "the sum it had cost the said testator to obtain for him his discharge from the Royal Regiment."

TABLE 3–1
Montauban Testators' Choice of Heir, 1775–1824

	Date of Testament		
Heirs Chosen	1775–1793 Faculté de Tester	1794–1799 Equal Inheritance	1800–1824 Limited Choice
Eldest male heir*	33%	4%	22%
Other legal heir	30	4	22
Coresident heir	10	1	11
Nonkin heir	8	1	6
Spouse as heir	16	37	15
Equal inheritance	3	53	24
N	320	104	423

Note: Significance level = .01, contingency coefficient = .437.

*Eldest male heir encompasses eldest sons, brothers, and nephews but also grandsons and cousins in cases where it was apparent that there were closer female heirs. A few testators probably had no male kin known to them and therefore were prevented from following primogeniture. We may assume that they are balanced in the sample by those few testators whose only legal heir was a son or brother and who were therefore practically forced to follow primogeniture.

of special favor but because of the modesty of [her daughter's] re-sources."[12] In most wills, such a legacy would rightly be read as a "mark of special favor." Although family priorities, as reconstructed from these documents, lean heavily on material bases, their slant indicates the direction of other kinds of favor as well. As Alain Collomp has argued, affective interest and material interest were not two distinct poles; division of goods and emotional attachment went hand in hand.[13]

For these reasons, a couple's choice of marital settlement or a testator's choice of heirs and legatees gives a skewed, blurry, and partial picture of Montaubaners' family priorities. But, for all of that, it is a rich and nuanced picture that permits comparisons across time, class, and gender, a view, albeit restricted, of the intentions and beliefs of ordinary people for and about their families.

The issues raised in the legislative debates over inheritance law corresponded to some of the realities of Montaubaners' behavior. As Mirabeau and Robespierre maintained, equality was rarely the object of Old Regime testaments; only 3 percent of the wills recorded between 1775 and the

[12] AD T-et-G 5E 2356 Martin no. 241 29–4–1809 testament Barrière v^c Boé. Three days later the daughter made a will appointing her mother as her heir. AD T-et-G 5E 2356 Martin no. 251 2–5–1809 testament Boé.

[13] Alain Collomp, "Tensions, Dissensions, and Ruptures Inside the Family in Seventeenth and Eighteenth Century Haute-Provence," in Medick and Sabean, eds., *Interest and Emotion*, p. 146.

enactment of statutory equal inheritance in 1793 called for the equal division of the succession among the heirs. Nor was primogeniture a figment of their revolutionary ardor; 33 percent of these wills favored the eldest male heir. But many Montaubaners used their legal prerogatives with more creativity than any of the legislators imagined. For example, in a will written in 1779, Nicolas Bassoul, a stocking bleacher, left his son only the légitime and made his wife his heir. He explained he was doing this to compensate her for her goods, which he had sold to pay for a trip to Flanders. In a 1788 will, a laborer's widow appointed her eldest son her heir, not from any concern for primogeniture but because he was providing her with room and board.[14] These and other wills suggest that popular concepts of family obligation and justice were flexible and dependent on more than law and custom.

Unfortunately, few testators were as forthcoming as Nicolas Bassoul; most recorded no explanation for their choices. We do not know the alternatives they considered or how or why they made their choices. However, we do know of alternatives to the heirs suggested by the wills themselves, the legatees. Although testators did not choose the latter as heirs, they acknowledged their importance. We might imagine a testator selecting an heir from a small pool of candidates composed of the heir and legatees. By comparing the heir with the legatees, we can speculate about the testator's family priorities and the strategies that informed them. For example, an eldest son chosen over his younger siblings or a nephew over a sister suggests that the testator was influenced by principles of lineage and primogeniture; a wife chosen over a father or a husband over a son indicates the priority of the marital bond. Wills from the Old Regime were most revealing because Montaubaners were relatively free to pick and choose their heirs and legatees as they wished. The period of mandatory equal inheritance, by eliminating most of the testators' choices, reduced the amount of information most wills contained; often testators did not even bother to name their heirs but simply left their property "as the law requires." Wills from the period after the relaxation of equal inheritance fell midway between, usually containing more information than Revolutionary wills but less than wills recorded during the Old Regime.[15] Nonetheless, throughout the entire period, Montaubaners incorporated into their wills some of their intentions for their families.

[14] AD T-et-G 5E 2009 Garrigues no. 272 20–5–1788 ouverture Bastoul. This is the record of the formal reading of Bastoul's will, written nine years earlier. AD T-et-G 5E 1944 Caminel no. 638 17–12–1788 testament Popis v.e Trumel.

[15] From 1775 to 1793, 79 percent of wills named at least one heir and one legatee; from 1794 to 1799, only 47 percent of wills named an heir and a legatee; from 1800 to 1824 this figure rose to 63 percent (significance level = .01, contingency coefficient = .317).

As the opponents of Roman law maintained in 1791, the most popular use of the faculté de tester was to concentrate property in the hands of the eldest male heir. However, this was by no means the majority choice; almost as many testators chose kin who were *not* designated by primogeniture. Two other arrangements were popular, too. Ten percent of testators chose heirs with whom they lived, testifying to some truth in Saint Martin's vignette of the invalid peasant patriarch. Sixteen percent named the surviving spouse as heir, a choice that neither the legal reformers nor the defenders of Roman law envisioned.

In conjuring up eldest sons who lolled in luxury while their brothers languished in poverty,[16] the advocates of equal inheritance exaggerated both the prevalence of primogeniture and the degree of inequality that resulted from the faculté de tester. Montaubaners rarely placed their non-inheriting children at as great a disadvantage as permitted by law. The Custom of Montauban allowed testators to satisfy the claims of their heirs with the meager légitime, but in the late eighteenth century few Montaubaners did so. Only 36 in a sample of 320 pre-Revolutionary wills assigned légitimes, and not invariably to daughters or younger sons.[17] Neither primogeniture nor any other general notion of family priorities influenced these testators; rather they used the légitime to respond to a number of specific family circumstances. First, with the légitime they could punish a child short of total disinheritance. In 1770, Daniel Rattier, a wealthy merchant, left his younger son thirty thousand livres with the stipulation that if he caused his mother any trouble, this amount would be reduced to the légitime. Second, the légitime could correct an injustice. In 1776, when merchant Pierre Huegla died, his younger son received only one thousand livres. The following year Pierre's widow made a will that left the eldest son, her husband's heir, the légitime and made the neglected younger son her heir. Third, the légitime was the standard legacy to posthumous children. Finally, testators used it when they wished to leave their property to someone who was not by law an heir, especially to a spouse. In 1788 clerk Jean-Baptiste Claret left the légitime to his father, who was his legal heir, and appointed his fiancée to inherit the rest of his

---

[16] The fate of overprivileged *aînés*, contrasted with that of underprivileged *cadets,* was a powerful image in the speeches of both Mirabeau and Robespierre, but a less prominent legislator, Pethion de Villeneuve, said it best: "How can you see without indignation the opulence of one brother contrasted with the indigence of the other? The one acquires the habit of arrogance; the other languishes in abject poverty: both are corrupted." *Moniteur Universel*, April 3, 1791.

[17] The 36 wills assigned 66 legatees the légitime. The breakdown was 29 percent daughters, 27 percent younger sons, 23 percent eldest sons, 11 percent posthumous children, 9 percent parents, and 1 grandson.

property. In another will of the same year, Jean Gleze, a shoemaker, left the légitime to his three minor children and appointed his wife as his heir.[18]

There was another legal avenue open to Montaubaners who wanted to enrich their sons at the expense of their daughters; with a token remembrance of five *sols* they could satisfy the legal claims of any daughters they had already provided with dowries.[19] However, although Montauban wills included more legacies of five *sols* than they did legacies of the légitime, testators did not always use them to exclude endowed daughters. Five *sols* did not necessarily connote exclusion from the succession; it merely confirmed legacies and gifts already made or promised, usually in marriage contracts. In 1788, Jean Bordier, a farm worker, left five *sols* to his eldest son, one quarter of his goods to his second son, and the rest to his wife to provide for their two younger children. The eldest son had already received one quarter of his father's goods in his marriage contract. Bordier's will actually established equal inheritance among his four children.[20]

In 1791 in the National Assembly, Cazalès argued that a *père de famille* should be able to reward children who obediently remained subservient in the paternal household. Ten percent of Montauban testators in the period before the Revolution left their property to heirs with whom they lived. However, situations besides filial submission contributed to this choice. One was the existence in the Garonne valley of what historians Lutz Berkner and John Shaffer have called "joint families."[21] For example,

---

[18] AD T-et-G 5E 2262 Caminel sn 22–5–1770 testament Rattier. Jeanne de Garrisson, wife of a local nobleman, wrote a similar clause into her will, 5E 2263 Caminel sn 22–10–1789. AD T-et-G 5E 1995 Garrigues no. 209 30–4–1776 testament Huegla and 1996 Garrigues no. 501 25–9–1777 testament Delbreil v^c Huegla. AD T-et-G 5E 2008 Garrigues no. 452 9–6–1788 testament Claret and 2337 Martin no. 334 23–8–1788 testament Gleze; similarly, 10877 Martin no. 521 20–10–1788 testament Lacroix.

[19] According to the Custom of Montauban, if a woman accepted her dowry from her parents she was not entitled to seek any further legacy from their estates, even if her dowry was less than the légitime. Lebret, *Histoire de Montauban* 1: 110. By the eighteenth century, however, the Parlement of Toulouse no longer upheld this exclusion and regularly recognized the claims of women who sued for a supplement to dowries worth less than the légitime. Maillet, "De l'exclusion coutumière des filles dotées," p. 519.

[20] AD T-et-G 5E 2008 Garrigues no. 256 24–3–1788 testament Border. The will of civil engineer Alexis Bergis provides another example: AD T-et-G 5E 2007 Garrigues no. 145 2–2–1787. Fifty-four out of 320 wills included legacies of 5 *sols*, totaling 108 legacies of 5 *sols* in all, 16 percent of all legacies in the pre-Revolutionary period. The recipients were the following: 50 percent daughters, 14 percent younger sons, 13 percent eldest or only sons, 9 percent grandsons, 6 percent granddaughters, 6 percent grandsons' wives, 1 percent brothers, and 1 percent grandfathers. These token legacies were four times as common in peasant wills as in elite wills.

[21] Berkner and Shaffer, "The Joint Family in the Nivernais," pp. 150–162.

Etienne Aché, a farm hand, married Gerande Mouméja in 1806 and moved in with her parents and sisters. Gerande's father gave the young couple a piece of land and half of his animals and tools. The two couples agreed to live "*au même pot et feu*," at the same pot and hearth, to share the work, and to divide profits and losses equally. In the following years, the other daughters left home and married, with their father and brother-in-law jointly providing their dowries. In 1820 Mouméja made a will that appointed as his heir Gerande, the daughter with whom he lived.[22] Before the enactment of the Civil Code, 21 percent of Montauban marriage contracts established "pot and hearth" communities between the nuptial couple and one set of parents.[23]

Another reason for choosing an heir who lived in the same household was dependence; testators who chose live-in heirs were disproportionately elderly and ill. For example, Catherine Desclaux made her niece's husband, Augustin Moineau, her heir "because of the great services he has done especially since his marriage and particularly in the last six years when the said Augustin Moineau has lived with the testator and provided her with all necessary food and maintenance."[24] Inheritance in such a case was less a reward for good conduct than an attempt to repay a debt.

The Revolutionaries who argued for equal inheritance, on other occasions (most notably in the debates over divorce) waxed poetic about companionship in marriage and conjugal love. Their opponents were almost equally vociferous about the importance of the marital bond and the indissoluble unity of husband and wife.[25] However, neither group raised the issue of a spouse's obligations or rights as a testator or heir. The spouse was a "stranger" with no right to the family property.

By the Custom of Montauban, too, a spouse was a stranger who inherited only if there were no children and then only an amount determined by the size of the dowry. "Nuptial gains" for the husband was his wife's dowry, and for the wife a sum equal to one half of her dowry. Almost all pre-Revolutionary marriage contracts followed this Custom. However, when Montaubaners made wills, a sizable minority modified the provi-

[22] AD T-et-G 5E 2133 Latreille-Olivié no. 123 31–1–1806 contrat de mariage Aché-Mouméja; 2141 Latreille-Olivié no. 115 10–2–1813 contrat de mariage Larroque-Mouméja and no. 194 22–3–1813 contrat de mariage Descazaux-Mouméja; 2149 Latreille-Olivié no. 176 2–56–1820 testament Mouméja.

[23] See table 7–1. Thereafter the frequency fell, in the decade 1805–1814 to 16 percent, in the decade 1815–1824 to 10 percent (significance level = .01, contingency coefficient = .125).

[24] AD T-et-G 5E 1943 Caminel no. 342 13–6–1787 testament Desclaux. Although notaries described 5 percent of all testators as old and 31 percent as ill, for testators appointing heirs in the same household these figures were 15 percent and 41 percent respectively (significance level = .01, contingency coefficient = .181).

[25] Traer, *Marriage and the Family*, pp. 91–94, 108–110.

sions of their marriage contracts to increase the share of their spouses. Sixteen percent appointed the spouse as heir and 19 percent left the spouse a pension, an annuity, or life rights to some portion of the estate.[26]

In the last decades of the Old Regime, Montaubaners did not rigidly follow any one model of succession; neither the eldest son nor all children equally nor the child who remained under the parental roof and authority prevailed as the automatic choice. Nor did testators create great gulfs in economic status between their heirs. In general, Montaubaners used the faculté de tester judiciously to carry out their ideas of equity in their families, ideas that differed from Roman models both in the minimum established for noninheriting children and in the treatment of spouses as strangers to the succession. Parents were concerned to provide sufficiently, if not equally, for all their children and married people to rectify the Custom of Montauban's neglect of surviving spouses. The faculté de tester also gave Montaubaners latitude to respond to diverse family situations, to repay services and correct injustices, to reward and punish behavior. As testators, Montaubaners were flexible and creative; their choices resulted as much from their individual family circumstances as from legal or cultural notions about succession.

The revolution in inheritance law that began in 1791 and did not end until the adoption of the Civil Code in 1804 initially confused both notaries and their clients. The family courts, created in 1790 to resolve familial conflicts, became the testing ground of the new laws. The years 1791–1794, when the principle of equal inheritance was declared but the law was in a state of flux, produced a spate of suits and more than a few bizarre decisions.[27] The suit brought by Jeanne Tandol against her father and adjudicated in the family court of Castelsarrasin in the summer of 1794 is an example.

Jeanne's suit was the result of a long-standing familial conflict that, during the Terror, developed political overtones. Before the Revolution, Jeanne had married against her father's wishes. After the wedding Tandol had grudgingly given his consent but had refused to give his daughter a dowry. So the matter stood until the Terror tipped the balance in Jeanne's favor. Her husband became a member of the local governing junta and her father was arrested. Jeanne sued to obtain a portion of his property, now sequestered by the government, as her dowry.

The family court clearly approved of endowing the wife of a good Patriot with the goods of a suspected Aristocrat. However, to base such a decision in law required a feat of legerdemain that reveals the confused state of legal practice. The arbiters cited a clause of Roman law sanctioned

---

[26] Significance level = .01, contingency coefficient = .354.
[27] Traer, "The French Family Court," pp. 220–223.

by the Parlement of Toulouse—"the father is obliged to support the expenses of marriage"—and the law of 17 *nivôse*, as well as "common Justice" to support their decision. The anomaly of appealing simultaneously to the Parlement of Toulouse and the Convention of Year 2 did not, apparently, occur to them.[28]

Most Montaubaners adhered to the new rules of inheritance. Only 6 percent of wills still used the term *légitime*[29] and only 9 percent clearly favored one heir over others. Marriage contracts were much more likely to contravene the law than wills. Fifty-six percent continued to follow the Custom of Montauban despite the fact that nuptial gains had become illegal. However, nuptial gains came into play only after the death of one spouse if the couple had no children, a set of unhappy circumstances that was probably far from the thoughts of a marrying couple and their parents. It was only after the couple married and the new family was a functioning reality that the fate of the surviving spouse became a concern.

The major novelty in these years was the almost exclusive use of the testament to provide for widowhood. Thirty-seven percent named the spouse as heir, a clause that was legal only if the couple had no children, and 46 percent, although agreeing to equal inheritance, like Barreau left the spouse life rights to a portion of the estate. This situation was a direct result of the changes in inheritance law. First, the law so restricted the faculté de tester that almost the only legitimate reason for making a will was to provide for a spouse. And second, the law created a need for making new provisions for a spouse or confirming ones already made. If a person died without having made a will or with an invalid marriage contract or will, the entire estate could go to the legal heirs, and the surviving spouse would have no legal claim on it. Because the vast majority of Montaubaners' marriage contracts and wills recorded before the Revolution included clauses that were illegal under the new laws, many couples were faced with this possibility. And so they wrote new wills or codicils to circumvent it. For example, Guillaume Rigal, a cloth dyer, was both a member of the Patriots Club and a devoted husband. In 1791 he made a will leaving his wife usufruct of his entire estate so that his son would inherit only upon her death. The law of 17 *nivôse* Year 2, however, invalidated this provision. Rigal revised his will on his deathbed in 1802 with the sole purpose of providing for his wife. "Wishing to favor his wife as much as the law permits," he left her life rights to one half of his estate and exempted her from legal fees and keeping accounts.[30]

[28] AD T-et-G L 456 Tribunal de famille, Castelsarrasin, 8 thermidor Year 2.

[29] For example, AD T-et-G 5E 2343 Martin no. 534 14–7–1795 testament Rochin and 2344 Martin no. 1058 8–8–1796 testament Lacoste ép Segouzac.

[30] AD T-et-G 5E 12882 Grelleau no. 304 7–5–1791 testament Rigal and 12897 Grelleau no. 363 10 floréal Year 10 codicil Rigal.

Montauban's notaries did not follow the rules of mandatory equal inheritance rigorously. They continued to draw up marriage contracts according to the Custom of Montauban and, although less commonly drawing up blatantly illegal wills, they pushed the one remaining loophole in the law—the provision for a spouse—as wide as possible.[31] If they were able to express their clients' wishes within the framework of the law, however, they adapted to the new formulas. The notaries reacted quickly and positively to the law of 4 *germinal* Year 8, which reintroduced the option of a favored heir. This law changed traditional terminology and format, but most of Montauban's notaries adopted the new forms almost immediately.[32] Four years later they were just as prompt to conform to the requirements of the Civil Code. Roman law terms such as *légitime* disappeared entirely.[33]

Notaries were slower to change their way of drawing up marriage contracts. Throughout the Revolution, the Custom of Montauban prevailed even though the changes in inheritance law had made it manifestly illegal. Only with the introduction of the Civil Code did notaries radically change their practice. The Civil Code spelled out three marital regimes, none of them identical to Montauban's Custom. Notaries and their clients who might never have considered arrangements other than the local custom were then confronted with a choice. Although only 16 percent continued to marry under the outdated provisions of the Custom of Montauban, Montaubaners remained faithful to dower arrangements. The marital community of property and the separation of property that the Civil Code offered as alternatives to a dowry system did not become popular in the early years of the nineteenth century.[34] The most common arrangement was the Civil Code's dower regime, which left the surviving spouse with-

[31] It is extremely unlikely that all of the testators who appointed a spouse as heir were childless. Perhaps these wills were intended, like Guillaume Rigal's deathbed statement, to favor the spouse as much as the law permitted and thus to obviate the need for a new will each time the law changed.

[32] The typical pre-Revolutionary will began with specific bequests to legatees and concluded with the appointment of the *hériter universel et général*. It was assumed that this residual heir would inherit the bulk of the estate. The law of 4 *germinal* Year 8 gave testators the option of creating a favored heir by appointing a *légataire particulier* who, *par préciput*, inherited a share of the estate. The focus shifted from naming the heir, determined by law since 1794, to naming a legatee. The wills of Valette and Barreau illustrate these changes.

[33] From 1775 to 1793, 11 percent of wills mentioned a légitime; between 1794 and 1800, this usage fell to 6 percent; after 4 *germinal* Year 8 it fell to less than 1 percent (significance level = .01, contingency coefficient = .219).

[34] The overwhelming predominance of dowries declined only slightly. Between 1775 and 1794, 96 percent of marriage contracts included dowries; between 1804 and 1824, 88 percent included dowries (significance level = .01, contingency coefficient = .139). Sicard, however, discovered in Toulouse that by midcentury dowries had ceased to be popular, especially with poorer couples. See Sicard, "Les Contrats de mariage à Toulouse," pp. 318–319.

TABLE 3–2
Montaubaners' Choice of Marital Property Arrangements, 1775–1824

	Percentage of Marriage Contracts		
	1775–1793	*1794–1803*	*1804–1824*
Choice of Contracts	*Custom of Montauban*	*Revolution*	*Civil Code*
Custom of Montauban	83%	56%	16%
Napoleonic dowry	0	0	29
Dowry reverts	2	1	2
Dowry and legacy	2	4	7
Half estate	1	23	27
Life rights	1	4	6
Marital community	0	1	5
Separate property	8	8	4
Other	3	3	4
N	314	166	343

Note: Significance level = .01, contingency coefficient = .576.

out any rights on the estate; almost as popular was a settlement that gave the spouse the most advantageous terms allowable by inheritance law. If one of the couple died and there were surviving children, the spouse retained life rights to one half of the estate. If there were no children, however, the spouse inherited one half of the estate, that is, the portion disponible. Versions of this regime had appeared during the Revolution as some Montaubaners realized the illegality of the Custom of Montauban. Once the Civil Code made it plain that marital settlements had to be compatible with inheritance law, this regime quickly gained in popularity.

The law of 4 *germinal* Year 8 and the Civil Code restored to the testator some choice of heir and resulted in a diversity of testamentary arrangements absent since 1794. This diversity did not entirely reproduce pre-Revolutionary patterns (see table 3–1). Although the incidence of spouses, coresident kin, and nonkin as heirs returned to pre-Revolutionary levels, the frequency of wills that favored one legal heir over another declined and equal inheritance increased to account for nearly one quarter of wills. This certainly suggests that family concepts had become more egalitarian and that the Revolutionaries' effort to reform the family by reforming inheritance law was in some degree successful.

Changing inheritance law explains only partly the diversity of Montaubaners' marriage contracts and wills. Many of these documents did not follow the officially endorsed models either before, during, or after the Revolution. Before the Revolution, the majority of Montauban wills established neither equal inheritance—the intestate option—nor primogeniture, the supposed southern tradition. During the Revolution, when official endorsement of equal inheritance was clear and when deviation from it might conceivably have been dangerous, many testators tried to bend the rigidity of the law to benefit their spouses. Although equal inheritance gained in popularity, it never accounted for a great majority of wills, and the marital community endorsed and promoted by the Napoleonic Code accounted for only 5 percent of marriage contracts. During the period when the law did not permit much individual choice, some Montaubaners were willing to risk illegal arrangements that expressed their wishes better than those mandated by law.

Despite the frequent and confusing changes in inheritance law, throughout the entire half-century Montauban testators continued to follow their own concepts of familial justice and responsibility. Between rigid conformity to the law and the infinite variety of individual opinions, a number of factors intervened. Marital status, gender, age, and class all influenced the way Montaubaners viewed their families and consequently the provisions they made in their wills and marriage contracts.

Parenthood was the circumstance that most influenced the way Montaubaners left their property. Marital regimes almost always distinguished between two futures: if the couple had children and if they did not. In the former case, their families of origin lost any rights to the couple's property and the surviving spouse saw his or her nuptial gains curtailed or eliminated. Children came first in wills, too. Both before and after the Revolution, 81 percent of parents appointed one, several, or all of their children (equal inheritance) as their heirs.[35] The only person who took priority with or over children was the surviving spouse. Only 4 percent of parents chose an heir who was neither a child nor a spouse.

Before the Revolution, parents were far more likely to favor their eldest sons than any other child or than all their children equally. Mandatory equal inheritance abruptly but temporarily curtailed this preference; it reappeared, only slightly weakened, under the law of 4 *germinal* Year 8 and the Civil Code. Although equal inheritance tripled in popularity and spouses were also increasingly favored, two thirds of parents continued to single out one child as heir and that child tended to be the eldest son.

Childless Montaubaners differed significantly from parents as testators. First, of course, they could not appoint children as heirs; this role was filled to a certain extent by siblings and siblings' children. But childless testators made choices among their kin different from those that parents made among their children. Primogeniture did not much influence them.

---

[35] It was not always possible to determine whether a testator was a parent or not. Forty percent of the testators in the sample were probably parents and 41 percent were probably not; in the remaining 19 percent of cases, there was too little information to make a judgment. Most of these last were from the period after 1794 and were wills written only to provide a legacy or life rights to a spouse.

TABLE 3–3
Parents' and Nonparents' Choice of Heir, 1775–1824

| | Testators | | | |
| | 1775–1793 | | 1800–1824 | |
Heir Chosen	Parents	Nonparents	Parents	Nonparents
Child	77%	0	68%	0
(Son)	(48%)		(42%)	
Other male kin	1	24	0	25
Other kin	5	45	1	44
Nonkin	0	20	0	15
Spouse	13	9	18	10
Equal inheritance	4	2	13	6
N	175	128	151	187

Note: Significance level = .01, 1775–1793 contingency coefficient = .652, 1800–1824 contingency coefficient = .656.

Although one quarter chose as their heir an elder male kinsman—usually a brother or brother's son—in fact more chose sisters than brothers, and nieces as heirs were nearly as popular as nephews were.[36] Only 9 percent of testators before the Revolution chose their spouses as heirs. This rose precipitously to 58 percent during the period of mandatory equal inheritance and then returned to the pre-Revolutionary level. Even during the Revolutionary period, equal inheritance was not popular with childless testators who preferred spouses as heirs or made illegal bequests.

The most striking difference between the wills of parents and childless Montaubaners was the frequency with which childless testators appointed heirs who were unrelated to them. Nonkin were virtually absent from the wills of parents; in the wills of nonparents, they appeared as heirs 20 percent of the time before the Revolution and 15 percent afterward. They were more popular heirs than were spouses and far more popular than equal inheritance. Most testators did not specify what their connection was to the heir they selected, but a few were employers, landlords, or servants.

The diversity of choices reflected the diversity of these childless testators. Antoine Besombes, formerly a potter of Montpezat, had been conscripted into the army of the Empire, and in March 1809, on the eve of his departure for the front, he made a will leaving all his property to his young

[36] In the pre-Revolutionary period, childless testators chose the following as their heirs: 19 percent nephews, 10 percent nieces, 9 percent brothers, and 16 percent sisters. After the Revolution, from 1800 to 1824, their choices were as follows: 13 percent nephews, 11 percent nieces, 10 percent brothers, and 15 percent sisters.

nephew and godson. Paul Caussat, an elderly bachelor, left his estate to his brother-in-law who was his partner in a retail business. Jeanne Sauret was the widow of a field hand and a farm servant herself. Bedridden in her employers house, she left all her goods to her employers children. Surveyor Paul Griffoul returned to his father the portion of a house given him in his marriage contract and left modest legacies to six nephews and nieces; he named his wife as his general heir. In preparation for her entry into the order of St Ursula, Catherine Pradel assigned to her mother her rights in her father's estate.[37] Elderly bachelors and childless widows, soldiers off to war, servant women, and newly married couples—as their circumstances differed, so did their families and their concepts of familial obligations.

A major difference among them was age. Unfortunately notary documents rarely gave the precise ages of the parties. We can only infer testators' ages in a few cases from the circumstances in which the wills were drawn up. In thirty-nine wills in the sample, the notary described the testator as "old" or "old and ill" but nonetheless in sound mind. These were elderly people about whose mental condition there might have been some question. In twenty-four wills, the notary identified the testator as "on the eve of his departure for military service." Because only men between the ages of twenty and twenty-five were called up for military service, presumably these testators were fairly young. These two small groups of testators, the notably elderly and the young men off to war, behaved differently from each other and from most other testators. Most wills distributed property as a corollary to bestowing favor and transmitting power. But the very old and the young often had little property and less power to distribute. Many of them were dependents, living in someone else's household at someone else's expense. The elderly testators were most likely to choose as their heirs the people with whom they lived—children, siblings' children, and, in the few cases of old servants, their employers. One example was Jeanne Pradel, a servant for more than thirty years of merchant Samuel Vidallet. Ill and lying on a bed in an antechamber of Vidallet's Villebourbon apartment, Pradel named her master's eldest son as her heir.[38] The departing soldiers, however, were most likely to choose their peers—their brothers and their friends. Two named their fiancées as their heirs. Few chose their parents.[39] Elderly testators used

---

[37] AD T-et-G 5E 2106 Franceries no. 218 2–3–1809 testament Besombes; 2009 Garrigues no. 286 10–2–1778 solemn testament Caussat; 10877 Martin no. 27 12–2–1788 testament Sauret; 2067 Delmas no. 637 24–11–1788 testament Griffoul; 10877 Martin no. 290 15–5–1788 testament Pradel.

[38] AD T-et-G 5E 13179 Deray no. 200 12–10–1783 testament Pradel.

[39] The twenty-four departing soldiers appointed as their heirs the following: 7 brothers, 4 friends, 3 mothers, 2 nephews, 2 fiancées, 2 sisters-in-law, 1 sister, 1 wife, 1 father, and 1 godfather.

bequests to try to compensate for the dependency their advanced age and ill health had brought. By contrast, the young man used his will to assert his independence of familial obligations. On the eve of his departure for military service, the young man declared his emancipation from his father's authority.

The ages of the marrying couple also made a difference in the type of property arrangement they chose. Unfortunately, most marriage contracts gave the ages of the couple only in relation to legal majority. The bride and groom were either *mineur* or *majeur* and rarely did the notary record an exact age.[40] Therefore we cannot compare extremes as we can for testators. Nonetheless, there were slight differences between the frequency with which minor and major brides and grooms chose some of the less popular marital settlements. Minor couples were five times as likely as major couples (6.4 percent to 1.2 percent) to arrange that, if the bride died without offspring, her dowry would return to her family. The contracts of minors were also more likely to name specific property as dower rights (17 percent to 5 percent). Both of these provisions showed the young bride still under the authority and protection of her family. Her marriage contract was often signed in her family's home amid a large gathering of relatives.[41] Through the marriage contract her family protected her and the property entrusted to her from the strangers with whom her marriage would necessarily associate her. Such was the alliance in 1788 of Claire Rouffio and Jean Graves, both children of merchant tanners. Although the bride was an orphan, a large circle of her relatives attended the signing of her marriage contract. Her aunt and her brother-in-law mutually pledged to deliver to her her inheritance from her parents, worth more than four thousand livres. Claire constituted this as her dowry, but if she died without children, her husband would inherit only five hundred livres of it; the rest would return to her relatives. Like Claire Rouffio, a disproportionate number of minor brides were daughters of Montauban's elite of property owners, merchants, and magistrates.[42] Their marriages and their marriage

---

[40] Fifty-eight marriage contracts recorded the age of grooms and forty-seven that of brides. However, most of these were merely numerical translations of majority, 21 and 25 for women, 25 and 30 for men.

[41] Fifteen percent of minor brides contracted marriage in their own homes, 43 percent were attended by at least one relative besides their parents, and 13 percent were attended by at least four relatives. By comparison, only 9 percent of adult brides' contracts were signed in the home; in only 23 percent were any relatives present, and in only 5 percent were more than three relatives present. (These comparisons were significant at .01 although the associations were weak, with contingency coefficients ranging from .136 to .199.)

[42] AD T-et-G 5E 2008 Garrigues no. 612 20–8–1788 marriage contract Graves-Rouffio. Twenty-one percent of minor brides' fathers were members of Montauban's mercantile and professional elite; only 9 percent of adult brides' fathers were from this group (significance level = .01, contingency coefficient = .196).

contracts were part of intricate strategies of familial advancement in which the bride was the tenuous link; she remained dependent on her own family even as she was allied to her husband's family.

Adult couples made choices with other considerations in mind. Before the advent of the Napoleonic Code, three times as many adult brides as minor brides retained their property under their own control (12 percent versus 4 percent). When the Civil Code deprived all wives of the administration of their property, separate property arrangements declined in popularity and were replaced by marital communities. Brides who chose these options tended to be widows and working women with property or businesses of their own.[43] Jeanne Segon Fournier, who contracted to marry Charles Gatereau in 1778, was such a woman. Daughter of a music teacher, Jeanne had saved two thousand livres, in the words of the contract, "by the work of her hands and her industry and notably by a commerce in sewing materials [*mercerie*]." Jeanne constituted a dowry in silver, furniture, and linens worth twelve hundred livres but retained the remainder of her goods, "notably her merchandise and stock-in-trade," as personal property under her control. As the contract stated, she intended to continue her business after her marriage.[44] Couples like this tended to contract their marriages at the notary's office without many family members in attendance. Their marriages were not familial alliances but individual partnerships in which both parties expected to contribute and from which they hoped to benefit.

Age was closely linked to marital status. Older couples were likely to be making second or third marriages and, especially if they had children by their previous marriages, had different intentions and obligations from those of young people marrying for the first time. Wicked stepmothers certainly existed in fact as well as in fairy tale, but a stepfather who had control of his wife's property could be a more serious threat to a child's future.[45] For inheritance purposes at least, Montaubaners did not treat stepchildren as their own children. They rarely appointed them heirs or even legatees so that if property passed into the hands of the spouse, in all likelihood it would eventually benefit that person's children or relatives.[46] Antoinette Teissières's marriage contract with gardener Pierre Soulié tried to prevent this from happening. Teissières, a widow with one child,

---

[43] Eleven percent of major brides were marrying for a second time; only 1 percent of minor brides were remarrying (significance level = .01, contingency coefficient = .170).

[44] AD T-et-G 5E 10867 Martin no. 178 9–4–1778 contrat de mariage Gatereau-Segon Fournier.

[45] Flandrin, *Families in Former Times*, pp. 40–43; David Warren Sabean, "Young Bees in an Empty Hive: Relations Between Brothers-In-Law in a South German Village Around 1800," in Medick and Sabean, eds., *Interest and Emotion*, pp. 171–184.

[46] In the sample, only four wills named stepchildren as heirs or legatees.

Catherine, had reclaimed her dowry in household goods from her late husband's estate and delivered it to her new husband, once more as her dowry. However, she also brought other goods into Soulié's household, goods that belonged to Catherine as her father's heir. The marriage contract identified these items and bound Soulié to turn them over to his stepdaughter at her marriage or majority.[47] But such an arrangement, although it guaranteed Catherine her paternal inheritance, denied her any rights on her mother's estate. If Antoinette and Pierre had children, they would inherit Antoinette's dowry; if Antoinette predeceased Pierre without children by him, Pierre would inherit the dowry. Only if the couple had no children and Pierre died first could Catherine inherit anything from her mother. A strict separation of property or a limitation of nuptial gains to life rights provided better safeguards of stepchildren's rights. Both regimes were more popular in remarriages than in first marriages.[48]

The marriage contract meant somewhat different things for women and men. Although concluded between a man and a woman, often it was more important to the bride's family than to the groom's. When the bride's parents were alive, they witnessed the contract in 93 percent of the cases. By contrast, in 18 percent of the cases where the groom's parents were alive, they did not attend. The contract was sometimes signed at the bride's home, almost never at the groom's, and the bride's relatives were present more often than were the groom's relatives. The bride's parents and sometimes other relatives gave her gifts or promised her legacies.[49] Besides defining the bride's relationship to her future husband and his family, the marriage contract provided an occasion to reaffirm and celebrate the bride's relationship to her own family.

Marital status was an important determinant in individual decisions about succession. Married testators were most likely to leave their property to their spouses or equally to their children. Widowed testators tended to choose one child or another relative as heir. Nearly one third preferred the eldest male heir. Single testators, those least enmeshed in familial obligations, were also least influenced by legal concepts of family priorities. Neither equality nor primogeniture rated very highly with them.

[47] AD T-et-G 5E 13179 Deray no. 207 16–10–1783 contract de mariage Soulié-Teissières.

[48] Separate property regimes appeared in 9 percent of contracts where the bride was remarrying compared with only 6 percent of first marriages. Contracts that limited nuptial gains to life rights occurred in like percentages for both men and women, 13 percent for remarriages compared with only 3 percent of first marriages (significance level = .01, contingency coefficient = .162).

[49] Ten percent of the sampled marriage contracts were recorded in the bride's home, less than 1 percent in the groom's home. In 31 percent, the bride's relatives witnessed the contract; in 25 percent the groom's relatives were witnesses. In 8 percent, the bride received a gift from a relative other than her parents. In 2 percent the groom received such a gift.

TABLE 3–4
Marital Status and Choice of Heir

	Percentage of Testators		
Heir Chosen	*Single*	*Married*	*Widowed*
Eldest male kin	25%	21%	32%
Other kin	35	14	37
Coresident	17	3	21
Nonkin	19	1	7
Spouse	0	30	0
Equal inheritance	4	31	3
N	177	482	178

Note: Significance level = .01, contingency coefficient = .551.

Instead, the common interactions of daily life influenced many of their settlements. Seventeen percent left their property to persons with whom they lived and 19 percent appointed nonkin—friends and neighbors—as their heirs. Seamstress Anne Carbouet chose a priest; Jean Pierre Coste, "coachman's apprentice, actually a beggar," chose his landlady. Marie Loup left small legacies to a friend and a fellow servant and named her employer to inherit the remainder of her possessions, probably consisting mostly of unpaid wages. Pierre Nouaille, a retired weaver from Bias, declared he had no descendants and left his estate to the widow of his best friend.[50] These people played a greater role in the testators' daily lives than the distant kin who were their legal heirs.

Because of the inequities of law and demography, men and women made wills at different points in their lives. Although some men made them when they were young and unmarried—young recruits, for example—most did so after they married and, like Antoine Barreau, once they had fathered families. Few male testators were widowers. Because of the ease with which men remarried and their tendency to marry women younger than themselves, there were far fewer widowers in the population than widows. Also, many widowers had made wills when their wives were alive and had no need to change them. Law and demography worked in the opposite direction for women. Before the Revolution, more than half of female testators were, like Françoise Valette, widows, and nearly one third were single women, many of them elderly. During the Old Regime, the law denied the legal competence of married women or of single women if their fathers or guardians were alive. Only in rare circumstances,

---

[50] AD T-et-G 5E 2008 Garrigues no. 742 13–10–1788 testament Carbouet; 1943 Caminel no. 117 22–2–1787 testament Costes; 1944 Caminel no. 494 29–9–1788 testament Loup; 2356 Martin no. 67 1–2–1809 testament Nouaille.

Table 3–5
Marital Status of Male and Female Testators, 1775–1824

	Period		
Male Testators	*1775–1793*	*1794–1799*	*1800–1824*
Single	21%	3%	22%
Married	66	95	67
Widowed	13	2	11
N	182	64	216
Female Testators			
Single	31%	7%	23%
Married	17	88	49
Widowed	52	5	28
N	136	40	199

Note: Significance level = .01, men contingency coefficient = .215, women contingency coefficient = .409.

for example, if a woman's father emancipated her or if her marriage contract specified a separate property regime, could a young woman or a married woman make a will.[51] Mandatory equal inheritance, however, encouraged both men and women to make wills in order to ensure some protection for their spouses. As a result, almost all the testators of the Revolutionary period were married. After the Revolution, the differences in marital status between the genders reappeared, although not as markedly as before.[52] Single women and widowed women continued to outnumber single and

[51] Timbal, "La Succession testamentaire," pp. 295–296. Formal, notarized emancipations of women were rare but they did occur, in most cases so that the woman could carry on a business. See, for example, AD T-et-G 5E 10867 Martin no. 174 7–4–1778 emancipation Tiers à Tiers. François Tiers, a cloth shearer's apprentice of Montauban,

> recognizing the prudence and capacity of Marie Tiers, his daughter, wife of Guillaume Deleil, retailer, . . . and wanting to make it easier for her to carry on her business, the said Tiers has emancipated the said Marie Tiers, present, accepting and humbly thanking her father, and [he has] placed her outside of his paternal authority so that she may from this time forward work for her own profit and advantage, acquire, sell, trade, contract, make a will, appear in court and generally act in her own name . . . the said Tiers, father, reserving to himself the honor and respect that his said daughter owes him following divine and human law from which the said Tiers [daughter] has promised never to stray.

[52] The difference in marital status between male and female testators did not entirely disappear even during the Revolution and fewer women made wills during this period. Both before and after the Revolution about 55 percent of testators were men and 45 percent women; during the period of equal inheritance, 62 percent of testators were men and 38 percent women.

TABLE 3–6
Men's and Women's Choice of Heir

Heir Chosen	Percentage of Testators	
	Men	Women
Eldest male kin	27%	20%
Other kin	16	32
Coresident	9	10
Nonkin	4	8
Spouse	20	15
Equal inheritance	24	15
N	469	378

Note: Significance level = .01, contingency coefficient = .228.

widowed men, and they continued to be the majority of female testators; however, far more married women than before made wills.

Men and women had different purposes in making their wills, too. Most men intended their wills to help sustain the family and preserve the family property. The typical male testator made his will shortly after he first married. He appointed his wife as his heir, trusting her to pass the couple's property on to their children in due course. It was the widow who then made the ultimate decision as to how the property would be distributed. Through her will, she dispersed the family and its possessions.

This pattern was clearest before the Revolution. During the Revolution, men and women acted almost identically as testators; both were married people concerned with providing for a spouse. The Revolutionary period gave birth to the practice of making reciprocal testaments. Shortly after marriage, husband and wife would go together to the notary's office to make their wills, setting up identical legacies in life rights or assigning each other the portion disponible. The custom grew in popularity after the Revolution and accounted for the increase in will making among married women, who, under the Civil Code, were at least as incapacitated in law as they had been under Roman law. These wills were as similar in intent and provisions to the wills of married men as they were different from the wills of unmarried and widowed women.

Men and women had different priorities in choosing an heir, differences that did not entirely depend on marital status. More men than women favored the eldest male heir and, in fact, when not choosing their wives or their heirs equally, two thirds of male testators chose men as heirs. Women were as likely to choose other women as they were to choose men. Thus, the beneficiaries of patrilinear inheritance—men—were the major perpetrators of it.[53]

The connection between the gender of the testator and the gender of the heir was due in part to the different types of property that men and women tended to own. In much of the world, male and female property is separate and distinct. As anthropologist Jack Goody has pointed out, preindustrial Europe differed from other traditional societies in this respect because property could pass between men and women and women could inherit land.[54] Nonetheless, there was a gender division of property, which although far from absolute was significant. In the sample of wills, 82 percent of legacies of household furnishings went to women and 69 percent of Montauban marriage contracts included dowries in household goods, principally beds, wardrobes, and linens. Even large dowries were often composed partially or even wholly of such *effets*. The dowry of Augustine Aimée, fiancée of a justice of the peace, was worth one thousand livres; it included the standard items, as well as such luxuries as a piano, a chaise longue, and place settings in silver.[55] By contrast, only 7 percent of dowries included real estate whereas 60 percent of legacies of land and other realty went to men.

The rough division of property by gender accounts for some of the differences between wills made by women and those made by men. For example, not only did women receive legacies of furniture, linens, and clothes more often than men did, women made such legacies more often than male testators.[56] If a woman's estate was composed of "feminine" property, she was more likely to leave it to a woman. Men, more likely to own land in the first place, were also more likely to leave this "masculine" property to men. Even after the Revolution, when the popularity of spouses as heirs and of equal inheritance should have accelerated the exchange of property between the sexes, the identification of property and gender remained. Shortly before his death in 1823, peasant Jean Gineste made a will leaving "by preference" his house and land to his son, Bernard;

---

[53] From the sample of wills, excluding cases where the testator chose the spouse or all heirs equally, in the period before the Revolution, 69 percent of men chose male heirs whereas 45 percent of women chose women (significance level = .01, contingency coefficient = .145). In the period after the Revolution from 1800 through 1824, 62 percent of men chose men and 55 percent of women chose women (significance level = .02, contingency coefficient = .161).

[54] Jack Goody, "Inheritance, Property and Women: Some Comparative Considerations," in Goody, Thirsk, and Thompson, eds., *Family and Inheritance*, p. 10.

[55] AD T-et-G 5E 2112 Franceries no. 300 10–11–1824 contrat de mariage Martin-Aimée. See also 5E 13182 Deray no. 1195 5–3–1793 contrat de mariage Boujol-Langlade.

[56] Twenty-four percent of legacies to women included *effets*; 25 percent of legacies from women included *effets*. For men these percentages were 7 percent and 16 percent.

the rest of his estate was to be divided equally between Bernard and his daughter, Marie. This legacy was far greater than the legal portion disponible, and Marie challenged it when the will was read. In 1824 she and Bernard reached an agreement whereby she ceded to him all her rights in her parents' succession in return for furniture and linens worth 240 francs and 4,486 francs in cash. She had received about 800 francs as her dowry, but the rest her brother was to pay her over the next nine years. Although Bernard had to mortgage everything he owned, he did manage to retain all of his father's real estate.[57] Obviously agreements like this could be disastrous if the heir was eventually forced to sell his inheritance in order to pay off his siblings' claims. Nevertheless, they were common and they maintained the association of *effets* with women and landed property with men.

The type of property, but also the amount of property and a person's occupation and social status, influenced decisions about succession. Peasants, merchants, artisans, and poor workers all had somewhat different intentions as testators. The reign of equal inheritance briefly erased these differences, but once the law again permitted some choice of heirs, many Montaubaners returned to pre-Revolutionary preferences—many but not all. Although landowning peasants, city workers, and the elite of merchants and professionals reestablished old inheritance patterns, the successions of the region's land-poor peasants and Montauban's artisans and shopkeepers changed radically.

Before the Revolution, the champions of primogeniture in the Montauban region, or at least its most diligent practitioners, were the peasants. More than half of self-sufficient landowning peasants left the bulk of their property to their eldest sons, brothers, or nephews. Farm workers and tenant farmers behaved similarly. Although these peasants did not own enough land to qualify as farm owners, many owned a few acres, their only possessions of value.[58] Like the wealthier landowners, they left their property to one heir, most often the eldest son. Very few peasants requested an equal division of their land and only land-poor peasants ever left its distribution to their spouses.

Comfortably off city residents—artisans and shopkeepers, as well as Montauban's elite of professionals, merchants, and manufacturers—also tended to favor one heir but not inevitably the eldest son. They chose

[57] AD T-et-G 5E 2153 Latreille-Olivié no. 131 12–5–1824 accord Gineste-Gineste ép Solleville. A similar case on a smaller scale unfolds in 5E 2143 Latreille-Olivié no. 216 18–5–1815 vente Ruelle ép Miquel and 2150 Latreille-Olivié no. 519 3–12–1821 cession Ruelle ép Miquel, in which a peasant woman sold and ceded her maternal and paternal inheritance to her brother.

[58] A peasant who accumulated any capital purchased land. Peasants without land rarely owned anything of value and rarely made wills. This was less true of urban workers, who also invested in furniture and linens as well as the tools or merchandise of their trades.

TABLE 3–7
Choice of Heir by Testator's Occupation, 1775–1824

Heir Chosen	Farm Worker	Peasant Owner	City Worker	Artisan Retailer	Merchant	Bourgeois
Eldest male						
1775–1793	44%	52%	15%	31%	47%	30%
1800–1824	21	47	20	14	6	19
Other kin						
1775–1793	27	24	25	36	47	38
1800–1824	23	17	20	15	44	33
Coresident						
1775–1793	4	5	19	11	6	7
1800–1824	12	9	11	10	0	16
Nonkin						
1775–1793	3	5	15	7	0	7
1800–1824	1	0	14	6	0	14
Spouse						
1775–1793	22	9	23	10	0	7
1800–1824	18	8	15	19	38	4
Equal inheritance						
1775–1793	0	5	3	5	0	11
1800–1824	25	19	20	36	12	14
N	208	100	155	227	41	83

Note: Significance level = .01, 1775–1793 contingency coefficient = .393, 1800–1824 contingency coefficient = .407.

other kin as frequently as they chose the heir designated by primogeniture. Their heirs of choice were descendants—children, grandchildren, nephews, and nieces. Their property was patrimony, received from parents and passed on to offspring. Their families were lineages which property supported in a continuing relationship between the past and the future. Like landowning peasants, Montauban's middle and upper classes did not leave property to their spouses; nor were their marriage contracts generous to the surviving spouse. They kept the patrimony out of the hands of "strangers."

For poorer city workers, lineage and patrimony had little significance. Their property consisted of, at most, a room and more often merely clothes, linens, and household furnishings. Few followed the dictates of primogeniture. A poor man was more likely to choose an heir who lived with him than he was to favor his eldest son. The most common heir was the spouse. In marriage contracts, too, poor couples often devised settlements that exceeded the Custom of Montauban. Their highest priority was the marital relationship, and the couple's property supported day-to-day survival. Unlike other Montaubaners, when poor workers had no spouse they were as likely to leave their property to friends and neighbors as they were to kin.

For all groups the period of mandatory equal inheritance brought significant changes. Equal inheritance with some provision for the spouse was the rule. Only a few peasant landowners attempted to follow pre-Revolutionary priorities by writing illegal wills that favored their eldest sons. When the law of 4 *germinal* Year 8 restored some discretion to testators, the inheritance patterns of different economic groups diverged once more. For all groups, equal inheritance, which had accounted for only 3 percent of wills before the Revolution, grew in popularity. But many Montaubaners returned to writing wills very like those of their predecessors although using new terminology and new forms. Peasant landowners continued to favor the eldest male heir in nearly half their wills; the elite of merchants and professionals also favored a single heir, often the eldest male but more often not. City workers once again chose among their spouses, housemates, and friends, with equal inheritance providing a newly popular option. For all of these groups, the ideology of the Revolution as codified in inheritance law changed the degree of preference that a testator might show but did not change the preferences themselves. The hierarchies inheritance confirmed within families—eldest son over younger son, nephew over niece, wife over brother, neighbor over distant kin—remained the same.

The same cannot be said for land-poor and landless peasants and for artisans and shopkeepers. For both of these groups, the Revolution marked a profound change in inheritance patterns. Before the Revolution, two thirds of these testators had selected one relative over others to inherit the bulk of the property. After 1799, less than one half of poor peasants and less than one third of artisans made this choice. For both groups, equal inheritance became the most popular solution. Except for the fact that peasants and artisans rarely left property to nonrelatives, their choices began to resemble those of the urban poor. They stopped behaving like the trustees of family property. The change in their family priorities was linked to a real decline in their economic position; their property was ceasing to be patrimony.

The vicissitudes of family law between 1775 and 1825 only partially governed the distribution of power and property within Montauban families. As a rule, Montaubaners' wills did not conform to primogeniture before the Revolution or to absolute equal inheritance after the Revolution. The legal changes did bring about changes in practice, but the law's impact was mitigated by personal and familial priorities and circumstances. Montaubaners' decisions about their wills and marriage contracts were predicated upon their positions within their own families, their property, and their idea of the proper relationship between the two. And this was not a simple relationship as if all the property owners did one thing and all the propertyless another. Nor did similar choices always result from similar circumstances and intentions. Decisions about family and property were tied together in a complicated interrelationship in which work, gender, marital status, age, not to mention unique personal considerations, each played a part.[59]

Consider the eighty-one testators in the sample who chose heirs who lived with them. Why did these people make this choice, a distinctly minority choice since they comprised only 10 percent of all Montauban testators? It was not a choice determined by gender because half were women and half were men; nor was marital status a significant factor because the single, married, and widowed chose it in about equal numbers. Two thirds were city dwellers and one third were peasants, a ratio similar to that of all Montauban testators. By looking simultaneously at gender, marital status, and social class, two patterns emerge. The majority of married testators of both sexes and of widowed men were peasants. The heirs they selected, the heirs with whom they lived, were almost always sons and usually eldest sons. The majority of single persons of both sexes and of widowed women were city dwellers, mostly elderly and mostly poor. Half of the widows lived with one of their children, with daughters as often as sons. The rest of the widows as well as the single testators lived with siblings, siblings' children and friends, with women as often as with men.

Two different circumstances produced apparently similar choices, but the intentions of the testators were as different as the circumstances. The circumstances behind the peasant's choice was the pot-and-hearth community. The peasant couple, headed by the husband, had taken a son into partnership, to live and work together, to share and share alike. The father's will confirmed the contract; the patrimony that they shared would pass to the son and partner. By this choice, the peasant intended to preserve and continue the unity of household, work, and property, which, if all went well, maintained the dignity and self-sufficiency of his family. The poor elderly testators who lived with friends or relatives in the city did not

---

[59] Given sex, marital status, age, parental status, occupation, and the date of the will, the statistical technique called discriminant analysis accurately predicted how testators had left their property in 36 percent of the cases. Parenthood, occupation, date of will, and marital status, in that order, provided the bulk of the predictive strength. Testators who chose nonkin as heirs and testators who chose equal inheritance were the easiest to predict (with 68 percent and 60 percent accuracy), whereas testators who chose heirs who lived with them and testators who chose other kin were the least well-defined groups (only 25 percent and 20 percent predicted accurately). Wilks's lambda = 0.558, significance level = .01.

make the same choice. They were not in partnership with their heirs but dependent on them for a place to live, for services, perhaps even for food. Their choice of which relative to live with was limited by who would take them in. For security, some had signed contracts trading the promise of inheritance for the promise of care, like Marguerite Bessede, widow of a wool comber, who promised to make her cousin her heir "on condition that [he] come to the aid of the said Bessede with food and care if she be in need of it."[60] These wills attempted to repay past kindness, service, and expenses whether these had resulted from a formal contract or from merely a tacit obligation. Although these testators did not conceive of their family priorities as a unity of household and property as did the peasants, by their choice of heirs they did buttress the crucial relationships with as much material support as possible. Survival of the household, survival of the individual—two different priorities generated by two different circumstances influenced Montaubaners to choose heirs who lived with them.

The revolution in inheritance law did induce Montaubaners to distribute their property more equally. Fewer testators chose to favor one heir over another; fewer upheld the rights of primogeniture. These changes were significant and they affected all types of testators, women and men, married and single, rich and poor. Statutory equal inheritance accomplished in Montauban what Mirabeau intended it should; it made material equality a foundation of family life.

The success of equal inheritance was not unqualified, however. It did not win an absolute victory in Montaubaners' wills. First, equal inheritance was distinctly more popular in some social groups than in others; for example, it was more popular with married people than with single testators and with artisans than with Montauban's professional and mercantile elite. Second, equal inheritance was not nearly as radical a reform as Revolutionary rhetoric claimed. It was a change only for testators; equal inheritance had always been the rule in Montauban for intestate successions. Nor was it such a wrenching change for testators, especially in its final modified form in the Civil Code. If before the Revolution few testators had left their property equally to their heirs, few had left it as unequally as the faculté de tester permitted. Montaubaners' rapid and uncomplaining adoption of the portion disponible suggests that the Civil Code accorded better with their ideas of family order and justice than the légitime had done. Finally, Montaubaners' sense of familial obligation and equity included a person left out by Old Regime, Revolutionary, and Napoleonic law, the spouse. An increasing formal recognition of spouses' rights ac-

---

[60] AD T-et-G B 420 no. 60 9–10–1782. The *Registres des dons entre-vifs* kept by the *sénéchaussée* in the eighteenth century are full of these contracts. See AD T-et-G series B and series Q and chapter 6.

companied the growing popularity of equal inheritance. During the Revolution, concern for the spouse led notaries to devise new formulas and, in fact, to create a new type of will with the sole purpose of awarding the spouse the maximum benefits the law allowed. Couples added a new custom to the marriage ritual and a new set of documents to the marriage contract: reciprocal wills. For these Montaubaners, equality in the family went beyond *fraternité*, the bond between brothers, to touch the nuptial bond as well.

Montaubaners' experiences in their own families shaped their responses to the radical change in family law. The laws of equal inheritance meant different things, posed different problems (or solutions) to people of different ages, genders, marital status, and socioeconomic groups. To answer the question of why the inheritance choices of some Montaubaners changed so dramatically while others returned to Old Regime patterns requires more than a survey of notary documents. We must now plunge below the surface trends to investigate Montauban's families in greater depth and detail.

CHAPTER FOUR

The Merchants and the Magistrates

MONTAUBAN IMPRESSED eighteenth-century visitors with its unostentatious yet imposing public buildings: the Jesuit school, the bishop's palace, the intendance, the Cour des Aides, and the neoclassical cathedral, which Arthur Young described as "modern and pretty well built, but too heavy."[1] The men who served these institutions were no less impressive and dominating, but unless a tourist had a letter of introduction, he would have to content himself with viewing the buildings. On a few great occasions, such as the visit of the king's brother in 1777, Montauban's notable citizens showed themselves in solemn procession and archaic costumes, but normally they spent their days behind the closed doors of courtrooms, offices, and warehouses. They traveled through the streets in carriages and sedan chairs and relaxed in the privacy of their homes.[2]

The homes of Montauban's important men were very private indeed. Shuttered on the street side, they faced inward onto shady, walled courtyards. To further exclude the world, some had thick, oak doors rather than wrought-iron gates which closed the courtyard to the street. Even within these houses, the eighteenth century had brought greater privacy. Except for the bishop's palace, which still operated as a kind of public office,[3] the great rambling households of kin, retainers, and servants were things of the past. Although the town houses of the well-to-do were large, they were divided into several apartments, each with its own entrance and small serving staff. Male servants, who publicly displayed their masters' ranks and wealth with their fancy liveries and conspicuous idleness, were far outnumbered by female domestics who worked within the household.

[1] Young *Travels*, 2: 40. Also see Guilhamon, *Richeprey* 2: 188–189.

[2] To welcome Monsieur, the municipal officers, dressed in their consular robes and hoods, met his carriage at the gates of the city. Accompanied by the captain of the guards and "all the noblity of the town," they escorted the royal visitor to the bishop's palace for a ceremonial banquet. AM Mont AA 11 Livre rouge neuf, pp. 64–65. By contrast, a dinner invitation from the intendant to a M. de Ste Croix expressed "mortification" that a carriage could not be sent to convey him in respectable privacy. AD T-et-G 9–J–5 papiers de famille. Garrioch, in *Neighbourhood and Community in Paris*, pp. 60–61, 94, 201–204, 255–256, concludes that the elite gradually withdrew from neighborhood sociability over the course of the eighteenth century.

[3] For example, on the occasion of Monsieur's visit, the municipality held a banquet in his honor in the bishop's palace. "In order to satisfy the public enthusiasm, the dining room doors were left open during the entire dinner." AM Mont AA 11 Livre rouge neuf, p. 64.

The first president of the Cour des Aides employed only eight servants; the wealthiest merchant only six.[4]

Nobles, magistrates, clerics, merchants, lawyers, *rentiers*—Montauban's elite made up about 10 percent of the population.[5] These families shared a life-style that set them apart from the rest of the city's inhabitants. The most distinguishing factor was wealth. Judging from the sample of marriage contracts, the average dowry of a working woman at the end of the eighteenth century was 232 livres and that of an artisan's bride 1,330 livres, whereas the average elite dowry was worth 15,452 livres. Almost all of the elite paid at least 20 livres in capitation tax, which indicated incomes of 2,000 livres a year or more. By contrast, few skilled workmen earned more than 1 livre a day. And, while even respectable artisans and retailers made do with a minimum of serviceable possessions, elite families lived in comfort and even luxury. Mme d'Alies de Cieurac, widow of a prominent magistrate, left in her estate marble-topped tables, gilt-framed mirrors, armchairs upholstered in silk petit point, inlaid sideboards, and a half-dozen card tables. Her bedroom was entirely furnished in Louis XVI furniture and decorated in gold and white.[6]

With a comfortable income went a certain amount of culture and education. Whereas peasants and working people spoke patois and shopkeepers, traders, and minor officials attempted to speak correct Occitan, the historic language of southern France, the elite could speak French. And although the bulk of the population was illiterate, Montauban's elite read and wrote both Occitan and French.[7] Montauban boasted several reading

---

[4] Ligou, "Montauban des lumières," pp. 177–179; Ligou, "La Cour des aides de Montauban," p. 319; AM Mont 1 G 1 capitation 1790 and 10 HH 1 dénombrement de Villebourbon, 1774. When, during the Revolution, the government sequestered and sealed the property of suspects and emigrés, separate entrances permitted other family members to remain in residence in their sections of the house. The Molières family was one such case. Des Rochettes, "Familles montaubanaises," 7: Molières. See Fairchilds, *Domestic Enemies*, and Maza, *Servants and Masters*, two excellent studies of the changing nature of service in the eighteenth century.

[5] Ligou, "Etude fonctionnelle de la population de Montauban," pp. 579–602. The eighteenth-century term *bourgeois* gave way in the nineteenth century to *rentier* and *propriétaire sans profession*, the first deriving income from investments and the second from land.

[6] AM Mont 5 CC 9 capitation, 1788; MS 20 no. 84 arrête du conseil général Year 2; Ombret et al., *Villes et campagnes du Bas-Quercy*, B3.

[7] A British visitor to Toulouse in the 1780s reported: "The French Language (except by the best sort of people) is most insufferably spoken, the lower class making use altogether of the Patois which is very soft and agreeable to the ear, but so different from the French that there are many persons here who do not understand it." Cited in John Lough, *France on the Eve of Revolution: British Travellers' Observations, 1763–1788* (Chicago: Dorsey Press, 1987), p. 7. Also see Castan, *Honnêteté*, p. 18; Le Roy-Ladurie, *Les Paysans de Languedoc*, p. 334; Armengaud, *Populations de l'est-aquitain*, pp. 330–331; and Furet and Ozouf, *Reading and Writing*, pp. 25–34.

TABLE 4–1
The Value of Dowries in Montauban Marriage Contracts

Dowry in Livres/Francs	Groom's Occupation					
	Farm Worker	Peasant Owner	City Worker	Artisan Retailer	Merchant	Bourgeois
No dowry	5%	9%	13%	8%	3%	5%
1–199	31	16	33	9	0	3
200–499	28	17	30	21	0	3
500–999	20	9	19	32	0	3
1,000–4,999	16	30	5	26	22	36
5,000–9,999	0	17	0	3	25	12
10,000+	0	2	0	1	50	38
N	264	57	194	203	35	64

Note: Significance level = .01, contingency coefficient = .634.

clubs and Masonic lodges as well as the prestigious Academy of Arts and Belles-Lettres, in which well-to-do citizens discussed literature and tried their hands at literary creation. They also regularly purchased books and paintings and patronized the theater. Between 1774 and 1783, merchant Pierre Lacoste-Rigail bought more than three hundred livres' worth of books and borrowed many more. He was also an avid theatergoer. When he was at home in Montauban he went to the theater every week; on business trips to Bordeaux or Toulouse, he frequently saw a different play every night.[8]

Many Montaubaners traveled about the region and beyond. Boatmen made frequent trips to Bordeaux; journeymen went on working tours throughout southern France and into Italy and Spain. But the elite's contacts beyond Montauban were more extensive and more regular. Most well-to-do men visited Paris as well as Toulouse and Bordeaux and corresponded with friends, relatives, and business acquaintances in these and other cities. Some also had far-flung international connections. The noble branch of the Garrisson family, for example, had relatives with whom they exchanged letters and visits in Amsterdam, Dublin, and New York. And well-to-do Montaubaners who rarely left home kept abreast of national and international political, economic, and literary currents by reading

[8] Extracts of his journal are cited in Ombret et al., *Villes et campagnes du Bas-Quercy*, D6. Inventories of Montauban merchants' private libraries reflect their classical education—Ovid, Cicero, Caesar, Plato—and their conservative taste for seventeenth-century pious works. The most common contemporary works were Voltaire's *Zaïre* and *La Henriade*, Rousseau's novels, and the ubiquitous *dictionnaires* on every subject. Ligou and Garrisson-Estebe, "La Bourgeoisie reformée montalbanaise," p. 403.

TABLE 4–2
Ability of Couples to Sign Their Marriage Contracts

	Groom's Occupation					
Percentage Who Signed	Farm Worker	Peasant Owner	City Worker	Artisan Retailer	Merchant	Bourgeois
Grooms	9%	37%	31%	66%	97%	100%
Brides	1	9	8	27	91	77
N	265	57	193	205	35	64

Note: Significance level = .01, grooms contingency coefficient = .523, brides contingency coefficient = .539.

newspapers. In 1790, Montauban subscribers received sixteen different journals, mostly from Paris, but also from Strasbourg and Marseilles and one that reported on West Indian affairs.[9]

In Nantes, Rouen, Montpellier, and other cities of comparable size and fortune to Montauban, shared literacy, culture, and levels and sources of income had led to intermarriage between different segments of the elite and the creation of a veritable ruling class.[10] By judiciously investing in offices, titles, and seigneurial property, over several generations families transformed wealth into social status. For example, few successful merchant families remained in commerce longer than three generations. The grandchildren and great-grandchildren of the merchants who had made the family's fortune were usually landowners, officials, and magistrates often with noble rank. The regular movement from the mercantile and financial elites into the nobility guaranteed a continual, although gradual, renewal and a progressive integration at the summit of society.[11]

[9] Henry de France, *Les Montalbanais et le refuge* (Montauban: Imprimerie Edouard Forestié, 1887), pp. 276–289. Fajn, "La Diffusion de la presse révolutionnaire," pp. 299–314. Marinière, in "Les Marchands d'étoffes," p. 298, cites one merchant who spent an average of one hundred livres a year for letter carrying.

[10] Jones, *Charity and Bienfaisance*, pp. 20–21; Richard, *Noblesse d'affaires*, pp. 18–19, 93–95, 109–115.

[11] The intendant of Languedoc advised in 1715 that only two merchants be appointed to the municipal council because they would "suffice to uphold the interests of the manufacturers and enhance that profession; but experience has shown that if, on the one hand, it is the prerogative of some, it is bad for commerce because the children of such merchants, thinking themselves noble, leave their fathers' profession in which it is important that they persevere." Cited in Lacave and Lacave, *Bourgeois et marchands*, p. 231. Richard, *Noblesse d'affaires*, pp. 109–115. Deyon, *Amiens*, p. 294; Goubert, *Familles marchandes*, p. 17; and Forster, *The Nobility of Toulouse*, p. 24, all trace the same three-generational pattern of movement up and out of commerce. Chaline, *Bourgeois de Rouen*, pp. 100–117, found the pattern continued in the nineteenth century, perhaps even accelerated by the Industrial Revolution.

Montauban merchants had ascended in this way in the seventeenth century; branches of the Garrisson and Vialette families, for example, purchased nobility through the sinecure of a *sécrétaire du roi*.[12] Then the Revocation of the Edict of Nantes placed an insurmountable barrier in their path. Montauban's merchants were Protestant almost to a man; although for much of the eighteenth century they maintained a public silence and outward compliance to the law, most steadfastly refused to abjure.[13] Therefore they could not practice law, hold office, serve in the army, in short, engage in any of the "honorable" professions that were the usual routes to official social status and ennoblement. Thus, religion created two elites in Montauban, one Protestant and commercial and the other Catholic and official. At the core of each group were Montauban's wealthiest citizens, the magistrates of the Cour des Aides and the *négociants* of Villebourbon.[14]

As members of a sovereign court, the magistrates of the Cour des Aides

[12] Des Rochette, "Familles montaubanaises," 5: Garrisson, 10: Vialette. Ligou, "La Cour des aides de Montauban," p. 314.

[13] According to Ligou and Garrisson-Estebe, "La Bourgeoisie reformée montalbanaise," p. 380, of the 123 merchants and manufacturers in the 1788 capitation list taxed at more than ten livres, only 27 were Catholic. Montauban was similar to La Rochelle in this Protestant domination of commerce. Clark, *La Rochelle*, pp. 5, 43–44, 51–53, found that Protestant merchant families in La Rochelle, like those in Montauban, remained in commerce. He found no evidence, however, of a longing for ennoblement and concluded that they were merchants by choice rather than because they were excluded from other careers. Nonetheless, he points out that career patterns in Catholic merchant families were more diverse and that they sought and accepted titles and offices not open to Protestants.

Elsewhere either Catholics dominated or Catholic and Protestant merchant communities rivaled each other. In these cases, although Protestants still remained a group apart, the elite as a whole was better integrated because Catholic merchants had closer ties with Catholic officials. See Carrière, *Négociants marseillais* 1: 286, and Butel, *Négociants*, p. 335. In some cities, La Rochelle, for example, some merchants did convert to Catholicism. See Forster, *Depont Family*, pp. 18–20. Missionary efforts in Montauban were not successful, according to Ligou, "Protestants et sans-culottes," p. 185.

After a century of silence, Montauban's merchants responded to the Act of Toleration in 1787 as a call to proclaim their allegiance to their religious heritage. The act legalized non-Catholic marriages and set up offices to record vital statistics. By the end of its first month in operation in Montauban, the Non-Catholic Register was recording twenty marriages a day. These were not current weddings but re-registrations of marriages often celebrated years earlier in the Catholic church. Whole families came in to declare their faith. On March 27, 1788, for example, Jean Garrisson *aîné*, merchant of Villebourbon, his cousin Marie Mariette, his second cousin's widow, her daughter, and niece all registered their marriages and the births of their children and witnessed one another's statements. AD T-et-G E Etat Civil Protestant no. 366 3-27-1788.

[14] At the end of the Old Regime there were 56 families of nobility of the sword, 98 robe families, 170 other officials and professionals, and about 370 members of the clergy for an official elite totaling about 2,000 people. The commercial and manufacturing elite included about 250 families, or 1,200 to 1,500 individuals. Ligou, "Etude fonctionnelle de la population de Montauban," pp. 579–602.

TABLE 4–3
Religious Affiliation in Montauban Marriage Contracts, 1775–1793

Religious Mention	Groom's Occupation					
	Farm Worker	Peasant Owner	City Worker	Artisan Retailer	Merchant	Bourgeois
None	28%	39%	29%	30%	36%	26%
Catholic	41	28	65	46	12	42
Protestant*	31	33	6	24	52	32
N	100	18	99	50	25	19

Note: Significance level = .01, contingency coefficient = .343.

*After 1787, Protestants contracted to marry "under the November Edict"; before toleration they had agreed to marry "Christianly" (*chrétiennement*).

were at the top of the legal profession. Admission to the bench automatically ennobled them, and they claimed power and privileges to match their dignity. Although their official business was to adjudicate tax disputes, they also claimed to share in the right to advise or remonstrate the king, which was held by the Parlements. In general, they used these prerogatives to uphold seigneurial rights and noble privileges and to defend the jurisdiction of their court from the "encroachments" of Toulouse, Bordeaux, and Cahors.[15] However, in the late eighteenth century the bench of the Cour des Aides began to interpret its role more broadly. In 1763 the magistrates initiated an undercover investigation of the financial administration of the province with the intention of documenting abuses and corruption even if—especially if—perpetrated by royal officials. They defended this campaign as necessary to the public welfare, which the court was honor bound to protect.[16] In 1785, the magistrates protested the opening of French West Indian ports to foreign trade, an issue that directly interested Montauban's merchants and manufacturers but not its landowning nobles and officials. By championing it at Versailles, the magistrates of the Cour des Aides once again proclaimed themselves the leaders of the city as a whole.[17]

[15] The major business of the Cour des Aides was the *cadastre*, the record of land holdings used to compute the *taille*, the basic royal tax. The court also had final jurisdiction over various customs and excise taxes like the salt tax, but the intendant administered the "modern" taxes, the *capitation* and the *vingtième*. The Conseil du Roi also directed sundry other matters to the Cour des Aides. For example, in 1723 the village of Bourrel sued its seigneur for illegally cutting down trees. After two years of litigation, the Conseil du Roi referred the case to Montauban's Cour des Aides, where, it so happened, the seigneur in question was a magistrate! Des Rochettes, "Familles montaubanaises," 6: Lacaze. See Ligou, "La Cour des aides de Montauban"; Ford, *Robe and Sword*, p. 39; and Carrière, "Le Recrutement de la cour des comptes," pp. 157–158.

[16] Cuillieron, *Contributions à l'étude de la rebellion des cours souverains*, pp. 61–101.

[17] Tarrade, *Le Commerce colonial* 2: 578–579.

The commercial community had its own sources of prestige. To be a *négociant*, therefore engaged in *Le Négoce*, carried a mystique barely perceptible in the English words *merchant* and *commerce*. In 1772 a Marseilles merchant wrote that the *négociant* "is the natural inhabitant of all the parts of the globe in which he keeps his goods and his agents; he sits between the two tropics where he finds his suppliers and his customers."[18] The perfumes of oranges, tropical flowers, sugar cane, and sea voyages clung to Montauban's dealers in such mundane items as woolens and flour.

Merchants and magistrates inhabited different physical and social worlds. Almost all of the magistrates of the Cour des Aides lived within a few blocks of the courthouse; their neighbors were their colleagues and their kin as well as other nobles and officials. The community of wealthy merchants was even more geographically concentrated. The 1774 census of Villebourbon's main street reads like a roster of Montauban's leading mercantile families. It begins with the wealthiest of them all, Rigail *aîné*, in the big house on the corner near the bridge, and then continues with Rigail *neveu*, Dumas *aîné*, Dumas *cadet*, Bergis *jeune*, Lacoste *aîné*, Lacoste *fils aîné*, Izaac Lacoste, Molles, Garrigues, Mariette, Bergis *aîné*, Garrisson, Vidallet *frères*, Garrisson *aîné*, and a dozen others.[19] Those who were not blood kin were connected by marriage, business associations, and friendship.

For the most part, merchants and magistrates frequented different clubs and Masonic lodges. The Academy of Arts and Belles-Lettres was the preserve of the magistrates; its founder and most famous member had been Voltaire's foe, Le Franc-Pompignan, also a first president of the Cour des Aides.[20] The leading merchants gathered to discuss literature

---

[18] Lacave and Lacave, *Bourgeois et marchands*, p. 203. In the early eighteenth century, a *négociant* was simply a wholesaler. By the end of the century, however, distinctions were made between "true *négociants*," who participated in international commerce, and mere wholesalers for regional markets. Savary, in *Le Parfait négociant* (1712), argued that "la grande commerce" was inherently noble since it did not bring the taint of derogation and discussed the possibility of establishing a *noblesse de commerce* to supplement the robe and sword. Louis XIV rejected this notion, as did his successors, although they gave special privileges and exemptions to nobles who engaged in commerce. See Richard, *Noblesse d'affaires*, pp. 37–38.

[19] AM Mont 10 HH 1 dénombrements circa 1774. In December 1773 the municipal council ordered a "general enumeration of all the inhabitants of the city, its suburbs and countryside." The committee charged with this task reported in June 1774, giving figures for the entire city but mentioning specifically only the census of Villebourbon. This is the only one of the enumerations that has survived; possibly it was the only one completed. AM Mont 2 BB 13 Délibérations du Conseil Général, pp. 204–205, 276–281.

[20] Other magistrates who aspired to literary reputations included Cathala-Coture, author of a history of Montauban, and Pierre Louis de Besombes, who wrote devotional poetry. Jean Louis de Cahusac, son of a magistrate, abandoned his allotted career to write plays for the Théatre Française and the Opera. Mathurin de Blazy was another magistrate's son who

and politics in private clubs like *le bal de la Concorde*, which met in Lejeune's wineshop. Freemasonry had initially promised broader social intercourse. The first lodge, founded in 1745, included magistrates, nobles, and some of the wealthiest *négociants*. However, by the 1780s, Montauban supported four different lodges with membership dependent on profession and religion. The most venerable of the lodges, *La Bonne Foy*, was the most prestigious and still had a mixture of the town's wealthiest inhabitants. *La Constance*, however, was resolutely Catholic and official; military officers joined *La Bonne Intelligence* while Protestant merchants met in *La Parfaite Union*.[21]

Officials and merchants also maintained different social and professional contacts outside of Montauban. Magistrates, as lawyers and royal officials, had closest ties to Toulouse and to Paris. Toulouse was the terrain of professional training. Most had studied at the Toulouse law school and had professional and familial connections to the parlement there. Paris, and especially Versailles, was the arena of social advancement, if not for the magistrate himself, then for his children. For example, Jacques de Molières, a president of the Cour des Aides from 1720 to 1760, had attended law school in Toulouse. He sent one son to the Jesuit school there, then transferred him to the Collège de Louis le Grand in Paris. He sent two daughters to prestigious Parisian convents, the Maison Royale de l'Enfant Jesus and St. Cyr.[22] Charles Gabriel Dubu, director of the Twentieth Tax in Montauban, used his younger brother, who was the administrator general of the Post in Paris, to intercede for him and his family with the appropriate officials at Versailles to get special consideration or to expedite his petitions. The family's "Parisian" obtained military commissions for two nephews and in 1780 was using his connections "in the entourage of M d'Autun" (Talleyrand, the bishop of Autun) to find something attractive for a third nephew who had entered the clergy.[23]

Montauban's merchants, too, had business in Paris and Toulouse—when the Montauban firm of Delon Cousin et fils went bankrupt in 1781, the receiver general of Toulouse and a Parisian banker were among its

---

was a devoted academician although an uninspired poet. Des Rochettes, "Familles montaubanaises," 1: Besombes; 2: Blazy, Cahusac; 3: Cathala-Coture. Ligou, *Montauban*, pp. 156–160.

[21] Ligou, "Montauban des lumières," pp. 187–190.

[22] Des Rochettes, "Familles montaubanaises," 7: Molières. The Collège de Louis le Grand was a favorite with Parisian parlementary families. By the end of the eighteenth century, provincial magistrates tried to enroll their sons there as well. Doyle, *The Parlement of Bordeaux*, p. 24, and R. R. Palmer, ed., *The School of the French Revolution: A Documentary History of the College of Louis-le-Grand and Its Directory Jean-François Champagne, 1762–1814* (Princeton: Princeton University Press, 1975), pp. 45–47.

[23] AD T-et-G 11 J 616 papiers de famille Dubu.

creditors[24]—but their interests allied them more closely with Marseilles, Bordeaux, and the West Indies. For example, in 1793 merchant Bernard Garrisson requested a passport from the municipal government because, "having arrived from America only a few days ago, urgent commercial affairs compel me to go to Bordeaux."[25] Many also had connections in Holland and England, using correspondents in both places to facilitate their commercial transactions and to invest for them.[26]

On the eve of the Revolution the social separation of Montauban's elite was more extreme than in most provincial cities, yet there were signs that integration was possible. The "amalgam of landlords, administrators, and professional men,"[27] which Robert Forster has identified as the embryo of the nineteenth-century society of notables, was beginning to form. The wealthiest merchants had begun to adopt the leisurely life-style of nobles and officials. Merchant-manufacturer Jacques Vialette-Daignan, for example, sold his premises in Villebourbon and moved the family textile manufacture to splendid new quarters in Montauban proper. His son changed his name to Vialètes d'Aignan, claiming that the family "descended from a Noble family of Rouergue where there still exists a castle which bears their name and which has their arms carved on the entrance."[28] He established himself as a leading member of the Masonic lodge *La Bonne Foi* and became the administrator of the hospital, a common first step to ennoblement. Other merchants built mansions in the new quarter of Moustiers, bought country houses to stage fashionable *fêtes champêtres*, sent their sons to law school, or bought them military posts. Michel Delon invited the entire officer corps to an elegant celebration dinner when his son was admitted into the regiment.[29]

[24] AD T-et-G 5E 2000 Garrigues nos. 135 and 183, 1781 dettes Delon Cousin.

[25] AM Mont 5 i 4 passeports. Historians Lucile Bourrachot and Jean-Pierre Poussou have counted at least one hundred Montaubaners who traveled to the West Indies in the eighteenth century. See "Départs de passagers quercynois," p. 432.

[26] Delvit, "La Cour de la bourse des marchands de Montauban," p. 202. Butel, *Histoire de la Garonne*, p. 353. According to des Rochettes, "Familles montaubanaises," the Garrisson, Rigail, Lacoste, and Vialette families all had branches in Amsterdam. Local merchant families also invested money in the London Stock Exchange. See AD T-et-G 5E 2263 Caminel sn 17 vendémiaire Year 7 testament Garrisson and 12 J 7 lettres missives Lagravère. There was a small community of English resident visitors in Montauban, which in 1764 included Laurence Sterne's wife and daughter. When France and England went to war in 1793, several English and American visitors were interned in Montauban. See AD T-et-G 96 l'état des reclus.

[27] Forster, *Depont Family*, p. x.

[28] AM Mont AA 77 Livre rouge neuf; des Rochettes, "Familles montaubanaises," 10: Vialette, p. 47.

[29] Ligou and Garrisson-Estèbe, "La Bourgeoisie reformée montalbanaise," pp. 402–403; Gausseran, "La Bourgeoisie montalbanaise," pp. 100–101, and AD T-et-G 5E 1943 Caminel no. 425 14–8–1787 contrat de mariage Lacoste-Payes. Clark, in *La Rochelle*, p. 54, cites criticism of some La Rochelle merchants in the 1780s who indulged in a fashionable social life to the detriment of their commerce.

More significant is the fact that merchants and magistrates came to have common interests as major landowners. Although judicial office was the source of a magistrate's prestige, it was not normally very remunerative and it began to appear insecure. In the 1750s, when the Cour des Aides tangled with the intendant, rumors flew that the court would be suppressed. Instead, the king merely exiled its two most obstreperous members. Nevertheless, the magistrates had been reminded of their vulnerability and had learned a lesson of caution. In 1763, when the court began to examine the intendant's fiscal administration, it kept the investigation secret and quickly backed off when the government got wind of its activities.[30] Then the Maupeou reforms in 1771 sent tremors through the ranks of all venal office holders.[31] For example, Henry de Darassus, son and grandson of treasurers of France, was negotiating to contract marriage to Marie Anne Dubu. Her father, Montauban's director of the Twentieth Tax, held up the match while he checked out the security of his prospective son-in-law's office. His brother who pursued the investigation for him reported that because the king had recently assigned the treasurers some of the jurisdiction of the recently suppressed parlements, "it does not seem as if it is His intention to suppress these companies." Nonetheless, he commented, "for myself, I would keep back during these tempestuous times when they are trying to diminish jurisdictions and offices."[32] As a result, the price of offices fell. According to a complaint the magistrates of the Cour des Aides sent to the royal chancellor, their offices lost half their value. Such a climate encouraged magistrates and other officials to protect their positions with more secure investments, especially in land.[33] In 1782, Jacques Antoine de Molières, son of magistrate Jacques de Molières, owned a town house behind the Cour des Aides, a large country

---

[30] Cuillieron, *Contributions à l'étude de la rebellion des cours souverains*. According to Doyle, "The Price of Offices in Pre-Revolutionary France," pp. 836–838, controversy, whether within the ranks of magistrates or between the courts and the Crown, usually resulted in falling office prices.

[31] After a series of confrontations with the Parlement of Paris, Chancellor Maupeou arrested and exiled its magistrates in January 1771 and then embarked on a wholesale reorganization of the judicial system by suppressing venal offices and restructuring jurisdictions. His reforms deprived thousands of magistrates, prosecutors, and other court personnel of their offices and reduced the jurisdiction and thus the revenues of many more. Louis XVI, shortly after he ascended the throne in 1774, restored the parlements and swept away most of Maupeou's other reforms. See Mousnier, *Les Institutions de la France sous la monarchie absolue* 2: 619–627. See Bien, "Les Offices, les corps et le crédit d'état," and Doyle, "The Price of Offices in Pre-Revolutionary France," for examinations of venal office as a financial investment in the eighteenth century.

[32] AD T-et-G 11 J 616 papiers de famille Dubu. Consternation within the *bureaux de finances* was general. See Doyle, "The Price of Offices in Pre-Revolutionary France," pp. 840–842.

[33] Cuillieron, *Contributions à l'étude de la rebellion des cours souverains*, pp. 21–22; Ford, *Robe and Sword*, p. 148; Doyle, *The Parlement of Bordeaux*, p. 30.

estate in Aussonne, a castle and seigneury in Monteils, three mills, and seventeen farms around Montauban and Espanel.[34]

By the 1760s, Montauban's merchants, too, began to buy land, a safer investment in what were uncertain times for commerce as well. Not only had they lost an important market in Canada, but the royal government defaulted on debts it had incurred there, sending shock waves through the French mercantile system. Bankruptcies followed one another as the major *négociants* of the ports brought down their suppliers in a chain reaction of ruin. With their confidence shaken, Montauban's merchants and manufacturers turned more often to land to secure the future of their families. In the 1780s, when the national fiscal crisis depleted sources of credit, the pattern repeated itself. Prudent merchants invested more and more of their capital in land. Farms bearing the names of many prominent merchant families, like Garrisson, Dumas, Albouy, Mariette, and La Motte, dotted the countryside around the city.[35]

By shifting investments into real estate, Montauban's merchants and magistrates acted from a similar understanding of their prerogatives and duties as heads of their respective families. Typically, the well-to-do husband and father ran his family according to his own wishes. The moral voice of both Catholicism and Protestantism exhorted his children to be dutiful and his wife submissive.[36] Moreover, he had control of the family's considerable material resources. Unlike elite families in England, who frequently entailed property in the male line so that its current beneficiary had no say over its ultimate disposition, wealthy families and even noble families in the Montauban region rarely entailed property and then only if the successor had no legitimate heirs of either sex.[37] Therefore, almost all elite men could leave their property as they chose and could use the faculté de tester to control their children.

[34] Des Rochettes, "Famillies montaubanaises," 7: Molières. Also see AD T-et-G 5E 10909 Martin no. 77 26–5–1788, the will of magistrate Jean Jacques de Colon, who included among the legacies twenty-five thousand livres due from the Clergy of France and twenty-nine thousand livres invested in the Hôtel de Ville of Paris. Joseph Duval de Varaire, a president of the Cour des Aides, owned a pottery as well as a chateau in Ardus. Guilhamon, *Richeprey* 2: 239–240.

[35] Clark, *La Rochelle*, pp. 105–109; Ligou, *Montauban*, pp. 120–121, 183–184; Gausseran, "La Bourgeoisie montalbanaise," pp. 94–102; Bosher, "Success and Failure in Trade to New France." The move into landowning was typical of commercial fortunes in the preindustrial period. However, the timing depended on the economic cycle. See Thomson, *Clermont-de-Lodève*, pp. 1–20. Marinière, "Les Marchands d'étoffes," p. 303, found an interesting trend in the land purchases of Toulouse merchants. Until the beginning of the severe economic crisis in the late 1770s, merchants had bought large estates usually from nobles or bourgeois; after the onset of the crisis, they continued to be buyers but of small properties whose sale was forced on debt-ridden peasants.

[36] Ozment, *When Fathers Ruled*, pp. 50–72, 132–177, and Flandrin, *Families in Former Times*, pp. 112–161.

[37] Augustin, *Les Substitutions fidéicommissaires*.

Elite patriarchs shared family goals and strategies as well. Two not entirely compatible desires shaped their choices. First, they wanted to preserve the family as a lineage by passing the patrimony to the next in the line. Second, they wanted to establish each of their children within the elite. Both goals were important to the survival of the elite family because to dissipate either the family's property or its respectability would diminish its status in the future.

Montauban's elite believed that honorable genealogies enhanced and supported the present and future status of their families. Although they had detached themselves from the powerful "houses" of kin and clients which had fought the Wars of Religion, they still participated in important, if sometimes mythical, ancestral chains and extended families of collateral relatives who shared the same family name. Well-to-do Montaubaners honored their family names in ways foreign to artisans and working people, who often went by nicknames. Merchants called their enterprises by the family name and tagged their merchandise with the family insignia. Magistrates and other nobles displayed their coats of arms in bas-relief above their doors or in the wrought iron of their balconies and gates.[38] This identification was not confined to the male line; merchants who married advantageously often were called "son-in-law of . . ." and nobles displayed the quarterings of wives, mothers, and even remote ancestresses. Both merchants and magistrates formed new branches of the family by adding the name of a wife or mother to the family name. For example, a seventeenth-century alliance of the daughter of one textile manufacturer and the son of another produced the Vialette-Daignan family.[39]

The family name was not all that connected elite families to an honorable past; there was also the patrimony, both the material inheritance and the legacy of status. As the Bordeaux parlementarians wrote in 1778, "the most cherished hope of magistrates who have grown old in the laborious discharge of their duties, is to Transmit the rank which they have occupied in Society to their posterity."[40] However, as Lawrence Stone has observed, the supposedly complementary desires to conserve the patrimony and to pass it on in the male line often proved contradictory. Because infant death was so common, a man had to have several children to ensure

---

[38] Gausseran, "La Bourgeoisie montalbanaise," p. 97. See examples on the Hôtel d'Allies de Réalville, now the Hôtel de Ville, and the Hôtel Mila de Corbarieu in the rue des Carmes.

[39] Here are other examples: Noble Pierre Debia became Debia de Moncau when he married Mlle Monteils de Moncau. The second son of merchant Jean Jacques Combes, who married Marie Brassard, took the name Combes-Brassard, a practice followed in turn by his second son, who became the Revolutionary leader Combes-Dounous. Des Rochettes, "Familles montaubanaises," 1: preface, 3: Combes, 4: Debia, 10: Vialette.

[40] Cited in Doyle, *The Parlement of Bordeaux*, pp. 12–13. See also d'Arvisenet, "L'Office de conseiller," pp. 538–539.

that one son would survive. Yet if several children survived, he had to divide the patrimony to provide for them. The career of the heir posed few problems; he would replicate that of his father and ancestors before him. But providing for noninheriting children involved a father in complex decisions. For example, should they remain single to reduce the strain on family resources or should they be married in the hope of improving the family's position through judicious alliances and greater chances for survival? In true lineages, these questions were solved by managing and tapping the resources of many relatives and patrons.[41] In Montauban's elite families in the late eighteenth century, such kinship systems were attenuated. Most merchants and magistrates faced the task of resolving the dilemma—how to conserve the patrimony yet provide for all children— with their own ingenuity.

The wills written by Montauban's elite before the Revolution demonstrated that the primary concern was to preserve the integrity of the patrimony to the lineage; almost all testators appointed a single blood relative as the universal heir (see table 4–8). Many also acknowledged the rights of primogeniture by appointing the eldest son, brother, or nephew as heir. Nonetheless, Montauban's elite agreed that all members of the family, even the youngest of numerous children, had some legitimate claim on the family's resources. Even patriarchs who left the bulk of their property to their eldest sons recognized and attempted to satisfy the lesser claims of their younger children and wives with legacies and usufruct. The forty-two testators in the sample named 60 general heirs, 105 legatees, and 20 liferights beneficiaries. Typical is the 1781 will of merchant Louis Garrisson, who appointed his eldest son as his heir, left eight thousand livres apiece to his two younger sons, six thousand livres each to two daughters, and four thousand to his youngest daughter, left his wife furniture worth twelve hundred livres, and even thought to provide for any posthumous children.[42] Sometimes the testator had already endowed his heir by purchasing him his office or setting him up in business and giving him sufficient property or investments to maintain his status. In this case, he used his will to provide for his younger children or other relatives who had a claim on his generosity.[43] As a result, elite families usually succeeded in providing adequately, although not equally, for all.

One solution would have been for elite couples to limit the number of

---

[41] Stone, *The Family, Sex and Marriage*, pp. 42–43.

[42] AD T-et-G 5E 1999 Garrigues no. 408 17–5–1781 testament Garrisson. He later raised the amounts left to the younger children so that all but the youngest daughter received ten thousand livres. See 5E 2008 Garrigues no. 203 7–3–1788 codicile Garrisson and 5E 13181 Deray no. 309 12–9–1790 testament Garrisson.

[43] See A D T-et-G 5E 1949 Caminel no. 258 21–5–1792 testament of merchant-dyer Alex Bergis, for example.

children they had and thus the number of claims on the patrimony. This was certainly part of the strategy of both the French court nobility and the provincial nobility of nearby Toulouse and probably of some Montauban noble families as well. John Clark has concluded that La Rochelle's merchants had fewer children after midcentury in an effort to scale down demands on family resources in a commercial climate that was becoming increasingly stormy.[44] However, family limitation was not a strategy adopted by most Montauban's merchants. In the 1770s, merchants had fewer children on the average than did artisans, but a sizable minority had numerous children who survived into adulthood. According to the Non-Catholic Register, Protestant merchant families with four, five, and six surviving children were common. Paul Butel has found families of similar sizes among Bordeaux merchants.[45] These families, apparently, found sufficient benefits in having numerous children to outweigh the worry and cost of providing for their futures.

One strategy that both merchant and magistrate families adopted was to limit what constituted the patrimony. Some French legal customs divided property into *patrimoine*—what was inherited in the direct line—and *acquêts*—what was acquired by purchase, gift, or other inheritance. Although Montauban custom did not require this, wealthy Montaubaners made a similar distinction. However, it was not patrilineal succession alone that clothed property in patrimonial garb; patrimony was property that gave the family its social status in the present and connected it to its past and future. The obvious example was the noble family that drew its honors, titles, and even its name from its fiefs. For magistrates and other officials, the patrimony was the office because its prestige determined the family's social position. For example, the Darassus family was known for the positions its members had held within the Bureau of Finances, and the names Malartic, Molières, and LeFranc de Pompignan immediately called to mind the Cour des Aides. At least one son or nephew had to maintain the connection into the future.[46]

<hr>

[44] Darrow, "French Noblewomen," pp. 41–65; Forster, *The Nobility of Toulouse*, pp. 129–130; des Rochettes, "Familles montaubanaises"; Clark, *La Rochelle*, pp. 54–56. Elite men may also have had other reasons for having fewer children, such as an increasing respect and concern for their wives. Mme d'Albis de Belbeze wrote repeatedly to her husband before the birth of their third child that it was a "wretched business" (*vilain métier*) always to be having children, that childbirth was very painful and she was afraid of dying. Afterward she cautioned him not to try to make love to her. Puis, *d'Ablis de Belbeze*, pp. 57, 63, 65, 72, 77, 95.

[45] Ligou, *Montauban*, p. 173; Butel, "Comportements familiaux," pp. 150–151, and AD T-et-G E Etat Civil Protestant.

[46] Bien, "Les Offices, les corps et le crédit d'état," p. 384. According to Ligou, "La Cour des aides de Montauban," p. 316, only 10 percent of counselorships in Montauban's Cour des Aides in the eighteenth century were inherited. However, he does not include in this figure the cases in which a new office was purchased for the heir. According to Doyle, *The*

If, like the judgeships on the Cour des Aides, the office was more honorific than remunerative, a family had to provide the heir with other property as well—a town house and farms or investments—to maintain a standard of living commensurate with his dignity. For example, in 1792 when notary Jean Benais retired, he passed the office on to his eldest son along with a house, lands, and vineyards, which he noted were to support his son in his new station.[47] For families whose status came mainly from their position as seigneurs, specific seigneuries and estates habitually passed to the heir. This was less true in magistrate families for whom rural property was more financially than socially significant. Although some official families had become identified with particular town houses such as the Hôtels de Scorbiac, Malartic, and Duval de Monmilan, even these were not sacrosanct. Jacques de Molières sold his family's mansion to purchase another nearer the courthouse. Both the Duc and the Blazy families built new mansions in Moustiers.[48]

For merchants, the patrimony was the business that bore the family name. This was usually a *société générale*, a formal partnership in which each party invested and for which each was legally responsible. Twelve percent of merchant grooms in the sample of marriage contracts entered into such societies at their marriages; others were associates already. These merchants were partners in, and heirs to, the patrimony.[49]

Magistrates and merchants could divide all other property—land, cash, investments—among their noninheriting children without endangering the family's social or economic status. In the first half of the eighteenth

---

Parlement of Bordeaux, p. 13, this was a common practice in the Bordeaux Parlement. In Montauban, six counselors in the Cour des Aides in the two decades before the Revolution served concurrently with the father or uncle from whom they might have expected to inherit the office. Another variation was when a father died or retired before his heir was old enough to succeed him. His office was then sold and another purchased later for the son.

[47] AD T-et-G Q 406 donations 4–2–1792.

[48] Des Rochettes, "Familles montaubanaises," 2: Blazy, 3: Duc, 7: Molières. AD T-et-G 5E 2263 Caminel sn 22–10–1787 testament Garrisson vᶜ Bonnecarrere; 12856 Grelleau no. 392 15–9–1769 testament Janolz. Ford, in *Robe and Sword*, p. 170, concludes that magistrate families tried to keep land undivided to pass to the eldest son while the office went to a younger son. However, Doyle found that in Bordeaux, magistrates regarded the office as the symbol of familial continuity and passed it to the eldest son. *Parlement*, p. 124. Montauban's magistrates followed this pattern.

[49] Commercial communities had been common in the sixteenth and seventeenth centuries but in the eighteenth century were replaced by societies. See, for example, AD T-et-G L324 Tribunal de commerce 14–6–1793 for the contract regulating a commercial society between Jean Rochin and his son Michel. Merchants evidently found the community too inflexible, especially when they acquired distant correspondents. See Hilaire, "Vie en commun," p. 32. Montauban merchants also participated in *sociétés en commandite*, which limited their liability to the amount they had invested, and in joint stock companies. The most important of the latter was the Three Mills Company.

century, Protestant merchants rarely invested much in real estate, preferring to provide for their children with investments in government bonds and commercial societies both in France and abroad. One favorite local investment was the Three Mills Company, which until 1764 had a monopoly on grain milling in Montauban. By the end of the century, however, most merchants succumbed to the dictum "As long as you have only money, you are always on the brink of having nothing" and bought land as security for their children.[50]

Separating family property into patrimony—reserved for the heir—and other properties that could be distributed among other claimants was not the only strategy for reconciling the desires to sustain the lineage and to establish all children suitably. Parents also attempted to acquire additional property for their noninheriting children from sources outside the immediate family. One such source was the dowries brought by sons' wives, which could offset the portions paid out to daughters' husbands. For example, Jacques de Molières's daughter-in-law brought his son the seigneury of Espanel as part of her dowry; in the next generation, his granddaughter took the domain of Monteils to her husband.[51]

Fathers tried to take in as much or more property from daughters-in-law as they paid out to daughters, but this was not always possible. In order to obtain a particularly advantageous match, an elite family could be pushed to the limits of its resources.[52] In these cases a call went out to relatives, especially to wealthy and childless relatives, to help make up the requisite sum. Kin contributed to 15 percent of elite marriage contracts. For example, Noble Pierre David du Roy gave his cousin Dlle Elizabeth Gautier six thousand livres as a token of his approval when she married in 1772. When Jean-Pierre Belbeze married, his uncle, aunt, and brother joined his mother to pledge the sixteen thousand livres needed to guarantee his bride's dowry.[53]

[50] *Tant que tu n'auras que de l'argent, tu seras toujours à la veille de n'avoir rien.* Cited in Chaline, *Bourgeois de Rouen*, p. 147. See AD T-et-G 5E 12856 Grelleau no. 392 15–9–1769 testament Janolz; 13179 Deray no. 410 2–7–1784 transaction Duc; 13206 Deray no. 269 11–9–1812 vente Ratier; 2263 Caminel sn 17 vendémiaire Year 7 testament Garrisson ép Garrisson. Even merchants with no pretensions to bourgeois status bought land; for example, merchant-dyer Jacques Urbain Bergis, 5E 2008 Garrigues no. 826 17–11–1788.

[51] Des Rochettes, "Familles montaubanaises," 7: Molières.

[52] Berlanstein, *The Barristers of Toulouse*, pp. 65–66; Doyle, *The Parlement of Bordeaux*, pp. 57–58. See, for example, AD T-et-G 5E 2067 Delmas no. 633 23–11–1788 contrat de mariage Bordaries-Capmar. Castan, in *Les Criminels de Languedoc*, p. 182, notes that when elite dowry negotiations had "winners" and "losers," too much disparity between benefits and costs soured alliances.

[53] AD T-et-G B 418 donations 22–9–1772 and 5E 2337 Martin no. 183 22–4–1788 contrat de mariage Campan de Belbeze-Lagravère. Also see 5E 1943 Caminel no. 207 17–4–1787 contrat de mariage Sartre de Salir-Baillio and no. 425 14–8–1787contrat de mariage Lacoste-Payes; 2008 Garrigues no. 635 30–8–1788 contrat de mariage Molinet de

Wealthy Montaubaners often bequeathed legacies to numerous relatives, especially to godchildren, women, and relatives in the female line who were excluded from patrilineal succession. Similarly, a childless testator often chose a niece or younger nephew as heir when the eldest nephew was heir to his own father. For example, military officer Michel Dupin de St André had two nephews, sons of his older brother, a magistrate in the Cour des Aides. He chose the younger nephew as his heir since the elder was heir to his father.[54] In the sample of wills, the twenty-six elite testators who had no children of their own left their property as frequently to their sisters and their nieces as they did to their brothers and nephews.[55]

Godparents were another source of material as well as spiritual support for children. Like parents, godparents had a sacred duty to their godchildren. Wealthy families used this pseudo-parentage to strengthen already existing ties of blood and marriage to create a set of patrons for each child. Parents chose one godparent from each side of the family, with the godparent of the same sex as the child giving his or her first name to the baby. The grandparents, if living, usually sponsored the firstborn. Aunts, uncles, cousins, and occasionally more distant relatives spoke for later children.[56] After his own children, a man's godchildren had first claim on his attention and fortune. Unmarried and childless testators often bequeathed more to godchildren than to other kin. Seventeen percent of bourgeois testators appointed godchildren as their heirs or legatees. For example, in 1770, François Mariet Debia left two nephews legacies but appointed a third who was also his godson as his heir. Similarly, the wealthy spinster Anne Garrisson gave her brother's younger son six thou-

---

Lavaur-Rival; 2106 Franceries no. 271 3–6–1809 contrat de mariage Ricard-Boyer; 2109 Franceries no. 296 9–4–1816 contrat de mariage Foissac-Linon and Q 406 donations 19–5–1792. Kin contributed to 17 percent of bourgeois marriages, 15 percent of merchant marriages, 7 percent of peasant marriages, 7 percent of artisan marriages, and in 2 percent of poor workers' contracts (significance level = .01, contingency coefficient = .184).

[54] AD T-et-G 5E 10869 Martin no. 240 2–5–1780 accord Dupin de St André. See also 5E 2263 Caminel no. 5 14–9–1787 in which priest Joseph Carrere made his niece his heir and 10909 Martin no. 77 26–5–1788 in which noble Jean Jacques de Colon also appointed his niece.

[55] These testators left their property as follows: to their nieces (6), nephews (5), nonkin (5), brothers (4), sisters (3), equal inheritance (2), and mother (1).

[56] This pattern of choosing a godparent was nearly universal among wealthy Montauban families. Bordeaux merchants often chose godfathers for their sons from the international branches of the family, ensuring future apprenticeships under their benevolent supervision. Butel, "Comportements familiaux," p. 153. I found only one such directly opportunistic choice of a godparent among Montauban families. Pierre Paul Garrisson, a merchant-bourgeois, was related through his mother to the powerful Mariette family who had recently constructed a new mill in Montauban. He asked the head of this family, who was his mother's cousin, to sponsor his second son. AD T-et-G E Etat Civil Protestant no. 366 26–3–1788.

sand francs to use in commerce and named her niece and goddaughter as her heir.[57]

Although an elite father tried to provide all his children with sufficient capital to sustain a dignified standard of living, he planned that his sons should have careers as well. In fact, if a younger son was fortunate in his career, he would require less family capital and could prove to be a valuable resource of capital and patronage for his nieces and nephews. Most careers, whether in law, the church, the military, or commerce, required education, an initial investment of capital, and some years of support while the neophyte learned his job and attained sufficient rank to be self-supporting. All of this was expensive but probably less expensive than supporting young men in idleness, even in the short run.

In merchant families, virtually all the sons became merchants (see table 4–7). In most official families, however, career followed birth order. Unless the family was unusually well-to-do, only the eldest son followed his father onto the bench or into the royal bureaucracy. The Dubu family is such an example. Gabriel Dubu, *sécrétaire du procureur général des recettes*, and later *sécrétaire du roi*, was able to start two of his four sons on the road to lucrative careers in the royal bureaucracy. However, his third son, Charles François, entered what proved to be a dead-end career as an inspector of commerce and his fourth son became a clergyman with only a very meager benefice. Charles François's sons followed a more common pattern. The eldest son was intended for an official career. His two younger brothers were purchased military commissions, and the youngest, like his youngest uncle, went into the church. Similarly, in the Verdier family, the eldest son of magistrate Jean Baptiste succeeded to his father's office, the second became a priest, and the third joined the army.[58]

Although apparently schematic, career planning did not always go smoothly. Sometimes sons did not fit into the niches prepared for them, nor were fathers always able to prepare the niches very comfortably. Parents plotted and worried over the future of their children. In the letters exchanged in the Dubu family from 1763 to 1785, schemes for the advancement of children, their progress, and their setbacks elicited much

[57] By comparison, 9 percent of peasant testators, 8 percent of poor workers, 7 percent of merchants, and 5 percent of artisans appointed godchildren as heirs or legatees (signficance level = .05, contingency coefficient = .116). See AD T-et-G 5E 2262 Caminel sn 12–2–1770 testament Debia; 2263 Caminel sn 30–5–1788 testament Lagravere; 13179 Deray no. 191 10–10–1783 donation Cinfraix and Q 414 donations no. 11 8 nivôse Year 2, AD T-et-G E Etat Civil Protestant no. 366 26–3–1788 and 5E 2263 Caminel sn 17 vendémiaire Year 7 testament Garrisson; Q 414 donations no. 13 13 nivôse Year 11. AM Mont 5 CC 9 capitation 1788 assessed Anne at ninety livres, among the top 1 percent of taxpayers.

[58] AD T-et-G 11 J 616 papiers de famille Dubu; des Rochettes, "Familles montaubanaises," 10: Verdier. See Ford, *Robe and Sword*, pp. 138–139, and Berlanstein, *The Barristers of Toulouse*, p. 64.

concern and even anguish. Charles François experienced the most difficulty. Compared with his two older brothers, he had the largest family—five children—and the smallest income. Already in 1771, he wrote to his eldest brother, Charles Gabriel, that his financial problems were threatening his children's future. By 1775, he was panic-stricken. The free-trade philosophy of the current Ministry of Commerce had cost him more than half his revenue, which he saw no hope of recuperating. Meanwhile, his children rebelled against their suddenly restricted expectations. The eldest son, apparently deprived of the position he wanted, ran away from home. His mother wrote to Charles Gabriel in the hope that he could get the boy to listen to reason. "I only ask that he consider what is to become of him. At his age one must choose a station in life. [Make him] look over his fortune and his expectations." His father later wrote to complain of the expenses this son had incurred as well as his disinclination to settle in life. Meanwhile, he could not support his two sons in the King's Guard, and his youngest son lost the reversion of a lucrative clerical appointment. Charles Gabriel in Montauban and the second brother, Pierre Michel, in Paris frequently came to his aid with money, advice, and a word in high places; they also commiserated with each other about their brother's lack of financial acumen and his "numerous family."[59]

Career plans began with the appropriate education. Sons of the well-to-do began their schooling in Montauban, but for specialized training boys had to leave home. Although most future lawyers and magistrates and other sons of the elite attended law school in Toulouse,[60] Montauban merchants sent their sons as apprentices to relatives in Bordeaux and as business representatives to England, Holland, Germany, Canada, and especially the West Indies. There they learned firsthand of the problems of suppliers and markets and met the merchants with whom their families corresponded. Perhaps more important, they met the heirs of these merchants and consolidated by personal friendship what could become crucial business relationships in the future. In these cases, as when Guillaume Rigal bound his son to his merchant cousins so that they might "teach him the trade," education and career placement merged.[61]

---

[59] AD T-et-G 11 J 616 papiers de famille Dubu. *Tresorier de France* Paul-François Depont considered his grandson lazy and scatterbrained. Although he did not think the boy would amount to anything, he never considered a life of idleness; a career had to be found for him. Forster, *Depont Family*, pp. 32–33.

[60] Not all young men who received the *license* from the *faculté de droit* and who were admitted to the bar practiced law. Not only was legal training traditional for magistrates, it was a prestigious credential for a bourgeois. See Berlanstein, *Barristers of Toulouse*, p. 16, and Olwen H. Hufton, *Bayeux in the Late Eighteenth Century: A Social Study* (Oxford: Clarendon Press, 1967), pp. 62–63.

[61] AD T-et-G 5E 12876 Grelleau no. 642 8–10–1786 apprentissage Bergis-Rigal. Thomson, *Clermont-de-Lodève*, p. 65; Clark, *La Rochelle*, p. 52. Bourrachot and Poussou, "Départs de passagers quercynois," pp. 424, found a "cascade of departures in the same family, a

The choice of a career was closely connected to decisions about marriage. Here, the strategies of magistrates and merchants differed. Just as all the sons of a merchant could expect to be merchants in their turn, all could reasonably expect to marry and head their own households eventually. This was not the case with the younger sons of magistrates and officials, many of whom entered celibate careers and remained single all their lives.[62] Religion was an important factor in this difference; careers in the army and the church were closed to Protestants and therefore to most of Montauban's merchants' sons. Also, marriage played a role in merchants' family strategies different from the one in official and seigneurial families. For commercial families, although the marriages of younger children drained family capital, the expense was outweighed by the opportunities they offered to consolidate and extend networks of business associates and correspondents.[63] In noncommercial elite families, however, only the heir's marriage was essential to preserve the family and advance its status. Once the family line was secure, it was more advantageous for noninheriting children to remain single to prevent the disbursement of the patrimony.

The cheapest way to provide for children was for them to take religious vows. Religious dowries were substantial but generally less than the légitime because the Toulouse Parlement had ruled that "monks and nuns are not counted among the number of children" for the computation of inheritance and were entitled to no more than the agreed settlement, which was "a sort of alms or charity."[64] When François Duc died intestate in 1784, his heirs signed an agreement with "Demlle Jacquette Duc, his other daughter, nun in the convent of Ste Claire in Alby, so that the said Demlle Jacquette Duc cannot inherit because of her religious vows."[65]

---

younger brother following the elder, a nephew following the uncle." Thirty-nine percent of these travelers were boys and young men between the ages of sixteen and twenty-five. AM Mont 5 i 1 no. 4 passeports. AD T-et-G 5E 1943 Caminel no. 158 2–5–1787 is an inventory of the estate of Jean Pierre Janolz Garrisson, who died in his midtwenties while on a trip to the West Indies. AM Mont 7 HH 5 commis des négociants 1775 shows that sons were rarely formally employed as clerks but that cousins and nephews frequently filled this position.

[62] In the sample of wills, only one merchant testator out of seventeen was unmarried, whereas nine out of forty men of the noncommercial elite were single. They included three clerics, two property owners, two military officers, and two lawyers.

[63] Bosher, "Success and Failure in the Trade to New France," pp. 455–458. Marriage remained an important business strategy even after the Industrial Revolution. See Chaline, *Bourgeois de Rouen*, pp. 102–117, 286.

[64] Sol, *Révolution en Quercy* 1: 395; Forster, *The Nobility of Toulouse*, p. 125; Aron, "Etude sur les lois," p. 489.

[65] AD T-et-G 5E 13179 Deray no. 410 2–7–1784 transaction Duc. See also 5E 2067 Delmas no. 103 9–2–1788 dotation en religion in which Perette Gatereau formally renounced all claims to paternal or maternal inheritance in return for three thousand livres paid to the convent of Ste Claire, where she was a novice.

Children who did not take vows were, of course, legally entitled to the légitime, but this was rarely enough to permit marriage and a standard of living in keeping with the family's social position. For example, Gabriel de Lantrom, president of Montauban's Royal Bureau of Finances, had two sons, the elder who succeeded him and the younger who became a cavalry officer, never married, and returned to Montauban late in life to retire on a small pension. Unmarried daughters who did not take the veil remained in their fathers', then their brothers', and then their nephews' households. The eldest daughter of Jean François de Caumont, for example, died single at the age of eighty-five in Montauban, where she had been living with her nephew. By the common formula of wills, most women should have received their inheritance "upon marriage or majority," but as long as a woman remained in the heir's household, it is unlikely that he ever actually paid it to her. Even legacies left her by other relatives normally went to the head of the household for her maintenance unless the testator gave explicit instructions to the contrary.[66] Unmarried persons then "returned" their portions to the heir when they willed their goods to nieces and nephews.

The marriage of children involved the family, especially the father, in considerable trouble and expense. To attract a suitable match, a father usually had to promise a portion exceeding the légitime. Thirty-eight percent of bourgeois brides and half of merchants' brides brought dowries worth ten thousand livres or more (see table 4–1). The largest dowries were those provided by magistrates of the Cour des Aides; First President Pullignieu gave his daughter a dowry in cash and land worth forty thousand livres.[67] Nor was all the expense borne by the bride's family. According to the Custom of Montauban, the groom had to possess property worth at least half the value of the dowry in order to guarantee the nuptial gains. When one of Jacques de Molières's daughters married an army officer with a reputation as a gambler, her family required that the groom put up fifteen thousand livres in security.[68] Because capital was usually tied

66 Des Rochettes, "Familles montaubanaises," 3: Caumont, 6: Lantrom; Forster, *The Nobility of Toulouse*, p. 126–127. See AD T-et-G 5E 10909 Martin no. 77 26–5–1788 testament Colon for a will that forbade the heir administration of legacies to his minor children.

67 AD T-et-G 5E 1943 Caminel no. 512 29–9–1787 contrat de mariage Bailet de Berdolle de Goúdourville-Pullignieu. This was slightly less than the average dowry of daughters of parlementarians although above the dowries of magistrates in lesser courts and barristers. Dawson, *Provincial Magistrates*, p. 96; Doyle, *The Parlement of Bordeaux*, p. 120; and Berlanstein, *The Barristers of Toulouse*, pp. 40–42.

68 Des Rochettes, "Familles montaubanaises," 7: Molières. Montauban merchants were not immune to suspicions of insolvency, either. When Jean Serres of the textile manufacturing family married the daughter of a Bordeaux merchant in 1739, his family contributed more than double the value of the dowry to secure it. Poussou, "L'Immigration quercynoise à Bordeaux," p. 413.

up in land or business, families often had to borrow money to meet the obligations of marriage contracts or to delay payment indefinitely. Pulligneu, for example, paid only fifteen thousand livres of his daughter's enormous dowry, reserving the rest until after his death. Marguérite Rivals's father paid her husband, Antoine Molinet de Lavour, only the interest on her dowry of twenty-four thousand livres during his lifetime. Thus, dowries and gifts to grooms were usually major debts that encumbered estates and complicated successions.[69]

Although its short-term costs were high, marriage could have important long-term advantages for the family; marital alliances could form new connections or confirm old ones, thereby increasing the family's social and even financial resources. Marriage to the daughter of a magistrate could give the groom and his family entrée into official circles. Louis de Savignac used his wife's dowry to buy a presidency in the Cour des Aides, and her cousin, a treasurer in the Bureau of Finances, to sponsor his candidacy.[70]

Such alliances were especially important in merchant families. In the eighteenth century, commerce was based on personal connections and depended as much on cooperation as on competition. As inlanders on the peripheries of the Atlantic trade, Montauban merchants depended as much or more on the cooperation of "foreign" merchants as on their fellow Montaubaners. In this they differed from the merchants of La Rochelle studied by John Clark. At the center of colonial commerce, Rochelais *négociants* engaged in fierce competition with other ports and drew together into tight clans to defend their interests against outsiders. Only 18 percent of marriages in La Rochelle merchant families involved parties not from La Rochelle.[71] By contrast, Montauban merchants depended not only on local business associations but also on Bordeaux ship owners, Parisian bankers, and foreign correspondents, and, during the Revolution, on army commissioners and government officials. They needed many friendly connections outside Montauban to do a profitable business. For example, the Lagravère brothers exchanged news of Montauban merchants—especially the bad news of deaths, debts, lawsuits, and

[69] AD T-et-G 5E 1943 Caminel no. 512 29–9–1787 contrat de mariage Bailet de Berdolle de Goudourville-Pullignieu and 2008 Garrigues no. 635 30–8–1788 contrat de mariage Molinet de Lavour-Rivals. For other examples see 13179 Deray no. 476 16–11–1784 contrat de mariage Rachou-Serres; 2067 Delmas no. 633 23–11–1788 contrat de mariage Bordaries-Capmar and des Rochettes, "Familles montaubanaises," 7: Molières. See also Sentou, *Fortunes et groupes sociaux*, p. 110, and Berlanstein, *The Barristers of Toulouse*, pp. 65–66.

[70] Jean de Saux-Peyrille of the Cour des Aides purchased the office of Garde-Sceaux in the court for his son-in-law. Des Rochettes, "Familles montaubanaises," 9: Saux-Peyrille, Savignac. Doyle, in *The Parlement of Bordeaux*, pp. 15–17, noted similar use of kin to incorporate new blood into the Parlement of Bordeaux.

[71] Clark, *La Rochelle*, pp. 58–59.

rumors of bankruptcy—for similar inside information from their correspondents in Carcassonne, Bordeaux, Paris, Bayonne, Oleron, and Pamplona.[72] Montauban merchants frequently arranged marriages for their children with the children of merchants in other cities, especially Bordeaux. In the sample of marriage contracts, one quarter of the marriages arranged for merchants' daughters before 1800 were with out-of-town merchants.[73]

Marriage instantly created a new set of contacts; subsequent intermarriage strengthened the network. The history of the Janolz family's progression from bourgeois of the country town of Négrepelisse at midcentury to Montauban merchants by the onset of the Revolution demonstrated the successful application of marital strategies. Their ascent began when the eldest daughter married Izaac Garrigues, the heir of a wealthy Villebourbon merchant. Their younger son, Pierre, who had been working as a clerk for the merchant house of Joseph Serres, soon joined Izaac in a business partnership and eventually married his sister. Antoine Janolz, the eldest son, remained a landowner in Négrepelisse and married a local woman against his family's wishes. On his wife's death, however, he too succumbed, marrying a cousin of the Garrigues and moving to Villebourbon. In 1809 his daughter continued the connection by marrying a Garrigues relative.[74] Another example was the alliance of the Garrisson and Lacoste

[72] AD T-et-G 12 J 7 lettres missives Lagravère frères.

[73] See, for example, AD T-et-G 5E 21880 Grelleau no. 172 9–4–1789 contrat de mariage Pourscillie-Milhau, in which the daughter of a Montauban merchant married a merchant from Caussade, and 5E 12856 Grelleau no. 392 15–9–1769 testament of merchant Michel Janolz, which assigned the légitime to his daughter Cathérine, wife of a Bordeaux *négociant*. The sons of Montauban merchants also married the daughters of merchants elsewhere. For example, the youngest son of merchant Jean Garrisson married the daughter of a merchant from Santonge. AD T-et-G E Etat Civil Protestant no. 370 20–10–1788. Henri Duroy, son of a Montauban merchant, married Marie Anne Rocaute, daughter of a Bordeaux merchant, and established himself as a merchant in Bordeaux, investing the 23,000 livres he had earned in society with his father and brother in a new venture with his in-laws. A younger son of the Serres family of merchant manufacturers also established a branch firm by marrying into a Bordeaux merchant family. See Poussou, "L'Immigration quercynoise à Bordeaux," p. 413. Because the marriage contract was usually drawn up and signed in the bride's hometown, such matches have escaped my sample of marriage contracts, which shows only one Montauban merchant marrying into a "foreign" merchant family.

[74] Both Marie and Pierre Janolz's marriage contracts were witnessed by numerous relatives. Antoine's first marriage was witnessed only by his cousin and had neither his mother's presence nor her consent. His second marriage, to Marie Noalhac, was witnessed by the whole Janolz-Garrigues clan. AD T-et-G 5E 1993 Garrigues no. 612 9–10–1774 contrat de mariage Garrigues-Janolz; 1996 Garrigues no. 632 7–12–1777 contrat de mariage Janolz-Garrigues and no. 419 24–8–1778 contrat de mariage Janolz-Couhert; 2001 Garrigues no. 793 20–12–1782 contrat de mariage Janolz-Noalhac; 2106 Franceries no. 180 4–1–1809 contrat de mariage Garrigues-Blumat-Janolz. Etat Civil Protestant no. 366 12–3–1788; no. 367 10–4–1788 and 2–5–1788. AM Mont 7 HH 5 commis des négociants 1775. In general, the textile industry tended to recruit merchant-manufacturers from small towns like

families, two of the wealthiest merchant houses in the city. In 1755 Jean Pierre Garrisson, eldest son and heir of Jean Garrisson, married Jean Marie Lacoste. Their eldest son, Bernard, married Magdelaine Payes, whose elder sister was married to Jeanne Marie's brother Izaac Lacoste. Bernard and his wife lived with his widowed mother only a few doors away from his uncle, who was also his brother-in-law.[75]

It is impossible to determine with any degree of certainty the relative prevalence of marriage and celibacy among Montauban's elite families. Robert Forster, in his study of Toulouse nobility, concluded that in the eighteenth century only one child of each sex married.[76] The genealogies of several Montauban noble families suggest a similar configuration, but the experience of merchant families was quite different. Although daughters in both mercantile and official families often remained unmarried, merchants' sons usually married even if they were younger sons.

Celibacy was most common among women of both commercial and official families although perhaps not as common as among Toulouse nobility. For example, at least two of Jacques de Molières's five daughters married, two others may have died in infancy, and only one definitely became a nun. Jean Duc, receiver of the *tailles* for Montauban, had three daughters, all of whom married. On the other hand, only one of Joseph de Blazy de Firmy's three daughters married; one became a nun and the other remained in her father's household.[77] Montauban's female religious orders continued to admit daughters from elite families right up to the Revolution. Of the twenty-five choir sisters of the prestigious order of Sainte Claire, seven had entered in the 1770s and six in the 1780s.[78]

The convent was not an option for Protestant families; their single daughters remained at home. Anne Garrisson's life was particularly well documented because she had control of her own fortune and participated in various transactions. Jean Garrisson's daughter Jeanne was more typical. In 1774, when she was at least thirty years old, she was living in her father's household in Villebourbon. Fourteen years later she was still

---

Négrepelisse, which were heavily involved in cottage industry. See Chaline, *Bourgeois de Rouen*, pp. 56–57.

[75] AM Mont 10 HH 1 dénombrement Villebourbon 1774 and AD T-et-G E Etat Civil Protestant no. 366 29–3–1788.

[76] Forster, *The Nobility of Toulouse*, pp. 128–130.

[77] Des Rochettes, "Familles montaubanaises," 1: Blazy; 3: Duc; 7: Molières. In the sample of wills, sixteen, or 24 percent, of all female elite testators were single compared with only 17 percent of male elite testators. Half of these women were daughters of the official elite, whereas only one was the daughter of a merchant. However, the rest were identified merely as *propriétaires sans profession* or *bourgeoises* who might as easily have come from commercial families as from official families.

[78] Sol, *Révolution en Quercy* 1: 395. The Ursulines and the Carmelites, too, continued to attract novices. Ligou, *Montauban*, pp. 60–62.

there, even though her father was dead and the house belonged to her brother. The only other mention of her was when she sponsored her brothers' children at baptism. Because she appeared in no property transactions, her fortune—she was taxed at nine livres in 1788—was probably in her brother's hands.[79]

In most elite families, the patriarch arranged a marriage for his heir and usually for at least one of his daughters as well. In noble, official, and legal families, the younger children of both sexes commonly remained unmarried. Merchants, however, followed different strategies, juggling the need to conserve the patrimony and the desirability of extending the network of alliances. With careful planning and long delays, they married most of their sons and set them up in business.

In the 1780s, merchant Jean Garrisson of Villebourbon was the very image of a patriarch. Eighty years old and still dominating the family business, he had four surviving children including three sons—his eldest son had died in 1775—seventeen grandchildren (two illegitimate), and four great-grandchildren. Jean-Pierre, his eldest son, had, at age twenty-nine, married the daughter of another Villebourbon merchant. Garrisson had given the couple a separate apartment in his house, had taken his son into partnership, and had made him his heir. His other three sons had left the family home and business when they married. The second, Louis, had married at thirty-four, eight years after his elder brother. The third, Pierre, had married ten years later, at age thirty-seven, and the youngest, Jean-François, had married five years after Pierre, at age thirty-eight. In 1788, just before Jean Garrisson's death, Jean-Pierre's eldest son and heir to his father was assessed at fifty livres in capitation tax, Louis was assessed at thirty, Pierre at fifty, and Jean-François at sixty. Louis had recently alienated a substantial portion of his capital to endow a daughter and a son, hence his lower assessment. As these tax rates show, by delaying the marriages and the financial independence of his younger sons, Garrisson *père* had been able to establish them all at comparable levels of affluence.[80]

Other merchant families created different patterns but aimed at the same result. For example, merchant-dyer Jean Izaac Bergis married and established his three younger sons first, one at age twenty-two and two at age twenty-seven. His eldest son and heir did not marry until age forty-three, ten days after Jean Izaac's death.[81]

[79] AM Mont 10 HH 1 dénombrement Villebourbon 1774; 5 CC 9 capitation 1788; AD T-et-G E Etat Civil Protestant no. 368 9–5–1788.

[80] Garrisson himself paid 110 livres in tax. AM Mont 5 CC 9 capitation 1788; 10 HH 1 dénombrement Villebourbon 1774; AD T-et-G E Etat Civil Protestant no. 377 28–3–1788, no. 368 9–5–1788, no. 370 20–10–1788.

[81] AD T-et-G E Etat Civil Protestant no. 366 21–2–1788, 3–4–1788, 10–4–1788; no. 367 18–4–1788; AM Mont 10 HH 1 dénombrement Villebourbon 1774.

These strategies contrasted with those of La Rochelle's merchants. Threatened by commercial crises and stagnation, merchants in that city limited the number of children they had to provide for but usually established each son when he was in his early twenties.[82] In Montauban, merchants continued to have large families but long delayed their sons' independence. By spacing their sons' establishments, Montauban merchants husbanded the patrimony. And single young men played a significant role in the family business. Distant as they were from the commercial centers on which their fortunes depended, Montauban merchants used their sons as traveling agents. In this way, sons not only learned the business, but also protected it from the risk of trusting important affairs or large sums of money to hired clerks.[83] Presumably if they had been young husbands and fathers of their own families, they would have been less available to travel to Holland or the West Indies or even to Bordeaux on their fathers' business.

The celibacy of magistrates' sons and the long-delayed marriages of merchants' sons succeeded in conserving the patrimony of wealthy families but often entailed less desirable side effects. Having no status in society, *fils de famille* sometimes idled and gambled and caused trouble. Charles François Dubu complained that although "our Lifeguards" were bored at home, they were extravagant when they were with their regiment. He worried that his brother in Paris would be put to yet more expense bailing them out of their foolishness.[84] At least they had not become involved with working women, a common occurrence for young men of good family but small means. If the woman had support in the working community, an elite family could find itself embroiled in a lawsuit. The law required a pregnant woman who was not married to declare her condition to the sheriff and, if possible, to name the father. The municipal authorities could then charge the putative father with the cost of the midwife and pressure him to support the child.[85] In the 1780s, Jean Garrison, a grandson of Jean Garrisson *père*, was the subject of at least two such paternity claims. In both, the women did not name him to the sheriff but used public pressure to obtain a settlement. In return for an unspecified sum, each withdrew her claim, declaring that she "had never had carnal commerce with the said Sr Garrisson, that it is unjust that he be accused in public of being the author of the said pregnancy. For such cause, the plaintiff, desiring to render homage to the truth, declared before us Nota-

---

[82] Clark, *La Rochelle*, pp. 54, 61–62, 82–83.

[83] Bosher, "Success and Failure in the Trade to New France," pp. 450–451.

[84] AD T-et-G 11 J 616 papiers de famille Dubu.

[85] Depauw, "Amour illégitime," pp. 1155–1182; Lottin, "Naissances illégitimes," pp. 278–322.

ries and witnesses today . . . that the said Sr Garrisson never had any courtship or acquaintance with her."[86]

Under the Custom of Montauban, illegitimate children had no legal claim on their parents' property unless the latter had no legitimate heirs. For children born of working women and elite men, this usually meant that although they might inherit from their mothers, they could rarely inherit from their well-to-do fathers. Nonetheless, the threat of a paternity suit often obtained a lump sum, which provided some endowment although much less than if the child had been legitimate.

Revolutionary inheritance law appeared to increase the rights of illegitimate children but in fact severely curtailed them. By the law of 12 *brumaire* Year 2 (November 2, 1793) the child of an adulterous union was to receive one third of a legitimate share of his parents' successions; if the child was merely illegitimate, he was to inherit as if he were legitimate. However, the law was interpreted to prohibit legal actions to establish paternity. Thus, if the father formally acknowledged his child, the child had a legal claim to a reasonable share in his estate. If the father ignored or denied paternity, neither the child nor his mother could bring legal action to prove it.[87]

The law of 12 *brumaire* Year 2 freed Montauban elite families from the claims of unwed mothers and illegitimate children. Men who had willingly acknowledged their illegitimate children had usually provided for them anyway. For example, Jean-François Garrisson, Jean Garrisson *père*'s youngest son, eventually adopted his two illegitimate children as his heirs. These children now had a legal claim they had not had before, but in practice their situation had not changed. They had been and continued to be the privileged minority of illegitimate children. By contrast, children whose fathers refused to acknowledge them had no claim at all, not even to the expenses of childbirth or minimal support. The practice of Montauban elite families of purchasing a renunciation of paternity claims rather than admitting paternity and paying what were probably much smaller costs rebounded to their advantage. The notarized statements extorted from the mother effectively eliminated any claim the child might have had under the new law. And women or children who had not brought suit to prove paternity now could not do so. As the law of 12 *brumaire* came to be interpreted, a *fils de famille* could no longer be pressured into making a

---

[86] Some years earlier, Pierre Garrisson, Louis's younger brother, had been involved in a similar case and had paid the woman in question seventy-two livres to extricate himself. AD T-et-G 5E 12858 Grelleau no. 394 13–10–1770 accord Riviere-Garrisson; 2002 Garrigues no. 450 12–7–1784 déclaration Pouramour; 2005 Garrigues no. 226 19–3–1786 déclaration Dellac.

[87] Traer, *Marriage and the Family*, pp. 156–157. See Brinton, *French Revolutionary Legislation on Illegitimacy*.

settlement or proved in court to be responsible. If a man denied paternity, that was the end of the story.

Nonetheless, the affairs of a *fils de famille* could have significant repercussions in his family. Some irregular relationships did not end with the birth of a child or even with the eventual marriage of the man. Some men, like Jean-François Garrisson, willingly acknowledged paternity, thereby forcing their families to accept the illegitimate children and their mothers as claimants on family resources. And the law of 12 *brumaire* Year 2 did catch out some families who had not been as prescient as to obtain a renunciation. For example, merchant Jean Izaac Saint-Genies left his legitimate heir with the financial problem of buying off an illegitimate half-brother whom Jean Izaac had acknowledged but not provided for, and the social problem of sharing his name with a poulterer.[88]

Perhaps as serious as the drain on family property and social status was the strain such affairs could create between husbands and wives. If elite marriages had been merely practical partnerships as appears to have been the case in earlier centuries, then a husband's infidelity would have had little impact. However, although marriages between Montauban's well-to-do families remained carefully negotiated exchanges of property and status, in the late eighteenth century they acquired considerable emotional content. Engaged couples talked not only of the suitability and advantageousness of the projected match but of the strong affection they felt for their future partners and the happiness they expected their marriages to bring. In 1773, noble Antoine Soulé de Besins declared to the Ecclesiastical Court that "having for so long been deeply inclined toward his cousin Mlle de Garrigues" he could not conceive of contracting marriage to anyone else. Merchant Bernard Julia stated that "given his inclination for Dlle Caladguez, he does not believe he will find happiness in any other alliance."[89] Such an exclusive and emotionally charged commitment would not easily admit the husband's maintaining a second establishment or casually presenting society with proof of his infidelity. Unfortunately, elite couples did not air their problems in the streets or the courts as did poorer families. We must remain in ignorance about how young Jean Garrisson's wife felt about her husband's premarital escapades, but we can speculate about how Jean-François Garrison's long-term relationship with a laundress affected his marriage. Jean-François married Henriette

[88] AD T-et-G 5E 2016 Garrigues no. 563 12 pluviôse Year 12 testament Garrisson; E Etat Civil Protestant no. 370 20–10–1788; B 418 donations no. 70 19–9–1772. Also see 5E 1934 Caminel no. 285 7–7–1780 testament Delcasse and no. 294 14–7–1780 testament Ramond de Redon in which a barrister left the légitime to his three natural children by the daughter of a stevedore.

[89] AD T-et-G G 459–460 procédures devant l'Officialité; Darrow, "Popular Concepts of Marital Choice," pp. 261–272.

Gareche, daughter of a merchant of Santonge, in 1773. Two years later his first child was born—to laundress Jeanne Bessey Soulas. The following year, he and Soulas had another child. His marriage was still childless in 1788, perhaps as a consequence of his extramarital establishment.[90]

Nonetheless, as marriage contracts made clear, the conjugal bond in Montauban's elite families connoted neither a complete unity of persons nor of property. A woman's rights in her husband's family depended on how much her own family was willing to invest. Sometimes, if her marriage ended without having produced heirs, her dowry reverted to its donors.[91] Such a marriage was above all an alliance of families in which each partner retained rights as a member of his or her family of origin.

This view of marriage had both advantages and disadvantages for women. It protected a married woman's property and her separate identity, but it also made her a "stranger" in the interests and concerns of her husband and children. Paul Butel has argued that the close cooperation of the merchant and his wife in Bordeaux was based, in part, on the Bordelais marriage custom, which created a *communité des acquêts* making all possessions acquired by a couple after marriage joint property.[92] Conversely, one could argue that the lack of such close partnerships in Montauban derived from the custom that kept the property of husband and wife separate and that denied the wife an interest in her husband's business except as it secured her dowry and nuptial gains. That wealthy Montaubaners interpreted the Custom of Montauban in this way is evident from the restrictions they placed on the husband's administration of his wife's property. Many contracts stipulated that the dowry be used only to buy real estate. Others set aside the bulk of the bride's property to remain under her sole control. Jeanne Garrigues's marriage contract even anticipated a legal separation in case her husband went bankrupt.[93]

[90] AD T-et-G E Etat Civil Protestant no. 370; 5E 2016 Garrigues no. 563 12 pluviôse Year 12 testament Garrisson.

[91] See, for example, AD T-et-G 5E 10867 Martin no. 212 27–4–1778 contrat de mariage between the comte de Pluvie and the daughter of the comte de Guibert of Fontneuve. Her parents gave the bride a dowry worth twenty-five thousand livres, but if she were to die without children, half of this amount would revert to her parents' estate. See also 5E 1943 Caminel no. 512 29–9–1787 contrat de mariage Bailet de Berdolle de Goudourville-Pullignieu; 2106 Franceries no. 271 3–6–1809 contrat de mariage Ricard-Boyer and 2109 Franceries no. 296 9–4–1816 contrat de mariage Foissac-Linon.

[92] Butel, "Comportements familiaux," pp. 143–146. Clark also found that merchants' wives and especially widows actively participated in commercial societies in La Rochelle in the eighteenth century. *La Rochelle*, pp. 60–61, 72.

[93] AD T-et-G 5E 1991 Garrigues no. 210 29–6–1771 contrat de mariage Lacaze-Garrigues; 13179 Deray no. 476 16–11–1784 contrat de mariage Rachou-Serre; 10877 Martin no. 258 27–4–1788 contrat de mariage Bernard-Tuffeau; 2008 Garrigues no. 831 17–11–1788 contrat de mariage Bergis-Lacaze; 2106 Franceries no. 65 19–4–1808 contrat de mariage Pellet-Martin; 2356 Martin no. 293 18–5–1809 contrat de mariage Pendaries-

A wife kept her own family name, adding her husband's name to it. On the marriage contract of Izaac Lacoste and Ester Payes, for example, the bride's mother signed herself as Gales Payes, her sister as Magdeleine Payes Garrisson, the groom's mother as Laressenjanie Lacoste, and his aunt as Lacoste vᶜ Garrisson. Even her husband continued to refer to her by her family name as when merchant François Mariet Debia bequeathed a legacy to "my wife Dlle de Belveze."[94]

Because one of the purposes of marriage was to gain alliances with other wealthy families, a wife was important as the link to a new set of relatives. She retained close contact with her own family although she usually lived in her own household or with her husband's family. This contact was in part ceremonial—her relatives cosponsored each of her children at baptism and witnessed their marriage contracts, and she did the same for her siblings' children. It was also financial; her relatives often left her or her children legacies or gave them gifts. Her dowry, usually paid in installments, necessitated regular, if not always agreeable, contact with her family. Less formal relationships are more difficult to document. Many elite brides moved some distance from home when they married, but they or their husbands owned or could easily hire comfortable transport and had the time to travel and to visit even if family visiting was combined with business. For example, when merchant Mouisset went to Bordeaux, he stayed with his sister and her husband. Grave illness and especially pregnancy were crises that often caused relatives to gather. When Louis Garrisson's wife was pregnant with their sixth child, her sister moved in to take charge of the household. When her third child was born, Mme d'Albis de Belbeze, wife of a Toulouse magistrate, received extended visits from her parents and her brother even though a dispute over her dowry had caused a rift between them.[95]

The lack of marital community protected a married woman's property and thereby bolstered her position in her husband's family and secured her future. It did not, however, guarantee her the right to govern her own affairs. Her dowry was invested according to the provisions of the marriage contract that had been negotiated by her family. The income from this investment went to her husband. Similarly, a married woman's identi-

---

Chené; 2109 Franceries no. 296 9–4–1816 contrat de mariage Foissac-Linon; 2001 Garrigues no. 793 20–12–1782 contrat de mariage Janolz-Noalhac; 1943 Caminel no. 512 29–9–1787 contrat de mariage Bailet de Berdolle de Goudourville-Pullignieu; B 418 donations no. 70 22–9–1772.

[94] AD T-et-G 5E 2262 Caminel sn 12–2–1770 testament Debia and 1943 Caminel no. 425 14–8–1787 contrat de mariage Lacoste-Payes. Also see 5E 2263 Caminel sn 24–5–1787 testament Debia.

[95] AM Mont 5 i 1 passeports; 10 HH 1 dénombrement Villebourbon 1774 and AD T-et-G E Etat Civil Protestant no. 368 9–5–1788. Puis, *d'Albis de Belbeze*, pp. 90–91, 119–120.

fication with her family of origin prevented her from being entirely sub-sumed into her husband's identity, but it did not recognize her in her own right. While she was Madame A wife of B, her husband was Monsieur B son-in-law of A; it was her family, especially her father, not she, who commanded respect.

When her husband died, a woman could become somewhat more inde-pendent. First, she gained control of her dowry, sometimes augmented by half. Elite dowries were usually large enough to produce an adequate income (see table 4–1). Although some elite widows experienced a decline in living standard, the majority were comfortably off and some were very wealthy indeed. Dlle Olympe Gasc, widow of one of Montauban's wealthiest landowners, was taxed at seventy-two livres; the widow of merchant Daniel Rauly paid one hundred and sixty livres, one of the highest assessments in the city.[96]

Second, although elite husbands rarely made wives their heirs, they often supplemented their dowries with the usufruct of the familial apart-ment and ownership of its furniture. For example, when Charles Gabriel Dubu married Dlle de Gironde, he promised his wife the use of his town-house and furnishings after his death provided that she abandon part of her ample dowry to his heirs. And these circumstances eventually trans-pired. When Charles Gabriel died only five years after their marriage, his widow maintained her own establishment in Montauban and successfully fended off the importune claims of her stepdaughter and her brother-in-law to take charge of her affairs.[97]

Many of the elite widows who headed the 1774 census entries were not dependents but heads of households. In Villebourbon, 32 percent of bourgeois and merchant households were headed by women, whereas only one widow lived as a dependent in her child's household. The same was true in noble and official families; like Madame Dubu, most widows headed their own households. For example, Madame de Malartic *dou-aurière* (dowager), the widow of a first president of the Cour des Aides, lived on the Place des Monges, whereas her eldest son and his wife lived on the Rue du Vieux Collège and her three younger children lived together on Grande Rue. Similarly, Madame de l'Escure, also the widow of a magistrate, maintained a separate household for herself and her daughter while her son, who had inherited his father's office, lived several streets

---

[96] AM Mont 1 G 1 capitation 1790.

[97] AD T-et-G 11 J 616 papiers de famille Dubu. Also see AD T-et-G 5E 2262 Caminel sn 15–9–1769 testament Janolz and 12–2–1770 testament Debia; 2263 Caminel sn 13 ven-démiaire Year 2 testament Garrisson and 17 messidor Year 8 testament Debia; 2356 Martin no. 434 11–7–1809 testament Tandol; 1999 Garrigues no. 408 17–5–1781 testament Garrisson.

away. The children who remained in their mother's household were dependent on her, not vice versa. For example, Madame de Colon, *seigneuresse* of St Nauphary, supported her son, a military officer, in her town house on the Rue de Monmurat. In such circumstances, adult sons remained dependent *fils de famille*.[98]

Gifts from well-to-do widows to their children in return for support revealed their financial independence. In such transactions among the artisans, the support contracted generally exceeded the value of the property the widow had to offer (see chapter 5). They were a form of aid from children to dependent parents. Among the widows of merchants and magistrates, the reverse was true. For example, in 1794, Anne Martin, widow of merchant Jean Leygue, gave all her goods to her two sons in return for an annuity of five hundred francs. Her property included a house in the center of town, two large farms, and livestock, worth in all more than twenty-four thousand francs. Since the annuity represented a return of only about 2 percent when the standard return on an investment was 5 percent, this transaction was a gift to help the sons rather than to provide for the mother.[99]

Most women lived off their property without participating in business. Of course, a lawyer's widow could not carry on her husband's profession; nor could a magistrate's widow fill his office, but wealthy women were not particularly active in the areas of business that were open to them, such as property management and commerce. In fact, they were less involved in property transactions than were poorer women. As Anne Martin's gift indicates, many widows were willing to leave the management of their property to others.[100]

Some wealthy women carried on business themselves. Rachel Huegla, daughter of financier Gervais Huegla, continued her father's business, making loans to merchants and peasants and foreclosing when her terms were not met.[101] In *négociant* families, daughters and sisters often invested in the family firm or used the facilities of the firm to carry on their own

[98] AM Mont 10 HH 1 dénombrements circa 1774.

[99] AD T-et-G Q 414 donations no. 35 13 floréal Year 2; similarly, B 418 donations no. 85 18–12–1772. In the same volume, no. 52 4–8–1772, a widowed mother gave her son money to purchase the office of a *Tresorier de France*.

[100] Age was probably a factor. In the Dubu family, Gabriel Dubu's widow, who was at least sixty when her husband died, employed an agent to manage her property, and when he proved dilatory, turned matters over to her sons. On the other hand, her daughter-in-law, who was widowed in her midtwenties, apparently managed her own affairs. AD T-et-G 11 J 616 papiers de famille Dubu.

[101] AD T-et-G 5E 12856 Grelleau no. 403 28–9–1769 quittance Huegla-Janolz and no. 405 dette Bardou-Huegla; 12867 Grelleau no. 85 6–3–1779 désistement Huegla-Bardou; 12875 Grelleau no. 149 7–3–1785 quittance Huegla-Peries.

TABLE 4–4
Women as Parties to Property Transactions

	Socioeconomic Status of Party				
	Farm Worker	Peasant Owner	City Worker	Artisan Retailer	Elite
Percentage of sales by women	30%	14%	57%	30%	29%
Percentage of purchases by women	25	13	33	21	25
N	53	56	21	49	66

Note: Significance level = .02, sales contingency coefficient = .234, purchase contingency coefficient = .134.

ventures. For example, Pierre Lacoste-Rigail noted in his journal on June 2, 1780, "Settled accounts with my sister. Loss on the saffron she sent to Holland, 15£ 3s."[102] Marie Vidallet, the widow of merchant Raymond Bergis, was even more active, comparable to the women historian Bonnie Smith has found so important to the textile industry in the Nord at this time.[103] Marie was the daughter of Izaac Vidallet, one of Villebourbon's grain dealers. In 1781, when she was eighteen, she married Bergis, the eldest son of a merchant-dyer, who used his wife's dowry and her family connections to become a grain merchant, forming with her brother the society of *Vidallet ainé Bergis maîtres et compagnie.* From the first, Marie followed the day-to-day activities of the warehouse, and when her husband died, leaving her with two minor children, she continued to run the business. In 1812, when her son Charles was twenty-seven, Marie was still the senior partner in the business, now called *Messieurs Ve Bergis et compagnie fils ainé.*

Marie Vidallet's daughter, Marie Bergis, also became a merchant. In 1806 she married a Villebourbon merchant who went bankrupt nine years later. Marie Bergis fought a long and ultimately successful court battle to protect her property from seizure. In this, her mother was her staunch supporter and witness. As part of this procedure she separated from her husband; by 1823 they were living apart, separate *de personnes* as well as *de biens* although by law she still needed his consent to do business. During this period Marie Vidallet finally allowed her son to take over the business, but apparently he proved incompetent. In 1826 Marie Bergis bought out her brother's lease of the warehouse, and so the family business became, in

[102] Cited in Ombret et al., *Villes et campagnes du Bas-Quercy*, B6. See Clark, *La Rochelle*, pp. 67–79, on familial investment in Rochelais commercial ventures.

[103] Smith, *Ladies of the Leisure Class.*

reality if not in name, *Ve Bergis et fille ainée* although Charles would inherit it after his mother's death.[104]

In theory and in practice, wealthy husbands had only limited authority over their wives. Neither a woman's property nor her person became completely identified with her husband when she married. The notion of marriage as a contracted alliance rather than a complete union prevented women from becoming dependent on their husbands and permitted some women, such as Marie Vidallet, scope for their talents and ambitions. During the Revolution, it enabled the wives of suspects and emigrés to protect large parts of the family's property from confiscation. It was only through the tenacity of his wife and mother that Jacques Antoine Molières retained any property at all in Montauban, to name one example.[105]

There were, however, less positive aspects of the separation of husband and wife. Because a wife remained a stranger in her husband's family, her interests were ambiguous and she could become a target for familial hostility. One source of tension was her dowry, first its payment to her husband or his family and then its return to her when she was left a widow. In both situations, the woman's position was ambiguous. A series of letters between Mme d'Albis de Belbeze and her husband written in 1783 and 1784 illustrates the first situation. The couple had been married for several years—they had two children and were expecting a third—but the wife's dowry had not been paid. D'Albis de Belbeze expected his wife to pressure her parents for payment. She sent her parents' unsatisfactory

---

[104] AD T-et-G E Etat Civil Protestant no. 370 15–10–1788; 5E 2005 Garrigues no. 955 3–12–1786 désistement Bringou-Bergis; 2013 Garrigues no. 36 20–8–1791 accord Graves-Roque; 2134 Latreille-Olivié no. 546 9–6–1806 contrat de mariage Lafon-Bergis; 2136 Latreille-Olivié no. 268 5–6–1809 quittance Vidallet v^e Bergis-Petit; 2140 Latreille-Olivié no. 245 8–4–1812 dette Izalie v^e Bergis et compagnie; 2141 Latreille-Olivié no. 268 23–4–1813 achât Nuly-Bergis ép Lafon and no. 644 23–11–1813 bail Bergis ép Lafon-Goulard; 2143 Latreille-Olivié no. 264 12–5–1815 accord Bergis ép Lafon; 2145 Latreille-Olivié no. 249 17–8–1817 donation Vidallet v^e Bergis and no. 250 17–8–1817 bail Vidallet v^e Bergis-Bergis; 2152 Latreille-Olivié no. 104 19–3–1823 autorisation Lafon-Bergis ép Lafon; 2156 Latreille-Olivié no. 20 31–1–1826 transport et cession Mouméja-Bergis ép Lafon and no. 367 23–12–1826 bail Vidallet v^e Bergis-Bergis ép Lafon. Marie Bergis's main concern was to protect a farm she had purchased in 1813. She claimed that she had paid for it with her dowry; however, because the price was twelve thousand francs and her dowry was only five thousand, her husband's creditors argued that it had been purchased with her husband's money and thus was liable to seizure. Marie Vidallet testified that she had given her daughter the price of the farm as an addition to her dowry. Although the deed of gift supporting this claim had been signed only in 1817, the court was satisfied with this explanation.

[105] Des Rochettes, "Familles montaubanaises," 7: Molières. Also *citoyenne* Rigal-Garrisson, wife of a *ci-devant sécrétaire du roi*, applied for a legal separation in order to protect her property when her husband was jailed as a suspected Aristocrat. AD T-et-G L 95 régistres de suspects et détenus. See Ligou, *Montauban*, pp. 562–563.

reply to her husband with this comment: "I hope you will not throw the blame on me and that you are well convinced that your interests are dearer to me than theirs. I avow I am truly angry with them and that I never expected them to act in this way toward you." Later, after a visit from her family at the birth of her child, she saw her position differently.

> My father and all my family arrived Saturday night and they left me only a moment ago, covering me with the most tender caresses. I was most touched and I tell you it is annoying for me that you insist upon always telling me your business. These things should not concern me, so don't speak of them to me any more. . . . You would say the same in my place, for if I railed at your father every day, you would turn me out. . . . My health is not good enough for me to be worried like this, and also, no one has the right to embroil me with the family I have always cherished and that deserves cherishing. This is the result of my reflections; they are just and my secretary approves of them. My father looks everywhere for the money to pay you but I repeat again I don't want to be involved.[106]

The reverse problem might occur when a widow claimed her dowry and nuptial gains. Often, to prevent the loss of invested capital, a husband made the legacy of the use of his house and furniture contingent on his wife's abandoning her dowry. Sometimes, even when she insisted, she could not reclaim her property. For example, when Jean-Pierre Janolz-Garrisson died, his brother and heir was supposed to pay the widow's dowry and nuptial gains out of the estate. However, this obligation amounted to twenty-four hundred livres and the entire estate was worth only two thousand. The brother quickly repudiated the inheritance as did his cousin, the next in line. It took the widow a long and expensive lawsuit to get even part of her dowry released to her from her husband's depleted estate.[107]

---

[106] Puis, *d'Albis de Belbeze*, pp. 79, 119–120. Jeanne Garrigues, supported by her husband, sued her brothers for a supplement to her dowry when the inventory of her father's estate showed that it had increased in value since the date of her marriage contract. AD T-et-G 5E 1993 Garrigues no. 205 25–3–1773 accord Garrigues frères et soeurs. Similarly, 5E 13180 Deray no. 498 25–2–1788 accord Espinasse frères et soeur; B 420 donations no. 10 25–2–1782 and Q 414 no. 3 22 nivôse Year 2. Castan, in "Criminalité familiale," p. 95, reports a case tried before the Parlement of Toulouse in 1718 in which a bourgeois of Fleurence accused his wife of adultery and tried to have her incarcerated. The wife insisted she was innocent and that he wanted to get rid of her because her dowry was unpaid.

[107] AD T-et-G 5E 2002 Garrigues no. 415 24–6–1784 répudiation Janolz; 1942 Caminel no. 158 2–5–1787 inventaire Janolz-Garrisson. See 2092 Franceries no. 392 28–5–1788 testament Garrisson and 2356 Martin no. 434 11–7–1809 testament Tandol for examples of wills in which legacies were contingent on the abandonment of the dowry. In 5E 13179 Deray no. 410 2–7–1784 transaction to settle the intestate succession of merchant François Duc, the inheriting children granted their widowed mother maintenance at their pot and hearth only if she did not demand the return of her dowry.

TABLE 4–5
The Relationship of Proxies to the Men Who Appointed Them

	Occupation of Man Appointing Proxy					
Proxies	Farm Worker	Peasant Owner	City Worker	Artisan Retailer	Merchant	Bourgeois
Child	5%	24%	4%	13%	12%	14%
Sibling	21	18	16	18	7	21
Parent	21	0	21	12	7	7
Wife	16	3	21	12	14	12
Nonkin	37	55	38	45	60	46
N	19	33	56	77	43	81

Note: Significance level = .02, contingency coefficient = .314.

Although often a party to her husband's daily concerns, a merchant's or a magistrate's wife could never be completely identified with his interests and therefore was not acceptable as his partner or representative. In Bordeaux, where the customary marital community unified the material interests of husband and wife, merchants' wives usually acted as their husbands' proxies, or *procureurs*, when their husbands were away from home.[108] This was not the case in Montauban. Only 14 percent of merchants and 12 percent of other elite Montaubaners appointed their wives to represent them in any capacity.

Husbands sometimes expressed opinions of their wives in their wills. Prevented by the Civil Code from making his wife his heir, Charles Janolz instructed his children "never to quarrel, to love and cherish their mother, to obey her in all things, and not to default in any of the obligations herein. Be persuaded that anything they do against their said mother will be against the will of their father, who desires with all his heart to be able to do much more for his dearest half, but the law prevents him."[109] For every such expression of conjugal confidence and affection, however, there was one of mistrust. Joseph Chevalier Chambert left his fortune in trust for his infant son under the control of his lawyer and forbade his wife any say whatsoever in its administration.[110]

[108] Butel, "Comportements familiaux," pp. 143–145. In La Rochelle, too, merchants' wives were intimately involved with their husbands' businesses because some marriage contracts specified that the wife was to have a say in the investment of her dowry. Clark, *La Rochelle*, p. 61.

[109] AD T-et-G 5E 12889 Grelleau no. 344 30 floreal Year 3 testament Janolz. Also see 5E 2262 Caminel sn 22–5–1770 testament Ratier and 2139 Latreille-Olivié no. 221 19–3–1795 testament Seguy.

[110] AD T-et-G 5E 10877 Martin no. 134 9–3–1788 testament Chambert. See also 5E 13174 Deray no. 653 21–6–1776 compromise Mariette.

TABLE 4–6
Comparative Social Status of Brides and Grooms, 1775–1799

| | Groom's Occupation | | | | |
Bride's Father	Peasant	City Worker	Artisan Retailer	Merchant	Bourgeois
Peasant	88%	35%	12%	4%	0
City worker	3	41	19	4	0
Artisan retailer	8	22	58	19	23
Merchant	1	0	5	42	23
Bourgeois	0	2	6	31	54
N	176	102	67	26	22

Note: Significance level = .01, contingency coefficient = .722.

One reason that merchants may have doubted their wives' competence was that often they were not from commercial families. In Bordeaux and La Rochelle, merchants almost invariably married merchants' daughters,[111] but this was no longer strictly true in Montauban. Many merchants' wives were the daughters of noncommercial families; their fathers were lawyers, officials, magistrates, and landowners. This may explain why Marie Vidallet was an extraordinary figure. She was unusually well qualified to continue her husband's business because she was a merchant's daughter as well as a merchant's wife.

By the end of the Old Regime, Montauban's merchants and magistrates were well on the way to forming a single integrated elite. Intermarriage, the official toleration of Protestants and merchants' investments in land, and a "less laborious" life-style, all demonstrated a gradual erosion of the barriers that stood between Catholic magistrates and Protestant merchants. They shared wealth, culture, and many family strategies as well.

The Revolution accelerated the progress toward integration but did not achieve it. The extremes—magistrates and merchants—collapsed into a mass of elite landowners, *propriétaires sans profession*, and local notables. However, although unified in economic interests and in social and political preeminence, Montauban's elite in the nineteenth century remained divided by the ideological and political heritage of the Revolution. This division replicated in some ways the fissure caused by the Revocation of the Edict of Nantes. There remained two elites, more similar than ever, but separated by a chasm of memories.[112]

[111] Clark, *La Rochelle*, pp. 58–59; Butel, *Négociants*, pp. 329–332.

[112] Nîmes was another city in which the Revolutionary experience overlaid religious and economic divisions with political hostilities. See Hood, "Protestant-Catholic Relations," pp. 245–275, and "Revival and Mutation of Old Rivalries," pp. 82–115. Although the Revolu-

The Revolution affected Montauban's magistrates and merchants very differently. The balance of power weighed briefly but terrifyingly against the magistrates and other *ci-devants*, former royal officials, who were silenced and occasionally persecuted. Far more serious for familial prestige and for elite family strategies, however, was the abolition of seigneurial rights and venal offices. Families lost not only substantial investments and revenues, but also the public status that had constituted the family's patrimony.[113] For merchant families, on the other hand, the Revolution provided great opportunities. At the same time as patrimony in public office vanished, careers in public service multiplied. The leading merchant families who, like the Garrissons and the Vialette-Daignans, had overstayed their three generations in commerce, rushed into politics and public administration.

Already during the Maupeou reform in the 1770s, official families had become anxious about the security of their patrimony. In the 1780s, in the climate of repeated clashes between the Parlement of Paris and the royal government, many people suspected that venal offices were becoming a risky investment. Prices for positions on the bench of Montauban's Cour des Aides plummeted as did the price of offices in general.[114] Nonetheless, when the blow finally fell, some tried to fight back. The magistrates of the Parlement of Toulouse resisted the abolition of their court and their offices in a formal remonstrance to the king. In Montauban the prosecutors discussed the possibility of organizing a nationwide assembly to protest and possibly resist the abolition of their offices. M. Selves, a prosecutor in the Cour des Aides, wrote to a colleague in Paris to sound him out about the idea. His correspondent cautioned against such a move. "Such a meeting would have the look of a coalition, which would displease the [National] Assembly." And, in fact, the National Assembly had already ordered the arrest of the Toulouse parlementarians for their resistance.[115]

The prosecutors' vague plans came to naught, and Montauban's elite succumbed to the loss of their offices without public protest and consequently without much persecution. Nonetheless, the climate of opinion was so hostile to *ci-devants*, especially after May 1790, that most felt it prudent to withdraw from the public eye. The two groups who suffered most were actual or suspected counter-Revolutionaries like the members

---

tion did not produce such virulent rivalries in Rouen, political affiliation as well as religion and degree of religiosity created social eddies within the elite throughout the nineteenth century. Chaline, *Bourgeois de Rouen*, p. 286.

[113] Sewell, in *Work and Revolution*, pp. 114–142, discusses the revolution in property rights and its implications for those who had possessed a public function in the Old Regime.

[114] Ligou, *Montauban*, p. 34; Doyle, *Parlement*, p. 30; Mousnier, *Les Institutions de la France* 2: 335–338.

[115] AD T-et-G 11 J 284 papiers de famille Selves, 1790–1791; Higgs, *Ultra*, pp. 29–30.

of the Aristocrat government of 1790,[116] and, as everywhere, the clergy. The vast majority of national properties auctioned in and around Montauban were church properties; when the priests were exiled, their personal property was auctioned as well.[117]

Most of Montauban's former officials withdrew to their country estates and survived with their property more or less intact. Most received at least partial compensation for the loss of their investment, and some were even able to recoup the loss of official salaries by deducting them from their Revolutionary taxes. They did not, however, profit from the losses of their former colleagues; they were conspicuously absent among the buyers of national properties.[118]

After the coup d'état of 1799, many *ci-devants* gradually reentered public life. Both of Jacques Antoine de Molières's sons were officers in the Imperial Army. Michel de Satur, a former magistrate in the Cour des Aides, became an imperial judge in Agen, and another former royal official, Pascal Duc-Lachapelle, became mayor of Montauban. Throughout the Empire and the Restoration, old noble and magisterial families, such as Gironde, Scorbiac, and Caumont La Force, played prominent roles in local and regional politics. However, the public functions and prestige that had formerly belonged to them as patrimony, inherited from their ances-

[116] The duc de Gironde and the marquis de Cieurac, who had been the mayor in the Aristocrat government, were apprehended trying to emigrate and were executed. Seven former magistrates of the Cour des Aides as well as other nobles and former officials were imprisoned during the Terror, most suspected of being members of the "Club Noir," a secret counter-Revolutionary society. Jacques Antoine de Molières and Pierre Ambroise de Savignac, both sons of magistrates, were allegedly the leaders of this club. None was executed, however, and the club itself may have been a figment of Revolutionary imagination. Ligou, *Montauban*, pp. 160, 319–320; des Rochettes, "Familles montaubanaises," 7: Molières, 10: Savignac.

[117] Sol, *Quercynois de la période révolutionnaire*, pp. 380–381; Ligou, "Biens nationaux," pp. 361–387, and *Montauban*, pp. 558–559. Merchant Pierre Garrisson bought the Capuchin convent for 30,300 francs, used it to house a spinning factory, then resold it to the Catholic church in 1825 at a profit of 14,700 francs. Some priests tried to forestall confiscation by formally giving their property to relatives and friends before they left. Pierre Boë, for example, gave one nephew a farm and appointed another to receive his inheritance from his parents. Since such eve-of-departure gifts were invalid, Boë carefully noted that he had promised his nephews these properties in their marriage contracts. See AD T-et-G Q 406 donations no. 39 5–6–1792, no. 65 20–9–2792, and no. 67–70, 2–10–1792.

Of the 145 persons on Montauban's emigré list, 99 were members of the elite. Fifty-six were nobles and 6 were non-noble officials, 29 were priests, 3 were bourgeois, 2 were lawyers, and 3 were merchants. Thirty-one were artisans and shopkeepers, 9 were textile workers, and the occupations of the remaining 6 were not given. Many of the working people were probably like wig maker Duluc, who had gone to Spain to find work as Montaubaners had been doing for generations, and found himself declared an emigré. AM Mont 7 i 1 emigrés.

[118] Ligou, *Montauban*, pp. 357–358, and Ligou, "Biens nationaux."

tors, they now had to compete for in the ministries in Paris and even at the polls. The self-confidence and tolerance that had been engendered by owning public power as family property never returned. As a group they belonged to the reactionary faction known in national politics as the Ultra-Royalists; in rhetoric and policies, they were simultaneously defensive and vindictive, continually fighting the political battle of 1790.[119]

For the merchants the story was quite different. In Montauban they were the driving force of the Revolution. They led the National Guard and the Patriots' Club and were heavy purchasers of national properties. Of the thirty-six properties sold for more than twenty thousand francs, two thirds were purchased by merchants. They also leaped into local and regional politics and administration. From August 1790 until well into the Empire, merchants and manufacturers dominated Montauban's government.[120]

The career of Paul-Elie Vialette-Daignan epitomized the new routes from commerce to landowning and public office. Paul-Elie was the second son of Montauban's foremost textile manufacturer. Whereas his elder brother gradually dissociated himself from commerce at the end of the Old Regime, Paul-Elie married the daughter of a rival manufacturer and expanded his enterprise. The Revolution and especially the Empire offered other opportunities. He acquired a large estate whose name he attached to his own, becoming Vialètes de Mortarieu. He became a municipal, then a departmental councillor, and finally Louis XVIII made him a chevalier de Saint Louis. His son became mayor of Montauban, deputy from the Tarn-et-Garonne and prefect of the Ariège and was eventually knighted. The textile factory had closed in 1802.[121]

Many of Montauban's commercial families repeated this pattern, if not with this degree of success. Before the Revolution, although merchants called themselves bourgeois when they retired, their sons remained merchants. During the Revolution, the older merchants carried on their businesses, but the younger men turned to new careers as bureaucrats and landowners. Their sons rarely entered commerce. Examples abound in the Rigail family, before the Revolution Montauban's wealthiest merchants, among the Bergis clan of merchant-dyers, and among the descendants of Jean Garrisson; where fathers and grandfathers were *négociants* and proud of the title, sons and grandsons became civil servants and *propriétaires sans profession*.

---

[119] The election of June 1830 pitted M. de Gironde, a leading Catholic landowner and descendant of the last provincial governor, against M. de Preissac, a "martyr of May 10." In 1848 the leaders on the Right were still a Scorbiac and a Gironde. Valmary, "Une Révolution montalbanaise," pp. 18–33.

[120] AD T-et-G L 407 membres du club patriotique; Sol, *Révolution en Quercy* 2: 341–342; Ligou, "Biens nationaux," and *Montauban*, pp. 206–283, 313–315, 393–395.

[121] des Rochettes, "Familles montaubanaises," 10: Vialettes.

In his book on the textile industry in Clermont-de-Lodève in the seventeenth and eighteenth centuries, J.K.J. Thomson describes an economic cycle of expansion, consolidation, and contraction after which textile manufacture regrouped on a smaller scale to expand once more. He argues that in Clermont, however, government intervention in the form of a highly regulated royal manufacture turned contraction into collapse. Unable to adjust to more competitive market conditions in the second half of the eighteenth century, Clermont's merchant-manufacturers abandoned commerce en masse.[122]

In Montauban, the preindustrial economic cycle ended even more dramatically during the French Revolution. Loss of the West Indian market, government requisitioning, loss of army contracts, and competition from Great Britain followed one another in quick succession. Small manufacturers went under while *négociants* withdrew and the Industrial Revolution prevented others from rising to take their place. In 1745 an initial registry of textile manufacturers in Montauban listed 170 names; by the 1780s, there were only about 80, but of these a dozen or more were large operations. In 1809, a list of all the town's textile manufacturers contained only 35 names and only 5 were major producers. By 1812, 3 of the 5 had ceased production.[123]

After 1800, Montauban's commercial elite shrank to insignificance. The most telling evidence comes from the sample of marriage contracts. In the 1770s and 1780s, 90 percent of the sons of merchants were themselves merchants and 18 percent of merchant grooms had risen from the ranks of artisans and shopkeepers. After 1800, no "new men" succeeded in commerce, and almost half of merchants' sons turned to law, the civil service, and landowning instead of pursuing commercial careers. In the 1810s and 1820s, landowning and professional grooms outnumbered merchants by seven to one.

The loss of patrimony in public office, the abandonment of commerce and industry, and the new opportunities in politics and public administration entailed some adjustments in elite family strategies. Although secure investments in land or government bonds became more important than ever because familial prestige was now more directly dependent on its wealth, public position remained crucial to elite family status. In his notes for a family biography, for example, the comte de Preissac carefully recorded every step of his public career, from municipal councillor in Montauban in 1811 to deputy, to prefect, to his ascent to the peerage and his nomination as grand officer of the Legion of Honor in 1838. It was this

---

[122] Thomson, *Clermont-de-Lodève*, especially pp. 1–20, 374–460.

[123] Forestié, *Fabrication des draps*; AM Mont 8 HH 3 registre des fabriquants and AN F[12] 559 L'Etat général et précis des manufactures 1783.

TABLE 4–7
Elite Recruitment, 1775–1824

| | Groom's Occupation | | | |
| | Merchant (N = 35) | | Bourgeois (N = 56) | |
Father's Occupation	1775–1799	1800–1824	1775–1799	1800–1824
Peasant	7%	0	0	3%
Artisan retailer	18	0	10	8
Merchant	61	100	5	19
Bourgeois	14	0	85	70

Note: Significance level = .01, 1775–1799 contingency coefficient = .584, 1800–1824 contingency coefficient = .536.

| | Groom's Father's Occupation | | | |
| | Merchant (N = 35) | | Bourgeois (N = 60) | |
Son's Occupation	1775–1799	1800–1824	1775–1799	1800–1824
Peasant	0	0	4%	0
Artisan retailer	5	12	8	31
Merchant	90	44	17	0
Bourgeois	5	44	71	69

Note: Significance level = .01, 1775–1799 contingency coefficient = .593, 1800–1824 contingency coefficient = .511.

distinguished public career, rather than his ancestry or wealth, that made his family history worth recording.[124] But a public position could no longer be passed on as patrimony; it had to be acquired anew by each succeeding generation.

As before the Revolution, elite families depended on connections of blood, marriage, and patronage to maintain their status and to place their children. However, with primary concentration now on careers in the bureaucracy, the network of useful connections diminished to include only those in the immediate region and in Paris. Elite families who had previously sought allies and marital alliances in Toulouse or in Bordeaux shifted and narrowed their focus. Fewer Montauban brides married Bordelais merchants and Toulouse magistrates; more married local officials and landed proprietors from nearby country towns, and ambitious young men sought brides in well-placed families in Paris. Jean Hyacinthe Bastard, for example, son of a former magistrate in the Cours des Aides, became an auditor in the Council of State and married a Parisian bride as

---

[124] AD T-et-G 11 J 614 papiers de famille Preissac.

his first steps on the road to a successful career in the upper reaches of the bureaucracy.[125]

Fathers continued to plan and worry over their sons' careers, but now more depended on the sons' ambitions and abilities. One could no longer automatically give the eldest son pride of place; it might prove to be a younger son who would ensure the family's prestige in the next generation. Such was the case in the de Blazy de Firmy family, formerly counselors in the Cour des Aides. Although the eldest son led the undistinguished life of a country gentleman, the second son maintained the family's position within the governing elite. His appointment as prefect of the Tarn-et-Garonne during the Restoration capped a successful career in the imperial bureaucracy, during which he had secured not only his own promotion but that of relatives and clients as well.[126] In this new climate of opportunity and competition, the future head of the family depended less on birth order than on a successful career. As a result, elite testators were less likely to follow the dictates of primogeniture automatically and more likely to pick and choose among their heirs.

Changes in inheritance law, on the other hand, did not seriously challenge the way elite families distributed power and property. Equal inheritance as moderated in 1800 and by the Civil Code corresponded quite well to their belief that it was a father's duty to establish each of his children within his class while transmitting the patrimony to a favored successor. Almost all elite testators continued to favor one heir over the others, doubly endowing him or her with the portion disponible. For example, in 1809 merchant Jean Laurents divided the portion disponible among the eldest son of his first marriage, the eldest son of his second marriage, and his widow.[127] Such solutions were more individual and in a sense more arbitrary than pre-Revolutionary primogeniture. They remind one of Cazalès's and Saint-Martin's opposition to equal inheritance in 1791, that a patriarch must have the power to reward and punish his children with his bequests. Post-Revolutionary elite testators were quite as patriarchal as their forefathers had been.

The restrictions that the Napoleonic Code placed on a wife's control of her property and of her rights on her husband's property also accorded well with Montauban's elite family strategies. The Napoleonic Code treated wives as strangers to their husbands' successions in much the same way as Montauban's well-to-do families did. The new dowry regime, included in the Napoleonic Code at the insistence of southern jurists, gave

[125] M. O'Gilvy, *Nobiliaire de Guienne et de Gascogne*, 2 vols. (Paris: 1856–1883), 1: 445–459.

[126] Des Rochettes, "Familles montaubanaises," 1: Blazy.

[127] AD T-et-G 5E 2263 Caminel sn 17 messidor Year 8 testament Debia and 2353 Martin no. 511 30–8–1809 testament Laurents.

TABLE 4–8
Elite Choice of Heir Before and After the Revolution

| | Testator's Occupation | | | |
| | Merchant (N = 31) | | Bourgeois (N = 70) | |
Heir Chosen	1775–1799	1800–1824	1775–1799	1800–1824
Eldest male	47%	6%	30%	19%
Other kin	47	44	38	33
Coresident	6	0	7	16
Nonkin	0	0	7	14
Spouse	0	38	7	4
Equal division	0	12	11	14

Note: Significance level = .01, merchant contingency coefficient = .550, bourgeois contingency coefficient = .201.

them an arrangement even superior to the Custom of Montauban in reducing a wife's claims on the estate. In the sample of marriage contracts, few elite couples established a marital community of goods, and only a small minority tempered the Napoleonic *régime dotal* with provisions for usufruct. The vast majority followed a strict dowry arrangement that admitted no nuptial gains at all.[128] And bourgeois couples demonstrated only a slightly greater sense of unity at the end of their marriages than at the beginning. Although many husbands supplemented their wives' dowries with usufruct rights on the estate—substituting, in many cases, for the nuptial gains that had been customary in the Old Regime—few named their wives as their heirs.

In other ways, too, elite families changed little. Celibacy and long-delayed marriage continued to figure in their family strategies. Female celibacy in particular remained high. The return of religious orders like the Ursulines and the revitalization and increasing militancy of Catholicism in Montauban made religious vows as spiritually attractive to elite women as they were financially attractive to their families.[129] On the other hand,

[127] Seventy-seven percent followed the Napoleonic *régime dotal*, 15 percent modified it by adding usufruct rights, 5 percent kept separate property, and only 3 percent created a marital community. In comparison with all marriage contracts, significance level = .06, contingency coefficient = .263.

[129] Estèbe, "La Vie politique," p. 251. Religious dowries were not cheap, however. Landowner Antoine Bessac paid the Ursulines 4,000 francs in 1820 as an endowment for his daughter. In 1823 the dowry of another novice was 4,600 francs. See AD T-et-G 5E 13517 Martin fils no. 223 27–6–1820 dotation religieuse Bressac and 13520 Martin fils no. 189 5–1823 bail de nourriture Delpon. In the sample of wills, 37 percent of elite testators from 1800 to 1824 were single, but only 23 percent of the men were single compared with 52 percent of the women (significance level = .02, contingency coefficient = .400).

male celibacy declined as honorable careers that did not require it prolifer-
ated.

The major change in elite families was not the distribution of power and
property within the family but the number and quality of connections
between families, the ties of blood, marriage, and shared business interest
that wove Montauban's elite into the fringes of world commerce. With the
virtual disappearance of *négociant* families, the distinctive strategies of
alliance and career placement that had supported and been supported by
commerce disappeared as well. After 1800, the samples of notary documents can no longer contrast the strategies of the commercial and noncommercial elite because the commercial elite almost ceased to exist.
Among grooms, merchants were outnumbered by seven to one; among
testators, commerce was represented more often by merchants' widows
than by merchants themselves. The family strategies of the commercial and
noncommercial elite had been sufficiently similar before the Revolution so
that the abrupt migration of numerous families from the first group into
the second was accomplished without familial upheaval or the loss of
power or status. What was lost was Montauban's entrée to a wider world
through the national and international connections of the city's *négociants*.
As the elite chose to become provincial landowners and administrators,
the city followed into eclipse as even a regional center, overshadowed by
Toulouse.

In his study of the Depont family in eighteenth-century La Rochelle,
Robert Forster noted that their move from commerce to administration
and landowning did not mean a broadening of horizons; a more "honorable," more leisurely life-style meant they became more provincial and
conservative.[130] The Revolution, the simultaneous opportunities in politics and land, and the collapse of commerce and industry had a similar
effect on Montauban's elite. The goals of family strategies remained the
same: to establish all children within the elite while transmitting the patrimony undiminished to a single heir. However, stripped of the need to
maintain commercial networks and divided into two irrevocably hostile
camps, Montauban's well-to-do families became more closed and exclusive
than ever. And, as *Le Négoce* dwindled to mere trade, merchants slid out of
the elite altogether.

[130] Forster, *Depont Family*, p. 17.

CHAPTER FIVE

The Artisans and the Shopkeepers

THE ABBÉ EXPILLY observed in his *Dictionnaire géographique* that Montaubaners were "livelier and more brilliant" than many Frenchmen. "Equally well suited to science, to war, to commerce and the arts, they succeed easily in everything they undertake and do not neglect any honest means that might lead them to their goals."[1] He was thinking, perhaps, of magistrate-poet Le Franc-Pompignan; Duc-Lachapelle, the astronomer; or Vialètes d'Aignan, the royal manufacturer; but his encomium could also apply to less famous Montaubaners. Louis Gasc, nicknamed Saint-Araille, for example, although hardly a national figure, was a well-known local success story. After inheriting his father's carpentry business in 1787, he built an addition to the family house and opened an inn. By 1793 it was one of the busiest, if not the most respectable, in the city. Standing in the brick arch that led into his courtyard, he could survey the comings and goings of his guests—boatmen, hog merchants, tinkers, a troupe of dancers and acrobats—with complacence. For he was indeed prosperous. In 1788 he paid twelve livres in *capitation* tax, placing him in the upper quarter of taxpayers. The estate he left on his death in 1821 was worth more than eight thousand francs. It included two houses, stables, a warehouse, and a lumber yard plus gardens and pasture.

Nor was Saint-Araille's success confined to material acquisitions. He was as socially and politically ambitious as he was financially shrewd, and in his Villebourbon gateway, he was as well informed as any bourgeois in his club. When the Revolution offered the opportunity to participate in public affairs, he took it. He was an early member of the Patriots' Club; during the Terror, he served as neighborhood police commissioner, reporting on emigrés and suspects to the municipal Surveillance Committee.[2]

Lumber merchant, innkeeper, and Patriot, Saint-Araille was also a family man. In many ways, he was first a family man because throughout his life his politics, his work, and his property were embedded in his family.

---

[1] Expilly, *Dictionnaire* 4: 805.

[2] AD T-et-G 5E 1995 Garrigues no. 315 22–5–1775 codicil Gasc; 2150 Latreille-Olivié no. 304 20–7–1821 partage Gasc; 2159 Latreille-Olivié no. 129 26–4–1829 vente Gasc; AM Mont 4 i 15 voyageurs de passages; 5 CC 9 capitation 1788; AD T-et-G L 407 le club des patriots de Montauban.

He had begun his working life as an apprentice in his father's carpentry shop. When he married in 1771, he and his wife contracted to live "at the same pot and hearth" with his parents and to share the work and the profits and losses of the family business with them. For sixteen years, until his father's death, the two couples lived and worked together. Only upon his father's death did Saint-Araille cease to be Gasc *fils* and become Gasc *père*. Only on his father's death, too, did he gain control of the family business and the capital with which to begin the innkeeping venture that would make his sons wealthy. For Saint-Araille, as for most artisans and shopkeepers, the property of the business and the property of the family, be it capital or contacts or labor, were one and the same. Work, property, and family formed one intricate pattern.[3]

The 1802 inventory of the estate of Raymond Mouméja demonstrates the degree to which family and business were materially inseparable. Raymond Mouméja was a gardener, but his sons were craftsmen, members of a large clan of Protestant gardeners, and artisans in Montauban's Lacapelle district. Three months before his death in 1802, Raymond estimated that his property, consisting of a small garden and a large house, was worth ten thousand francs. Two thirds of the house was rented out while the family lived in the remaining wing. Their apartment had on the ground floor a bakery shop operated by the eldest son, Pierre, a kitchen rented to a tavern keeper, and three sheds built onto the back of the building. On the second floor were two rooms where the family lived. The second-hand dealers who conducted the inventory estimated the worth of Raymond's furniture at six hundred francs. Raymond had helped his son furnish the bakery by providing a cauldron, several pots, a candlestick, a lamp, assorted tin spoons and forks, eight chairs, and two folding tables plus Pierre's bed and linens. Probably because the tenant furnished the kitchen, Raymond's possessions there were limited to two spits and their weights and chains, a table, and some dishes. The main room on the second floor contained a large bed, two wardrobes of clothes and linens, two tables with cane-seated chairs, a buffet holding tin plates, a couple of irons, and a branched candlestick. Fire irons, pothooks, a salt box, a frying pan, a copper pot, and a kettle equipped the hearth. The second room held only two beds with inexpensive fittings. Above were attics used for storage—two half-barrels of vinegar, old furniture, and a trunk. The sheds contained Ray-

---

[3] AD T-et-G 5E 1991 Garrigues no. 404 15–11–1771 contrat de mariage Gasc-Debia; 1995 Garrigues no. 315 22–5–1775 codicile Gasc; 2007 Garrigues no. 507 26–2–1787 accord Gasc. A month after Saint-Araille joined the Patriots' Club, so did his two sons. An uncle and three of his cousins also became members, although neither his father-in-law nor his brothers-in-law joined. AM Mont L 385 Société des Amis de la Constitution and L 407 le club des patriots. See Sonenscher, *Hatters*, pp. 3–11, for a discussion of the implications of the notion of labor as property to eighteenth-century craftsmen.

mond's wine-making equipment, some old furniture, a shotgun, and a salting tub.[4]

Despite the value of Raymond's estate, the Mouméjas' standard of living was not luxurious. First, there was no mention of gold or silver, no upholstered furniture, no mirrors, rugs, tapestries, or books. Even the cooking utensils were meager, and although these were supplemented by his widow's possession, her entire estate, worth only two hundred francs, could not have made an appreciable difference.[5] Second, although the house was commodious, a good portion of it was taken up with business and storage. Raymond rented out one whole room and allotted a second to Pierre's bakery shop. The property of the artisan family, even its residence, was devoted to business.

The head of the family business was more than simply the owner of its property; he was also its master. Mastership, and especially membership in a guild, signified recognition of mastery of a craft or trade. Like the magistrate's office or the *négociant*'s trading company, mastership gave a man an official place in society, a place of public authority and trust. Mastership turned mere property into patrimony and the owner of a small business into something like a trustee. For although technically the owner of the business and its assets—equipment, materials, stocks, credit, real estate—the artisan or retailer was constrained in the use and disposition of this property by the regulations of his trade and by his ideas of the family. The family business, as patrimony, belonged not only to him in the present but to his heirs in the future.[6]

The small business supported the artisan's family but also shaped the family's organization and internal dynamics. Unlike Montauban's merchants who cushioned their families from the vicissitudes of commerce with noncommercial alliances and investments, the resources of artisan and shopkeeper families were totally bound up in the family business. Most of the capital was immobilized in work space, equipment, and materials. Major expenditures, whether to expand the business or to pay off noninheriting children, burdened the business with debts. Anything that touched the health or direction of the business soon had repercussions in the family. The loss of a few good customers or the closing of a market jeopardized the survival of both the business and the family. This intimate

---

[4] AM Mont 10 HH 1 dénombrement Villebourbon 1774; AD T-et-G 5E 1973 Latreille-Olivié no. 104 17 brumaire Year 10 contrat de mariage Mouméja-Mouméja; 1975 Latreille-Olivié no. 524 20 ventôse Year 11 partage Mouméja; 2143 Latreille-Olivié no. 287 27–7–1815 achât Saligné ép Pujol; 2131 Latreille-Olivié sn 16 fructidor Year 10 accord Mouméja.

[5] AD T-et-G 5E 2150 Latreille-Olivié no. 149 26–3–1821 vente Mouméja.

[6] Sewell, *Work and Revolution in France*, pp. 117–119. Steven Laurence Kaplan, "Social Classifications and Representation in the Corporate World of Eighteenth Century France: Turgot's 'Carnival,' " in Kaplan and Koepp, eds., *Work in France*, pp. 182–183, Sonenscher, "Journeymen, the Courts and French Trades," p. 83.

connection made artisanal families particularly responsive to economic change, whether it was the upsurge of the textile industry in the eighteenth century or its subsequent collapse in the early nineteenth century.

Artisans did what they could to reduce the risks. They demanded that competition be controlled and markets be protected, and they tried to enforce guild regulations on the merchant-manufacturers upon whom many of them depended for work. But the core of artisans' business strategy was a family strategy. They protected the family business by refusing to acknowledge the claims of their noninheriting children and of their wives. Since they could not, like the merchants, expand the business to embrace all their sons, they tried to reduce the family to a size and a structure compatible with the resources of the business.

The Revolution disrupted the organization of artisan businesses and families in three important ways. First, it abolished the albeit rather feeble but still cherished craftsmen's guilds. Second, and even more important, was the collapse of Montauban's export industry at the turn of the century. Both developments threatened the businesses around which artisans' families revolved. Third, the enactment of mandatory equal inheritance attacked family organization directly by lessening the artisan's ability to adjust the claims of his dependents to the resources of the family business. The aggregate of all three trends resulted in the absorption of some artisans, especially textile artisans, into the ranks of the working poor and the transformation of artisan family strategies. Whereas in the eighteenth century Montauban's artisanal families had approximated the concerns and inheritance patterns of the propertied elite, in the early nineteenth century their family strategies were more analogous to the survival strategies of the working poor (see table 3–7).

Artisans and shopkeepers were a large and active force in the daily life of the city. With their families, they numbered about fifty-five hundred Montaubaners in the 1780s, or 20 percent of the city's population.[7] And with their families they produced and sold most of the city's goods from the ordinary staples of bread, shoes, and sheets to the luxuries of chiming clocks and silk judicial robes. Although geographically close to Toulouse and commercially intimate with Bordeaux, Montauban had a full complement of craft and retail shops which served the local population, the surrounding countryside, and produced and processed grain and textiles for export.

All these different craftsmen and retailers did not operate or conceive of themselves as a single group. First, as table 5–1 shows, their work was extremely varied. So was their wealth, ranging from the likes of master cooper Antoine Garrigues, who, when his daughter married in 1782,

---

[7] AM Mont 5 CC 9 capitation 1788.

TABLE 5–1
Occupation of Artisans Who Made Wills, 1775–1793

N = 86			
Weaver	10	Fuller	1
Shoemaker	9	Stocking knitter	1
Retailer	9	Wig maker	1
Cloth shearer	5	Innkeeper	1
Carpenter	5	Stonecutter	1
Baker	4	Mason	1
Cloth dresser	3	Tiler	1
Saddler	3	Chandler	1
Wineshop keeper	3	Wheelwright	1
Apothecary	3	Locksmith	1
Tailor	3	Loom builder	1
Cabinetmaker	2	Goldsmith	1
Cooper	2	Miller	1
Tanner	2	Surgeon	1
Ironsmith	2	Boat master	1
Jeweler	2	Carter	1
Cookshop keeper	2	Butcher	1

could give her only thirty livres, to Pierre Terrens, a master pastry chef who, two years earlier, had endowed his daughter with four thousand livres. (see table 4–1).[8] Artisans and retailers were geographically dispersed as well, unlike the closely knit communities of merchants and professional elite (see table 2–1). Some trades concentrated in a few locales, such as the cloth shearers and the boat masters in Villebourbon, but others, like wineshop keepers, shoemakers, and bakers, were scattered all over the city.

Although officially all the *arts et metiers* practiced in Montauban were organized into guilds, in practice many of the corps had never been organized or had ceased to function. The clerk who drew up a list of the corporations in 1756 indicated with marginal notes that twenty of the seventy-four corps did not exist. These included upholsterers, tilers, tinkers, and wool combers. In the weakness of its guilds, Montauban was a typical southern city. Corporate regulation had come late to the south; most guilds dated only from the late seventeenth or early eighteenth cen-

---

[8] AD T-et-G 5E 10869 Grelleau no. 259 16–5–1780 contrat de mariage Bouquet-Terrens. Dlle Terrens married a merchant, son of a Sarlat bourgeois. 5E 12871 Grelleau no. 222 24–5–1782 contrat de mariage Habart-Garrigues, Garrigues's son-in-law to be was a *maître ès arts* with only fifteen livres to his name. Eighteen artisanal households (5 percent) in the Villebourbon census AM Mont 10 HH 1 were noted as *pauvres*. See also Sewell, *Work and Revolution in France*, pp. 20–22, and Cerutti, "Du corps au Métier," pp. 331–340.

tury, when they had been formed in concordance with Colbertian economic policy.[9] And by the second half of the century, many of these guilds were disintegrating due to lack of participation and crippling debts. The Tailors' Guild, for example, issued repeated notices from the 1750s on, condemning its members for neglect of duty and enjoining them to attend the guild's meetings, funerals, and church services on pain of fines.[10] The Bakers' Guild withered under a debt of 1,320 livres contracted in 1745 to purchase an inspectorship so that no outsider could meddle in its affairs. In 1759 the bakers had to borrow 650 more livres to pay a surcharge on the price of this office. Both debts were still running when guilds were abolished in 1791. In the meantime, the number of masters had dwindled because the guild required "aspiring masters" to sign an agreement to pay a prorated share in the debt's liquidation. In 1792, this share came to 240 livres apiece.[11]

Textile production in Montauban was virtually a "free industry," that is, it was run by the Merchants' Corporation and the government inspectors without the intervention of craftsmen's guilds.[12] In the seventeenth century, before woolen cloth came to dominate Montauban's economy, there had been only one guild of textile artisans, the linen weavers. When the woolen industry began to grow, textile workers became more specialized and sought to protect their particular "art" and share in the market with corporate privileges. The Merchants' Corporation successfully opposed these efforts, even branding the *sargeurs* (wool weavers) crypto-Protestants in order to prejudice the royal government against them.[13] By the early eighteenth century, workers involved in the preparatory processes of carding and combing wool had lost all status as independent artisans, and by the middle of the century, the *sargeurs* had suffered the same fate. They rarely used the title *maître*; nor did they often formally apprentice helpers.[14]

[9] Coornaert, *Les Corporations*, p. 26; Thomson, *Clermont-de-Lodève*, pp. 244–245.

[10] AM Mont AA 10 Livre gris 1752–1774, pp. 52–54, 324–325. Castan, *Les Criminels de Languedoc*, pp. 256–258.

[11] AM Mont 8 HH 1 boulangers.

[12] This was also the case in other textile towns. See Thomson, *Clermont-de-Lodève*, pp. 318–328, and Garden, *Lyon et les lyonnais*, pp. 181–183.

[13] Toujas, "Vie des apprentis," 2: 335–337, 344–345. AN F[12] 776 Mémoire 30–4–1728 summed up the merchants and manufacturers' objections to the incorporation of *sargeurs*. It cited a precedent—the *sargeurs* had been denied letters patent three times in the past—and the good of the industry, and called attention to one article of the *sargeurs'* proposed statutes, which included *nouveau convertis*, that is, Protestants, among the guild's officers. This, said the Merchants' Corporation, many of whom were themselves very "newly converted," was an act of rebellion against the Crown and an attempt to reintroduce heresy in France.

[14] In a sample of twenty-eight apprenticeship contracts from 1779 to 1788, three *peigneurs*, two *cardeurs*, and two *sargeurs* apprenticed their sons—two to shoemakers, two to stocking knitters, and one each to a plasterer, a cloth shearer, and a potter—but no one was apprenticed to a *peigneur, cardeur*, or *sargeur*. AM Mont 10 HH 1, the 1774 census of

The growth of a cottage industry in the production of unfinished common cloth, which the Merchants' Corporation did little to regulate, was the main reason for Montauban's textile workers' loss of autonomy. Carders, combers, spinners, and weavers came into competition with part-time peasants who could produce ordinary cloth more cheaply because of their other sources of income. The only way to earn a living as a textile producer in Montauban was to work on fine cloth as an employee or subcontractor of one of the manufacturers.[15]

The story of the craftsmen involved in the finishing processes—cloth shearers, fullers, and dressers—was somewhat different, although by the end of the century it was heading toward the same conclusion. Early in the century, the Merchants' Corporation had managed to frustrate their attempts to gain official recognition, but the cloth shearers did finally register their corporation in 1752. However, in the chaotic state of the industry following the Seven Years' War and the growing government partiality to free trade, the Cloth Shearers' Guild had difficulty persuading the manufacturers to abide by their statutes or the government inspector to enforce them.[16] In particular, the guild could not control the number of apprentices accepted for training in the large *fabriques* for which many of their members also worked. These "apprentices" were in fact wage laborers rather than cloth-shearers-in-training.[17]

It is doubtful, however, that a stronger corporate structure would have provided a sense of unity to Montauban's craftsmen and shopkeepers since

---

Villebourbon, the center of Montauban's textile industry, listed only 1 *garçon cardeur* for 115 carders and only 7 *garçon sargeurs* for 45 *sargeurs*. There were, by contrast, 3 apprentice stocking knitters for 11 stocking knitters, 5 apprentice shoemakers for 5 shoemakers, 15 apprentice dyers for 14 merchant-dyers, and 55 apprentice cloth shearers for 49 cloth shearers.

[15] Ombret et al., *Montauban, cité drapière*, p. F1; AM Mont 8 HH 7 manufacture 1754–1785. Arthur Young observed the extent of the cottage industry around Caussade and also noted the competiton between town and country in textile production for Montauban's export trade. *Travels* (1794 edition), 1: 542.

[16] Forestié, *Fabrication des draps*, p. 14; AM Mont 8 HH 7 manufacturers 1754–1785. Similar difficulties beset the Cloth Shearers' Guild of Clermont-de-Lodève, where royal edicts gave the manufacturers the right to do their own finishing despite the guild's legal monopoly. Thomson, *Clermont-de-Lodève*, p. 327. See Cynthia M. Truant, "Independent and Insolent: Journeymen and Their 'Rites' in the Old Regime Workplace," in Kaplan and Koepp, eds., *Work in France*, pp. 139–141, and Sonenscher, "Journeymen, the Courts and French Trades," pp. 100–105, regarding the relaxation of enforcement of guild regulations after 1750 by both government officials and the courts.

[17] Coornaert, *Les Corporations*, p. 195. AM Mont 10 HH 1 dénombrement Villebourbon 1774 recorded fifty-five *garçon tondeurs* of whom only seven lived with masters. The remaining forty-eight lived in their own households, many with wives and children. They were, in fact, textile workers like their *cardeur* and *sargeur* neighbors. Proletarianization was the common lot of French textile artisans in the second half of the eighteenth century. See Deyon, "La Production textile à Amiens," pp. 201–211; Reddy, "The Textile Trade," pp. 62–89; and Trénard, "The Social Crisis in Lyon," pp. 68–100.

many of the strong and active corporations devoted their energies to ceaseless struggles with other artisans. The Tailors' Guild spent large sums to drive seamstresses out of business, whereas litigation between shoemakers and cobblers was a permanent source of income to the local legal profession. Denied legal status, the two rival journeymen's organizations, the Compagnons du Dévoir and the Gavots, fought their fratricidal battles in the streets with cudgels and knives. Government action to resolve or repress these disputes was rarely successful.[18]

And guilds themselves were rarely unified. Although imagined as brotherhoods, corporations were hierarchically structured, with journeymen as postulants at the bottom and a small and often closed circle of guild officers at the top. Between them were the mass of master artisans, who, although legally full members of the guild and admitted to its privileges, were often excluded from governance. Many of the revisions of guild statutes in the eighteenth century resulted from long and acrimonious campaigns by militant minorities of masters to muscle their way into the inner circle. Sometimes they forced the revision of statutes in a democratic direction; if they failed, the elite was in a position to institute more exclusive policies.[19]

Perhaps the most important reason for the disunity among artisans was the increasing difficulty of the climb up the hierarchy of the crafts from apprenticeship to mastership. Corporate discourse—in apprenticeship contracts, for example—was familial and paternalistic. Just as a son was to grow up in the family under his father's authority, marry with his father's consent, and become a father in his own right, so too was an apprentice to grow and learn within the corporation under the masters' supervision and authority until he was admitted to mastership with their consent. In fact, the two developments were synchronized, because marriage and *maîtrise*

[18] AM Mont AA 10 Livre gris, 1752–1774; AA 11 Livre rouge neuf, 1775–1790; 7 HH 2 –7 HH 5 corporations; 6 FF 47 dossiers des procédures consulaires 1776. In 1775, the king, in recognition of "the many disputes that continually arise between the two communities and the exorbitant debts they have contracted because of these disputes," ordered the shoemakers and the cobblers to amalgamate. The shoemakers resisted this order, continuing to function as a separate guild. AM Mont AA 11 Livre rouge neuf, 2–9–1775 Lettres patentes; 7 HH 2 cordonniers et savetiers. Intertrade warfare was ubiquitous in the eighteenth century. See Sewell, *Work and Revolution in France*, pp. 27–29. Under pressure from the intendant and from the Joiners' Guild, Montauban's municipal government repeatedly issued ordinances against journeymen's organizations although by their own admission these had little effect. AM Mont 7 HH 3 menuisiers; 7 HH 5 corporations. The rivalry between these two sects of journeymen joiners also erupted in violence in Nantes in the 1780s. See Truant, "Independent and Insolent," p. 155.

[19] Kaplan, "The Character and Implications of Strife Among the Masters," pp. 631–647. In Montauban, the leading example of such strife was the Manufacturers' Corporation, in which the presence of two royal manufacturers exacerbated the friction. AM Mont 8 HH 7 manufacture; Forestié, *Fabrication des draps*, pp. 30–31.

were often assumed to go together; many guilds forbade apprentices to marry. In the last half of the eighteenth century, however, the analogy of guild to patriarchal family was a fiction, used by the masters to assert their authority over workers and to deny them more rights than those of a dependent *fils de famille*.[20] Throughout the eighteenth century the statutes of many guilds became more restrictive, increasing the price of a *maîtrise*, raising the requirements of a chef d'oeuvre, or limiting access to mastership to the sons and sons-in-law of masters. Some guilds severely reduced the number of formal apprenticeships and filled their labor needs by hiring helpers. Others, like the cloth shearers, multiplied the number of apprentices. Both practices created a large number of workers who would never be permitted to "grow up" to be masters.[21]

The increasing exclusiveness of guilds in the late eighteenth century both responded to and accelerated the growth of production and sale of goods outside corporate regulation. In trying to impose their monopoly privileges, many of them of fairly recent origin, guilds revised their statutes over and over to plug loopholes and tighten their grasp. Montauban's Tailors' Guild, for example, revised its statutes in 1756 and then again in 1764, the second revision expressly to prohibit "apprentices who have left their masters and anyone else to do any work of master tailoring in Montauban and its faubourgs, be it in a workshop or a home, if he is not received into the corps" on pain of a six livres' fine and confiscation of his work. However, the battle was not merely with such unauthorized workers, called *chambrelans*, but with the guild's own members who employed

[20] Coornaert, *Les Corporations*, p. 198; Toujas, "Vie des apprentis," pp. 339–340; Kaplow, *Names of Kings*, pp. 34–35; Sewell, *Work and Revolution in France*, pp. 31–32; Sonenscher, *Hatters*, pp. 46–47; and "Journeymen's Migrations and Workshop Organization in Eighteenth Century France," in Kaplan and Koepp, eds., *Work in France*, p. 76. Defending themselves against Turgot's reforms, corporations lauded the master's paternalistic authority and its superiority to the "brutal" regime of police and law. Kaplan, "Social Classification and Representation in the Corporate World," pp. 190–193.

[21] Sewell, *Work and Revolution in France*, pp. 31–32; Kaplow, *Names of Kings*, p. 36; Mitteraurer and Sieder, *The European Family*, pp. 107–109; Castan, *Criminels de Languedoc*, p. 259; Farge, *La Vie fragile*, pp. 127–131; Garden, *Lyon et les lyonnais*, pp. 189–191. AM Mont AA 10 Livre gris 1752–1774, pp. 324–325; AD T-et-G 5E 2001 Garrigues no. 523 16–7–1783 accord records an out-of-court settlement between four would-be master shoemakers and the Shoemakers' Guild. The four requested admission into the guild in 1774. After long delays they finally were permitted to submit their chef d'oeuvres in 1781. Two years later, they had still not been accepted; the guild kept creating new hoops for them to jump through and new fees to pay. Finally they sued the guild for admission. However, greater exclusiveness was not the general trend everywhere. Where economies were local and stable or expanding gradually, guilds continued to admit new members. See Edward J. Shephard, Jr., "Social and Geographic Mobility of the Eighteenth-Century Guild Artisan: An Analysis of Guild Receptions in Dijon, 1700–1790," in Kaplan and Koepp, eds., *Work in France*, pp. 97–130.

chambrelans or subcontracted work to them. The guild was unwilling or unable to discipline its own members; in 1774 some masters petitioned that the police be required to enforce this statute because the corporation's bailiffs were ineffective.[22]

As opportunities increased for journeymen to earn a living outside corporate authority, masters complained of their workers' "infidelity" and "rebelliousness."[23] Both terms derived from the paternal model of their relationship, which, if it ever had been applicable, was no longer. The situation was particularly "unnatural" in the joiners' trade, where, according to the Joiners' Guild, illicit journeymen's organizations had acquired the upper hand. "Under the outer pretence of a pious Devotion or Confraternity, [the journeymen assemble] to appoint judges to execute their pretended rules by acts of violence, to make themselves the masters of the price, conditions, and hours of work, and the quality and quantity of food and to deprive Masters who displease them of journeymen."[24] Although no such *compagnonnage* existed in the textile industry, in 1785 a group of cloth shearers' apprentices had the effrontery to report their employers to the royal inspector for making cloth that did not conform to the government standards.[25]

From the 1770s on, the Merchants' Corporation alternately grumbled and thundered about the "infidelity" of their workers until during the Revolution they finally obtained the legal control they sought. A new manufacturing code enacted in 1803 forbade workers to leave their masters without a written release assuring that their contract had been fulfilled and their debts paid. However, this law immediately ran into the problems that had bedeviled the tailors' attempts to eliminate the *chambrelans;* it

[22] AM Mont AA10 Livre gris, 1752–1774, pp. 324–325. See also Kaplan, "Les Corporations, les 'faux ouvriers' et la Faubourg Saint-Antoine."

[23] Kaplan, "Les Corporations, les 'faux ouvriers' et le Faubourg Saint-Antoine," p. 354. In the second half of the eighteenth century and especially after Turgot's abortive reforms, conflict between masters and journeymen became endemic in many French cities. See Kaplan, "Social Classification and Representation in the Corporate World," Truant, "Independent and Insolent," and Sonenscher, "Journeymen, the Courts and French Trades."

[24] AM Mont 7 HH 3 menuisiers. Sewell, *Work and Revolution in France*, pp. 40–61. It was a common tactic among employers to paint journeymen's confraternities and *compagnonnage* activities with the same brush, attempting to condemn the legal existence of the first by linking it to the illegal existence of the second. However, as David Garrioch and Michael Sonenscher have pointed out, the two were quite different organizations even though they may have shared some members. "Compagnonnnages, Confraternities and Associations of Journeymen," pp. 25–30.

[25] AM Mont 8 HH 7 manufactures 1754–1785. In Lyons, silk workers had organized mutual aid societies similar to confraternities which would later be the seed of political organization. See Garden, *Lyon et les lyonnais*, p. 328, and Louis Trénard, "The Social Crisis in Lyon on the Eve of the French Revolution," trans. Jeffry Kaplow, in Kaplow, ed., *New Prespectives on the French Revolution* (New York: John Wiley and Sons 1965), pp. 68–100.

required the adherence of the manufacturers and masters who, as suit after suit demonstrated, were often disposed to disregard it. For example, Fabré, a foreman for the manufacturing firm of Depuntis et Raby, brought suit against *sargeur* Raymond Laflorentie for having illegally left his employ to work for another manufacturer, Lamothe, who had given him a substantial advance. The court ruled that Laflorentie was to refund Lamothe's money and return to Fabré to complete his contract. Instead, Laflorentie found employment as a bargeman and left town. Both Lamothe and the boat master had connived at Laflorentie's dereliction, yet neither was prosecuted. After an initial spate of litigation, employers ceased to file suits under this law. They recognized, perhaps, that after they themselves had undermined the "natural" patriarchal relationship of master to worker, they could not impose it artificially either on their workers or on themselves.[26]

The portrait of the artisan family painted by contemporaries like Restif de la Bretonne and Jacques-Louis Ménétra bears a great resemblance to the idealized guild in which patriarchal authority reigned benignly over fraternal harmony. Ménétra contrasted the family and workshop in the provinces where mutuality still held sway with the Parisian world of corruption and competition that he inhabited. In the provinces, the Golden Age of corporate democracy still obtained; the master/father supervised both family and business with the active collaboration of his wife and the willing cooperation of his sons, apprentices, and journeymen who would, in time, inherit or replicate both his business and his family.[27]

Although the evidence of *Sturm und Drang* in eighteenth-century manufacturing has redrawn this picture of artisanal labor relations, family relations have remained enveloped in the ideology of solidarity—one for all and all for one, the one being the patriarch.[28] Yet, just as corporate solidarity was built over exclusion and conflict, so was domestic solidarity. For example, among the Latreille millers near Sapiacou mill lived the widow of miller Antoine Latreille and her two daughters, who worked for their living as spinners. They were the remnants of an artisan's family who

[26] AM Mont 8 i 3 tribunal de police 1791 Year 3.

[27] See Restif de la Bretonne, *Monsieur Nicolas*, and Ménétra, *Journal of My Life*. Also Daniel Roche, "Work, Fellowship and Some Economic Realities of Eighteenth-Century France," in Kaplan and Koepp, eds., *Work in France*, pp. 54–73.

[28] Babeau, in *Les Artisans*, pp. 77–78, 166–167, 177–187, 216–218, and 229, wrote movingly of the harmony and hard work that bound together eighteenth-century artisanal families. Both Strumingher, "The Artisan Family," pp. 214–215, and Tilly and Scott, *Women, Work and Family*, pp. 21–22, concur, although in less nostalgic language. One dissenter is Lawrence Stone, who labels eighteenth-century child rearing in British artisan families "brutal but careful." However, he too emphasizes the companionship and economic solidarity of husband and wife. *The Family, Sex and Marriage*, pp. 362–367, 468–469.

had been plunged into the ranks of the working poor. Neither corporate nor familial solidarity had protected them.[29]

Saint-Araille's family history indicates how this could have happened. When Louis Saint-Araille married, he, his parents, and his two sisters, Marguérite and Perrette, were living together in the Gasseras district of Villebourbon. Shortly thereafter Marguérite married a locksmith and moved to Mas Grenier, a country town about twenty kilometers away. Six years later, Perrette married a law clerk and moved across the river to Montauban's city center. Saint-Araille was the only child to remain in the household and the only one to remain in Gasseras. Moreover, the separation between brother and sisters was not purely geographic. In 1787, Marguérite sued Saint-Araille for an increase in her dowry. Her later donations and wills further illustrate the divisions between sisters and brother. In 1809 she gave Perrette all of her real property in Mas Grenier—two houses, a shop, a stable, a pigeon coop, and fields worth four thousand francs—in return for care in sickness and health. She followed this gift by a will leaving her brother's two sons five hundred francs apiece, not payable until seven years after her death, and making Perrette her heir. On her deathbed in 1815, Marguérite made a second will again appointing her sister as her heir but replacing Louis's sons with Perrette's grandson, whom she left one thousand francs. She did not mention her brother or his sons, not even to leave them the traditional five sous.[30]

Solidarity and continuity were one side of Saint-Araille's family, separation and conflict the other. Saint-Araille's marriage contract expressed both by regulating the composition of the household and the work force of the family business and by allocating the patrimony. Saint-Araille with his future wife and children were embraced within the household and the business. Saint-Araille was named heir to all his father's goods. The contract set aside only one thousand livres in cash and five hundred livres in furniture to endow each sister. Obviously their parents expected them to marry and leave home. The contract made no provision at all for Saint-Araille's mother should she be left a widow; presumably, like his future wife when Saint-Araille died, she could reclaim her dowry.[31]

There were many reasons that one family might be closely knit whereas another was strife-torn. Temperament was certainly important; Saint-

---

[29] AM Mont 10 HH 1 dénombrement Villebourbon 1774.

[30] AD T-et-G 5E 1991 Garrigues no. 404 15–11–1771 contrat de mariage Gasc-Debia and no. 412 6–11–1771 contrat de mariage Pradel-Gasc; 1996 Garrigues no. 175 22–3–1777 contrat de mariage Begué-Gasc and no. 366 10–7–1778 codicile Gasc; 2007 Garrigues no. 507 26–6–1787 accord Gasc; 2135 Latreille-Olivié no. 131 17–2–1809 donation Gasc vᶜ Pradel and no. 141 19–2–1809 testament Gasc vᶜ Pradel; 2143 Latreille-Olivié no. 305 27–8–1815 testament Gasc vᶜ Pradel.

[31] AD T-et-G 5E 1991 Garrigues no. 404 15–11–1771 contrat de mariage Gasc-Debia.

Araille's ambition, and perhaps his revolutionary activism as well, set him apart from his sisters and their husbands. Demographic accident could also have effects. Saint-Araille was considerably older than his sisters, and he had no surviving brother to whom he might have felt closer. Nonetheless, the material conditions of survival in an artisanal or retail trade also weighed in the balance. The nature of the patrimony—the small family business—made certain kinds of family dynamics more likely than others.

Before the Revolution, many of Montauban's artisans and retailers were small independent operators who owned their own homes, workshops, and tools, hired their own workmen—rarely more than four or five—and produced for a relatively small, static market such as the immediate neighborhood or the city's few luxury consumers.[32] Such a business could be shared or perhaps expanded but it could not be divided. Consider Saint-Araille's estate, the result of an unusually successful career. He could (and did) divide it into two portions—a house, a lumberyard, and a warehouse in one lot, the inn, stables, garden, and pasture in the other—because he had two businesses.[33] But each was in itself indivisible. The inn without the stables and pasture would not be viable, nor would the lumberyard without the warehouse. In families that owned businesses like this, the values of cohesion and continuity contradicted each other in the same way as lineage and patriarchy did in elite families. For the family business to survive as an ongoing concern, it was usually entrusted to one heir while the claims of other household members, family as well as apprentices and other employees, were strictly limited.

There was another variety of artisanal business that was more conducive to family coherence than that of the small independent producer or retailer. Among the *chambrelans* prevalent in shoemaking and tailoring and among artisans in the textile industry, the family business was merely an assortment of skills and contacts that secured regular employment. Shoemakers, cloth shearers, even weavers, invested little capital in their work. Their tools were relatively inexpensive; sometimes they were leased from their employers.[34] Many of these artisans worked in the rented rooms where they lived or else in large workshops owned by the manufacturers. The markets for which they produced, especially in the textile industry, were elastic. They could expand to employ the labor of the whole family and they could contract suddenly to throw everyone out of work simultaneously. In such circumstances, it made no sense to try to protect the family business by excluding some family members from it. Instead, whole

---

[32] Forty percent of the purchases of urban realty in the years before the Revolution were made by artisans, attesting to their status and activity as property owners. Compared with other occupation groups, significance level = .01, contingency coefficient = .415.

[33] AD T-et-G 5E 2150 Latreille-Olivié no. 304 20–7–1821 partage Gasc.

[34] Thomson, *Clermont-de-Lodève*, pp. 316–317.

families worked in the same or related trades and often lived in close proximity. All the sons followed their father into the same trade; daughters, also trained in the craft, married other practitioners. The René family of weavers is a good example. On one side of Villebourbon's main street lived the eldest brother with his wife and four children. Across the street lived his two younger brothers, both weavers as well. One lived with his wife and five children plus a woman employed to help spin because his daughters were young; the other was single and "working with his sister," a weaver in her own right and also widow of a weaver. An even greater clannishness existed in the loom-making business. There were a dozen loom makers in Villebourbon in 1774 and at least eleven of them were closely related. They included three Bourel brothers and the widow of the fourth brother, whose eldest son was also a loom maker, three Prat brothers plus two sons of the eldest of them, and the two Roques, father and son. All three families were linked by marriage and all lived clustered in a few blocks.[35] These families achieved both craft continuity and family cohesion, although the secure niche of the independent family business was missing. All of them were directly dependent on the merchant-manufacturers and Montauban's export trade. Although these were families of skilled craftsmen, very little separated them, in either work or family experience, from the working poor.

A shopkeeper or master artisan, even if he were only a subcontractor or employee of a manufacturer, was the head of both the family business and the household. And just as a patriarch could not and did not share his authority over the family, neither did a master artisan or shopkeeper share his command of the family business. Although commercial partnerships and associations were common among Montauban merchants, business associations were rare among artisans. Formal associations of father and son or son-in-law were uncommon and tended to be short-lived. One example was the society of Negre *père et fils aîné*, wagoners, which, formed in April 1791, collapsed in March 1792 when Negre *père* withdrew his investment of two wagons, five horses, and a mule, the society's main capital, leaving his son with debts. Partnerships between other kin were even less common and perhaps even more prone to acrimonious dissolution.[36] Most business associations between artisans and shopkeepers were

---

[35] AM Mont 10 HH 1 dénombrement Villebourbon 1774. There were also kin clusters of cloth shearers, masons, and boat masters. Simona Cerutti found similar residence patterns in the tailoring trade in Turin. See "Du corps au métier," pp. 326–328.

[36] In a sample of twenty-eight apprenticeship contracts from 1779 to 1788, only three involved partnerships of masters, a father and son who were tailors, two brothers-in-law who were potters, and two apparently unrelated plasterers. See AD T-et-G 5E 12871 Grelleau no. 356 11–8–1782 apprentissage Requiers à Charles père et fils, 2009 Garrigues no. 284 28–7–1788 apprentissage Lespinet à Feral et Rebouille, beaufrères and 2083 Franceries no. 334 8–6–1779 apprentissage L'hoste à Mathaly et Delport. See also AD T-et-G 1 U 369 tribunal

short-term and informal. For example, several sabot makers might jointly purchase a load of wood or lend each other tools or workmen. Brothers provided surety for loans, brothers-in-law rented property together, or a sister-in-law invested her inheritance in the family business, but none of these agreements created an extensive network of family and business connections.[37]

Nor did most master artisans or retailers retire. Only textile artisans—*fabriquants* and cloth shearers, in particular—showed any disposition to retire, and probably this was not by choice but because merchant-manufacturers ceased to give them orders. Even in old age, blind or incapacitated, the master artisan retained the ownership of the business and his position as head of the household. Very few elderly artisans appeared in the census or in their wills as dependents in someone else's household.[38]

Although the master artisan or retailer was the head of the family business, he was rarely the only person employed in it. In many trades, the whole household—wife, children, apprentices, servants, even grandparents and orphaned nieces—worked in the family business. As a result, most artisans and retailers ruled over larger than average households. Few artisans lived by themselves or with only a wife, sibling, or servant because the work of only one or two people was insufficient to carry on most businesses. Nearly three quarters of Villebourbon's artisan households were composed of husband and wife and two or three children. Fourteen percent included an apprentice or two as well, and 10 percent housed extra kin, especially siblings, siblings' children, and grandchildren, many of whom were also employed in the family business.

In some family businesses, the work of women was essential, particularly in textile production. A weaver, for example, needed several spinners to keep him supplied with yarn. If the family could not supply enough female labor, he had to hire servants to spin for him. In the households of

---

correctionnel 29 fructidor Year 9; 5E 1949 Caminel no. 160 15–3–1792 dissolution Negre père et fils ainé. Similarly, 5E 13179 Deray no. 514 10–12–1784 accord Mouméja père et fils and 17173 Deray no. 474 11–9–1781 transaction Prat père et fils. An exception is 5E 2153 Latreille Olivié no. 128 1–5–1824 dissolution Larroque père et fils of a society of wheelwrights that had lasted twenty-three years.

[37] Garrioch, *Neighbourhood and Community in Paris*, pp. 101–102, and Garden, *Lyon et les lyonnais*, p. 279; AD T-et-G 5E 12853 Grelleau no. 270 30–5–1768 quittance Mouméja à Acquié; 12882 Grelleau no. 564 6–9–1791 quittance Faure à Mouméja; 12897 Grelleau no. 527 14 messidor Year 11 quittance Py à Mouméja; 12851 Grelleau no. 706 30–9–1765 bail à ferme Delpech à Malfre et Gasc; 10872 Martin no. 371 2–6–1783 partage Durand frère et soeur; AD T-et-G L 324 tribunal de commerce.

[38] Only thirteen testators reported that they lived in someone else's household. Five of these were young men making their wills on the eve of departure for the military. In the Villebourbon census, there was only one widower living in his offspring's household. By contrast, widowers headed 8 percent of artisan households. AM Mont 10 HH 1 dénombrement Villebourbon 1774.

Table 5–2
Household Size in Villebourbon, 1774*

	Households		
	Workers	*Artisans*	*Merchants*
Number of individuals per household			
Range	1–9	1–11	1–14
Mean	3.3	4.1	3.9
Median	4	5	5
Percentage of individuals in households of			
1–2 members	16%	10%	13%
3–5 members	66	52	38
6+ members	18	38	49
Percentage of households with			
children	73%	70%	41%
servants	0	4	52
apprentices	1	14	8
N	551	381	103

*AM Mont 10 HH 1 dénombrement Villebourbon 1774. Census includes fifty-seven households (containing 181 individuals) for which no occupation is given.

the twenty-two weavers who lived on the Villebourbon's main street lived sixty-three women and only forty-five men. The "extra" women included widows, daughters, nieces, granddaughters, and servants. For example, Sr Presseq lived with his wife and four daughters, and Pierre Borios, a widower, lived with his five daughters; his son, the census reports, did not live at home. Sr Jean René *cadet* lived with his wife, three sons, two daughters, and a servant. His younger brother housed their widowed sister, a weaver in her own right, and her three children, all of whom must have been useful because he had no children of his own nor any servants.[39]

In other trades, women may have been less involved in production but their work was often essential to the business as a whole.[40] The master craftsman who took on apprentices depended on his wife to fulfill the part

[39] AM Mont 10 HH 1 dénombrement Villebourbon 1774.

[40] In present-day French artisanal businesses, wives and daughters are found particularly in clerical and customer service activities. They are more likely to be unsalaried than male relatives employed in the business. See Christine Jaeger, *Artisanat et Capitalism: L'Envers de la roue de l'histoire* (Paris: Payot, 1982), pp. 134–144. In the eighteenth century, it is likely that women were more often involved in production as well. Their work was often essential in preparing tools and materials and in finishing products. This was the case, for example, in hat making. See Sonenscher, *Hatters*, pp. 20–25.

of the contract that required that the apprentice be lodged and fed and that his clothes be laundered. Retailers and artisans who both produced and sold goods, like butchers, bakers, and shoemakers, all depended on wives and daughters to serve the customers. Denunciations and prosecutions for contravention of the market and price regulations during the Terror indicated that women sold while men produced. When a customer denounced a master baker, it was for making poor-quality bread, and when a butcher was charged, it was for infractions in purchasing or slaughtering animals; women were denounced for selling overpriced merchandise. They sometimes tried to evade the charge by claiming to be temporary assistants, unfamiliar with the business. For example, Marguérite St Faust, daughter of a draper, accused of charging eight francs for cloth that should have sold at six francs seven sous, pleaded "that finding herself alone [in the shop] and not knowing the Maximum, she had accepted what the said Citizeness Faure [the customer] offered." The court was not impressed with this defense because several witnesses testified that Marguérite often tended the counter. Other women, especially the wives of butchers and bakers, were charged with infractions over and over again, making it clear that the retail side of the family business was in their hands.[41]

Some adult sons also remained in the household as workers in the family business. In very small enterprises, they took the place of apprentices and journeymen. In Villebourbon in 1774, one quarter of the artisan households without children had resident apprentices, whereas only 8 percent of households had both children and apprentices. In larger businesses, sons also provided useful labor, more reliable and probably less troublesome than journeymen. To employ sons might also be less expensive than to hire workers, for while under paternal authority, they were fed and housed but not usually paid a wage. However, neither could they be so easily dismissed when work was short, and few businesses, small or large, could afford to maintain a large work force when it was not working.

Although marriage and mastership coincided in the patriarchal scheme of the small family business, in reality marriage did not always bring independence from paternal control. For example, when cloth shearer Pierre Prunetis married in 1778, his father promised to give him tools

---

[41] AM Mont 8 i 3 tribunal de police 1791 Year 3. Marie Etié, wife of Mounié, a butcher, was charged six times in Year 2, paid a total of 37 francs 11 sous and 6 deniers in fines, and spent five days in prison for using false weights, overpricing, selling mutton as lamb, and other such crimes. Also see AD T-et-G 1 U 1 tribunal correctionnel 27 nivôse and 15 thermidor Year 8; 1 U 369 tribunal correctionnel 29 fructidor Year 9; 1 U 370 tribunal correctionnel 16 fructidor Year 10 and 1 U 368 tribunal correctionnel 12 ventôse Year 8, when a suit was brought by one Villeneuve, wife of a joiner, against a shoemaker who had taken her for a prostitute in a tavern. The tavern keeper was absent; his son-in-law was getting wine from the cellar and his wife and daughter were serving customers.

worth three hundred livres, but only after Pierre had served for three years as his apprentice and only if his father was satisfied with his work after those three years. Unlike merchants, artisans did not often emancipate their sons at marriage, nor did they set them up in business. Of artisan grooms whose fathers were alive, only 12 percent were emancipated and only 18 percent received any property from their fathers, whether cash, tools, furniture, or real estate. This was even fewer than poor working men, whose fathers presumably had much less to give.[42]

Nor did artisans transfer property and authority at any other time, except after death. By law, any gift worth more than one thousand livres and any gift of real estate regardless of its worth had to be registered with the *sénéchal*. Although both the elite and the poor were frequent givers, artisan gifts were rare. In one of the few exceptions, the wealthy pastry chef Pierre Terrens emancipated his twenty-five-year-old son "in recognition of his prudence and good conduct" and gave him a house in Montauban. However, Terrens retained possession of the house until his death and stipulated that the gift was void should his son predecease either himself or his wife. The gift was no more than a guarantee of inheritance.[43]

And unlike peasant fathers, artisans did not often formally associate their sons in the family business. Although 42 percent of artisan grooms followed the same trade as their fathers, only 8 percent were taken into partnership. Even when such an association occurred, it was little more than a promise of future inheritance; it committed the son to the family business while leaving the father in control of the business. It is significant, for example, that Saint-Araille did not begin his expansion of the family business until after his father had died.[44] Most artisans, like young Terrens, had to wait until their fathers died before they could attain professional or economic independence.

[42] AD T-et-G 5E 1996 Garrigues no. 626 13–12–1778 contrat de mariage Prunetis-Gasc. In the sample of marriage contracts, 38 percent of merchants emancipated their sons, compared with 12 percent of artisans (significance level = .01, contingency coefficient = .256). Thirty-seven percent of merchants made gifts to their sons, as did 42 percent of peasants, 20 percent of working men, and 18 percent of artisans (significance level = .01, contingency coeffiecient = .230).

[43] AD T-et-G Q 406 donations no. 92 5–12–1792.

[44] For example, as half-owner of the family property, Saint-Araille should have ratified his sisters' dowries, which cost eight hundred livres more than allowed for in his contract with his father. In his sisters' marriage contracts, however, his father acted as if he were the head of the family and sole owner of its property. AD T-et-G 5E 1991 Garrigues no. 404 15–11–1771 contrat de mariage Gasc-Debia and no. 412 16–11–1771 contrat de mariage Pradel-Gasc; 1996 Garrigues no. 175 22–3–1777 contrat de mariage Begué-Gasc. Simona Cerutti found similar patterns among tailors in Turin. Very few young married tailors lived with their fathers. When young men did live at home, they were the eldest sons. Younger sons lived as apprentices in the households of other masters. "Du corps au métier," pp. 326–329.

The patriarchal control of artisan families and the family business was often more absolute and the household more isolated from kin and community than was the case in merchant families. Merchant businesses were nearly always partnerships or associations, and merchant strategies for placing and providing for children depended on a large network of cooperating kin. As a result, Montauban merchants were connected through family and business to a local, a national, and even an international commercial community. By contrast, artisan families and businesses operated, or attempted to operate, as self-sufficient units, and artisanal corporations were exclusive rather than inclusive. The tensions so evident within the artisanal working world pervaded artisans' families as well. Like the guild, the unity of family business and household simultaneously privileged some individuals and excluded others. Unity on the one hand created conflict on the other.

The central bond in the artisan household and family business was between the master and his chosen heir. The relationship between them was, like most relationships in the artisanal world, both mutual and hierarchical. Both the master and his heir were embraced within the fraternity of the artisanal corps. A spiritual bond doubled the bond of blood or alliance and the promise of property. Both were privileged practitioners of the same art and members of the same moral community; they served in the same confraternity and offered devotions to the same patron saint.[45] Yet, at the same time, the master kept his heir in submission to his authority. He promised—but rarely contracted—that if his heir served him well, he would eventually reward him. Unlike peasant fathers who legally committed themselves to their heirs in their marriage contracts, the master artisan could change his mind. He could and did use the faculté de tester to control his business and his family.

A son might chafe under this arrangement, but he rarely directly challenged it because it was so greatly in his interest to tolerate his father's rule. For, not only had he the prospect of future inheritance, he benefited from current advantages. As the heir apparent, he could attract a better-connected and better-endowed bride than could his brothers. Whereas 31 percent of all the sons of artisans married working women, the daughters of poor peasants and workers, 81 percent of artisans married the daughters of artisans and landowners (see table 5–3).[46] The solidarity of interest

---

[45] Sewell, *Work and Revolution in France*, pp. 32–36. See Reddy, *The Rise of Market Culture*, pp. 34–38, on the anti-entrepreneurial nature of corporations. See Agulhon, *Pénitents et francs-maçons*, and Garrioch and Sonenscher, "Compagnonnages, Confraternities and Associations of Journeymen," for discussions of the importance of the devotional side of corporate life.

[46] This is not an exact comparison between inheriting and noninheriting sons because artisan fathers rarely designated their heirs in their marriage contracts. It is rather a com-

between master and heir was most evident after the master's death. Then his heir emerged as his late father's champion, struggling to carry out his last wishes, which were to keep as much of the patrimony as possible in his heir's hands.

After his heir, a master artisan's wife was the person most closely associated in the family business. As with the heir, the association was informal. Before the Revolution, artisans rarely appointed their wives as their official proxies or joined them in legal business partnerships. Nonetheless, the wife's contribution to the family business was often essential. Her dowry furnished the household, and any cash she brought to the marriage was invested in the business.[47] In addition, she usually managed the household, dealt with customers, and even supervised the workshop in her husband's absence. If a master artisan died, most guilds permitted his widow to continue the business, although she could not accept apprentices, until his heir could take over.

As tacit partner, an artisan's wife operated under several disadvantages when compared with his heir. First, since few women married men with the same trades as their fathers, she was usually untrained in the family trade. And second, her formal education was inferior. The elite of both sexes was literate, the poor and the peasantry illiterate, but the "literacy line" ran right through the middle of artisan couples. Seventy percent of artisans signed their marriage contracts compared with only 25 percent of their brides. In nearly half of the artisan couples, the husband could sign his name and the wife could not.[48]

The solidarity of the artisanal couple grew in their daily commitment to the family business, but for some couples, it was rooted in their commit-

---

parison of all grooms who were sons of artisans with those grooms who were themselves artisans. I assume that the former group included both inheriting and noninheriting sons whereas the latter group included a greater number of inheriting sons.

[47] AD T-et-G 5E 2008 Garrigues no. 612 20–8–1788 contrat de mariage Graves-Rouffio specified that the dowry was to be used to buy a wig maker's license for the groom; in 10877 Martin no. 357 9–7–1788, contrat de mariage Benoit-Tayac, the dowry was to be invested in a wineshop. Since artisan grooms were often still *fils de famille*, it was common for dowries to be paid to their fathers. See, for example, 5E 2140 Latreille-Olivié no. 457 24–8–1812 contrat de mariage Capelle-Mouméja.

[48] This was the case in only 12 percent of peasant couples, 17 percent of elite couples, 25 percent of urban working couples, and 43 percent of artisan couples (significance level = .01, contingency coefficient = .621). According to the study by François Furet and Jacques Ozouf, the ability to sign one's name was a reasonably good measure of literacy in eighteenth- and nineteenth-century France. However, it was probably a better measure for men than women because female literacy was often confined to reading. See *Reading and Writing*, pp. 11–18, 25–34, 71–76. It is possible that the small percentage of artisans' brides who signed their names could both read and write, although many more could read but not write. Nonetheless, for keeping accounts, giving receipts, taking inventory, and many other tasks, the inability to write hindered a woman's full participation in the business.

ment to each other. Although economic considerations were certainly paramount in artisan marriages, they were not as restrictive as in elite families. In a city the size of Montauban, there were many more suitable matches for artisans' children than there were for the sons and daughters of the elite. Nor were their engagements distant or formal, even though they might well have been initiated by parental negotiations. When artisanal couples appeared before church magistrates in order to obtain a papal dispensation in order to marry, they emphasized the length and seriousness of their engagement, that they saw each other frequently, although always "honestly" and *en famille*, and that they knew each other well. Several applicants claimed that their attachments were unique, that they could find happiness together, and only together. Jean Louis Ligounhe, a weaver, and his first cousin Antoinette Boussarot stated that "the time they spent together and what they learned about each other formed a very tight bond of mutual inclination between them." Marie Vales, daughter of a master wig maker, was even more eloquent. Having come to know her fiancé over the past two years when he ate dinner regularly at her home, "she had been taken with such an inclination for him that she could not promise to be happy with anyone else."[49] Artisans' children could and did choose spouses whose families, character, and habits they knew well, whom they liked and respected. An artisan's wife was not his equal partner, but often she was someone he could trust. In their wills, artisans often confirmed their regard by providing for the care of their widows. Although artisans rarely named their wives to succeed them as heirs, they did acknowledge a widow's right to lifelong support by the family business (see table 5–4).[50]

Besides the artisan, his wife, and his heir, no one had rights on the patrimony. Other relatives were outsiders, perhaps outright competitors, whose importune claims artisans fought, when possible, and settled grudgingly. A sample of 250 quittances—receipts for loan payments— reveals 35 between artisan relatives. Of these, only 2 actually represented the repayment of loans. The rest resulted from property settlements against the patrimony, some obtained at law and many under the threat of legal action. Thirteen concerned the settlement of contested successions; 4 recorded the payment of court costs and damages resulting from intrafamilial law suits; the rest documented daughters and sons-in-law collecting dowries. Even the last, straightforward on the surface, could have

---

[49] AD T-et-G G 458–460 procédures devant l'Officialité 1760–1789, and Darrow, "Popular Concepts of Marital Choice," pp. 261–272.

[50] Usually a widow had to renounce her right to her dowry to claim this support. See, for example, AD T-et-G 5E 1952 Caminel no. 336 30–6–1793 testament Jean Moulis, *fabriquant*, who left his wife his furniture and a pension of three hundred livres a year on condition that she abandon her rights to her dowry and nuptial gains.

murky currents. In 1798, for example, weaver Jacques Ferral demanded a formal receipt from his son-in-law for the portion of his daughter's dowry, which his wife had paid ten years earlier. He brought witnesses with him to swear that the payment had been made. Apparently, since the death of Ferral's wife, the son-in-law had been trying to collect all over again.[51]

Sales and purchases tell the same story of property division—and family division—formalized and recorded. In the sample of property sales, ten sales show artisans and their children or siblings as joint sellers; only one had such a group as buyers. The circumstances that forced these sales explain the disparity. For example, bricklayer Pierre Mouméja, as heir to his father, and his mother, who had life rights to her late husband's estate, jointly sold land to a neighbor. They then paid the money they received to the husband of Pierre's sister as partial payment of her dowry.[52] The ultimate alienation of the patrimony occurred as each heir claimed his or her legal share.

The *accord*, or notarized out-of-court settlement, was a document familiar to many artisans. Long and detailed, *accords* recounted past family financial arrangements—marriage contracts, loans, informal associations—set down the facts as agreed to by the parties, and spelled out future commitments. A typical agreement was reached in 1794 in the Gasc family of Lacapelle, cousins of Saint-Araille. It involved the father, Antoine Gasc, a carpenter; daughter Marie and her husband, a cooper; daughter Elizabeth and her husband, a law clerk; two unmarried daughters, Marie and Gasparde; and sons Jean Paul, a tailor, and Izaac, a cooper. Elizabeth was the heir of their mother, Alexide Ferral. Since Ferral had made her will, two other of her children had died. At issue was the amount Elizabeth owed each of her siblings, taking into account what had already been paid at their marriages, the amount due her father as heir of the two dead children, her own unpaid dowry, plus the money due to her for loans she had made to her father after his wife's death, and the question of the value of furniture Gasparde had illegally taken from the parental home. Similar circumstances produced conflict among the survivors of bricklayer Jean Mouméja. In his will, he left only fifty livres each to three of his daughters as their legal portions. At the time of the agreement, two daughters had died, another had been born (posthumously), and the eldest was caring for the mother, who had become an invalid. This daughter, Françoise, representing also her minor sister, sued the eldest son, Pierre, claiming that the portions they had been left were smaller than the légitime. In 1788 Pierre

---

[51] AD T-et-G 5E 12893 Grelleau no. 202 18 prairial Year 6 quittance Ferral.
[52] AD T-et-G 5E 12859 Grelleau no. 372 5–8–1772 achât Mouméja.

agreed to an additional legacy and also a stipend to Françoise for the care of their mother.[53]

Like *accords*, *partages*—divisions—recorded property settlements, but these resulted directly from the death of the property owner and not necessarily from disagreements among the living parties. The death of the head of the family and holder of the patrimony often brought about a general family accounting in which past debts were formally recognized and future obligations recorded. Many of these divisions stipulated exact equity in such trivial detail that they suggest mistrust, tension, and even hostility among the parties. For example, in the division following the death of Pierre Mouméja, a distant relative of Jean, the bricklayer, the widow was allotted a pension that included the right to vegetables from the family garden. However, she was constrained to take these vegetables only as she needed them for her own personal consumption and in strict rotation from the plot of each child in turn. The death of Pierre's uncle, Jean David, resulted in at least three separate acts of division. The first, very straightforward, divided the real estate into two lots, one for Jean, the heir, the other to be shared by his brother and two sisters. These nonheirs forced the second division, claiming that because Jean was heir to half the estate, he owed half the funeral expenses, not the one quarter he had paid. He also owed his sister Marguérite the money she had spent during their father's terminal illness. The younger brother called for a third division, to include the expenses he also had incurred on behalf of their father.[54]

Behind the lawsuits and forced property divisions were artisans' younger sons and daughters, the noninheriting children who had experienced the other side of artisanal solidarity. The master artisan or retailer kept his chosen heir as a subordinate, even a dependent, within the family business with the promise that someday he would be head of the business and the

---

[53] AD T-et-G 5E 12887 Grelleau no. 185 5 ventôse Year 2 accord Gasc; 12859 Grelleau no. 311 24–9–1778 accord Mouméja. See also 5E 10869 Martin no. 155 24–3–1780 accord Benech-Pendaries; 13181 Deray no. 561 21–5–1790 accord Carenou-Prat; 2352 Martin no. 305 8 germinal Year 13 accord Lafargue frères et neveux; 10869 Martin no. 447 25–9–1780 accord Pons and 12868 Grelleau no. 236 6–7–1779 délaissement in which cloth bleacher Jean Ruelle, "menaced by his sister for debt," ceded his house to her.

[54] AD T-et-G 5E 2150 Latreille-Olivié no. 146 22–3–1821 partage Mouméja; 1970 Latreille-Olivié no. 204 11 fructidor Year 6 partage Mouméja and no. 218 15 fructidor Year 6 partage Mouméja. See also 5E 10869 Martin no. 418 15–9–1780 partage Marty frères, which includes the stipulations that each brother may use the well on alternate days and that the loose planks in the attic are to be apportioned between them, and 1975 Latreille-Olivié no. 524 20 ventôse Year 11 partage Mouméja, in which the division of Raymond Mouméja's house included a protracted discussion of *droits de passage*, which doors should be left open and which sealed, and what to do about the water that habitually collected in the end of the stable allotted to one heir.

household. The corporations made a similar commitment to the heirs of their members by admitting them as masters at a young age without formal apprenticeship and with a lower standard of professional achievement.[55] Few noninheriting children could look forward to such a secure position. Whether kept as workers within the family business or sent off with meager endowments to earn their living elsewhere, noninheriting children received much less than an equal share in the family's resources.

Artisans treated their noninheriting sons in a variety of ways. In the textile industry and in a few other trades, artisans did not differentiate among their sons because all "inherited" the skills needed to become subcontractors or employees of merchant-manufacturers like their fathers. In these families, all the sons could eventually establish themselves as masters in the trade.[56] In other families, the younger sons remained as dependent workers in the family business and permanent *fils de famille*. For example, in order to remain in the family bakery business after it had passed to his older brother François, Antoine Barriere promised "that during the time he shall remain in his [brother's] household he will work with all his might for his brother's profit and advantage, without demanding any recompense for his work or the interest on the legacy of fifteen hundred livres [due him from his father's estate], and in return the said François Barriere promises to keep his brother, the said Antoine Barriere, in sickness and in health, to feed him at his pot and hearth, and to provide for his needs."[57]

More commonly, artisans and retailers apprenticed their noninheriting sons outside the family trade. An uncle or a cousin without a son of his own might take a lucky young kinsman into his business, in which case the noninheriting son became an heir in another household. For example, Pierre Golse was the son of a textile artisan, but his uncle Izaac, a master bricklayer, took him on as an apprentice. Pierre's marriage contract was signed in Izaac's house with Izaac as witness and signatory even though Pierre's father was alive. Izaac made no formal promise to his nephew but his patronage was clear.[58] Most, however, became ordinary apprentices to masters unrelated to them and without any particular interest in their fate.

---

[55] Coornaert, *Les Corporations*, pp. 190–195; Sewell, *Work and Revolution in France*, p. 30.

[56] AM Mont 7 HH 2 records of the Shoemakers' and Cobblers' Guild show the easy and frequent entry of sons and sons-in-law. For one hundred masters there were eleven sets of brothers and one set of brothers-in-law, as well as eight fathers and sons. Shoemaking was one of the most overcrowded, least remunerative, and least respected trades. See Jacques Rancière, "The Myth of the Artisan: Critical Reflections on a Category of Social History," trans. David H. Lake and Cynthia J. Koepp, in Kaplan and Koepp, eds., *Work in France*, pp. 318–320.

[57] AD T-et-G 5E 2094 Franceries no. 354 5–10–1790 accord Barriere.

[58] AD T-et-G 5E 12876 Grelleau no. 478 20–8–1786 contrat de mariage Golse-Moutet. Also see 5E 1998 Garrigues no. 32 18–1–1780 apprentissage Gasc, and 1999 Garrigues no. 211 6–3–1781 resiliement d'apprentissage Gasc. The apprenticeship of seventeen-year-old

In the apprenticeship contract, the father delegated his paternal authority to his son's new master, who was to act *en bon père de famille*, not only teaching the boy a trade and providing for his room and board but also attending to his moral and spiritual education. Some apprenticeships, like that of Etienne Gasc to master shoemaker Pierre Martel, included formal instruction in reading and writing.[59] In material terms, too, the father turned over his son's future to his master. Sometimes the price of the apprentice constituted the boy's entire inheritance; usually it was deducted from the légitime. At completion of his apprenticeship, he received his brevet, a new suit of clothes, and possibly a set of tools and joined the ranks of journeymen. If he wanted to become a master or to marry, he had to save his wages because he could expect little or no financial help from his father or brother.[60]

A journeyman was still under the paternal authority of his master, yet that paternalism was more often rhetorical than real. Although in the good old days of corporate harmony journeymen lived in their masters' homes, ate at their tables, courted and married their daughters, in Montauban those days were past, if they had ever existed.[61] Only two artisans' households in Villebourbon in 1774 included *compagnons*; instead, journeymen lodged in inns and boarding houses. In the textile trades, many were married men with families. Others—joiners, bricklayers, tailors—traveled from town to town on a Tour de France, looking for work and, possibly, adventure. Even those who remained in one place did not work for one master long enough to become part of his family. Masters hired journeymen by the job, for a few days or a month at a time.[62] In Montauban, few

---

Izaac Gasc to his cousin Jacques, a master cooper, did not work out, perhaps because Jacques had a son to succeed him. In the sample of twenty-eight apprenticeship contracts, only one was of a boy to his uncle. It is possible, however, that such arrangements were usually informal.

[59] AD T-et-G 5E 12892 Grelleau no. 188 17 fructidor Year 5 apprentissage Gasc à Martel. Toujas, "Vie des apprentis," pp. 339–344. Both Toujas and Farge, *La Vie fragile*, pp. 138–139, point out that in practice this transfer of paternal authority was fraught with ambiguity and reluctance. Fathers did not hesitate to complain or to try to remove their sons from masters who they felt were not treating them correctly.

[60] See, for example, AD T-et-G 5E 10869 Martin no. 447 25–9–1780 accord Pons and AD T-et-G 5E 2331 Martin no. 691 and no. 697 1–11–1777 licitations Delbreil and 2083 Franceries no. 224 9–4–1779 licitation Delbreil.

[61] Ménétra, *Journal of My Life*, and Darnton, *The Great Cat Massacre*, pp. 78–82. Toujas, in "Vie des apprentis," pp. 339–340, reports that even in the seventeenth century, masters did not always act like *bon pères de famille*.

[62] Sonenscher, "Journeymen's Migrations"; Farge, *La Vie fragile*, pp. 127–131. AM Mont 9 FF 1 déclarations de séjour; 10 HH 1 dénombrement Villebourbon 1774. Journeymen implicated in connection with *compagnonnage* violence in 1776 included a tinsmith from Paris, a joiner nicknamed Bordelais, and another joiner, nicknamed Suisse. AM Mont 6 FF 47 jurisdictions consulaires.

journeymen married their masters' daughters—only 12 percent of artisan grooms had the same occupation as their fathers-in-law—although more may have hoped to do so. Nicole Castan, in her study of Toulouse judicial records, found that 29 percent of cases of seduction involved apprentices or journeymen and their masters' daughters.[63]

Some journeymen succeeded because they had been trained in trades that were expanding, because they traveled from job to job and from town to town until they found a niche for themselves, or, perhaps, because they were unusually capable. One quarter of the artisans who married in Montauban were relative newcomers to the city. Most were immigrants from nearby country towns, but a few had come from some distance, attracted by Montauban's industry. Silk stocking knitter Charles Philippe Ferrier, for example, was recruited in Berlin by a manufacturer eager to establish a silk industry in Montauban. Joseph Boé and François Jourdia, both wool comb makers from the Ariège, found work and brides in Montauban; they married cousins who were daughters of master comb makers.[64] Many, however, remained permanent journeymen, eking out a living at the fringes of a trade or falling into the ranks of the poor. When they married, they wed working women, daughters of poor peasants and city workers, who brought dowries only half the size of the dowries that went to their privileged brothers.

Artisans' daughters, like Saint-Araille's sisters, usually left the household and the family business when they married. If it was uncommon for an artisan's daughter to marry her father's journeyman, rarer still was the son-in-law who moved into his wife's family and family business; only 2 percent of artisans joined in partnership with their fathers-in-law when they married.

A small minority of artisans provided very well for their daughters, educating them and endowing them with portions large enough to enable them to marry merchants or minor officials. Most fathers gave their daughters enough so that, when supplemented by their own savings, their dowries were large enough to secure husbands who were artisans or retailers. But a sizable minority of artisans' daughters, 38 percent, could afford to marry only a laborer.

In theory, small business families devoted sufficient resources to their noninheriting sons and daughters to establish them within the ranks of their class. They provided their sons with training that was supposed to

[63] Castan, *Criminels de Languedoc*, pp. 269–270. David Garrioch found the story of the master's daughter marrying her father's journeyman "largely utopian" in eighteenth-century Paris as well (*Neighbourhood and Community in Paris*, p. 106).

[64] AD T-et-G 5E 2332 Martin sn 28–10–1779 contrat de mariage Ferrier-Lowantin; 13197 Deray fils no. 155 1–5–1807 contrat de mariage Boé-Beret; 2142 Latreille-Olivié no. 347 30–8–1814 contrat de mariage Jourdia-Beret.

TABLE 5–3
Social Mobility by Marriage of Artisans and Their Children

	Artisans	Artisans' Sons	Artisans' Daughters
Percentage who married* down	13%	31%	38%
Mean dowry in livres/francs	370	520	440
Percentage who married same	76%	57%	53%
Mean dowry in livres/francs	970	760	950
Percentage who married up	11%	12%	9%
Mean dowry in livres/francs	2,500	4,000	4,400
N	193	189	224

*Status differed by gender. An artisan who married a landowning peasant's daughter married down, but an artisan's daughter who married a landowning peasant married a social equivalent.

enable them to earn a living and to rise eventually to the status of their fathers. In addition, most artisans' sons, whether heir or not, learned to read and write. Their education and training were the essence—in some cases the totality—of their share of the patrimony. An artisan's daughter received little formal training or education, but her portion of the patrimony, the dowry, was supposed to obtain for her a position in an artisan's household comparable to her mother's.

Like elite fathers, artisans and retailers tried to establish all of their children within their class yet conserve the patrimony intact to pass to one privileged heir. In general, artisans were less successful in attaining these ends than were Montauban's merchants and magistrates. The success of artisans' strategies depended on either a static population or an expanding economy. In the eighteenth century, Montauban's population grew substantially, but from the 1720s to the 1760s the economy expanded as well, so it is possible that during this period artisans were able to attain both goals and maintain harmonious familial relations. In the last third of the century, as Montauban's economy faltered, if any such harmony had existed earlier it quickly eroded. As guilds became more restrictive, non-inheriting sons found it ever more difficult to attain mastership outside the family trade, and work outside the corporate structure brought neither the security nor the independent status that was the portion of their inheriting brothers. More and more sons and daughters found their allotted portions insufficient and disputed them as unjust and illegal.

Artisans' widows also sometimes disputed the allocation of the family's resources which, they claimed, shortchanged them. As brides they had brought substantial capital to the family business and as wives they had contributed valuable labor to it, yet in the years before the Revolution,

TABLE 5–4
Provisions for Widows in Artisans' Wills

	Legal System	
Provisions	*Old Regime*	*Civil Code*
Nothing	7%	7%
Use of percentage of estate	45	28
Annuity	24	2
Property of estate (heir)	24	63
N	29	43

Note: Significance level = .01, contingency coefficient = .407.

their husbands rarely acknowledged them as partners during their lifetime or their successors after death.[65] The most a widow could expect was that her husband would oblige his heir to support her as a dependent in his household. If her husband had not been generous enough to provide adequately for her maintenance, she would have to trade her dowry for a promise of care and support. We have already seen that this was the case between Saint-Araille's two sisters. Often such an arrangement was little more than charity, as was made clear in a property settlement between Guillaume and Antoinette Durand, children of a textile artisan. After dividing their father's estate, "the parties pass in silence over the few goods which the said Laulanie [their mother] had when she died and which she had taken into the said Antoinette Durand's home, being agreed that the said goods were absorbed by the expense of caring for the said Laulanie during her last illness and death."[66]

It was not only elderly women who were sometimes shunted out of the family business. If her husband had not yet inherited the business, a widow and her children lost any claim on it. For example, Antoinette Carenou, who married into the Prat family of loom makers, discovered that after her husband died not only were she and her daughter no longer

[65] In the samples of loans and property transactions for the period before the Revolution, 5 percent or less of artisan participants were married couples. In the sample of procurations, only 8 percent of artisans appointed their wives.

[66] AD T-et-G 5E 10872 Martin no. 371 2–6–1783 partage Durand. Also see 5E 2150 Latreille Olivié no. 146 22–3–1821 partage Mouméja; 21880 Grelleau no. 247 17–5–1789 donation Dejean. Nor did the legacy of support from the family business necessarily solve a woman's problems, as Marie Germa discovered when her husband's business passed to her nephew, who stopped paying the pension to which she was entitled because her care had become "onerous." AD T-et-G 5E 13189 Deray fils no. 573 14 prairial Year 10 accord Germa. Nonetheless, Marie was lucky compared with Noële Guelphe, widow of a Toulouse butcher who had left her life rights to his house. Her son and grandson killed her when she refused to cede her rights to them. See *Journal de Tarn-et-Garonne* no. 17, 27–2–1828.

welcome in her father-in-law's household, but that she would have to take him to court to get back her dowry.[67] In such a circumstance, a young widow and her children had little choice but to return as permanent dependents to the household of her father or inheriting brother. In Villebourbon in 1774, only fourteen artisans' widows headed their own households; an equal number lived in the households of their sons, daughters, fathers, and brothers.

The dowry system helped to perpetuate women's dependence in artisan families. Like elite couples, almost all artisans before the Revolution married according to the Custom of Montauban, and after the Revolution most chose the Napoleonic *régime dotale*. Although dowries provided adequate support for the widows of the wealthy, they did not do so for artisans' widows. First, their dowries were much smaller (see table 4–1). Second, most artisans' dowries were invested not in land or any other income-producing property but in furnishing a home.[68] The bulk of a widow's portion was likely to be the bed, wardrobe, buffet, linens, pots, tableware, and so on, that she had brought to the marriage, now several years old and well used. To sell them would deprive her of the standard of living to which she was accustomed without providing enough to support her for long.

As the lawsuits, the *accords*, and the *partages* attest, some women did not dutifully accept the secondary, supportive status that the artisan patriarchy assigned to them. They used two strategies: first, to force a redivision of the patrimony to give them a larger share, and second, to create an alternative set of relationships, independent of the family business, on which they could depend.

The lawsuits exemplified the first strategy. Women took their fathers and brothers to court, arguing that the patrimony was worth more than the heirs claimed and that therefore the women's portions were less than the légitime. In these cases, a woman's husband was often her ally and champion. As in elite families, the relationship between the groom and his father-in-law often soured by the nonpayment of the dowry, and the husband was willing to risk the expense and the bad feelings caused by a lawsuit in order to have the matter resolved. The prospect of a supplement was doubly tempting because, unlike the typical artisanal dowry, the supplement was usually in cash. For instance, Marguérite Gasc obtained two hundred livres in gold plus five livres' interest and the cost of the lawsuit when she sued her brother for a supplement. Husbands and wives in these cases appeared as partners pitted against the wife's father and his heir.

---

[67] AD T-et-G 5E 13181 Deray no. 561 21–5–1790 accord Carenou et beaupère.

[68] Seventy percent of artisans' dowries included furniture, 55 percent included some cash, and only 4 percent included real estate.

Widows had few legal claims on the patrimony, but neither were they backward about suing their fathers-in-law or their sons to secure the return of their dowries or to obtain any other rights that their husbands may have left them.[69]

Some women invested the little capital they possessed in independent enterprises that, although not in competition with the family business, were separate from it. Using skills they had learned when serving customers in the family business, they engaged in retailing on their own account. Most *marchandes* sold common consumer goods of the sort ordinarily purchased by women, such as sewing materials, pots and pans, food, and second-hand linens. For example, in her marriage contract to a journeyman carpenter, Marie Laplagne reserved six hundred francs as her own property "with which she intends to begin a little trade in groceries, *mercerie*, or something else," and in hers Angelique Baucopin obtained her husband's consent for her to continue to work as a hairdresser in a business partnership with her two sisters. Although some husbands granted their wives the right to do business on their own account, it was more common—and more necessary—for widows to launch their own businesses, using the return of their dowries as the initial capital. Saint-Araille's sister Perrett, for example, opened a retail shop after her husband died. Most such businesses were very small, rarely involving more than five hundred livres in merchandise. An exception was the tanning business of Catherine Ruelle, widow of butcher Jean Ramondis. In 1795, she borrowed more than twenty thousand francs from Montauban merchants to provision her tannery.[70] In these enterprises, women acquired an independent status and a source of income outside the family business; they also created relationships at odds with the patriarchal structure of the artisan household.

Women maintained a feminine support system within artisan families. Although the census showed dependent women living with male relatives, the women's own perceptions were that they were living with other women. In the sample of wills, all nine artisans' widows and daughters

[69] AD T-et-G 5E 2007 Garrigues no. 507 26–6–1787 accord Gasc. See also 5E 13215 Solon no. 112 13–4–1819 accord Padié; 12864 Grelleau no. 499 20–12–1776 accord Mouméja and 13181 Deray no. 561 21–5–1790 accord Carenou et beaupère and 12841 Delteil fils no. 281 25–10–1815 accord Gineste et mère.

[70] AD T-et-G 5E 13517 Martin fils no. 176 1–6–1820 contrat de mariage Bouet-Laplagne; 10877 Martin no. 606 29–12–1788 contrat de mariage Valadie-Baucopin; 12888 Grelleau no. 491 17 prairial Year 3 dettes Ruelle vᶜ Ramondis and L 324 tribunal de commerce. See also 5E 10867 Martin no. 178 9–4–1778 contrat de mariage Gatereau-Fournier and 2345 Martin sn 24 frimaire Year 5 contrat de mariage Taverne-Lavergne; 2065 Delmas no. 214 10–7–1785 contrat de mariage Sarrat-Pech and 13517 Martin fils no. 208 18–6–1820 contrat de mariage Massot-Mailhet.

who recorded that they lived with kin mentioned female relatives—mothers, sisters, daughters, and daughters-in-law. For example, in her will, Marguérite Gasc reported that she was living with her sister although the proprietor and head of the household was her nephew.[71]

Women in artisan families, especially artisans' widows, often appointed other women as their heirs.[72] Marguérite Gasc was only one such testator who preferred her sister and her sister's children to her brother; Geromie Arché, widow of a tailor, was another. In 1792 she gave all her property, worth 859 livres, to her sister Delphine, also a widow, in return for support. Because part of this property was three hundred livres that her brother's son owed her, we can conclude that she, too, turned to a sister rather than to a brother or his family. Saint-Araille's widow divided her property into thirds, leaving one portion to each of their sons and one to her daughter-in-law, wife of the son with whom she lived.[73]

Like the wives of the elite, an artisan's wife often lived too far from her mother, sisters, or married daughters to provide day-to-day help and companionship. Half of artisans' fiancées did not live in the same neighborhood as their future husbands.[74] Some artisan women were further separated from their families of origin by a difference in status between their husbands and their brothers. In the family of Jacques Gasc, master cooper, for example, both sorts of mobility operated to separate the women from their families. Jacques's only son, Alexandre, also a master cooper, married the daughter and sister of *commis négociant*. Marrying a step down in social status, she also moved away from her family's home in the center of the city to live near her parents-in-law in Lacapelle. Two of Alexander's sisters also married master artisans, one a cloth shearer and the other a cloth presser, but both moved to Villebourbon. The third sister moved to Ville-

---

[71] AD T-et-G 5E 2143 Latreille-Olivié no. 305 27–8–1815 testament Gasc v^c Pradel. See also 5E 12841 Delteil fils no. 486 28–3–1816 testament Labarthe v^c Revouilhac and 2002 Garrigues no. 752 22–11–1784 contrat de mariage Mouméja-Crouzatie. Three of the women testators lived with sisters, two with daughters, two with nieces, one with a female cousin, and one with a female friend.

[72] In the sample of wills, only 34 percent of artisan men appointed women as their heirs, whereas 51 percent of women appointed women as heirs (significance level = .08, contingency coefficient = .168).

[73] AD T-et-G Q 406 donations no. 46 30–6–1792; 5E 2150 Latreille Olivié no. 83 14–2–1821 testament Debia v^c Gasc. Also see 5E 2151 Latreille-Olivié no. 356 24–9–1822 testament Mouméja and 12866 Grelleau no. 213 14–6–1779 testament Sirven v^c Mouméja, in which a bricklayer's widow left her two sons the légitime and named her daughters as her heirs.

[74] Whereas 62 percent of poor workers lived in the same neighborhood as their brides, this was true of only 49 percent of artisan couples (significance level = .01, contingency coefficient = .483).

bourbon at her marriage as well, but her husband was a poor textile worker with only thirty livres to his name.[75]

Despite physical and socioeconomic separation, the women in artisan families still came to each other's aid in times of need. In August 1799, when Marguérite Gasc fell ill in Mas Grenier, her sister Perrette, then forty years old and already a widow, applied for a permit for herself, her son, and daughter-in-law to go to Marguérite's side. In the same month, the town's officials received several other similar requests. Cecille Moissac, aged fifty-four, applied for a passport to go to Albi to "bring succor to her sister who is dangerously ill." Her brother Antoine, a tailor, was to accompany her. Marguérite Boyer, aged fifty-seven, asked to go to Castelsarrasin on a similar mission, and Marthe Barbert, wife of a retailer, aged forty-six, also wanted to go to Castelsarrasin to nurse her sick daughter. Whether traveling alone, or as in the first two cases, accompanied by male relatives, the person who applied for these permits was a woman intent on bringing aid to another woman.[76]

The artisan family nourished two separate and not at all equal kinds of relationships. Authoritarian relationships dominated because the patriarch controlled the patrimony and through it his wife and children. But his authority was challenged by more cooperative relationships that prevailed between women and sometimes between husband and wife. The law also intervened to protect certain minimal rights of the subordinate parties, the *légitime* of noninheriting children and the dowry of the wife. Patriarchal power prevailed in artisanal families before the Revolution, but it was not absolute and unquestioned.

The Revolution gave new weapons to some of the family members who had disputed artisans' family strategies in the Old Regime. The challenge came in two forms on two fronts—free trade in the business arena and equal inheritance in the familial realm. Both undermined artisans' strategies to protect the patrimony by excluding most claims on it. Free trade—abolition of the guilds—reduced a master artisan's patrimony because it no longer secured an *état*, a guaranteed position within the city's economic and social structure. Equal inheritance greatly increased the size of claims on the patrimony. Together they revolutionized artisans' family strategies.

Although Montauban's merchant-manufacturers and *négociants* opposed free trade when it meant opening the West Indian market to foreign commerce, they chafed under both royal and local manufacturing regula-

---

[75] AD T-et-G 5E 2001 Garrigues no. 865 19–12–1783 contrat de mariage Pere-Gasc; 1996 Garrigues no. 626 13–12–1778 contrat de mariage Prunetis-Gasc; 2007 Garrigues no. 83 20–1–1787 contrat de mariage Vincent-Gasc and no. 652 18–9–1787 contrat de mariage Gasc-Belluc.

[76] AM Mont 5 i 3 registre des permis.

tions. During the prolonged crisis provoked by the Seven Years' War, some of Montauban's wealthiest merchants had sought out new markets and new products. They had begun to deal in cheaper, lighter-weight fabrics, which could be sold in Spain and the West Indies. Because this material was too loosely woven to conform to Montauban's manufacturing code, merchants employed rural weavers, who were outside the code's jurisdiction. They wanted, however, to regularize this industry, to reform or abolish the regulations rather than to evade them. The Merchants' Corporation applauded the "liberation" of textile manufacture in 1779.[77]

Montauban's textile artisans, on the other hand, clung to their guilds and insisted that manufacturing codes be maintained and enforced. For them, the end of regulation meant submitting to the absolute control of the merchants. Lyons silk workers summed up the position of all textile artisans who saw mechanization and English-style factories lurking behind the merchants' enthusiasm for free trade.

> Among men equal in means and in power who, for this reason, cannot be subjected to the arbitrary will of the one or the other, freedom can only be to their mutual advantage. But with respect to silk workers, deprived of all resources and whose daily subsistence depends entirely upon their daily work, this freedom leaves them completely at the mercy of the manufacturer who can, without harm to himself, suspend operations and thus reduce the worker to the wages he chooses to offer, well knowing that the worker, driven by the superior law of necessity, will soon be obliged to give in to his demands.[78]

In some trades where guild officials had vigorously pursued and prosecuted *chambrelans*, journeymen applauded Turgot's abolition of guilds in 1776 and their final demise in 1791. This was the case among Montauban's journeymen tailors and seamstresses, whom the Tailors' Guild had repeatedly harassed with confiscations, fines, and legal action. However, most artisans, journeymen and masters alike, supported the corporate system despite its manifold problems and resisted its abolition. The *cahiers de doléances* of the artisan corporations demanded the return to local policies of protection for both the producer and the consumer and the enforcement of strict standards of craftsmanship. When the bourgeois and merchants who drew up Montauban's official *cahier* eliminated these demands and substituted a call for free trade, at least one guild, the carpenters', registered a complaint and sent a *mémoire* to the Estates General to that effect.[79]

---

[77] Ligou, *Montauban*, pp. 98–99; Forestié, *Fabrication des draps*, pp. 29–31; AM Mont 8 HH 7 manufactures 1754–1789.

[78] Cited in Trénard, "The Social Crisis in Lyons," pp. 80–81.

[79] Ligou, *Montauban*, p. 199. This also happened to the *cahiers* of artisans in Lyons and many other cities. Trénard, "The Social Crisis in Lyons," p. 98, and Coornaert, *Les Corpora-*

The final abolition of guilds and the institution of free trade coincided with the worst depression Montauban had known in the eighteenth century. In 1789–1790, nearly one third of the population was out of work. The Aristocrat faction cannily focused popular discontent on the Protestant merchants who dominated the Patriot party. Except for a few specialized trades—wool comb makers, for example—Montauban's working people were largely Catholic (see table 4–3). The Aristocrats' platform—militant Catholicism and economic protectionism—appealed especially to the Congregation of Artisans, a devotional and social organization that became the popular bulwark of the 1790 municipal government. The Aristocrats kept their promises to the extent of reviving controls on the grain trade and harassing the merchant-manufacturers, but they worsened the city's economic plight by isolating it from Bordeaux, its main market, and by driving out many of the artisans' best customers.

The beginning of the war and the army contracts it brought revitalized Montauban's export industry but did not boost small businesses. The contracts went to the *fabriques* of Vialettes-Daignan and Serres and to new protofactories, like the one Pierre Garrisson set up in the former Capuchin convent. The artisans employed in these enterprises were more like wage laborers than subcontractors. For example, master cloth shearers lost the right to negotiate apprenticeship contracts; their apprentices were to be paid a flat rate fixed by the merchant-manufacturers. As a result, textile artisans experienced a sharp reduction in income. The Maximum and the fall in the value of paper money, in which their piece rates were calculated, were partly responsible, but the increased power of the merchant-manufacturers was a major cause. Freed from the restraints of the guilds and the manufacturing code and assured a guaranteed market at lucrative prices, the merchant-manufacturers controlled Montauban's textile industry to a degree never possible in the Old Regime. Textile artisans, especially cloth shearers, protested and in 1791 invaded Vialette-Daignan's *fabrique*, but with the merchants in command at the Hôtel de Ville as well as in the Chamber of Commerce and on the benches of the Revolutionary courts, effective opposition was impossible. The collapse of the industry after the Peace of Amiens was only the final blow to the fortunes of Montauban's textile artisans.[80]

---

tions, pp. 173–174. Nonetheless, there was no public resistance to the abolition of the guilds in 1791 as there had been in 1776. See Kaplan, "Social Classification and Representation in the Corporate World," and Sewell, *Work and Revolution in France*, pp. 87–88, 93–94.

[80] Sol, *Révolution en Quercy* 2: 131; Ligou, *Montauban*, pp. 590–595; AM Mont 8 HH 7 manufactures and 4 F 3 Manufacture de draps. Although the Revolution did not spell the collapse of the textile industry in Lyons as it did in Montauban, it did abolish the *Grande Fabrique*. The merchant-manufacturers in the nineteenth century controlled the industry to a much greater extent than they had done in the Old Regime. See Robert J. Bezucha, "The 'Preindustrial' Worker Movement: The *Canuts* of Lyon," in Robert J. Bezucha, ed., *Modern European Social History* (Lexington, Mass.: D. C. Heath, 1972), pp. 97–98.

Textiles were not the only sector affected. Boat building and barrel making, the by-products of the grain trade, were mortally wounded by the English blockade. According to the subprefect in 1802, since the 1780s annual production of barrels had dropped from 150,000 to only 10,000. Leather and pottery, also produced for export in the eighteenth century, declined as well.[81] Luxury craftsmen, like jewelers and wig makers, found their businesses reduced by the emigration or rustification of their aristocratic clientele and by the trends toward simpler, "republican" fashions. All artisans and shopkeepers who sold primarily to working people were directly affected by the depression in the early years of the Revolution and by the later collapse of the textile industry.

For most master artisans and retailers, living standards rather than mere survival were the major concern of these years. Shortages, new regulations, new procedures, and new officials complicated the lives of both consumers and retailers. Although consumers and politicians rhetorically vented their hostility on wholesalers, speculators, and *agioteurs*, in practice their targets were local shopkeepers, especially bakers and butchers. The Terror magnified a traditional arena of social tension, the confrontation between merchant and customer.[82]

For Montauban's artisans, the political and social benefits of the Revolution were ambiguous. Although the artisans were important political actors, they were rarely leaders; nor were they able to impress their own interests on those whom they supported. Artisans elected the municipal government of 1790, yet the government, composed of nobles and Old Regime officials, did little for their artisan clients. Those on the other side of the political fence fared no better. Many artisans joined the National Guard and served as neighborhood police commissioners but always under merchant leadership. The Patriots' Club took on a somewhat popular coloring during the Terror when it functioned as a kind of friendly society as well as a political forum. However, the club was officered throughout by merchants and manufacturers and rarely voiced the artisans' demands for protected markets and trade regulations. Its fraternal aid, although important in individual cases, hardly compensated for failing businesses and falling incomes.[83]

The economic balance sheet of the Revolution in Montauban was less ambiguous. A few small entrepreneurs did extremely well—witness Saint-

---

[81] AD T-et-G 152 J notes sur le commerce.

[82] AM Mont 8 i 3 tribunal de police 1791–Year 3. See also Slavin, *The French Revolution in Miniature*, pp. 129–131, 180–183. The Terror certainly did not create this conflict, nor did the fall of Robespierre eliminate it as anyone familiar with the comedy routines of Fernand Reynaud will attest. As the classic American comic conflict scenario is played out in marriage, in France it occurs "chez le boucher."

[83] AM Mont 7 i 2 reports des commissionnaires de polices; Arches, "Garde nationale," pp. 303–314; Galabert, "Le Club jacobin de Montauban," 1: 142–143, 10: 313–314; Kennedy, *The Jacobin Clubs*, pp. 8–9, 73, 81–82.

Araille's success. Abraham Antoine Albert Samuel Mouméja was another. A candle maker and small-time loan shark before the Revolution, Mouméja made a considerable, if not exactly respectable, fortune during the Revolution by lending out sums in *assignats*, collecting them in hard currency, and investing in properties confiscated from the Catholic church.[84]. But such success stories were in the minority. For most artisans and retailers, the Revolution proved to be a period of retrenchment, not expansion. That few artisans participated in the major material opportunity of the Revolution, the sale of national properties, is evidence of this trend. Many of these properties, especially those formerly owned by religious orders, were small houses, apartments, rooms, workshops, and gardens, just the sort of realty that artisans had purchased in great numbers before the Revolution. Yet artisans and small retailers constituted only 12 percent of the purchasers of low-priced properties—under five thousand francs—and only 2 percent of purchasers of more expensive properties. Some were outbid by merchants—gardens, in particular, often sold for far above their evaluation; some may have been kept away by religious scruples. But for many, economic conditions precluded any such major purchase.[85]

The decline in artisanal fortunes can be charted in the dowries artisans were able to attract and that they could afford to offer. In the last quarter of the eighteenth century, the average dowry brought by an artisan's bride was worth 1,330 livres. In the first quarter of the nineteenth century, the average dowry was worth only 900 francs, a decline of nearly one third. At the end of the Old Regime, 37 percent of artisans married women who brought more than 1,000 livres to the marriage; in the early nineteenth century, only 26 percent of artisans' brides were so well endowed, whereas the percentage of brides who brought less than 100 francs doubled, from 7 to 14 percent. Artisans' ability to endow their daughters also declined over the same period despite the fact that a daughter's legal share in the patrimony had increased considerably. The mean dowry of artisans' daughters fell from 1,250 livres between 1775 and 1799 to 940 francs between 1800 and 1824.

Many, perhaps most, of Montauban's small family businesses were worse off in the early nineteenth century than they had been in the 1770s. Like the city's merchants, artisans and shopkeepers suffered from the retraction of the textile industry. They also felt the loss of a protected local market. The percentage of *soi-disant* artisans and retailers in Montauban's population increased as many former textile workers tried to earn a living

---

[84] AD T-et-G E Etat Civil Protestant no. 366 19–3–1788; 12882 Grelleau no. 209 18–2–1792 achât Mouméja; 12890 Grelleau no. 332 23 ventôse Year 3 dette Angé and no. 617 3 fructidor Year 3 dette Pauline; 12891 Grelleau no. 201 13 prairial Year 4 dette Pradine; 12896 Grelleau no. 264 10 ventôse Year 9 quittance Mouméja; 2135 Latreille-Olivié no. 485 14–6–1808 achât Mouméja.

[85] Ligou, "Biens nationaux," pp. 366–371.

as tailors, shoemakers, and in other crafts and as very petty retailers. With wages low and the city's population stagnating, however, there was little increase in demand.[86]

The revolution in inheritance law also dealt a heavier blow to artisan families than it did to elite families. The strategies of both groups had involved an unequal distribution of the family's resources, but whereas most noninheriting children in wealthy families had acquiesced to their position, many children in artisanal families had not. Before the Revolution, daughters and disinherited sons had gone to court to contest the distribution and to demand their meager rights; under the new laws of equal inheritance they claimed much greater benefits. An example is the *accord* signed in 1804 by the three children of gardener Etienne Mouméja. Etienne had promised one daughter a dowry of one thousand francs and the other fifteen hundred francs and had appointed his son as his heir. The daughters requested, and the law agreed, that the son's share be reduced to half the estate—the portion disponible. Because Etienne's estate was valued at nineteen thousand francs, the two women shared ninety-five hundred francs rather than the twenty-five hundred their father had intended.[87]

As artisans had not fought to defend their corporations in 1791, neither did they try to fight or to evade the new inheritance laws. They could have used subterfuges like undervaluing the estate to reduce the portions of noninheriting children or tactics like maintaining the estate undivided under the tacit control of one heir. To be successful, however, such expedients required the cooperation or at least the acquiescence of all the legal heirs. The histories of most artisan families mitigated against such an expectation, and most artisans assumed, undoubtedly correctly, that their heirs would not be satisfied with less than what the law accorded them.[88]

Neither did artisans and shopkeepers tailor their chosen heir to fit the Civil Code. Elite families used the facility of the portion disponible to continue to favor one heir over the others to maintain the integrity of the patrimony. But such an adaptation was not a solution for small-business families. Unlike merchants and landowners, few artisans or shopkeepers owned much property outside the family business. Even if there were only

---

[86] The fate of Montauban's artisanal businesses was not unique. See Sewell, *Work and Revolution in France*, pp. 157–161.

[87] AD T-et-G 5E 2131 Latreille-Olivié no. 443 1 ventôse Year 12 accord Mouméja; See also 5E 1949 Caminel no. 316 27–7–1792 accord Bede frères; 1952 Caminel no. 463 3–8–1793 accord Fraisines Latout et soeur; 2130 Latreille-Olivié no. 417 28 pluviôse Year 12 accord Charles-Geneste and 1962 Caminel no. 429 23 ventôse Year 6 accord Issanchou et soeurs, in which the sisters specifically called attention to the laws of 14 and 17 nivôse Year 2 to justify their action.

[88] This may also be the reason for the artisans' resignation before the Allarde Law, which abolished the guilds. Increasing conflict within the guilds in the preceding fifteen years may have convinced most artisans that, in the absence of a united front, resistance was impossible.

TABLE 5–5
Artisans' Choice of Heir Before and After the Revolution

| | Men | | Women | |
Heir Chosen	1775–1793	1800–1824	1775–1793	1800–1824
Eldest male	35%	23%	28%	4%
Other kin	23	8	49	23
Coresident	14	10	7	10
Nonkin	5	3	9	10
Spouse	16	25	5	11
Equal division	7	31	2	42
N	43	61	43	52

Note: Significance level = .01, men contingency coefficient = .339, women contingency coefficient = .495.

two children to inherit, the favored heir would have to liquidate one third of the business to pay his sibling's claim. If there were more children, of course, the portion of the patrimony that could be reserved for a favored heir was correspondingly smaller, and the bulk of the estate had to be divided among the claimants. Few small businesses could survive such a drain on their capital. For most craftsmen and retailers, the double share that could be constructed under the Civil Code was not a viable alternative to equal inheritance because it was rarely sufficient to ensure the survival of the family business.[89]

Perhaps even more important to the artisans' inheritance decisions was the sudden change in the nature of their patrimony. Without the corporate system, without the corporate world view, the family business was reduced to little more than its components—capital, labor, premises, stock, and so on. It no longer secured an artisan a definitive and privileged place in society, a place that, with the material accoutrements of the business, he could pass on to his heir.[90] Stripped of its ability to confer status, the designation "favored heir" was less meaningful; as a consequence, the integrity and survival of the family business was less worth defending.

Thus the response of artisans and shopkeepers to the rule of equal inheritance was very different from that of the merchants and magistrates. Whereas the elite modified the details of property distribution, they maintained the same basic strategies and the same goals. The inheritance strat-

---

[89] For example, AD T-et-G 5E 13512 Martin fils no. 24 7–8–1815 vente Rabastens, in which the death of Jean Rabastens resulted in the liquidation of his retail business in order to pay off his debts and the portions of two of his four children.

[90] See Sewell, *Work and Revolution in France*, pp. 114–142, for a discussion of the implications of the Revolution's redefinition of property. Kaplan, in "Social Classification and Representation in the Corporate World," shows that artisans were fully aware that free trade was an assault on their patrimony.

egies of artisans and shopkeepers, however, changed in their fundamentals, affecting not only the distribution of the patrimony after death but also the dynamics of their households and businesses.

When the goal of the master artisan was to pass his business to his heir, the core of the family and the business had been the duo of father and son, with the marital couple playing a secondary and supportive role. When the revolution in inheritance law made it difficult to ensure the life of the family business beyond the lifetime of the patriarch, the priority of these two couples was reversed. The assistance of the wife became essential not only to the day-to-day running of the business and household, but also to the survival of the business. By leaving his property in her hands, the artisan or shopkeeper could extend the life of the family business from his own death until hers. Only when both partners of what became a mom-and-pop business were dead were its assets distributed. Inheritance became a two-step process. First the husband left the patrimony to his wife, usually part in ownership (the portion disponible) and the rest in usufruct. Then the wife, in turn, left the property to be divided equally among their children.

In the Old Regime, the wife's cooperation had been important in running a small family business, especially the retail side, although her partnership was usually unacknowledged. After the Revolution, more artisan husbands recognized their wives' importance as their relationships with their heirs became weaker and less exclusive. The master artisan remained the sole official head of both the business and the household. Just as there had been few formal partnerships between father and son, there were few between husband and wife. In fact, the Civil Code made such partnerships difficult because it reinforced a husband's control over his wife and her property. Nonetheless, artisans and shopkeepers began to act more frequently in concert with their wives. Before the Revolution, only 5 percent of artisans' notarized property transactions were joint actions of husband and wife; after 1794, these rose to 16 percent. Husbands and wives also began to appear more frequently as joint borrowers and lenders, and men who before the Revolution were most likely to chose their sons as their business representatives began to prefer their wives. For example, in 1809 carter Jean Negre authorized his wife to "direct and administer his goods and affairs, to receive and furnish receipts for any sums that may be due him for whatever reason, to pursue his debtors . . . to sell and buy" while he was out of town.[91]

That in the late eighteenth century artisan couples began to acknowl-

---

[91] AD T-et-G 5E 2136 Latreille-Olivié no. 799 16–10–1809 authorization Negre. Negre so authorized his wife again in 1811; 2138 Latreille-Olivié no. 20 7–1–1811. Similarly, 5E 2135 Latreille-Olivié no. 484 14–6–1808 authorization Mouméja; 2143 Latreille-Olivié no. 287 27–7–1815 achât Saligné ép Pujol and 12893 Grelleau no. 616 29 frimaire Year 6 quittance Belloc.

edge a unique, emotional attachment undoubtedly underlay the greater sense of unity between husband and wife and encouraged husbands to recognize their wives' complementary contributions to their households and businesses. But in the absence of a change in their relationship to the patrimony, it is likely that the marital partnership would have continued to defer to the partnership of father and son as it did in elite families. The prod of equal inheritance shifted the priorities in small-business families, bringing the team of husband and wife to the fore. The picture of the couple as the core of artisan business and family life, so lovingly painted by nineteenth-century historians, was a portrait not of "traditional" artisanal family patterns but of families created in a large part by Revolutionary inheritance law.

CHAPTER SIX

The Poor

In the eighteenth century, Montauban was busy and crowded, with little unused space in either the substantial brick buildings or in the narrow streets and infrequent squares. Families rented rooms, not apartments; workshops spilled over into courtyards; and retailers encroached on the pavement. One observer remarked that Montauban was too populated; even the *Couverts*, the market square that today seems spacious, he described as small and cramped, overstocked with merchandise and chaotic with vendors, porters, livestock, and customers.[1]

One of the regular actors in this scene was Antoinette Corbières, a cheese peddler. Without a shop, a stall, or even a permanent bench in the market, she made the street her place of business. Along the Grande Rue Montauban and through the side streets around the *Couverts* she hawked her wares from a tray that hung around her neck. Between customers she gossiped in doorways with her friends and flirted with the butcher's son from across the street. Once a week she walked twenty kilometers to the country town of Molières, where, on market day, she shared a bench with her sister who sold bread.[2]

Corbières was one of Montauban's numerous poor working people, participants in what historian Olwen Hufton has called an economy of makeshifts.[3] They included domestic servants, boatmen, stevedores, construction workers, retailers of a multitude of goods and services, and even some craftspeople. Most poor workers were unskilled, like refuse collectors, or semiskilled, like boatmen, although some were highly skilled but poorly paid; seamstresses and cloth shearers are two good examples. Most, too, were wage earners or piece workers, unprotected by corporate statutes because, throughout the century, merchant-manufacturers had lobbied vigilantly to prevent textile workers from obtaining permission to organize.[4]

---

[1] Guilhamon, *Richeprey* 2: 188.

[2] AD T-et-G 1 U 1 tribunal correctionnel 27 nivôse Year 8; 1 U 369 cour d'assises 18 germinal Year 9 and 1 U 370 cour d'assises 9 thermidor Year 10.

[3] This apt description is the title of two chapters in Hufton, *The Poor of Eighteenth Century France*.

[4] AN F¹² 776 Memoire of the Corps des marchands et facturiers de la ville et jurisdiction de Montauban to M. Le Peletier, Comptrolleur général 30–4–1728, opposing the efforts of the *sargeurs* to incorporate. Besides arguing that custom, the interests of the customer, and

However, it was not skill or even guild membership that most divided artisans and shopkeepers from the poor; it was income and, especially, property.[5] Unlike most shopkeepers and artisans, workers depended completely on the daily earnings of their labor. Economic necessity defined them; they had no capital, no savings, and few resources. No matter what they did to earn a living, they could rarely earn more than what they needed immediately. Royal commissioner Henry de Richeprey observed in 1781: "One can count close to ten thousand workers [in Montauban] who live from day to day. The least accident reduces them to the almshouse. If they become sick, one sees them die without resources, and when times are hard, for example, when wars depress the [textile] industry, they become beggars and vagabonds."[6] In good times they were the working people, in bad the destitute, and there was very little that separated one state from the other.

Although apparently quantifiable and therefore comparable, degrees of property owning did not produce a continuum of working people from Corbières near the bottom to Saint-Araille near the top. At some point, the difference in quantity became a real distinction in quality. The artisans and shopkeepers and the poor workers were two groups (with, of course, some overlap) differing not only in the amount of property they owned but in their organization of property, work, and family.

Saint-Araille's wealth, work, and family organization all depended on the business and property he had inherited from his father and that he passed on to his sons. Daughters had no part in the patrimony; they married out—out of the business, out of the household, out of the family. His wife's position, as we have seen, was similar. When she married Saint-Araille, she cut her ties with her family of origin but never became a full member of her husband's family; nor did she become a full participant in his business or have an equal interest in his property. For the artisans and shopkeepers in the eighteenth century, family, property, and business were different views of the same small enclosure.

Antoinette Corbières's familial and work experience was much less cohesive. She owned no property beyond her clothes, probably some linens and cooking utensils and perhaps her wares. Her family in Montauban consisted of her sister, but they did not live together. She shared a top-

---

the health of the textile industry depended on the manufacturer's right to hire whom he chose for whatever wage he chose, the letter accused the *sargeurs* of religious heresy because their articles of incorporation stipulated that two of the four officials of the guild were to be *nouveaux convertis*, that is, Protestants. Because since a large majority of the merchants were themselves *nouveau convertis*, their willingness to use this weapon against the *sargeurs* indicates the strength of their opposition to the workers' incorporation. In 1765 the Merchant Corps moved quickly to suppress an incipient organization of cloth shearers. AM Mont 8 HH 7 Manufacture; Jugements sur les contraventions 20–12–1765.

[5] Kaplow, *The Names of Kings*, p. 28.

[6] Guilhamon, *Richeprey* 2: 207.

floor room with five or six women, none of them related to her. Each worked separately and presumably paid a share in the rent, fuel, and food. They were friends; for example, Corbières cared enough about them to go to court to testify on behalf of three of her roommates who were accused of beating up another woman.[7] If Corbières had made a will, it is likely she would have left her meager possessions either to her sister or to one of her roommates. Her decision would have been different in quality from Saint-Araille's and not simply because her possessions were of little value. As Richard Cobb has pointed out in his study of Paris suicides, when people had very little, a pair of shoes, even a shirt or a handkerchief was precious.[8] She would dispose of her belongings differently from the way Saint-Araille would his because she did not identify her possessions with her work or with her family but rather with the tasks of daily living. She would have bequeathed her possessions to the people to whom she most owed her day-to-day survival. If she had been married, most likely this would have been her husband; unmarried, it was her friends and neighbors and her sister (see table 3–7).

The poor did not have a family business to absorb and unify the interests of husband and wife and of siblings or patrimony to cement generation to generation. Historians have tended to view this circumstance as a source of familial instability. Louise Tilly and Joan Scott conclude: "The bonds holding the proletarian family together, bonds of expediency and necessity, were often less permanent than the property interest (or the inherited skill) which united peasants and craftsmen."[9] As we have seen, however, patrimony also divided families; strategies that divided the family between those with property rights and those without often led to disputes and lawsuits. The family ties of the propertyless were not necessarily weaker than those of the propertied, but they were different. Family relationships were built on different premises and had different meanings for people like Corbières from what they had for people like Saint-Araille. Whereas artisans calculated long-term advancement, the poor lived from day to day. Next to their strength and wits, their families were their most important resource in the struggle for survival.[10]

And, in the late eighteenth and early nineteenth centuries, survival was often difficult. The textile industry, shaken by the Seven Years' War, never

---

[7] AD T-et-G 1 U 370 cour d'assises 9 thermidor Year 10.

[8] Cobb, *Death in Paris*, pp. 21–22. An example is the 1787 testament of Anne Silhes, a seamstress of Villenouvelle. She left her bed, curtains, and an armoire, which she had inherited from her mother, to her elder sister Jeanne. However, if Jeanne were to sell the armoire, she was obliged to give half of what she received for it to her younger sister, Guillamette. AD T-et-G 5E 12877 Grelleau sn 25–5–1787 testament Silhes.

[9] Tilly and Scott, *Women, Work and Family*, p. 21.

[10] Michael Anderson, *Family Structure in Nineteenth Century Lancaster* (Cambridge: Cambridge University Press, 1971), pp. 162–167.

recovered its equilibrium. Unemployment and high prices periodically beset the city. The traditional source of temporary assistance, the Catholic church, supported the hospital and intermittent distributions of work and food from the tithe, feudal dues, and pious gifts and legacies. By the 1770s, however, few of Montauban's parish priests had the resources to corral their flocks through periods of hardship. The number of wage earners had grown and charitable funds had shrunk. Pious legacies were no longer as common as they had been in the early part of the century; only 26 percent of the sample of testaments between 1775 and 1790 left anything to charity at all, and most of these legacies were no more than tokens. In 1789 the priest of Montauban's central parish apparently threw up his hands at the hordes of the unemployed and devoted his meager funds to aiding the *pauvres honteux*, the impoverished members of the upper classes.[11]

The town sought a solution through a central agency, a charity bureau, which would receive all charitable donations and coordinate emergency poor relief throughout the city. Organized to meet the subsistence crisis in 1778, the bureau enrolled fifteen hundred families and rapidly ran out of money. A decade later poor harvests led the town to resuscitate the bureau. Again, it was only a very qualified success. Because voluntary contributions did not raise the amount needed, the bureau repeatedly had to reduce the bread ration and finally begged the town council for an emergency grant in order to remain in operation.[12]

As Alan Forrest has shown in his study of public assistance in this period, the Revolution made survival more difficult for those dependent on charity. The break with the Catholic church and the abolition of Old Regime institutions eliminated the leading sources of charity, and although the Revolutionary regimes were great innovators of proposals for poor relief, they never had the money to put these into practice. The charitable funds of the Jacobin clubs and the occasional forced loans assessed on the wealthy did not make up the difference.[13] In Montauban,

---

[11] AM Mont 29 GG 2 bureau de charité 1778–1790. In January 1789 the curé of St Jacques reported that he had used a grant from the Cour des Aides to support the *pauvres honteux* of his parish. See Gutton, *La Société et les pauvres*, pp. 23–29, for a discussion of the *pauvres honteux.*. See Jones, *Charity and Bienfaisance*, pp. 76–94, 209–212, for a discussion of the shrinking and shifting nature of charitable giving in France in the eighteenth and early nineteenth centuries.

[12] Sol, "Bureaux de charité en Quercy," pp. 260–284; AM Mont AA 11 Livre rouge neuf 1775–1790, pp. 63–64, 24–1–1778; AM Mont 29 GG 2 bureau de charité 1778–1790. These requests were made monthly from March through September. Charity bureaus were the favorite panacea to pauperism in eighteenth-century France. See Gutton, *La Société et les pauvres*, pp. 435–436.

[13] Forrest, *The French Revolution and the Poor*, pp. 35–71; Jones, *Charity and Bienfaisance*, pp. 162–175.

the main contributors to the charity bureau in 1789 had been the diocese and the Cour des Aides while the bishop had headed its administration. Deprived of these resources, the charity bureau of 1790 was forced to abandon its plans for public works projects. Private charity dried up almost entirely; for example, only 6 percent of wills from 1791 through 1799 included charitable legacies. The only sources left were the municipal and national governments, but in Montauban recourse to public funds immediately became an issue in the local political struggle. From 1790 until the Napoleonic era, the level of public assistance depended more on the political stripe of the municipal government and its relationship with Paris than to the needs of the poor, who were often left without an avenue of appeal.[14]

The long war was another burden that the Revolution placed on the poor. In Montauban as elsewhere, both volunteers and conscripts were recruited primarily from the urban poor. The only man guillotined in Montauban (the town ordered the equipment for the occasion) was a harness maker arrested as the leader of an antidraft demonstration in 1793. The police arrested about three hundred demonstrators in all, mostly textile workers, but according to the official who reported the incident to Jeanbon Saint-André, they released most of them because "being of the indigent class [they] cannot be deprived of their liberty without depriving their families of the means to subsist."[15] However, conscription had the same effect. Members of the local Jacobin club pledged to employ on their return any of their workers who enlisted and helped out the families of their own members who were conscripted, but this was a small drop in a large bucket. Most soldiers were not volunteers and few workers were members of the Jacobin club. The war simply became one more tribulation of poverty.[16]

But although the war brought grief and hardship for many, it also brought Montauban a brief period of full employment. With the textile industry as well as the output of the grist mills requisitioned by the gov-

[14] In January 1790, a town council, dominated by textile merchants, decided to impose a surtax to fund the charity bureau. The Aristocrat party vociferously opposed this measure, claiming it was a hidden subvention of workers' wages benefiting the manufacturers at everyone else's expense. Their proposed solution was to force the manufacturers to provide full employment. When they won the municipal election, they repealed the surtax. This began a long argument over the causes and remedies of unemployment, which often left the charity bureau with no funds at all. AM Mont 29 GG 2 bureau de charité 1778–1790; Ligou, *Montauban*, pp. 396–402.

[15] Ligou, "Les Suspects dans le district de Montauban," p. 214, and Ligou, *Montauban*, pp. 415–418.

[16] Kennedy, *The Jacobin Clubs*, p. 197; Ligou, *Montauban*, p. 268, 310–312; Galabert, "Le Club jacobin de Montauban," 1: 142–143, 10: 313; Forrest, *The French Revolution and the Poor*, pp. 118–119, 138–168; Jones, *Charity and Bienfaisance*, pp. 172–179.

ernment, everyone could find a job, even the most incompetent, if factory inspectors were to be believed. Although food shortages continued and wages were fixed at quite low rates, wage earners had some political recourse. Numerous working people reported fraudulent butchers and bakers as well as their better-off neighbors to the police for black-marketeering and contraventions of the Maximum,[17] and workers in the government-run industries petitioned for higher wages, not always in vain. In the summer of 1795, for example, apprentice cloth shearers requested a pay increase proportionate to the recently approved increase in piece rates to the masters. The workshop foremen opposed the petition, claiming that the town council had no business deliberating on what was a private matter between master and apprentice. The town council of merchant-manufacturers thought otherwise. Stating that it was "in the interests of just such as those as the apprentice cloth shearers" that they had increased the piece rate, they ordered the masters to raise the apprentices' wages.[18]

And in the spring of 1793 and after 1799, lucky young men who had escaped conscription could earn a considerable capital for themselves or their families by selling themselves as replacements for well-off conscripts. As Bernard Schnapper's work on Bordeaux has established, the bulk of the replacements were urban workers. In Montauban, they tended to be textile workers, casual laborers, and journeymen from overcrowded and poverty-stricken trades like shoemaking and tailoring. The price varied depending on the extent of the draft and whether the young man to be replaced had already been called up or had merely reached draft age, but it rarely fell below one thousand francs, an amount equal to about three years' wages for a laborer.[19]

One aspect of the Revolution that did not have a great impact on the poor was the new family law. With little property, the poor had little to

[17] AM Mont 8 i 3 tribunal de la police 1793–Year 3.

[18] AM Mont 4 F 1 manufactures: ouvriers. This file also contains petitions for higher wages from grist mill workers, masons, and construction workers, workers in the saltpeter works, and print shop workers. According to Forrest, *The French Revolution and the Poor*, p. 112, the grievance procedures established in the public workshops often benefited workers.

[19] Schnapper, *Le Remplacement militaire*, pp. 27, 118–122. In a sample of replacement contracts signed in Montauban from 1799 to 1819, the price ranged between a low of three hundred francs for a naval recruit in 1800 to a high of six thousand francs to replace a soldier in active duty in 1813. The prices held fairly steady at around one thousand francs from 1799 until 1812, rose abruptly to around five thousand francs for the draft of 1813 when virtually everyone was called up, and then fell to around five hundred francs after Napoleon's defeat. According to Antoinette Wills, in *Crime and Punishment in Revolutionary Paris*, pp. 82, 107–108, the Revolution also created new opportunities in forging and passing forged assignats and documents. See AD T-et-G 1 U 94 cour d'assises 1812 for evidence of a flourishing trade in false birth certificates.

leave and little to inherit regardless of the laws of inheritance. Changes in marital law offered new legal formulas but did not change the realities of married life when the only resource and only security was the "daily work" of both husband and wife. Even divorce in most cases merely cloaked in legal garb preexisting informal arrangements. As Roderick Phillips has shown for Rouen, the largest number of divorces were granted to long-deserted wives, many of whom quickly married men with whom they had already been living.[20] In fact, the Revolution affected the family organization of the poor much less than that of other Montaubaners.

The elite, the artisans, and the property-owning peasants all modified their family strategies in part because these groups had designed them with particular futures in mind, futures disrupted by the Revolution and the changes in inheritance law. Poor families were less concerned with the future than were property owners; the present posed sufficient problems. For many, the Revolution presented new obstacles and new opportunities. A husband arrested or a brother conscripted meant increased hardship; a daughter employed by the government spinning factory or a son hired as a military replacement meant easier times. But none of these occurrences was unprecedented. Unemployment, illness, bread shortages, wage cuts, conscription, imprisonment, as well as occasional windfalls, were all within the experience of the poor in eighteenth-century Montauban; the Revolution perhaps lengthened the odds but did not change the nature of the lottery.

What percentage of Montauban's population was poor? Estimates of the size of the poor working population in French cities in the eighteenth century vary between 20 and 50 percent.[21] Figures from three different sources suggest that Montauban was near the high end of the scale because of the large number of textile workers. And nearly half of this population of workers teetered on the brink or slipped over into the abyss of indigence.[22] Approximately 32 percent of the population was too poor to pay any capitation tax at all. Census takers in 1774 noted that 23 percent of the households of the Villebourbon district were "poor," and in 1778 the

---

[20] Phillips, *Family Breakdown*, pp. 44–50, 142–148.

[21] Gutton, *La Société et les pauvres*, pp. 51–53; Forrest, *The French Revolution and the Poor*, pp. 1–12; Hufton, *The Poor of Eighteenth Century France*, pp. 21–24; Jones, *Charity and Bienfaisance*, p. 22.

[22] In the sample of marriage contracts (1775–1793) 46 percent of Montauban's grooms were wage earners and journeymen. Approximately 55 percent of the population were assessed for the 1788 capitation tax at only three livres or less. See AM Mont 5 CC 9 capitation 1788. The 1774 census of Villebourbon shows that 45 percent of the district's population were day laborers, boatmen, textile workers, and servants. See AM Mont 10 HH 1 dénombrement 1774.

charity bureau enrolled fifteen hundred families, about one fifth of the city's population; a similar number enrolled in 1789 and 1790.[23]

Although they made up a large part of Montauban's population and often claimed the anxious attention of municipal authorities, the working poor were underrepresented in public records. Tax lists, of course, excluded the propertyless and notary documents also privileged the propertied. Guilds recorded the affairs of master artisans and entrepreneurs like Saint-Araille, rarely the concerns of the journeymen and day workers; hospital and workhouse registers catalogued the indigent, whereas police and prison records dealt mostly with petty criminals and transients. However, by comparing the information from notary records, hospital, police, civil and criminal court records, and the 1774 census, we can begin to see Montauban's working poor emerge.

Of all these documents, the sample of marriage contracts sketches the most attractive portrait of poor families. Those who planned to marry were already among the most fortunate of the poor. Marriage coincided with the apogee of prosperity because bride and groom were at the height of their earning power and most had no dependents. They had managed to save up the price of the marriage contract and their wedding clothes, and almost all—93 percent—had amassed a small stock of goods, usually composed of such items as a bed, a mattress and linens, a wardrobe, some pots and pans, and a few livres in coin (see table 4–1). Although their average dowry was worth only about 250 livres, often this represented the savings of years of work. Very few working couples were able to sustain this modest prosperity through the childbearing years; and beyond, old age threatened.[24]

Workers and their brides came from a variety of backgrounds. Although the majority of other couples came from families very like the ones they were founding, only about 40 percent of worker couples had grown up in urban working families. More than one third were the children of peasants and newcomers to Montauban. Forty-four percent of worker grooms in the sample of marriage contracts had lived in Montauban for less than five years.[25] Pushed out of their villages by a growing population and pulled to

---

[23] Ibid.; AM Mont 29 GG 2 bureau de charité 1778–1790. In March 1790, in response to a circular letter from the newly formed Comité de Mendicité, the intendant estimated that one sixth of Montauban's population was indigent. Bloch and Tuetey, eds., *Comité de Mendicité de la Constituante*, p. 485.

[24] In the sample of marriage contracts (1775–1799) the mean dowry of worker's bride was 248 livres (range 10 to 1317, median 186.5). By comparison, the mean dowry of an artisan's bride before the Revolution was 1431 livres. See also Hufton, *The Poor of Eighteenth Century France*, p. 32, and Garden, *Lyon et les lyonnais* p. 170.

[25] Another 18 percent were immigrants who had been in the city for more than five years. Only 38 percent of worker grooms, compared with 53 percent of other Montauban grooms, had been born in Montauban (signficance level = .03, contingency coefficient = .172).

TABLE 6–1
Social Origins of Montauban Workers, 1775–1824

Father's Occupation	City Workers		Brides of City Workers	
	1775–1799	*1800–1824*	*1775–1799*	*1800–1824*
Peasant	41%	14%	35%	21%
City worker	40	48	41	31
Artisan retailer	18	37	22	47
Elite	1	1	2	1
N	99	85	102	86

Note: Significance level = .01, grooms contingency coefficient = .295, brides contingency coefficient = .259.

the city by the promise of employment, the high percentage of immigrant brides and grooms was testimony to the opportunities that still existed in Montauban in the years before the Revolution for those who were young, healthy, and lucky.[26]

Because many workers were immigrants, fewer resided with their parents or other relatives than did other Montauban brides and grooms. Less than half of worker grooms lived with their parents at the time they contracted marriage. Their brides, although more likely to live with their families, also lived and worked away from home more often than did other Montauban brides. Just where "home" might be was problematic for people like peddler René Bournot, who contracted to marry a Ville-nouvelle woman in 1788. He had been born in Mâcon, but his father was dead and his mother, who had remarried, had left town.[27]

As wage earners, even if they lived with their parents, poor brides and grooms were relatively free from the dictates of familial advancement when they decided to marry. In general, they did not marry into a family business as did merchants, artisans, and landowning peasants. They met their future spouses in their lodgings and in the neighborhood streets and shops; they courted them in walks along the quay, in the gardens above the Tescou, or at dances under the *Couverts*.[28] Theirs was a choice over

[26] Fairchilds, in *Domestic Enemies*, pp. 64–66, argues that women were most likely "pushed" out of their villages by economic necessity whereas men were sometimes "pulled" by the greater opportunities of the city. This continued to be the case in the nineteenth century. See Sewell, *Structure and Mobility*, pp. 161–177.

[27] AD T-et-G 5E 2008 Garrigues no. 325 14–4–1788 contrat de mariage Bournot-Belmontet.

[28] Most of the accounts of courtship come from those that went wrong—paternity suits. See AM Mont 6 FF 46, 47, 59, and 60 dossiers de procédures jugées par les jurisdictions consulaires 1775, 1776, 1789, 1790. See also AD T-et-G G459[bis] procédures devant l'Officialité 1773–1779, petition of Rivière and Lombard. Very few urban workers petitioned

TABLE 6–2
Parental Mortality and Residence, 1775–1799

| | Groom's Occupation | | | |
	Peasant	City Worker	Artisan	Elite
Grooms with				
parents dead	38%	34%	18%	10%
parents alive				
live with parents	47	18	46	49
live on own	15	48	36	41
Brides with				
parents dead	28%	40%	22%	10%
parents alive				
live with parents	55	36	61	82
live on own	17	24	17	8
N	185	103	69	48

Note: Significance level = .01, grooms contingency coefficient = .282, brides contingency coefficient = .248.

which their parents had little influence. Some young immigrants arrived in Montauban thoughtfully provided by their parents with a blanket notarized consent to marry whomever they chose.[29]

Yet most of the poor brides and grooms were not isolated individuals; they were securely entrenched in their families and communities. Although immigrants, most were familiar with Montauban and had connections there. Thirty-five percent of workers' brides had been born in the countryside immediately surrounding the city. Their fathers were day laborers from the vineyards of Le Fau, for example, whose slopes overlooked Montauban from the south, or farm servants from Falguières to the north, or weavers in St Etienne de Tulmon, or boatmen from the numerous hamlets along the Garonne. Grooms tended to come from greater distances; only 17 percent came from Quercy, and 21 percent were natives of the surrounding provinces of Languedoc, Lomagne, and Aveyron.[30] Yet even they may well have worked in their native villages for

for dispensation to marry relatives—only three out of ninety-two petitions from 1750 to 1789. This suggests that workers in a city of Montauban's size had a large pool from which to choose a mate and that family pressures such as a desire to keep property within the family or to weld kinship-cum-business connections played little part in their considerations. See Darrow, "Popular Concepts of Marital Choice," pp. 261–272.

[29] See, for example, AD T-et-G 5E 2106 Franceries no. 200 25–1–1809 consentment Mondon à Mondon fils and 1942 Caminel no. 174 29–7–1787 procuration Dulau v^c Saint Roma à sa fille.

[30] Throughout eighteenth-century France, men tended to migrate greater distances than women. See Garden, *Lyon et les lyonnais*, pp. 107–108; Fairchilds, *Domestic Enemies*, pp. 61–64; and Hufton, *The Poor of Eighteenth Century France*, pp. 92–98.

TABLE 6–3
Geographic Origin of Montauban Brides and Grooms, 1775–1799

	Groom's Occupation			
Birthplace	City Worker	Artisan	Merchant	Bourgeois
Montauban				
Groom	39%	57%	86%	73%
Bride	42	75	95	82
Quercy				
Groom	17	13	7	18
Bride	35	17	5	9
Surrounding provinces				
Groom	21	15	0	0
Bride	19	6	0	9
Outside region				
Groom	23	15	7	9
Bride	4	2	0	0
N	82	54	20	11

Note: Significance level = .01, grooms contingency coefficient = .309, brides contingency coefficient = .393.

Montauban landlords and textile merchants and come to Montauban's markets and festivals. Landlords and textile merchants often acted as employment agents; peasant women, in particular, sometimes found their first jobs in the city working as servants in their landlords' town houses. Relatives and fellow villagers already working in the city were another important channel of recruitment.[31] And, as David Garrioch has shown, eighteenth-century French cities welcomed newcomers who were able to work and willing to socialize. An immigrant might be stuck with the nickname "Provinsal" or "Rodez," but he could quickly become a recognized member of the neighborhood community.[32]

[31] Valmary, *Familles paysannes*, p. 28. Merchant Pierre Lacoste-Rigail employed the daughter of one of his tenant farmers as chambermaid to his wife. Ombret et al., *Villes et Campagnes du Bas-Quercy*, B6. See also Maza, *Servants and Masters*, p. 139; Collomp, *La Maison du Père*, pp. 231–233; and Sewell, *Structure and Mobility*, pp. 159–160.

[32] Garrioch, *Neighbourhood and Community in Paris*, pp. 227–229. Many working people went by nicknames. Some, like "St Araille," were handed down in the family. Many, however, related to regional origins or occupations. AM Mont 10 HH 1 dénombrement 1774 lists, among others, a wineshop keeper Jean Dalmont *dit* Villefranche, an apprentice cloth shearer Jean Mauri *dit* Clermont, and a boatman called Paisant (peasant), as well as Bernard Sevegues, a teamster for the grist mill nicknamed "Barrel," and a boatman Pierre Noyes called "Barge." Female nicknames tended to be feminized forms of their husbands' names, like Baudonette and Capette, widows of Baudon and Capet, or sexual, like Marie Daubanes *dite* Marion Latarte, who was accused of abandonning a child in AM Mont 6 FF 46 jurisdictions consulaires 1775.

A measure of immigrant workers' ties to their families and to their new urban community was the ritual of witnessing the marriage contract. Although not the great familial occasions among the poor that they were for the wealthy, considering demography, the difficulties of travel, and the expense of taking time from work, the marriage contracts of many poor couples show an impressive degree of familial and community support. Most workers had lost at least one parent by the time they married; in the sample of marriage contracts, 38 percent of grooms and 28 percent of brides were orphans (see table 6–2). However, when parents were alive, they almost always came to witness the contract or delegated an official proxy to represent them. And, although the bride usually had saved most of her dowry herself, in 44 percent of the contracts her parents promised to contribute as well (see table 6–5). In one quarter of the contracts, the grooms' parents made gifts to the couple. The marriage of servant Antoinette Lamolle and gardener Jean Monat is typical. Antoinette was twenty-five years old, born in Cahors, but a resident of Montauban for more than ten years. Monat was a local man, born and raised in Sapiac, where his father grew vegetables and fruit for a local magistrate. When they contracted marriage in 1787, both sets of parents attended as did Antoinette's employer, a merchant's wife. Antoinette constituted a dowry worth 206 livres in all. To amass this sum, her employer contributed 100 livres owed her in back wages, her father gave her a bed worth 20 livres and promised goods worth 50 livres at his death, and Antoinette herself added a trousseau of linens worth 36 livres. The groom's father completed the household with a gift of furniture worth 60 livres.[33]

A very different picture of the urban poor emerges from the records of Montauban's hospital, the Hôtel Dieu. Entry into the Hôtel Dieu was the last resort of those who were unemployed, ill, and without resources; very often it was the immediate prelude to death and the paupers' grave. Hospital records giving information about the inmates exist only for the 1720s, a period when the hospital was better able to cope with the demands made on it than later in the century. In the 1780s and 1790s, the hospital was overwhelmed by a flood of abandoned infants and children, but in the 1720s half of the inmates were between the ages of sixteen and thirty, an age group corresponding to engaged couples. Some were young families struck down by disease, like the Quittard family whose four members were admitted within days of each other. More often they were single men and women.[34]

---

[33] AD T-et-G 5E 1943 Caminel no. 271 20–5–1787 contrat de mariage Monat-Lamolle. See also 5E 2014 Garriques no. 508 29–4–1792 contrat de mariage Bonnet-Garrisson and 2136 Latreille-Olivié no. 778 10–8–1809 contrat de mariage Duminy-Dupuy.

[34] Archives Hospitalières de Montauban (hereafter AH Mont) F 4 registre des entrés 1724–28; Ligou, *Montauban*, p. 400; Fairchilds, *Poverty and Charity*, pp. 83–84, 155; Jones, *Charity and Bienfaisance*, p. 193.

Young male inmates were different from the poor grooms of the marriage contracts. There were far fewer textile workers and apprentices among them and many more tinkers, peddlers, woodcutters, and terrace builders—itinerant workers from the mountains of the Rouergue, the Auvergne, and the Pyrenees. David Garrioch has pointed out that in eighteenth-century Paris the working population contained both people closely enmeshed in neighborhood communities and a number of transients with neither settled work nor residence, such as journeymen, casual laborers, boatmen, and beggars.[35] Montauban had its share of this population; the 1774 census of Villebourbon listed several families of beggars whose surnames were in fact soubriquets—Lauvergne, Provinsal—indicating their origins in distant provinces. Such people often ended up in the Hôtel Dieu or in jail. Some, like twenty-three-year-old Jacques Loquez from the Auvergne, visited both. Picked up by the police for begging, Loquez was initially placed in the Hôtel Dieu. However, the hospital administrators judged him a malingerer, a liar, and a vagabond and removed him to prison.[36]

Women inmates, however, closely resembled workers' brides. Jeanne, surname unknown, was a servant born in Molières who had entered the hospital voluntarily because of illness. Inmates Anne Paysou, aged twenty, and Marguerite Vales, aged twenty-eight, were spinners and natives of Montauban. Three quarters of the female patients came from the city or the nearby countryside, and almost all were servants or textile workers.[37]

The difference in origins suggests the different experience of male and female workers in Montauban. Young women were more vulnerable than were young men. Many of the women in the Hôtel Dieu were admitted in labor or because of postpartum debility or infection. As several historians have shown, childbirth was one of the most common and certainly the most serious risk to a working woman's health and livelihood.[38] As Marianne Dubosc discovered in 1790, few employers hesitated to fire a servant

---

[35] Garrioch, *Neighbourhood and Community in Paris*, pp. 147–148, 202–204; also Kaplow, *The Names of Kings*, pp. 30–31. Both Poussou, *Bordeaux et le Sud-Ouest*, pp. 167–172, and Sewell, *Structure and Mobility*, pp. 221–231, make the point that immigrants from farthest away, who were "on the road" in temporary or mobile occupations, were most likely to be convicted of crimes. This was true both in eighteenth-century Bordeaux and nineteenth-century Marseille.

[36] AM Mont 10 HH 1 dénombrement Villebourbon 1774; AH Mont F 4 registre des entrés 1724–1728. Also see Garden, *Lyon et les lyonnais*, p. 96, and Forrest, *The French Revolution and the Poor*, pp. 90–92.

[37] AH Mont F 4 registre des entrés 1724–1728. For similar cases see Fairchilds, *Poverty and Charity*, pp. 85–86, and Hufton, *The Poor of Eighteenth Century France*, pp. 318, 332–333.

[38] Hufton, *The Poor of Eighteenth Century France*, pp. 324–332; Tilly and Scott, *Women, Work and Family*, pp. 56–58; Depauw, "Amour illégitime," pp. 1155–1182; Tilly, Scott, and Cohen, "Women's Work and European Fertility Patterns," pp. 447–476.

they suspected was pregnant. While working as a serving maid at the Auberge de la Menuisière, Dubosc was courted by Jean Michel, the inn's stableboy. When the innkeeper discovered Michel hiding in Dubosc's room, she fired Dubosc; Michel kept his job.[39] Even for an independent working woman like Antoinette Corbières, pregnancy put her subsistence in jeopardy. Corbières appeared in the police records in a dramatic scene, played out in 1800. Pregnant from her affair with the butcher's son, she tried to force him to marry her by putting two pistols to his head.[40] The desperation of her action reflected the desperation of her situation. Hampered by an infant, she would have been unable to carry on her business and could not have afforded a wet nurse. On the one side lay the modicum of security offered by marriage; on the other loomed the wards of the Hôtel Dieu. A working woman needed better luck than was Corbières's portion to survive.

Leaving aside the issue of pregnancy, the typical circumstances of female employment also increased the risks for women. Almost all young female workers were spinners or servants, workers who lived and worked in their employers' households. In theory, domestic workers received their wages yearly, but in fact their pay was often years in arrears and sometimes never materialized. A sample of loans reveals that 13 percent of those in which a city worker was the creditor were in reality records of unpaid wages to women servants. When there was a slump in the textile industry, a woman could lose simultaneously her job, her room and board, and her savings.[41]

The registers of the Hôtel Dieu reveal other sorts of disasters as well. In times of crop failure, epidemic, and unemployment, the Hôtel Dieu admitted children and old people whom poor families could not support. In the 1720s, 16 percent of the inmates were under the age of sixteen and a similar percentage were sixty or older. Marie Delpont, an octogenarian widow, was one such case. Before entering the hospital she had lived with her son, a wool carder, but he could no longer feed her. Pierre Lagarde, aged eight, was admitted in June, collected by his parents one month later, readmitted in September, and released again to his family in May.[42] In the 1720s there were few truly abandoned children, but this changed as the century progressed. In the 1780s and 1790s, charity hospitals were flooded with foundlings. At nearly every Montauban town council meet-

---

[39] AM Mont 6 FF 60 jurisdictions consulaires 1790. When Dubosc discovered that she was indeed pregnant, the innkeeper did try to help her by pressuring Michel to pay the costs.

[40] AD T-et-G 1 U 1 tribunal correction 27 nivôse Year 8.

[41] Tilly and Scott, *Women, Work and Family*, p. 31, and Hufton, *The Poor of Eighteenth Century France*, pp. 27–31; Fairchilds, in *Domestic Enemies*, p. 70, notes that every year when noble employers shut up their town houses to move to their chateaus, they usually laid off most of their servants so that even a fairly secure job in a well-to-do household was subject to seasonal unemployment.

[42] AH Mont F 4 registre des entrés 1724–1728.

ing from 1788 through 1791, the city government voted to assume the financial responsibility of caring for infants and children who were orphaned or abandoned. In 1788, the twelve hundred livres budgeted for this purpose ran out in August; the following year it ran out in May. In 1791, the number of abandoned children on the public charge was three times that of the early 1770s.[43]

Marriage contracts recorded moments of security and optimism; the registers of the Hôtel Dieu testified to hopes deceived and security lost. The daily life of poor families usually poised between the two. Montauban's working men and women had little in the way of property and few expectations of betterment; they could expect to save little, inherit less. Their lives traced a fairly predictable trajectory.

Childhood was difficult and often short; only about 60 percent of workers' children survived to their fifth year.[44] Infant mortality was high in part because working mothers could not devote much time to child care. As a petition to Montauban's town council stated, Anne Brengou needed help supporting her two children because "her work is so often interrupted by the care she is obliged to take of her children, that she cannot afford to feed them."[45] Nor could Brengou or women like her afford to hire a wet nurse because the monthly charge was a week's income or more. In fact, some were wet nurses themselves; five Villebourbon women—two boatmen's wives, two wives of textile workers, and one servant's wife—nursed bourgeois infants in their homes. A few even poorer women took in foundlings from the Hôtel Dieu.[46] Women whose work took them out of the home left their children in the care of neighbors, older siblings, and especially grandmothers. At least one Villebourbon textile worker couple sent their infant to be raised by his grandmother in the countryside. El-

[43] AM Mont 2 BB 21 délibérations du conseil général 1788–1789; Ligou, *Montauban*, p. 400. This was the situation throughout France. See Fairchilds, *Poverty and Charity*; Hufton, *The Poor of Eighteenth Century France*, pp. 318, 332–333; Forrest, *The French Revolution and the Poor*, pp. 116–137; Jones, *Charity and Bienfaisance*, p. 193.

[44] Calculated from AD T-et-G E Etat Civil Protestant no. 366–374. The chances of survival for all Montauban infants were better than this. According to Ligou, *Montauban*, p. 172, of every 4.3 children born, 3 survived. See also Pinede, "La Population du Quercy," pp. 64–66, and Gausseran "La Population montalbanaise," pp. 60–66.

[45] AM Mont 2 BB 21 Conseil général 1788–1789.

[46] AM Mont 10 HH 1 dénombrement 1774; AN F[15] 1210 hospices, bureaux de bienfaisance (Tarn-et-Garonne). Although most of the nurses hired by the town lived in the countryside, a few lived in Montauban. In 1809 the town paid ten francs a month although the going market rate was twelve. The town later tried to cut the payment to eight francs, but hospital authorities reported that "the class of artisans who place their babies with wet nurses pay them at least twelve francs a month," and it was virtually impossible to hire nurses for less. Nurses told of the impending wage cut threatened to return the babies to the hospital. See also Sussman, *Selling Mothers' Milk*, pp. 19–27, 58–64, 101–104.

derly mothers and mothers-in-law taken into their children's households probably repaid at least part of their debt by baby-sitting.[47]

During adolescence and early adulthood a worker's lot improved as the family's income increased with the number of wage earners. Some parents formally apprenticed their sons in a trade. Unlike the apprenticeships of artisans' sons which often cost hundreds of livres, training for the sons of the poor was very inexpensive, costing at most one hundred livres and often nothing at all; the children reimbursed their masters with their own work. An example was the apprenticeship of Raimond de l'Hoste, son of a textile worker, to plasterers Antoine Mathaly and François Delport in 1779. Raimond was to work for them without wages for eighteen months while he learned the trade. His parents would continue to house and feed him, a simple arrangement because they all lived on the same street. Similarly, in 1782 laborer François Ressejac apprenticed his son to his next-door neighbor, a weaver. Young Ressejac ate and slept at home and the only extra expense to his family was the cost of a shuttle, a pair of scissors, and pincers "appropriate to the said trade."[48] Girls, too, worked although their training was usually less formal. The daughters of textile workers learned to sort, wind, and spin wool from their mothers. Peddler Marie Marre took her niece with her on her rounds to teach her the business.[49]

Although most young workers lived at home, as they grew older they began to move out on their own. Jeanne Dufau, for example, lived with her employer Marie Soulié for several months in order to learn more about the seamstress's craft; other girls left home to work as servants in the households of the well-to-do or as spinners and draw girls in weavers' households. Although most of the servants counted in the Villebourbon census were "strangers" from the countryside, one third were native Montaubaners.[50] Because poor households "exported" teenagers and young

[47] AM Mont 10 HH 1 dénombrement 1774 listed in faubourg Gasseras, *sargeur* Pierre Bonhoure and his wife and son with another son "at nurse in Gasseras with his mother-in-law." AM Mont 2 BB 21 conseil général 8–8–1788 and 5–9–1788 motions that the town assume care for two infants left with neighbors, one by a mother who decamped, the other whose mother was desperately ill.

[48] AD T-et-G 5E 2083 Franceries no. 334 8–6–1779 apprentissage Del'hoste à Mathalye et Delport and 12871 Grelleau no. 290 3–7–1782 apprentissage Ressejac à Tissendie; similary, 2083 Franceries no. 438 12–8–1779 apprentissage Coyne à Tieys; 12876 Grelleau no. 246 23–4–1786 apprentissage Baillet à Delboy and no. 398 22–7–1786 apprentissage Cassan à Eon.

[49] AD T-et-G 1 U 368 cour d'assises 2 fructidor Year 8. A sample of twenty-seven apprentice contracts notarized in Montauban from 1779 to 1789 includes not a single female apprentice even though police records and marriage contracts sometimes identified women as apprentice seamstresses, for example.

[50] AM Mont 10 HH 1 dénombrement 1774. This is a much higher percentage of urban-born servants than Maza found in Aix-en-Provence and Marseilles (16.5 percent) (*Servants and Masters*, pp. 30–31) and Fairchilds found in Toulouse (6 percent), Bordeaux (3 percent), and Paris (9 percent) (*Domestic Enemies*, p. 62). It is possible that both exaggerate rural-born

adults to the households of their better-off neighbors, working peoples' households were fairly small, usually containing only three or four people. According to the Villebourbon census of 1774, although 16 percent of all households had six or more members, only 8 percent of workers' households were that large.[51]

Whereas most young adults left home to be incorporated into another household, some boys went farther afield, either by force or by choice, leaving home and family behind. Some became immigrants through unemployment. Gerand Mouméja called "Viande," suspected of robbing a church, told the police that having been laid off from his work as a wool comber, he had spent three weeks in Castelnau-Montratier working on the roads. He had come to Montauban, he claimed, to try to get a job in the Vialètes factory.[52] Some were conscripted into the army, a fate that befell a large number in the 1790s and in the final years of Napoleon's reign. Some took up traveling occupations as peddlers or boatmen. In 1774 boatman Antoine Dalles reported to the census taker that one of his sons was in the merchant marine and he did not know whether he was alive or dead. Perhaps young Dalles had followed his father's trade on the river until, once in Bordeaux, he had felt the call of the sea.[53]

Whether living at home and contributing to the family income or supporting themselves on their own, most young workers hoped and planned for marriage and a family of their own. But from the high point of marriage, a downward curve began with the birth of children as dependents increased while income remained the same or declined. This was the point when unemployment, illness, and death were most devastating to a poor family. The illness or death of a young mother might leave the father with children he could neither supervise nor, if they were infants, feed. In July 1788 one father, confronted with the death of his wife, skipped town, leaving their infant with a wet nurse whom he could not afford to pay.[54] The illness or death of a father was even more serious because he was the

---

servants in the population, however, because their source—notary records—was more likely to mention a woman's occupation if she was away from her family. It is also possible that Montauban had more native servants than these cities because it was primarily an industrial city. Many of these "servants" were wool sorters, spinners, and draw girls who would have been recruited from the families of urban textile workers.

[51] AM Mont 10 HH 1 dénombrement; similar figures derive from AM Mont 29 GG 3 états nominatifs des pauvres 1778.

[52] AM Mont 6 FF 59 jurisdictions consulaires 15–4–1789. Other young men picked up by the police had similar stories; for example, journeyman mason Pierre Belmont's peregrinations are recounted in AM Mont 6 FF 47 jurisdictions consulaires 12–4–1773. Romon, in "Le Monde des pauvres à Paris," p. 735, reports that most of the male beggars arrested in Paris cited the loss of a job as the reason they took to the road.

[53] AM Mont 10 HH 1 dénombrement 1774.

[54] AM Mont 2 BB 21 conseil général 7–11–1788. Sussman, *Selling Mothers' Milk*, pp. 62–63.

family's main wage earner. To begin with, women earned less than men, and women with small children to supervise earned even less because, as a journeyman's widow reminded the town council in her petition for public assistance, they could rarely put in an uninterrupted day's work.[55] Although men were usually quick to replace a dead wife, especially if they had children to raise, remarriage was not as easy for women in the same circumstances, as the Villebourbon census demonstrated. In 1774, there were 111 households headed by widows with children and only 55 headed by widowers with children. The feminization of poverty is hardly a new phenomenon; in Villebourbon, 41 percent of female-headed households were listed as poor compared with only 17 percent of male-headed households.[56]

If a poor family was fortunate enough to survive these difficult years, it had another brief upswing, when most of the children were working. Then came the final downward plunge of old age, when decreasing capacities and earnings led at last to permanent indigence and dependence. Under these conditions, not only family but also friends and neighbors were essential props in the daily effort to survive.

Notary documents consistently shortchanged the importance of family ties among the urban poor because the kind of exchange they recorded usually involved property, whereas exchanges between the laboring poor were more likely to consist of services. Neighbors and female relatives, for example, often cared for the children of mothers whose work took them away from home. Such a "debt" did not appear in a notary's register. Whenever the records reveal family ties and exchanges of services, it is safe to assume that these represent only a small part of the raft of interdependence that kept poor families afloat.

---

[55] AM Mont 2 BB 21 conseil général 28–11–1788. Official wage lists from 1790 show that draw girls earned fourteen sous a day compared with general laborers in construction who earned one livre (twenty sous); most female work, however, was paid by the piece and so comparisons are difficult. A seamstress earned eight sous for a skirt and twelve sous for a man's shirt; a spinner earned eight sous for three and a half pounds of ordinary thread. The official value of a day's labor was set at one livre. It seems very unlikely that many women workers earned that much with any regularity. AM Mont M.S. 20 no. 84 Arrêté du Conseil Général de la Commune de Montauban; Ligou, "Montauban des lumières," p. 181.

[56] AM Mont 10 HH 1 dénombrement 1774. Widows headed 16 percent of all households and 10 percent of all households with children and made up 5 percent of the total population of Villebourbon, whereas widowers headed 5 to 11 percent of all households and 5 percent of households with children and made up only 1.5 to 3 percent of the population. The figures for the widowers are uncertain because although the census gave the marital status of almost all women it rarely did so for men, and this must be inferred from the composition of the household. Gutton, *Société et les pauvres*, pp. 36–37. See also Hufton, "Women and the Family Economy," p. 11, and Carlo S. Corsini, "Why Is Remarriage a Male Affair? Some Evidence From Tuscan Villages During the Eighteenth Century," in Dupâquier et al., eds., *Marriage and Remarriage*, pp. 385–394.

Relatives could provide financial aid. An urban worker was almost certain to be unemployed at one time or another. In order to buy necessities, workers sold or pawned possessions, lived on the credit extended by shopkeepers and landlords, and borrowed small sums.[57] They rarely notarized their debts because this service cost money; only 6 percent of debtors and 9 percent of creditors in the sample of notarized loans were workers. However, these formal transactions were consistent with more common, less formal lending behavior—that is, the sums involved were small (one third under one hundred livres), the time periods short (half for a year or less) or unspecified (to be repaid "from day to day"), and often the lender charged no interest. More than any other group, the city working people borrowed to cover daily expenses and borrowed in kind, especially grain. They also borrowed more often from relatives and from people like landlords, employers, and co-workers and less often from professional moneylenders than other Montaubaners. Most frequently, the loans were between siblings, particularly from sisters to brothers and also between siblings-in-law. Next in frequency were loans made by younger persons to older relatives, from children to parents especially. Predictably, because of the life cycle of the poor, there were very few loans that went in the opposite direction, from older persons to younger ones.[58]

One service recorded by notaries was the *procuration*, or power of attorney. As this was mainly a commercial device, the working poor were again underrepresented both as appointers and as appointees, but when poor workers did appoint proxies they chose family over professional help. Sixty-two percent appointed relatives to represent them; the most common proxy was the spouse. Older relatives often did services for younger kin—mothers and fathers acted for their children, uncles acted for their nephews, and so on. Brothers, sisters, siblings-in-law, and cousins also represented each other. For example, in 1780 Pierre Laborde, a carpenter's apprentice from the Auch region, contracted marriage to his cousin, the daughter of a Montauban textile worker. Laborde had been a resident of Montauban for only five months, staying with another cousin, Pierre Antoine Delaye, a blacksmith. Laborde's father appointed Delaye as his proxy to consent to the marriage.[59]

Families also shared lodging and provided temporary support as Delaye did for his country cousin. Unlike in artisan families, the recipients of

---

[57] Kaplow, *The Names of Kings*, p. 99.

[58] Margaret H. Darrow, "French Families and the Revolution in Inheritance Law: Montauban, 1775–1825" (Ph.D. diss., Rutgers University, 1981), pp. 234–235. See, for example, AD T-et-G 5E 2337 Martin no. 152 11–4–1788 testament of Catherine Espagna, a serving maid, who left her blind brother life rights to her inheritance from their parents.

[59] Ibid., p. 236; AD T-et-G 5E 12869 Grelleau no. 635 1–12–1780 contrat de mariage Laborde-Capdaze.

room and board were not likely to be newly married couples like Saint-Araille and his bride. Workers were less likely to need support at this point in their lives than earlier or later. Single people, old people, and children needed the most help and it was often forthcoming.

In April 1774 the population of Villebourbon included 546 households of working people and 113 servants living in the households of artisans, bourgeois, and merchants. Sixteen percent of the workers' households included "extra" people, that is, persons who were neither the spouse nor the child of the head of the household. Some were orphaned children, like the six-year-old girl who lived with her aunt, the widow Argeol, a wool sorter. Some were young adults, like the niece of textile worker André Estampes who was a spinner, and seamstresses Antoinette Prunetis and her friend Marie Legrand who lived with Antoinette's brother, his wife, and their four children. In many cases the extra person was an elderly parent like Thimothé Vidallet's disabled father, who lived with his boatman son and peddler daughter-in-law.[60]

Working families who took in needy kin were not always in secure economic circumstances. Ten were beggars and more than half were listed as "poor" in the census. Some of the relatives they housed also were beggars, as were, for example, boatman Samuel Gaillard's mother-in-law, who lived with her daughter and son-in-law, and widow Coustan, who lived with her apprentice son and his family. Since her daughter-in-law had five young children, Coustan probably had several small apprentices in her trade.[61]

Poor people most likely to need regular assistance were the elderly and the incapacitated, often one and the same. Because workers lived by their daily work and not from investments or family businesses, when they could no longer work they had no income. And the work many did wore them down before their time. Boatmen, stevedores, and casual laborers depended on strength and agility and textile workers and seamstresses

---

[60] Eighty-nine of the workers' households were extended, 64 by kin and 25 by unrelated persons. There was a total of 133 "extra" individuals, 87 kin and 46 nonkin. The most common were mothers and mothers-in-law (28), unrelated lodgers (24), sisters and sisters-in-law (19), brothers and brothers-in-law (18), unrelated orphaned children (12), and grandchildren (11). Others included fathers, nieces and nephews, aunts, daughters and sons-in-law, cousins, apprentices, and nurslings. AM Mont 10 HH 1 dénombrement 1774.

[61] Ibid. The census takers distinguished between beggars and "poor" families who probably also depended on charity. Several of the beggar households bore surnames that were in fact soubriquets—La Soleil, Baudonette, Lauvergne, Provinsal—often indicating origins outside Quercy. The census takers may have been making a distinction between respectable poverty, deserving of assistance, which had its roots in the community, and alien poverty, possibly dangerous and requiring repression. See Gutton, *La Société et les pauvres*, pp. 419–437; Romon, "Le Monde des pauvres à Paris."

needed nimble figures and good eyesight. Loss of these faculties pushed a poor worker over the brink into indigence.

Despite their limited resources, many poor families cared for invalid and elderly relatives at home. Richard Cobb and David Garrioch have emphasized the willingness of workers to abandon relatives who could no longer earn their keep, but this is a distorted image, derived from scrutiny of decisions of last resort.[62] In Villebourbon in 1774, forty-three workers' households, half of whom were further qualified as "poor," included members, often extra members, who were elderly or ill or both. For example, the household of poor wool comber Pierre Pougeol contained his wife, three children, and mother-in-law, who was described as infirm, and boatman Antoine Dalles gave shelter to his elderly invalid cousin.[63] Workers who temporarily became dependents tried to repay their benefactors as best they could. For example, in 1779, widow Anne Falga sold to her sister Marie, wife of a wool comber, her half of the two-room apartment the two sisters shared (presumably inherited from their parents). The price was sixty livres, from which Marie was to deduct forty-one livres and eight sous for "divers loans in money and services which her sister the said Marie Falga lent her in the past two months during her illness."[64] But family resources could quickly run out. If the household's wage earners lost their jobs or caring for the invalid proved more expensive than anticipated, the family might take the dependent relative to the Hôtel Dieu, as was the fate of Marie Delpont, aged eighty, and Catherine Bonet, aged seventy-six, both admitted to the hospital by their children, who could no longer care for them.[65] Yet the fact that their children had initially taken them in is important. The poor did not routinely abandon their relatives.

Some poor people tried to ensure their old age against abandonment by making contracts with their relatives, signing over their few possessions in return for care until they died. The agreement between Marie Bia, a former servant and widow of a servant, and her nephew Jean Mauries, a shoemaker, spelled out the nature of such a bargain: "Because the said Bia is very old and a chronic invalid, the said Mauries will care for her in all circumstances be it with money or with services, but the said Bia, recognizing that her resources are not sufficient to support her, especially in her present state of health, . . . prays her nephew the said Mauries, who has always given her proof of his attention and affection, to take her into his

---

[62] Cobb, *Death in Paris*, pp. 12–13, and Garrioch, *Neighbourhood and Community in Paris*, pp. 64–65.

[63] AM Mont 10 HH 1 dénombrement 1774.

[64] AD T-et-G 5E 2083 Franceries no. 356 24–6–1779 licitation Falga soeurs. Also see 5E 2337 Martin no. 119 25–3–1788 quittance Bonnal frère et soeur.

[65] AH Mont F 4 Entrées 1724–1728.

home." In return she signed over to him her property, which consisted of a pension from a former employer and the rent of a room.[66]

Other poor people wrote wills leaving their goods as inadequate recompense for the care they had received in their final years. Nineteen percent of the poor who made wills appointed as their heirs the relatives and friends with whom they lived (see table 3–7). For example, Joseph Furbeyre and his wife, Marie Caussade, left most of their goods to their younger daughter, who had taken care of them for several years before they died, bequeathing only fifteen livres to their elder daughter and cutting their son's child out of the succession altogether. The last omission allowed the neglected daughter to challenge the will in probate. However, by producing doctors' bills and estimating the cost of food and fuel for the old folks, the younger daughter was able to bill the estate for 380 livres, more than its entire worth.[67] It was rarely possible for working people to save enough to support themselves in old age; whether in formal agreements and wills or through informal arrangements, what the elderly had to offer in goods and services could not cover the cost of their care. One can easily imagine that even with a formal gift or a promise of a legacy, some families were not able to fulfill their part of the bargain. For the poor, old age brought dependence first on relatives and neighbors, and in extremis, on public charity.

The evidence of loans between kin, of support for the elderly and the needy does not mean that poor relatives always helped one another. Some families expelled or abandoned needy members. For example, although paternity suits demonstrated considerable family support for unmarried mothers-to-be, this was not invariably the case. When seamstress Anne Delbreil discovered she was pregnant, her father turned her out of the house. Fortunately, her aunt took her in or else she would have wound up in the hospital, as her infant was fated to do. In fact, many of the young single female inmates of the Hôtel Dieu who had been born in Montauban were probably in this condition.[68]

And assistance, when extended, did not always produce happy results. Poor people often shared households from necessity rather than choice, a circumstance that made disputes inevitable. In 1815, for example, Mar-

---

[66] AD T-et-G 5E 10867 Martin no. 287 24–6–1778 accord Bia v^e Delon-Mauries. The register of gifts kept by the sénéchal is full of such arrangements. See, for example, in January 1772, Jean Ramal, a boatman and his wife of Sapiacou who gave their son and daughter their room and garden in return for a weekly pension of eight livres. In November of the same year, Jeanne Soulie, widow of a sailor, gave her cousin and godson her room with fireplace and its contents, worth only two hundred livres, on her death in return for daily care. AD T-et-G B 418 Donations; 3–2–1772 and 23–11–1772.

[67] AD T-et-G 5E 21880 Grelleau no. 261 22–5–1789 accord Furbeyre soeurs.

[68] AM Mont 2 BB 21 conseil général 12–9–1788; AH Mont F 4 Entrées 1724–1728.

guérite Pinos brought suit against her brother Dominique for assault. Dominique, a porter, lodged with his sister, her barrel-maker husband, and their teenaged son. After a series of family quarrels, Dominique declared he was going to move out. His nephew taunted him saying, "Carnaval s'en va!" (The carnival is leaving!), to which Dominique replied, "Mais les p[utes] restent!" (But the whores are staying!) and hit his sister in the stomach. In 1801 two young women were arrested in a stairwell and charged with "libertinage." One of them, Anne Laporte, aged twenty, lodged in the house with her uncle. Instead of pleading for his niece's release, he told the police to lock her up because she was continually causing him trouble with the neighbors. Even the agreements carefully registered with the sénéchal were not immune to problems. In 1782 Pierre Presseq, a retired wool comber, gave all his goods to his nephew in return for lodging, food, and care in sickness and health. Three months later, Presseq went to court to reclaim his furniture and linens because the boy was not fulfilling his side of the bargain.[69]

When kin did not live together, they often lived in the same neighborhood. In Villebourbon in 1774, at least 15 percent of poor working families lived in close proximity to relatives, and many more had relatives elsewhere in Villebourbon or in other districts of the city.[70] Boatmen, in particular, lived in family enclaves in which ties of work and neighborhood reinforced ties of kinship. For example, in Sapiacou, widow Galan, spinner, her boatman son, and two daughters lived a few houses away from the widow of boatman Jean Galan, another Jean Galan, also a boatman with

---

[69] AD T-et-G 1 U 3 tribunal correctionnel July 1815: 1 U 369 tribunal correctionnel 8 floréal Year 9; B 420 donations 11–2–1782 and 8–5–1782.

[70] AM Mont 10 HH 1 dénombrement 1774. Fifteen percent is the minimum figure and probably a very low one, including only those households specifically linked by kin terms to other households (for example, on Villebourbon's main street lived Jean Reynal, stevedore, with his wife and two daughters next-door to Anne Cruzel, "sister-in-law of Reynal," and in the faubourg Gasseras, Jean Cougoureux, *père*, poor wool carder, and his wife lived next-door to carder Jean Cougoureux, *fils*, and his wife and daughter) or whose surnames were sufficiently unusual virtually to guarantee that close neighbors of the same name were related to them (for example, in Sapiacou, the widow of Goulard *père*, a spinner, lived with a grandchild next-door to the widow of Jean Goulard, *sargeur*, and her two children). Forty-one percent of workers' households had the same surname as other families in Villebourbon. Some of these were very common names like Marty and Benech and were probably unrelated. However, because this figure is based on patronyms only, it is certainly an underestimation. David Garrioch's research on Paris suggests that poor workers were more likely to live near the wife's family than the husband's. *Neighbourhood and Community in Paris*, p. 68. Phillips, *Family Breakdown*, pp. 190–191, found that the wife's parents were more likely to impinge on urban working couples than were the husband's parents. In Villebourbon in 1774, working-class households were more likely to include the wife's relatives than the husband's. Eighteen households included mothers-in-law, whereas only ten included mothers and only two included fathers.

his wife and son and Antoine Galan, boatman, with his wife and three children. When a group of drunken boatmen burst into the rooms shared by three young working women, one of the roommates managed to escape through a window into the house next-door. In her subsequent testimony she variously described the woman who gave her shelter as her friend, her neighbor, her godmother, and her aunt.[71]

Workers also maintained ties with relatives who did not live in the neighborhood. Siblings and cousins, in particular, were often important members of workers' circles of friends and supporters. Suspected thief Gerard Mouméja explained that he was in the church sacristy looking for his cousin Jean Pierre, who was the church janitor. A few months before, Jean Pierre had persuaded the priest to hire Mouméja for a few days to do some repair work and Mouméja was hoping he would do so again. As we have already noted, every week Antoinette Corbières and her sister shared a bench at Molières's market. Izaac Tieys, a cloth shearer, hired his cousin Pierre Coyne, a textile worker, promising to teach him his craft for free. Seamstress Jeanne Dufau spent her Sunday holiday visiting her sister in Sapiac. Lebrun, a dockworker, regularly drank and gambled with his younger brother and his father-in-law. Pierre Antoine Delaye, the blacksmith mentioned earlier who had witnessed a cousin's marriage contract, entertained guests on a summer evening in 1800, including a cousin from the countryside and another from the city.[72]

Relatives also interfered in each others' lives and fought each others' battles. In 1799, Antoinette Vidallet, a stocking knitter, brought suit against Marguérite Laflorentie, another stocking knitter, who was Vidallet's brother's mistress. She had gone to visit her brother to persuade him to stop seeing Laflorentie, but when she found Laflorentie in her brother's room, a fight ensued. In another case, a seamstress brought suit against a second-hand dealer (*revendeuse*) for having purchased goods that the seamstress' apprentice had stolen from her mistress. According to the seamstress, the *revendeuse* and her niece had cornered her and beaten her up. According to the *revendeuse*, the seamstress had threatened her and her niece had simply come to her aid. In 1819, a hapless widow, caught

---

[71] AD T-et-G 1 U 1 tribunal correctionnel 16 frimaire Year 13. The census reveals seven other "clans" of boatmen, the Chaubets and Pradels of faubourg Gasseras; the Mares, Seguelas, Blancs, and Azemas of Sapiacou; and the Ferries of Tour de la laquc. There were also a few clans of textile workers like the four Boredon households, all wool carders around the Place Villebourbon, and the Coynes, spinners and wool carders in the rue Caussat.

[72] AM Mont 6 FF 59 jurisdictions consulaires 15–4–1789; AD T-et-G 1 U 369 cour d'assises 18 germinal Year 9; AM Mont 6 FF 90 jurisdictions consulaires 22–4–1790; AD T-et-G 1 U 1 tribunal correctionnel 15 thermidor Year 8; 1 U 7 cour d'assises, August 1830. Also Garrioch, *Neighbourhood and Community in Paris*, pp. 87–93.

spanking a neighbor's child, was pummeled by the boy's mother, his grandmother, his aunt, and his uncle.[73]

In other instances relatives, seconded by employers and neighbors, acted to mediate quarrels. In order to redress material damage or insults to honor, most poor people looked first to the intervention of relatives and friends, which was cheaper and also more likely to bring restitution than a lawsuit. A good example was the paternity suit of seamstress Jeanne Dufau against merchant-dyer Urbain Bergis. Her neighbors testified that initially Dufau's employer and then her sister had met with Bergis to try to reach a settlement. Only when these negotiations broke down did Dufau file a suit.[74]

As Dufau's case illustrates, the poor turned to their neighbors as well as to their families for support. Studies of nineteenth- and early-twentieth-century working-class neighborhoods have emphasized the importance of neighbors in the life of the poor. In recent works on Paris, Arlette Farge and David Garrioch argue for even greater importance of neighborhood in eighteenth-century city life. The shared staircase and courtyard, the daily exchange of services—marketing, child care, nursing—of information, and of recreation built ties that paralleled, complemented, and sometimes replaced those of kinship. Property-owning families had patrimony to form a barrier between family and outsiders; as Ellen Ross has suggested, the edges of poor families were ragged, sometimes standing out in sharp contrast to the community and sometimes blending imperceptibly into it.[75]

Garrioch's work on Parisian neighborhoods describes the neighborhood as the setting and audience before which conflicts between individuals and families were played out but which rarely became directly involved except to break up a fight that was getting out of hand. Evidence from Montauban confirms this view. Although relatives as distant as aunts,

[73] AD T-et-G 1 U 368 tribunal correctionnel 6 frimaire Year 8, 2 nivôse Year 8 and 2 fructidor Year 8; 1 U 5 tribunal correctionnel 1819. See Castan, "La Criminalité familiale," p. 93, and Garrioch, *Neighbourhood and Community in Paris*, pp. 88–95.

[74] AM Mont 6 FF 60 jurisdictions consulaires 1790. The same dossier contains a similar suit by Marianne Dubosc against fellow servant Jean Michel. Her father and her employer had carried on the negotiations. In many such cases the lawsuit was a tactic to pressure the recalcitrant party rather than a direct means of seeking justice. Very often, a private settlement in the form of a notarized *accord* precluded a judicial decision. See the example cited in chapter 4. Garrioch, in *Neighbourhood and Community in Paris*, pp. 45–48, discusses the politics of making an official complaint.

[75] Ross, "Survival Networks," pp. 4–27; Michael Young and Peter Willmott, *Family and Kinship in East London* (Harmondsworth, Middlesex: Penguin, 1957); Garrioch, *Neighbourhood and Community in Paris*; Farge, *La Vie fragile*; Castan, *Honêteté*, pp. 282–283. Also see Chaytor, "Household and Kinship," pp. 25–60, and Harris, "Households and Their Boundaries," pp. 143–152.

cousins, and grandparents would leap in to second the combatants, neighbors rarely did so. Instead, they evaluated the performance and reported on it to others who were not present, constructing in the process a neighborhood judgment on what had occurred. Sometimes—but not always—they communicated this judgment to the police. Although the police inquiring into the abandonment of Marie Richard's baby had no difficulty elucidating the affair from the evidence and hearsay of numerous neighbors, those investigating a boat master's complaint that a sailor had slandered his two daughters found a curiously silent neighborhood. Only two people admitted hearing of the incident. In 1800, when the authorities tried to discover who had sung royalist songs in a wineshop in Sapiac, no one in the neighborhood knew who had been drinking there on the evening in question, nor had anyone heard the songs. In the first case, the neighborhood judged for Richard and supported her claims on her lover; in the second, the boat master's neighbors disapproved of his action and refused to second it; in the third, judicious ignorance protected not only the imprudent singers but also the reputation of the neighborhood as a whole.[76]

As a collectivity, the neighborhood witnessed and judged the behavior of individuals in ways that could bring considerable pressure to bear upon them. For example, "scandalized" neighbors often encouraged couples who had been courting too long and, perhaps, too intimately to make the trip to the altar. According to textile worker Jean Rivière and his fiancée, Philippe Lombard, talk in Sapiac where they both lived, "especially about the said Lombard," persuaded them to marry.[77] Without the influence of wealth or political power, the poor turned to the neighborhood's weapon, gossip, to obtain redress. When merchant Jean Garrisson's grandson acted to settle the paternity suit of Izabeau Dellac, he responded to the pressure not only of her wool comber father, brother, and two uncles but also to "public rumor" that flew through Villebourbon's busy streets and wharves.[78] If he had not acted promptly, Dellac's next move probably would have been to expose the infant on his doorstep, a "scandal" for the neighborhood to see. This was what seamstress Marie Richard did with her son by Pierre Mary *dit* Avignon, a master locksmith. When told there was a cradle in front of his shop, Avignon hastily removed it to the porch

[76] Garrioch, *Neighbourhood and Community in Paris*, pp. 41–53; AM Mont 6 FF 47 jurisdiction consulaires 1776; 1 U 3 tribunal correctionnel 6–6–1814; 1 U 1 tribunal correctionnel 15 thermidor Year 8.

[77] AD T-et-G G459[bis] Officialité 1773–1779; Darrow, "Popular Concepts of Marital Choice," p. 264; Phillips, in *Family Breakdown*, pp. 129, 139, 186, cites the use of neighbors as witnesses. For example, when a woman decided to leave her husband, she often called the neighbors in and turned out her pockets in their presence so that they could affirm that she was taking nothing with her.

[78] AD T-et-G 5E 2005 Garrigues no. 229 19–3–1786 declaration Dellac.

of the cathedral, the traditional spot to abandon infants. But he was too late. News of the exposure went quickly around the neighborhood, which, as the police investigating the affair discovered, stood firmly behind Richard. Such tactics could succeed, especially if the man had a reputation to maintain. Jean David Rauzet, clerk to his merchant father-in-law, paid off the servant who accused him of impregnating her because she threatened to expose the child in front of his father-in-law's house.[79]

Although neighbors and friends often helped working people in many of the same ways as did relatives, they could not be depended upon to the same extent, particularly in the event of quarrels within the family. When seamstress Anne Delbreil became pregnant, her father threw her out of the house. After going the rounds of the neighbors looking for help, she was finally taken in by her aunt. When Jean Cassac beat up his wife, Marianne Delfau, she sought refuge with a neighbor. Although the neighbor sent for her brother, he refused to let her in, not wanting to come between husband and wife. He also may well have been afraid of Cassac because it was not unknown for husbands to turn on neighbors who tried to intervene.[80]

That neighbors and even relatives hesitated to intervene between husband and wife indicates that here was a boundary, not inviolable, but nonetheless recognized, between family and outsiders. The conjugal couple was the core of the poor family. As Hufton, Tilly, and Scott agree, the economy of the working poor was essentially an economy of the couple; for their mutual survival, husband and wife had to be committed to supporting each other.[81] If one spouse died or deserted the family, indigence often quickly engulfed the spouse who remained. A large contingent of the destitute were widows and abandoned wives and their children, but the illness or death of the wife could produce the same unfortunate result, especially if there were small children. Jean Dumas, an apprentice cabinetmaker, petitioned the town council for assistance when his wife's long illness beggared the family and necessitated the hire of a wet nurse for their youngest child. Similarly, laborer Antoine Doumerc applied for aid when his wife's death left him with the care of three children under the age of

[79] AM Mont 6 FF 46 and 47 jurisdictions consulaires 1775–1776. Police records contain numerous instances of such exposures, and the babies' mothers were not the only ones to resort to it. In 1788 a wet nurse, left with a newborn when its mother died, exposed it in front of a dance hall patronized by the child's putative father. See AM Mont 6 FF 58 jurisdictions consulaires 1788. See also Castan, *Les Criminels de Languedoc*, pp. 168–169.

[80] AM Mont 2 BB 21 conseil général 12–9–1788; AD T-et-G 1U 369 cour d'assises 8 germinal Year 9. Also see 1 U 368 cour d'assises 2 nivôse Year 8; 26 frimaire Year 8. Phillips's work on divorce in Rouen suggests that women neighbors were less hesitant to intervene than were men. *Family Breakdown*, pp. 113–114, 184–186.

[81] Tilly and Scott, *Women, Work and Family*, pp. 43–44; Hufton, "Women and the Family Economy," pp. 1–22.

TABLE 6–4
Marital Property Arrangements of Montauban Workers

	Legal System	
	Custom of Montauban 1775–1803	Napoleonic Code 1804–1824
Dowry	74%	49%
Separate goods	16	1
Life rights	9	39
Community property	1	11
N	115	72

Note: Significance level = .01, contingency coefficient = .434.

four. The death or flight of one spouse often soon led to the flight of the other as the fragile security provided by the couple snapped.[82]

The marriage contracts of poor couples recorded their agreement to form working partnerships. Such contracts were not familial alliances; neither were they property settlements. More frequently than grooms or, especially, brides of other socioeconomic groups, poor workers entered into this contract alone, unsupported by parents or relatives.[83] And much more frequently than for other couples, poor workers married without any property at all, pledging only the "daily work of their hands" to each other's maintenance.

Before the Revolution, most Montaubaners married according to the Custom of Montauban even though it was ill adapted to the realities of workers' marriages. The Custom of Montauban assumed that marriage was a limited association in which each party would invest only a portion of his or her property and interest. It also assumed that each party had sufficient capital to provide for his or her own support. Neither assumption held for the working poor. Although most workers' marriage contracts followed the Custom of Montauban, 16 percent dispensed with the fictions of inalienable dowries and mortgages. Each retained economic autonomy through a formal separation of property, although many de-

[82] AM Mont 2 BB 21 conseil général motions in the town council meetings of 8–8–1788 and 8–2–1789. Also Gutton, *Société et les pauvres*, pp. 133–135.

[83] In the sample of marriage contracts, 36 percent of worker grooms contracted marriage without the presence of parents or other relatives, compared with 26 percent of artisans, 25 percent of the elite, and 19 percent of peasant grooms (significance level = .01, contingency coefficient = .152). Twenty-three percent of their brides contracted marriage without any family present, compared with 15 percent of artisan, 7 percent of elite, and 10 percent of peasant brides (significance level = .01, contingency coefficient = .156).

clared that they, in fact, had no property other than the income of their labor or that their belongings were too trivial to evaluate.

Revolutionary family law brought the concept of the marital community to Montauban. Before 1804, this type of arrangement had been confined, for the most part, to the contracts of immigrants from northern France, where community property was the legal custom.[84] After the enactment of the Napoleonic Code, marital communities quickly gained in popularity in the contracts of the poor, becoming second to dowries as the most common type of property arrangement.

Pooling resources in a marital community approximated the reality of working people's marriages. According to the law, however, the community ended at the death of one spouse; then the property was divided and the decedent's share went to his or her legal heirs. Again, the formula assumed that the property of each party was sufficient to his or her own maintenance, which was not the case for the poor. They could not afford to divide the meager property of their marriages; without the pots, linens, and furniture that were usually the sum of their goods, life for the widow or widower was untenable. For example, when Marie Magdeleine Rafine, widow of a journeyman shoemaker, contracted to marry for a second time, her children demanded an accounting of their father's estate. Rafine declared that at his death he had owned "neither gold nor silver" and that more than half of the couple's total goods was the furniture she had brought as her dowry. Nonetheless, the law required that the remaining items—some linens, pots and pans, and shoemaking tools—be divided among the couple's five children.[85] To prevent this, many workers modified the marital community to extend it until the death of both spouses by assigning to the surviving spouse life rights to as much of the estate as the law allowed. They did this in the marriage contract itself, or, less commonly, by written will. Both before and after the advent of the Napoleonic Code, married working people were more likely to name their spouses than their children as heirs.

Although the poor couple usually worked independently, in official financial matters they stood as a unit, one spouse acting for the other if need be. For example, in an effort to crack down on peddlers who were fencing stolen merchandise, the police began to require that *revendeuses* put up a deposit or that a "reputable" person agree to assume their liability. The person who most often filled this role was the woman's husband.[86] When choosing legal proxies, poor workers turned to their wives

[84] See, for example, AD T-et-G 5E 2008 Garrigues no. 391 5–5–1788 contrat de mariage Paul-Delsol and 10877 Martin no. 469 8–9–1788 contrat de mariage Joli-Meunier.

[85] AD T-et-G 5E 12897 Grelleau no. 159 30 nivôse Year 9 accord Rafine v^c Baisset et ses enfants.

[86] AM Mont 7 HH 4 état des revenduses (*sic*) et proxenettes d'effets 18–2–1779.

more readily than to any other relative and far more often than to professional representatives (see table 4–5). It was common practice for departing soldiers to authorize their wives to buy, sell, lend, collect debts, and so on, on their behalf in their absence. Often married volunteers who contracted to replace wealthy conscripts assigned to their wives the right to collect their replacement payment. For example, *sargeur* Louis Guillot appointed his wife, Jeanne Rafine to receive the interest on the eight hundred francs owed him by Jean Marty, a landowning peasant, for having replaced Marty's son in the draft. Rafine collected annually forty-five francs in cash and an equal amount in flour for the duration of her husband's service.[87]

Marriage was not a partnership of equals; custom, law, and religion placed the wife under her husband's authority. The police could imprison a wife at her husband's request and sanctioned his use of physical force to "correct" her. The neighborhood community also assumed that a husband had a right to extract obedience from his wife and that it was a wife's duty to be faithful to and to conciliate her husband.[88]

Nonetheless, poor working women had relatively greater weight in the working community than had women in elite circles. Working women were an integral part of the urban scene; their exchanges of goods, services and information formed the networks that bound the neighborhood together and constituted the "public rumor" that could damage a reputation or incite a riot. Whereas men left the neighborhood to work—casual laborers, for example, as well as construction workers and boatmen— women usually worked in their home or in the streets nearby. Sewing, spinning, and wool sorting were domestic work as were, of course, taking in lodgers and nursing infants, other common ways of stretching the household's income. And female peddlers—*revendeuses*—were a different breed from male *colporteurs*. Whereas male peddlers carried novelty items from the city to the countryside, women sold necessities like food, drink, firewood, and old clothes to their neighbors. In many cases the neighborhood as a collectivity was composed of women. They were often the major witnesses in police investigations because of what they saw as they were "just passing by" in the stairwell, shop, street, or square or because of what

---

[87] AD T-et-G 5E 1971 Latreille Olivié no. 1042 13 germinal Year 8 traité militaire Marty-Guillot; 2136 Latreille Olivié no. 462 15–10–1809 quittance Rafine-Marty. Another example is 5E 13206 Deray no. 293 30–8–1812 traité militaire Pradal-Bayou. In this agreement, Bayou's wife had the right to receive some of the capital as well. In 5E 2153 Latreille Olivié no. 47 4–2–1824 Francois Vidal, a shoemaker of Villenouvelle, named his fiancée as his heir so that she could receive the replacement money due to him should he be killed.

[88] Garrioch, *Neighbourhood and Community in Paris*, pp. 78–79; Kaplow, *The Names of Kings*, pp. 57–59; Philipps, *Family Breakdown*, pp. 110–114. Southerners defended the traditional right of husbands to an even greater extent than did men in northern France. See Castan, "La Criminalité familiale," p. 93.

they "happened to overhear" in the courtyard, wineshop, or corridor. In the paternity suit of Jeanne Dufau against merchant-dyer Urbain Bergis, every witness called was a woman. From their windows and doorways, on Sunday walks and in evenings passed in each others' rooms, they watched and judged the whole affair.[89]

Part of poor women's visibility was due to the fact that they were not simply relatives of workers but workers themselves. Unfortunately, notaries usually identified women by their husbands' or fathers' occupations rather than by their own. Despite this, in the sample of marriage contracts, the notaries noted an occupation for nearly one quarter of workers' brides and a similar number of workers' daughters, and in the sample of wills, 38 percent of working-class women were identified by their own occupations. Unlike notaries, the police usually noted a woman's own occupation as well as her husband's. The embattled seamstress mentioned earlier, for example, was married to a hat maker, and her opponent, the second-hand dealer, was married to a cook. Witnesses to the Dufau paternity suit included a stocking knitter married to a tailor, a seamstress married to a brigadier in the police, and a laundress married to a textile worker.[90] Unlike the wives of artisans and shopkeepers, these women did not work under their husband's authority in a family business; their work was a part of their identity as individuals rather than the result of their association with their husbands.[91]

Not only did poor women usually work independently of their husbands, they also owned most of the couple's "capital." It was the bride's dowry that in almost every case provided the essential furnishings of the household plus the linens, which through the judicious use of the pawnshop, were the only financial cushion most poor families possessed. In general, it was not a young man's responsibility to save for marriage; nor

[89] AM Mont 6 FF 90 jurisdictions consulaires 1790. Dufau presented as her witnesses a servant, a seamstress, and a cotton spinner; Bergis called a stocking knitter, two seamstresses, a laundress, a servant, a baker's widow, and a *revendeuse*.

[90] AD T-et-G 1 U 368 cour d'assises 2 fructidor Year 7; AM Mont 6 FF 60 jurisdictions consulaires 1790. In AM Mont 7 HH 4 état des revenduses (*sic*), 1779 husbands of peddlers included two tailors, two shoemakers, four textile workers, two shopkeepers, two tanners, three metalworkers, a plasterer, a butcher, a carpenter, a potter, and an invalid soldier; only one was also a peddler.

[91] Farge, *La Vie Fragile*, pp. 55–59. Sometimes working couples were unable to live together much of the time. Boatmen, for example, were absent for long periods. Married servants could rarely live together. There were at least two such divided households in Villebourbon in 1774, one in which a woman servant lived with her master while her boatman husband lived with his brother's family, the other in which a valet for the enormously wealthy merchant Rigail *aîné* rented a room for his wife in Montauban. AM Mont 10 HH 1 dénombrement. See Roche, *Le Peuple de Paris*, p. 108. Garrioch, in *Neighbourhood and Community in Paris*, pp. 82–83, points out that different work schedules interrupted life as a couple as well.

did the groom's family "set up" the couple as was common in merchant and peasant families. The groom and his parents contributed to only 40 percent of marriages, and only 14 percent contributed an amount equal to or more than what their brides contributed. Women, on the other hand, saved as much of their wages as possible, investing in furniture and linens or lending their wages to their parents or brothers against the day they would need a dowry (see table 6–5). For example, in May 1788, a woman serving in a bourgeois household in Montauban lent her brother, a farm worker, one hundred livres in cash which she had just received as her wages. He promised to repay it after the harvest whenever she demanded it.[92] The most fortunate of brides could count on some assistance from their parents, but 30 percent constituted the entire dowry from their own savings.[93]

Because of their autonomy as workers, perhaps even more because they owned most of the capital of the household, working women participated equally with men in formal property transactions. In the sample of debts, 46 percent of lenders and half of borrowers who were city workers were women. Similarly, in property sales one third of buyers and more than half of sellers were women. Working women participated to a greater extent in these transactions than did women of any other socioeconomic group (see table 4–4).[94]

That the marital relationship was central to the survival of the working poor and that wives had both more autonomy and more authority in the family did not mean that their married lives were free of problems or that workers' homes were havens of domestic unity. That both spouses' active cooperation was crucial to the well-being of the family made tensions inevitable. Public records are silent on routine marital discord, but when certain limits were breached, the couple could end up in court. Enough

[92] AD T-et-G 5E 12832 Delteil fils no. 392 12–5–1788; see also 5E 2004 Garrigues no. 854 10–11–1785 contrat de mariage Rozier-Gasc and 13184 Deray no. 228 11 nivôse Year 5 accord Vidal v͏ᵉ Delfour.

[93] Comparing the bride's and groom's contributions by the groom's occupation produces at the significance level of .01, a contingency coefficient for brides of .200 and for grooms of .301. The bride's average contribution was worth 302 livres/francs, the groom's only 63 livres/francs excluding contracts to which they did not contribute. Also see Castan, *Honnêteté*, p. 240, and Fairchilds, *Domestic Enemies*, p. 83.

[94] In a sample of 250 loans, half of workers who lent were women compared with 17 percent of peasant lenders, 30 percent of artisans, and 20 percent of elite lenders (significance level = .01, contingency coefficient = .248). Half of workers who borrowed were also women, compared with only 10 percent of peasants, 36 percent of artisans, and 38 percent of elite borrowers (significance level = .01, contingency coefficient = .369). In a sample of 250 property sales, 57 percent of worker sellers were women compared with only 30 percent of other sellers (significance level = .01, contingency coefficient = .234), and 47 percent of worker buyers were women compared with less than one quarter of other buyers (significance level = .08, contingency coefficient = .196).

cases of wife beating appeared before magistrates for us to assume that although women may have tolerated a certain amount of brutality, they did not hesitate to file a complaint if the beating became, in their eyes, excessive. In this they were often supported by their families, who sheltered battered wives and interceded for them with their husbands and in court.[95]

It is far more difficult to define exactly what constituted "excessive brutality" for the working poor. Wife beating and divorce cases generally described repeated, brutal beatings that left the wife in fear for her life. In the case of Cassac and Delfau mentioned earlier, neighbors confirmed Delfau's story of almost daily beatings and a surgeon's report catalogued the material evidence of the beatings in cuts, bruises, and broken bones.[96] But in the following divorce suit, the situation was more ambiguous. Marguèrite Rabaly and Jean Primo Valy were married in 1788. According to the brief Rabaly's lawyer filed in 1793,

> this marriage was not happy for long because soon the said Valy's violent character showed he no longer had any regard for the said Rabaly and almost daily, without any pretext whatsoever, treated her outrageously with the most offensive insults. To this he soon added terrible threats, waving his fists in her face and saying he wished he had a double-barreled shotgun to kill both her and her mother at the same time. And from these excesses the said Valy went on to strike the said Rabaly cruelly and often. And that similar scenes transpired almost every day and always with fury on Valy's part. The said Rabaly, fearing for her days, left the house six months ago to return to her mother, with whom she is now living.

In his short statement, Valy admitted that he was "content with the truth of the facts as advanced by the said Rabaly and, not being the master of his violent impulses," feared that if his wife returned he would commit only new "excesses."[97]

According to the divorce law of 1792, a simple agreement of incompatibility was sufficient grounds for divorce, but Rabaly and Valy seemed to feel that the charge of life-threatening violence was desirable, perhaps necessary, to make a strong case. They were reacting less to legal requirements than to community expectations. Because the unity of the couple was essential to the survival of the poor, workers disapproved of separation and desertion. They expected that, despite a working woman's practical autonomy, she would conciliate her husband to keep the couple to-

---

[95] See AD T-et-G 1 U 368 cour d'assises 2 nivôse Year 8; 1 U 369 cour d'assises 8 germinal Year 9; 1 U 104 cour d'assises 18–4–1815 and 8 i 5 tribunal de famille 26–4–1793; Phillips, *Family Breakdown*, pp. 108–124, 180–191.

[96] AD T-et-G 1 U 369 cour d'assises 8 germinal Year 9.

[97] AM Mont 8 i 5 tribunal de familles, 29–5–1793.

gether. It was only when the marriage, which was supposed to ensure her survival, instead threatened it that "public rumor" would condone her efforts to break up the couple. Working women initiated most divorce petitions and they also abandoned them more often than did men, suggesting the double pressures on working wives. They often had the most to gain from a divorce and also the most to lose.[98]

If, during the Revolution, wives occasionally divorced their husbands, husbands more frequently deserted their wives. According to Gutton's study of the Lyonais poor, desertion was more often the response to sudden hardship—the birth of another child, the loss of a job, the death of a spouse—or the final step in a descent to destitution than the result of wanderlust or marital disagreement.[99] Male workers were often mobile before their marriages, moving from job to job and from place to place. When they married, however, they intended to have a more settled future. For some it never materialized. Pierre Belmont *dit* Lapax, aged twenty-five, arrested for theft in Montauban in 1773, was a good example. Before his marriage he had been a wandering mason and boatman, on occasion traveling as far as Bordeaux. When he married a Montauban servant he was working at a grist mill. However, floods closed the mill and sent him on the road again searching for work in Moissac, Toulouse, Castelmoron, and Caussade. Such was the fate of many working men, especially in periods of industrial recession. Lapax returned to Montauban to see his wife and mother, but some men slid into lives of permanent vagrancy.[100]

As Lapax's history suggests, the relative independence of working women had both benefits and costs. When Lapax lost his job at the mill, his wife returned to her work as a servant so that she could support herself. On the other hand, a working woman's ability to earn an income probably facilitated desertion because a husband, particularly if he were unemployed or his earnings were minimal, could conclude that his family was better off without him. Unfortunately, although a woman could support herself, she could rarely earn enough to support their children as well. A deserted wife often, in turn, abandoned the children.

---

[98] Phillips, in *Family Breakdown*, pp. 56–60, 159–162, concludes that there was general acceptance of divorce, however only for good reason. For women, this usually meant life-threatening violence. Garrioch, *Neighbourhood and Community in Paris*, pp 78–80, cites evidence that neighbors disapproved of women who left their husbands. The 1774 Villebourbon census AM Mont 10 HH 1 identified only two women as *femmes separées*, both living with or near their mothers and both listed as poor.

[99] Gutton, *Société et les pauvres*, pp. 132–135; Also see Phillips, *Family Breakdown*, pp. 142–147.

[100] AM Mont 6 FF 47 jurisdictions consulaires 12–4–1773. In the sample of marriage contracts, the fathers of three worker grooms and one bride had deserted their families. See, for example, AD T-et-G 5E 2356 Martin no. 7 11–1–1809 contrat de mariage Rocquet-Descoux.

Working women's visibility and autonomy in the public world of the streets, markets, and police courts also had a cost. Garrioch has argued that because women were assumed to be less responsible for their speech or actions, they often could articulate public opinion and confront officials, which would have been dangerous for men to do. However, this license was not absolute, either with the neighbors or with the authorities.[101] And during the Revolution, official tolerance of "public rumor" decreased. Some women found that the license to speak out, which they assumed was theirs, had been withdrawn. Such was the case of Prexede Lauta, a peddler, one of the few working people in Montauban to be imprisoned for any length of time. According to the notes of the Surveillance Committee, she was the leader of a group of market women whose "patriotism is equivocal." Specifically, she was charged with "publicly, in the street, having voiced views that testify to her attachment to the former Queen" and making fun of the Republic's war efforts.[102]

For working women—and for the poor in general—life consisted of weighing opportunities against risks, in situations where the opportunities were never great and the risks often overwhelming. The Revolution added new items to the balance, new options like the marital community of the Napoleonic Code and the Revolutionary divorce law, new opportunities in the form of municipal workshops, price controls, and military replacement, and new dangers in massive conscription, inadequate charity, and the eventual collapse of the city's industry and commerce. Until the advent of the last, however, the good and the bad balanced each other, producing no significant changes in the imperatives of poverty or in the ways families attempted to meet them.

Before, during, and after the Revolution, workers were both the most autonomous of Montaubaners and the most dependent. Without the cement of patrimony, poor families were less cohesive than the families of the elite or of the artisans and shopkeepers. Their members detached themselves more frequently and more easily. Children left home even before marriage, husbands and wives worked separately, wives divorced husbands and husbands deserted wives, parents abandoned children and

---

[101] Garrioch, *Neighbourhood and Community in Paris*, p 86. Also see Castan, *Les Criminels de Languedoc*, pp. 25–36, who finds that in southern France women were much underrepresented among those arrested and convicted of crimes. Women were often released to the supervision of their fathers or husbands in instances where men would have been prosecuted. However, if a woman was outside a familial context, she was more likely to be convicted.

[102] AM Mont L 97 fiches du Comité de Surveillance; also imprisoned was Jacquette Garric, a cook, accused of having been in the crowd in front of the convent on May 10, 1790, and several other women whose occupations were not given, arrested for participating in this crowd or for holding "unpatriotic" opinions, such as supporting the Catholic church or making disparaging comparisons between the state of affairs in the Republic and the Old Regime.

vice versa. On the other hand, without the resource of property, the poor were more dependent on each other for daily survival than were other Montaubaners. Family and neighbors helped poor parents raise their children, helped individuals find jobs, lent them money, cared for them in illness, sheltered them in old age, and rallied around to fight their battles and protect their interests. Independence and interdependence suggest static polarities of family life; in reality, the lives of poor families were a constant, sometimes desperate, fugue on both themes.

Although flexible and adaptable, the poor family was not a well-oiled "fit" between the needs of its members on the one hand and available resources on the other. At times in most workers' lives, needs outran their families' abilities to meet them. A working couple might easily have found themselves obliged to contribute to the support of several children and an elderly parent just when their own strength was beginning to wane. Common disasters like unemployment, sickness, or the death of a wage earner could at any time swallow the family's income and savings. The relatives of poor families were usually poor too, although they often offered assistance. But the absence of property did indeed lead to the breaking of family ties, as Tilly and Scott maintain. This did not mean, however, that family ties were weaker among the poor than among other Montaubaners, only that their strength was not always up to the herculean demands life made on them.

The one way in which the French Revolution decisively tipped the balance of survival against Montauban's workers was that it undermined the city's industry and commerce. Whereas for Montauban's merchants and manufacturers, deindustrialization coincided with new opportunities in landowning and civil service, there were no such compensations for the poor, at least not in Montauban. Although the problem of unemployment had been briefly but artificially solved by government requisitions and army contracts, in the closing years of the century it returned in full force. The remedies proposed by the government, whether to revive the sagging economy or to initiate public works projects, were short-lived and wholly inadequate. The destitute began to include able-bodied "former textile workers" who scrambled for jobs as day laborers. By the mid-nineteenth century there were less than two thousand people employed in the textile industry in the whole city.[103]

Subsistence crises of varying degrees of severity remained a recurrent problem in Montauban and the surrounding countryside. In 1816 the departmental authorities anxiously tracked the price and availability of

[103] AN F15 2768 secours aux indigents et aux sinistrés 1811–1818 (Tarn-et-Garonne) letters from Prefect Villeneuve to the minister of interior, 29–10–1816 and 15–5–1817; Armengaud, *Populations de l'est-aquitain*, p. 118.

grain in Montauban's market and warned the population that any "seditious activities" such as market riots and interference with grain transports would be severely punished. In 1818 poor harvests again led the prefect to beg for relief from Paris. In the first half of the nineteenth century, the Tarn-et-Garonne was the only department in the region to experience periods in which the mortality rate rose above the birth rate. The cholera epidemic in the 1830s produced one such demographic disaster, but the other was due to crop failures and unemployment around 1820. Intermittent although less severe shortages continued to plague the city in the 1830s and 1840s.[104]

In the eighteenth century, poor people had flocked to Montauban because they had reason to believe that the balance of risks and opportunities was more favorable there than in the countryside. In good times, the textile industry, the wharves, the mansions and gardens of the wealthy, the markets and fairs had provided employment. In bad times, the city offered more in the way of relief than did their native villages. But by the turn of the century, especially after 1810 when the full extent of the industrial and commercial collapse made itself felt, Montauban ceased to attract many newcomers. In the first decades of the new century, Montauban's population grew slightly and then stagnated. Unemployment was high and wages were low by comparison with other cities in the region, particularly Toulouse. Already there began the stream of out-migration; at first only a trickle of artisans, merchants, and textile workers, it became a flood by midcentury.[105]

Meanwhile, for the workers who remained in Montauban, it became harder to "succeed." The profile of those who were able to marry changed subtly from before the Revolution in ways indicating that Montauban was no longer a place of modest opportunity. Before the Revolution, 41 percent of poor grooms and 35 percent of their brides in the sample of marriage contracts were children of peasants (see table 6–1). They had come to the city to find work, the men as laborers and construction workers, the women as servants, and both as textile workers. Many lived on their own, working, supporting themselves and, if they were lucky, saving for marriage and their household. After 1800, the picture changed. Thirty-seven percent of grooms and 47 percent of their brides were the children of artisans and shopkeepers, not recent immigrants but born and raised in Montauban. Rather than peasants on their way up—or at least

---

[104] Armengaud, *Populations de l'est-aquitain*, pp. 71–73; AD T-et-G MS no. 114. Reynaud, "Du mouvement de la population dans le départment de Tarn et Garonne de 1827 à 1851." Grèzes-Rueff, "Assoupissement économique," pp. 221–225.

[105] Armengaud, *Populations de l'est-aquitain*, pp. 71–72, 134; Grèzes-Rueff, "Assoupissement économique," pp. 221–225, 230–231; Pinède, "Migrations temporaire en Quercy," pp. 122–134.

TABLE 6–5
Contributions of Workers' Brides and Their Parents to Dowries, 1775–1824

Dowry Contributed By	Workers' Marriage Contracts*	
	1775–1799	1800–1824
Bride		
All	49%	26%
Some	58	31
Brides' parents		
All	35	48
Some	44	53
No dowry	7	21
N	105	90

Note: Significance level = .01, contingency coefficient = .273.

*Percentages add to more than 100 because those who contributed all are also included among those who contributed some.

out—of rural poverty, Montauban's workers were becoming the children of small business families sinking into urban poverty.

Fewer marriage contracts told proud stories of personal achievement. Whereas before the Revolution 49 percent of workers' brides contributed their entire dowries, after 1800 only 26 percent of workers' brides accomplished this. Working women fortunate enough to marry had parents who could afford to endow them—or they married with no capital at all, simply adding their labor to a marital community.

Peasants still came to Montauban looking for work. The countryside remained overpopulated and wages for rural laborers were even lower than for workers in the city. However, they were less likely to find regular work than in the past and thus were less likely to be able to marry. Instead, they joined the population who lived on the verge of destitution, the itinerant workers from the impoverished mountain provinces, the widows, and the elderly. The hospital took in seventy or more abandoned infants and children every year and housed two hundred or so destitute elderly as well as many incapacitated veterans, the legacy of two decades of war.[106]

However, for the young and strong, Montauban became simply a way station between their native village and better prospects elsewhere. At the same time that Montauban's population increased by less than 15 percent, the population of Castre, for example, went up by more than one third. The textile industry there, with the aid of mechanized spinning factories, employed more than thirty thousand people, many drawn from the same

[106] AN F15 1210, 1213 hospices, bureaux de bienfaisances (Tarn-et-Garonne) 1809–1814, 1824–1827; Pinède, "Migrations temporaries en Quercy," pp. 124–125.

countryside that in the eighteenth century had supplied Montauban with textile workers. Toulouse drew even more. The fastest-growing city in France in the first half of the nineteenth century, Toulouse absorbed thousands of immigrants into the production of ready-made clothes and shoes and many more as laborers on construction sites, wharves, and markets. Many of these newcomers were peasants from Quercy and workers from Montauban.[107]

[107] Armengaud, *Populations de l'est-aquitain*, pp. 22, 31–33, 118–120, 172. Montauban's satellite country towns grew even less: Moissac by only 7 percent, Castelsarrasin by only 3.5 percent.

CHAPTER SEVEN

The Peasants

On March 12, 1827, the public prosecutor of the Royal Court of Toulouse delivered an indictment of Arnaud Bouzeran, a plowman, for the murder of his elderly father-in-law, Etienne Sanson. The police investigation had quickly revealed Bouzeran as Sanson's "only known enemy in the region" and had painstakingly constructed the circumstances of the murder and its motive.

> Financial arguments had been going on between Sanson and Bouzeran for a long time. These began as the result of a gift made by the father-in-law to his son-in-law in return for a life pension of 60 francs a year payable semiannually, and became bitter at each due date, one of which was fixed as September 15 when some arrears were due. Sanson had not wanted to receive [partial] payment on account and had shown his intention to sue Bouzeran if he was not paid [the whole amount due] at the agreed time.[1]

To free himself once and for all from these demands, Bouzeran had taken a hatchet and murdered Sanson in his bed; so stated the indictment.

Before Sanson's murder, Bouzeran faced the collapse of the tenuous security he had worked for years to acquire. He had been a propertyless young man, probably a younger son, when he married Marie Sanson, heiress to a little land in the hills northwest of Montauban. After the marriage, Sanson and his wife had formed a "pot-and-hearth" community with their daughter and son-in-law, agreeing to pool their resources, share household expenses, and work together for the common profit. Four or five years before the murder, the partnership dissolved and Sanson retired by turning over half of his property to his son-in-law in return for a pension. During the ten years that Bouzeran had waited impatiently to inherit Sanson's property, he had saved, schemed, and gone deeply into debt to acquire enough land so that, added to Sanson's, it would make him independent, a *propriétaire*. However, when he finally acquired Sanson's land, he also assumed an annual debt, Sanson's pension, which cancelled out any profit.[2] Unable to support his family from land thus burdened, he had to continue to work for wages on neighboring farms, farming his own land only by stealing time from his employers and by hiring occasional

---

[1] AD T-et-G 1 U 137 assises 1827; acte d'accusation 12–3–1827.

[2] Sanson's property was worth 2,500 francs; the sixty-franc pension therefore represented approximately a 5 percent return on half of it.

help. Still he could not earn enough cash to pay his father-in-law's pension. Already Sanson had taken him to court once and had obtained a lien against his property for four hundred francs in arrears, interest and costs. Now Sanson was threatening to go to court again if Bouzeran did not pay up. Where would Bouzeran find four hundred francs? He would surely lose his land. Small wonder if he took an axe to the old man.

In the eighteenth and nineteenth centuries, social critics on both the Left and the Right envisioned the traditional French peasant household as an extended family, all living and working in common under the authority of a patriarch. The *Encyclopédie*, in an article entitled "Moraves ou Frères Unis," eulogized the equality, harmony, and productivity of the peasant familial community; conservative agronomists and moralists emphasized its economic self-sufficiency and deference to paternal authority.[3] Already in the eighteenth century, this peasant family was thought to be under attack and in decline. In the nineteenth century, Le Play depicted his famous Pyrenean *famille souche* as an endangered species that had managed to survive only because of its geographic and social isolation.[4] There is, of course, some truth to this nostalgic view, but as several historians have now shown, extended households of various sorts remained important forms of family organization throughout the nineteenth and into the twentieth century in many areas of rural France.[5] Familial labor in the

[3] Hartig, "Révolution et communautés familiales." As Le Play later identified one household, the Mélougas in the Pyrenees, as his model of an ideal peasant family, his eighteenth-century predecessors discovered and idealized the Quittard-Pinon family in the Auvergne.

[4] Frédéric Le Play began his campaign to repeal the law of equal inheritance and to restore paternal power in his pioneering work of sociology, *Les ouvriers européens*, first published in 1855. In this and in his subsequent major works, such as *La Réforme sociale en France* (1864), *L'Organisation du travail* (1870), and *L'Organisation de la famille* (1871), he argued that the spirit of individualism and competition promoted by the Enlightenment and Revolution and embodied by the Napoleonic Code was destroying family stability and social prosperity. He contrasted the modern "unstable family" with the patriarchal family and especially the *famille souche*, which he argued had been the traditional French family for twenty-five centuries. See Le Play, *L'Organisation de la famille*, pp. 1–114, and Assier-Andrieu, "Le Play et la famille-souche des Pyrénées," pp. 495–512. For utopian socialist Etienne Cabet, the modern family represented the triumph of self-interest over social welfare. In his *Voyage en Icarie* (1848), Cabet depicted the ideal family as composed of two dozen members ranging over four generations, all living together under the benevolent direction of the patriarch. Pierre-Josephe Proudhon, concerned with the atomization of working-class families, defended an ideal patriarchal family of the small-property owner. Like Le Play he advocated restoring paternal authority in the family by restoring the faculté de tester. Proudhon, *Programme révolutionnaire, Oeuvres Completes*, vol. 10 (Paris: Marcel Riviere et Cie, 1938), pp. 301–303.

[5] For example, Lehning, *The Peasants of Marlhes*; Smith, "Family and Class," pp. 64–87; Berkner and Shaffer, "The Joint Family in the Nivernais"; Goubert, "Family and Province," pp. 179–195; Lemaitre, "Familles complexes," pp. 219–224; Segalen, "The Family Cycle and Household Structure," pp. 223–236; Shaffer, *Family and Farm*; Zonabend, *The Enduring Memory*.

nineteenth century was not a quaint survival but, in certain circumstances, the most profitable way to farm the land.

In the eighteenth century, Quercy peasants farmed inefficiently, worked land under sharecropping contracts, and left what property they owned to a single male heir, a combination that, according to the studies of Franklin Mendels, supported the use of family labor and the existence of extended peasant households.[6] Traditional agriculture and sharecropping continued to dominate the rural economy in the early nineteenth century, but the Revolution had mandated equal inheritance and buttressed individual rights. As a result, economic realities combined with the law to pull peasant families in two directions. To attain the secure and independent status that Bouzeran coveted, he needed the income of all the family property and the labor of all the family members. But Sanson could not turn over all his property; he had another daughter who was legally entitled to inherit a share. And he refused to subordinate his own rights as an individual to the needs of his family. He wanted the income of his property to provide a comfortable and honorable retirement for himself. One ambition or the other would go under; the family simply did not have enough resources to satisfy the legitimate but divergent claims of both Bouzeran and Sanson. For Bouzeran and Sanson and for other peasant families, there was no happy solution.[7]

Sanson's tragedy illustrates an intersection of legal and economic tensions in peasant families in the years after the French Revolution. Behind the murder loomed both the change in family law—mandatory equal inheritance—and the ruthless struggle for land ownership that meant economic security. During the Revolution, the land market opened up slightly with the sales of land confiscated from the church, but this hardly satisfied the land hunger of the peasantry. In the early nineteenth century, the demand for land became even more pressing.

In Quercy in the eighteenth century, few peasants owned enough land to support their families, much less to provide for all their heirs. The bulk of the population that inhabited the countryside around Montauban were farm servants, hired hands, and day workers who either owned no land or, like Bouzeran, owned too little to support themselves on it alone. Some were also part-time artisans; many, like Sanson's other son-in-law, worked

---

[6] Mendels, "La Composition du ménage paysan," pp. 780–802. See Kertzer, *Family Life in Central Italy*, for a detailed study of the interconnections between sharecropping and extended households.

[7] Castan, in *Les Criminels de Languedoc*, pp. 183–184, discusses the potential for neglect, abuse, and murder in southern peasant households, especially in the case of parental retirement. Gaunt, "Rural Household Organization," pp. 136–139, found similar pressures and potential for violence in nineteenth-century Scandinavian peasant households.

as weavers for Montauban's merchant-manufacturers.[8] Only a minority of peasants owned or rented enough land for self-sufficiency.

Peasants with the most land under their control were the *métayers*, or tenant farmers, who rented large farms owned by Montauban's elite and worked them on sharecropping contracts. A typical *métairie* included a house, outbuildings, a garden, pasture and fields totaling between ten and twenty hectares, and a team of cattle or oxen to work them.[9] In personal capital, however, tenant farmers were as poor as day laborers. They endowed their daughters with only three hundred or four hundred livres on the average, slightly less than the average dowry of a day laborer's daughter.[10] All of the income of the farm went for the immediate needs of the family, to pay the landlord's share and to pay off the debts that rapidly accumulated in years when harvests were poor.[11]

Peasant proprietors, called *laboureurs* in the eighteenth century, owned farms, which were usually not as large as the average *métairie*. According to the word's etymology, a *laboureur* should have owned a plow and team; however, in the 1770s at least half of the so-called plowmen in the district of Montauban did not own cattle.[12] A peasant who owned enough land to support a plow team had reached the apex of village society. The average dowry of a farm owner's daughter was two to three times larger than dowries in day laborer and sharecropper families. Bouzeran called one of his *laboureur* neighbors "*la bourgeoise*."[13]

There were several patterns of landholding that predominated in the region around Montauban. Nowhere, however, did peasants own more

[8] For a detailed discussion of the nuances of rural occupational terminology, see Lefebvre, *Les Paysans du Nord*, p. 278; Ligou, *Montauban*, p. 79; and Valmary, *Familles paysannes*, pp. 17–18, 69.

[9] In the district of Montauban, *métairies* were generally between ten and twenty hectares in size, large enough to be worked efficiently by a single plow team. Few were so large as to require two teams, and only one had three. AM de Mont 10 HH 1 dénombrement rural sd (circa 1770).

[10] In the sample of marriage contracts, the mean dowry of a sharecropper's daughter was 405 livres and the median 300. The mean dowry of a farm worker's daughter was 529 livres and the median 250. The difference was the contribution of the bride herself. Farm workers' daughters were often wage earners themselves and contributed an average of 281 livres to their dowries. Sharecroppers' daughters rarely worked for wages because they were part of the work team of the *métairie*. They contributed on the average only 89 livres to their dowries.

[11] Ricalens, "Statut et revenus de métayers de Moissac," pp. 39–51.

[12] AM de Mont 10 HH 1 dénombrement rural; Ligou, *Montauban*, p. 79; Frêche, *Toulouse*, pp. 324–325.

[13] AD T-et-G 1 U 137 assises 1827; procès verbaux des déclarations des témoins 14–1–1826. Based on the sample of marriage contracts, the mean dowry of a farm owner's daughter was 1,706 livres and the median 625 livres.

than one third of the arable land, and the possibilities for self-sufficiency declined as the eighteenth century progressed. Between 1706 and 1776, the number of landowning peasants in the Consulat of Montauban declined by 10 percent whereas the total number of peasants increased by 20 percent. In the decades before the Revolution, only 10 percent of peasants owned the six, eight, or ten hectares necessary for self-sufficiency. When the harvest was poor, three quarters of the population went hungry.[14]

To supplement their insufficient fields, many would-be *laboureurs* rented land. Throughout the seventeenth and eighteenth centuries, the increasing demand for rental land allowed landlords to toughen the terms of the lease. Whereas in the sixteenth century landlords had received as a net profit 27 percent of the harvest and tenants 32 percent, by the end of the eighteenth century these figures were reversed. The village council of Léojac complained in 1771 that "the landlords from Montauban and elsewhere carry off a third and more of the grain."[15]

The scarcity of land aggravated an age-old rural problem, the scarcity of cash. The entire rural community lived on credit from one harvest to the next. Even craftsmen who did most of their work in the winter and spring waited until the harvest to bill their customers. Landlords lent their tenants seed, grain, and money to buy animals and to meet current expenses. A poor harvest could quickly reduce an entire community to bankruptcy. In 1780 Charles Janolz, a somewhat unscrupulous Montauban merchant, rented a farm to Pierre Gaubil, a peasant who also owned land of his own. Janolz included in the lease an accounting of his past loans to Gaubil totaling 320 livres. Gaubil was to pay in full after the harvest, but because the farm in question brought Janolz only 199 livres a year, Gaubil would probably have to sell his land to meet the debt. The crop failures of the early 1770s and especially in 1788–1789 forced many peasants to sell off their land and livestock to pay their debts.[16]

In the early years of the Revolution, the abolition of feudalism and the sale of national properties offered some peasants a brief moment of financial relief and an opportunity to increase their landholdings. Various seigneurial rights, for example, *lods et ventes* and *banalités*, were quite prevalent in the countryside around Montauban and some seigneurs had been suc-

[14] Of the six thousand hectares owned by peasants in the commune of Montauban, half were owned by almost fifteen hundred persons, an average of only two hectares apiece. Ligou, *Montauban*, pp. 76–77; Boutier, "Jacqueries en pays croquant," p. 779; Bergeon, "La Terre et le paysan dans le Consulat de Montauban," pp. 18–23; Ligou, "La Structure agraire de la banlieu montalbanaise," p. 36.

[15] Bergeon, "La Terre et le paysan dans le Consulat de Montauban," pp. 13–18; Frêche, *Toulouse*, pp. 188, 248; and Latouche, *La Vie en Bas-Quercy*, p. 349.

[16] AD T-et-G 5E 12868 Grelleau no. 415 1–10–1780 bail à culture Janolz-Gaubil; Ligou, *Montauban*, pp. 179–181; Frêche, *Toulouse*, p. 307; Ricalens, "Statut et revenus de métayers de Moissac," 39–51.

cessful in resurrecting inactive ones.[17] Although taxes soon increased to take their place, the suppression of such fees and of the tithe did benefit landowners. Peasants who rented land hardly benefited at all. In 1791 a group of tenant farmers from the district of Montauban petitioned the Legislative Assembly to adjust by statute their sharecropping contracts to add to the tenant's share the produce that had previously gone to pay the tithe. Not only was this economic justice, they claimed, but it was political justice because the tenant farmers were the only ones in the district who supported the Revolution. The government was not convinced, arguing that since the ultimate responsibility for paying taxes rested with the landowner, he also should receive the benefit of any tax reduction.[18]

Of greater economic importance was the sale of national property, which greatly benefited some well-to-do peasants in outlying areas. A few poorer peasants were also able to acquire land by collective buying although this was illegal. Groups of peasants bought land at auctions in Réalville, Bioule, and Albias. Around Montauban itself, however, the land was sold in large lots and peasants had little chance to acquire any. For the most part, the Revolution meant that they exchanged ecclesiastic or emigré landlords for Montauban merchants.[19]

The decline of Montauban's textile industry outweighed many of the economic benefits of Revolutionary legislation. In the eighteenth century, landless peasants had found work in Montauban, whereas the land-poor and the underemployed combined agriculture with spinning and weaving. In the nineteenth century, as these alternatives disappeared, peasants depended even more heavily on the land for their survival.[20] At the same

---

[17] For example, Jean-Léon Bonal, who had made a fortune as *controleur général* in Tours, purchased the barony of Caselnau-Montratrier north of Montauban in 1775 for more than four hundred thousand livres. He immediately attempted to recoup the cost by the "minute and sometimes childish extraction of feudal rights which were unknown until then," according to des Rochettes, "Les Familles montaubanaises," 2: Bonal. Nor were all seigneurial obligations abolished. In 1804, a group of peasants had to agree to pay more than four thousand francs to redeem the perpetual rent on their land retained by their ex-seigneur M. Descorbiac. See AD T-et-G 5E 12856 Grelleau no. 218 6–5–1769 vente Gales à Ruelle frères; 5E 2130 Latreille-Olivié no. 960 10 fructidor Year 12 abandon Descorbiac à Vales et al.

[18] Gerbaux and Schmidt, eds., *Comités d'Agriculture et de Commerce* 2: 455–456.

[19] Ligou, *Montauban*, p. 569, and Ligou, "Biens nationaux," p. 363.

[20] In the sample of marriage contracts from 1775 to 1825, the percentage of grooms who were textile workers remained stable at about 15 percent. However, the proportion of rural to urban textile workers shifted. At the end of the Old Regime and during the early years of the Revolution before the upheaval of the war economy (1775–1794), 16 percent of textile worker grooms were rural dwellers. The redirection of Montauban's textile industry to manufacturing coarse cloth for military uniforms and blankets (1795–1804) created greater opportunities for rural weaving, and the proportion of rural textile workers rose to nearly 40 percent. However, the decline of textile manufacture in Montauban in the years after 1800 hurt the cottage industry the most. After 1804, rural textile workers declined to only 11 percent of textile worker grooms.

time, merchants increasingly invested a much larger percentage of their fortunes in agriculture, competing both with ex-seigneurs and with peasants to purchase land. After a brief respite during the Revolution, the land market tightened up once more.

This was the vise in which Bouzeran was caught. Unable to survive on the produce of Sanson's land, at first he bided his time, working for wages while his wife and parents-in-law worked the family's few acres. Saving every sous, he purchased what additional scraps of land he could while watching the prices move steadily beyond his means.[21] This, he must have thought, was not all bad, because Sanson's land, when it finally came to him, would be worth that much more. But Sanson's land, when it did finally come to him, was encumbered with the pension, calculated from its increased market value. Sanson's "gift" in fact withdrew both his labor and his land from the family economy. Bouzeran gained nothing.[22]

The indictment explained Sanson's murder against the background of economic pressure, but the rural economy was not the only or necessarily the most significant context of the crime. Sanson's neighbors pointed to his relationship with his family to explain the murder. Sanson's murder resulted from a family quarrel, over land and money, certainly, but especially over power and status in the household. Sanson's widow complained that Bouzeran had expected his parents-in-law to work for him, had begrudged them food when they did not work, and had refused to treat them with respect. In other words, Bouzeran had acted like the head of the household. Sanson rebelled. Like King Lear, he wanted to retire yet at the same time to retain control. According to the arbiter who had tried to reconcile Sanson and Bouzeran, the old man had refused all efforts at compromise. He was determined to remain head of the family.

Each couple blamed the other for the quarrel. Bouzeran's wife said it was all her parents' fault. "They have always harbored resentment against him [Bouzeran] and against me." Because Sanson and his wife had refused to live under Bouzeran's authority, Sanson had "only his hot head and his wickedness" to blame if tragedy resulted. Sanson's widow told a different story. Bouzeran was a usurper who had "used every kind of trick to make my husband decide to make him a gift of his goods" and then provoked "daily disputes" with his father-in-law and heaped "daily humiliations" on

---

[21] One witness testified that eight years before Bouzeran had been negotiating to buy land from a peasant named Richard. He could not meet Richard's price and the land was sold to someone else. Shortly after Richard's house burned down and rumor named Bouzeran as the culprit. AD T-et-G 1 U 137 assises 1827; interrogation of Jean Flourens 23–11–1826.

[22] Held, in "Rural Retirement," p. 234, cites studies of retirement in Sweden and Austria that indicate that retirement often imposed a considerable burden on peasant holdings, absorbing up to half the farm's profits.

his mother-in-law.[23] The two couples, each claiming authority over the other, tore apart the unity of household, land, and labor that, according to Le Play, was the heart of the peasant family.

The extended household, the cause of Sanson's murder, was also the core of the peasant family and an important component of rural society. The household was expected to work together, to protect the status and reputation of its members, to establish its place in the social hierarchy, and to advance or decline as a unit. As Le Play fulminated, it was in this household that Revolutionary laws of marriage and inheritance intervened, to overthrow custom and to replace a stability and harmonious patriarchy with the individualism and selfishness of the *famille instable*.

Equal inheritance and marital community property did contravene the customary arrangements of peasants in the Montauban region. But, as Sanson's murder shows, the impact of the new laws was less clear-cut and one-dimensional than the opponents of equal inheritance allowed. Equal inheritance increased Bouzeran's problems but hardly created them. The conflict that erupted between the two couples was built into the power structure of the household, which rested directly on control of the land. Nonetheless, the changes in family law did lead to the restructuring of peasant families. Extended households like the Sanson-Bouzeran ménage became less common as it became less easy to "make an heir." This change, however, did not affect all peasant families in the same degree or in the same way. Day laborers were usually little affected whereas small-property-owning households like Bouzeran's were sometimes devastated. The extent and type of changes depended on the family patterns that had prevailed under the faculté de tester and the Custom of Montauban including household structures and familial behaviors rarely mentioned in marriage contracts and wills.

How can we define the peasant household and determine who was a member and who was not?[24] Shared residence was essential but insufficient; when Sanson and his wife stopped eating and working with Bouzeran, they left his household although they all lived in the same house. Even those who lived, ate, and worked together were not necessarily household members. Servants, for example, were usually only accessories.[25] A mark of their tenuous connection to the household was the

---

[23] AD T-et-G 1 U 137 assises 1827; interrogations of Jean Boyer, Marie Sanson ép Bouzeran and Jeanne Lisse v^e Sanson.

[24] See Gaudemet, *Les Communautés familiales*, pp. 11–13. Françoise Zonabend discusses the close interconnections of apparently nuclear households in a modern French village in *Enduring Memory*, pp. 36–38.

[25] In the Nivernais, where tacit communities were supposed to exist among any persons who lived and worked together for a period of years, masters filed "contradictions" to prevent servants from claiming shares. Berkner and Shaffer, "The Joint Family," p. 151.

fact that, like both Bouzeran and Sanson, male farm employees in Quercy normally slept in outbuildings rather than in the farmhouse. A farm servant thus housed might even be a poor relation, an uncle or a cousin partly earning his keep and partly dependent on the household but not a household member.[26]

Peasant households were built on ties of blood and marriage reinforced by shared residence, shared work or expenses, and, for many households, a shared interest in the land they worked. Such households were rather like artisanal family businesses. But peasant households in the region around Montauban were likely to be larger than artisan households and were much more likely to include two or more married couples.[27] In the words of their marriage contracts, these people "agreed to live at the same pot and hearth . . . in joint community."

A pot-and-hearth community was a contractual association among household members to live and work together for the common profit. This had been the arrangement between Sanson and Bouzeran. Although we do not have the contract itself, it was probably not very different from the community established between another farm worker, Etienne Aché, and his parents-in-law in 1806. Aché, originally of the Haute-Garonne, contracted marriage to Gerande Mouméja, daughter of Antoine Mouméja, a landowning farmer. Antoine Mouméja gave his daughter and son-in-law one half of his land and goods, the young couple assumed one half of his debts, and all agreed to live at the same pot and hearth, to share the work, profits, and losses equally.[28]

Pot-and-hearth communities like this were very common in central and southern France at the end of the eighteenth and in the early nineteenth century. Although such communities were occasionally found in artisan households, the institution was largely rural.[29] Peasant couples formed communities in separate acts of association, as part of sharecropping contracts and especially as part of marriage contracts. In the countryside

[26] According to Claude Rivals's study of rural architecture in the Bas-Montauban region, farms often had a room partitioned off in the stable known as the room of the *vieux garçon*. *Midi toulousain et pyrénéen*, Collection L'Architecture rurale français directed by Jean Cuisenier (Paris: Berger-Levrault, 1979), p. 74. See also AD T-et-G 5E Latreille-Olivié 2154 sn 13 and 14–9–1824 accords Ruelle and 1 U 97 1813, the indictment of Jean Lugan for murder. Lugan, a farm servant, slept in the stable while his girlfriend, also a farm servant, slept in the house.

[27] In the middle of the nineteenth century, the average household in the Tarn-et-Garonne included 2.53 related adults. Mendels, "La composition du ménage paysan," p. 801.

[28] AD T-et-G 5E 2133 Latreille-Olivié no. 123 31–1–1806 contrat de mariage Aché-Mouméja.

[29] See Goubert, "Family and Province," pp. 179–195; Lehning, *The Peasants of Marlhes*; Shaffer, *Family and Farm*, and also Hilaire, "Vie en commun," pp. 8–53; Fine-Souriac, "La Famille-souche pyrénéenne," pp. 478–487; Collomp, *La Maison du père*.

TABLE 7–1
Pot-and-Hearth Communities in Montauban Marriage Contracts, 1775–1824

| Groom's Occupation | Marriage Contracts Establishing Communities | | |
	All 1775–1824	*I* 1775–1793	*II* 1794–1824
Peasant (*N* = 323)	39%	51%	33%
Urban worker (*N* = 195)	3	1	4
Artisan (*N* = 204)	7	12	6
Elite (*N* = 100)	4	2	5
N	822	311	511

Note: Significance levels = .01, contingency coefficients = .401 (all), .486 (I), .343, (II).

around Montauban, 51 percent of marriage contracts in the years before the Revolution established such communities between the nuptial couple and one set of parents. The law also recognized tacit pot-and-hearth communities,[30] but these were rare around Montauban where the number of notarial acts that created communities suggests a high regard for written formalities. All in all it is likely that two thirds or more of peasants in this region spent part of their lives living and working in households organized as pot-and-hearth communities.

In Quercy, these familial communities were contractual associations providing shared residence, work, profits, and losses and often property as well. In almost every case, the contract that created the community also provided for its dissolution. Usually the young couple would take their share of the profits, pay their share of the losses, and receive some portion of the property given them in the marriage contract. For example, if Etienne Aché and his bride left the community, they were to take all the furniture and animals given them but only half of the real estate; the other half Antoine Mouméja reserved until his death.[31]

[30] In the absence of a formal contract, if the parties had acted as if they were bound by a community, the court could rule to enforce its tacit terms. See, for example, AD T-et-G 5E 2107 Franceries no. 225 12–1–1811 dissolution Souloumiac-Malfre. See Shaffer, *Family and Farm*, pp. 21–22.

[31] AD T-et-G 5E 2133 Latreille-Olivié no. 123 31–1–1806 contrat de mariage Aché-Mouméja; similarly, 12876 Grelleau no. 255 30–4–1786 contrat de mariage Pefourque-Mouméja, and many other contracts. In the fourteenth and fifteenth centuries in Languedoc, only the father could dissolve the community, and even in the eighteenth century, some contracts from this region penalized children who withdrew. Flandrin, *Families in Former Times*, pp. 82–83, and Castan, *Honnêteté*, pp. 229–235. I have not found a single Montauban marriage contract that included any penalty clause, and every contract was strictly proportional; for example, if the young couple were to receive a one-third share of the profits, they were to contribute only one third of the work.

The partners to the contract were married couples. Seventy percent of the pot-and-hearth communities formed in marriage contracts were between the nuptial couple and a parental couple. In a society in which much of the work was identified by gender,[32] an enterprise in which all work was to be shared equally required an equal number of men and of women. The need to balance the community by gender meant that pot-and-hearth communities were not well suited to all peasant families. Only 41 percent of peasant grooms and 51 percent of their brides in the sample of marriage contracts had both parents living when they married. A community with a widowed father was twice as likely as a community with a widowed mother, but neither was very common. The death of one of the male partners usually ended the community; the loss of one of the women was less serious but also could create problems. The community between two brothers, Paul and Pierre Fabie, was dissolved for just such a reason. Pierre had lost his wife, and one of Paul's children had reached an age to contribute substantially to the community. The partnership was no longer practical because Pierre was "no longer able to work in the same proportion and with the same profit as his brother, whose family is composed of three people capable of working while the said Pierre Fabie is alone."[33] An unbalanced community was a vulnerable community.

Peasants preferred sons four to one over daughters as partners in pot-and-hearth communities. The contract marked the beginning of a new relationship between father and son. The father first emancipated his son from his paternal authority, severing the "natural" hierarchical bond between them. He then gave his son a portion of his property, materially elevating his son to his own status. Finally, the father contracted a new bond with his son, a partnership in which the son was legally his father's equal while promising always to remember "those rights and duties toward their father to which children are held following divine and human law."[34] By this act the father created a partner who was to be his faithful reflection, an equal who always agreed with him.

---

[32] Segalen, *Love and Power in the Peasant Family*, pp. 78–111, distinguishes three divisions of work by gender throughout French peasant society. Some tasks were reserved for women alone. For others men had the primary responsibility although women often helped. Others, depending on the region, were carried out by either gender.

[33] AD T-et-G 5E 13184 Deray no. 284 1 ventôse Year 5 dissolution and accord Fabie-Fabie.

[34] AD T-et-G 5E 13180 Deray no. 350 13–6–1787 contrat de mariage Beluc-Charles includes a typical emancipation preceding the formation of a community.

In favor and contemplation of this marriage the said Antoine Beluc has emancipated and emancipates the said Jean Beluc, his son, the future husband, who accepts the present Emancipation and humbly thanks the said Antoine Beluc, his father, who removes his said son from his paternal authority, giving him the power to sell, buy and negotiate, work for his own profit and use, make a will, settle a suit, and generally do all the acts of a free, duly emancipated person, the said Beluc *père* reserving only the rights and duties

If parents had no sons, or their sons were too young to provide the necessary labor, they might then form a community with a daughter and son-in-law. Etienne Aché's bride, for example, had two sisters and no brothers. Sanson, too, had only daughters. Widow Marie Lieges took her daughter and son-in-law into community although she had three young sons. Apparently her husband's death had made the acquisition of an adult man to help on the farm a top priority. But sons-in-law were not as satisfactory as sons. No filial piety bound them to their fathers-in-law. Proverbs warned that "a son-in-law's love is winter sunshine." Plus there were material risks. As another proverb pointed out, "when the daughter dies, the son-in-law is lost."[35] A suit between Jean Bouye and his son-in-law François Malbreil illustrated the truth of this adage. When Malbreil married Guillamette Bouye in 1805, the couple joined Bouye's parents in community and received a fourth interest in their property. Unfortunately, Guillamette died shortly after, and Bouye, who had hardly profited from the association, had to pay Malbreil four hundred francs to settle his claim.[36]

Nor were all communities between parents and children. A few peasant couples with no children of their own formed communities with nephews or nieces. For example, in 1788 tenant farmer François Mespoulets took his brother's younger son into community with him, his own children having all died.[37] But such communities were not common and rural

---

toward their father to which children are held following divine and human law, from such rights and duties the said future husband has protested that he will never waver.

See also AD T-et-G 5E 21880 Grelleau no. 204 24–4–1789 contrat de mariage Padie-Herin and 13182 Deray no. 1307 9–5–1793 contrat de mariage Mauron-Mauron. This is quite a different convention from the one that prevailed in the Haute-Provence studied by Alain Collomp. There, fathers emancipated the sons who left the household (and who renounced their inheritance rights in the bargain); the son who married and remained in the household lived and worked legally "as a son of the family" completely under his father's rule. Collomp, "Tensions, dissensions, and ruptures inside the family," pp. 150–152.

[35] Cesaire Daugé, *Le Mariage et la famille en Gascogne* 1: 280. Other proverbs accused sons and daughters-in-law of bringing conflict into the house and of throwing out the parents.

[36] AD T-et-G 5E 13517 Martin fils no. 267 5–8–1820 accord Bouye-Malbreil. Alain Collomp suggests other reasons that communities with sons-in-law may have produced more problems than communities with sons. Because women married earlier than men, a son-in-law was often older than a son would have been and thus more likely to challenge his father-in-law's authority. Also a man who joined in community with his parents-in-law was often of lesser social status than they; this could create tensions with them and with his wife. Collomp, *Maison du père*, pp. 186–187.

[37] AD T-et-G 5E 2337 Martin no. 17 12–1–1788 contrat de mariage Mouraille-Bournet. See also AD T-et-G 5E 2067 Delmas no. 712 23–12–1788 contrat de mariage Gineste-Gineste and B 418 donations no. 43 27–5–1772. In the sample of marriage contracts, only 4 of 153 communities were formed with people other than the parents of one of the fiancés. One couple joined the groom's two uncles and one joined the bride's uncle, one formed a community with the groom's grandfather and one with the groom's employer.

wisdom cautioned against them. *A qui Diu nou da maynadyes, la diable qu'ou da nebouts* (To whom God does not give children, the devil gives nephews), ran a local proverb.[38] More common were communities between brothers or sisters, the remnants of earlier communities formed by the parents with two or more of their children (see table 7–4). When the old couple died, the children decided to continue to live and work communally rather than to divide the inheritance. Such was the history of Fabie brothers' household mentioned earlier.

The existence of pot-and-hearth communities depended in part on demography—the survival of the parental couple and the survival, sex, and age of their children. But it depended also on the willingness of parents and children to live and work together as partners. Not all fathers enjoyed the prospect of taking a son into partnership. A case of assault and battery that reached the assizes court in 1827 involved a father's refusal to take his eldest son into community. The parents testified that the son, Pierre Bouble, aged thirty, was debauched, idle, and violent. He stole from the family purse, frequented fairs and carnivals, shirked his work, and came home drunk. At various times he beat and choked his father and threatened to burn the house down unless he was given his share "now and not by testament."[39] In other cases it was the son who objected to the community arrangement. When weaver Jacques Crabon married in 1813 he joined in community with his farm worker parents. A year and a half later he initiated the dissolution of the community although the two couples continued to live together. The son felt that too much of his earnings at the loom had gone to support his parents and not enough to his own young family. He returned the property his father had given him and each man agreed to work for his own profit.[40]

When the household was organized as a community, not only did a child become the parents' partner, but so did the child's spouse. He or she had to be, in the conventional term, suitable (*sortable*) from economic, social and, in this region, religious perspectives and also compatible as a housemate and co-worker. This was most critical when the parents were contemplating forming a community with a son-in-law, but it was also a consideration with daughters-in-law. In fact, peasant proverbs commented more frequently on the evil effects of power struggles between mothers and daughters-in-law than on those between fathers and sons-in-law. Conflicts between the female partners rarely broke up the community but could poison daily life. As we saw in the Sanson case, hostility between

[38] Daugé, *Le Mariage et la famille en Gascogne* 1: 289.

[39] AD T-et-G 1 U 136 assises, 1827. See Castan, *Les Criminels de Languedoc*, pp. 187–190.

[40] AD T-et-G 5E 2142 Latreille Olivié no. 409 2–10–1814 dissolution de société Crabon père et fils ainé.

father and son-in-law quickly brought the community to an end. Peasants endured hostility between mothers and daughters-in-law and used proverbs to criticize it in an attempt to control it. Proverbs about fathers and sons-in-law advised against forming such communities in the first place.[41]

Parents often chose or supervised the choice of the spouse of the child they had decided to join in community. Bernard Cuquel, a farm worker from St Porquier, said his courtship of his cousin Blaise Grellou began when "his family having proposed this marriage, [he] acquiesced, visited the said Grellou, and became engaged to her."[42] Sometimes the marriage contract was more of an agreement between the groom and his parents or his future parents-in-law than between the bride and groom. In 8 percent of peasant marriage contracts in the sample, all of them establishing pot-and-hearth communities, the bride was not even present when the contract was signed. One such was the marriage contract of Etienne Aché to Gerande Mouméja. In this instance as in later transactions, Gerande appeared to be a catalyst, facilitating the bond between her father and her husband, rather than a full partner in the community.[43]

In a very few instances the groom was also absent and the whole marriage was arranged between the fathers, suggesting that besides creating new bonds within the household, the pot-and-hearth community could create or strengthen alliances with other households. In isolated villages of the Pyrenees or the Massif Central, these alliances are easy to trace as families consciously exchanged children and property, intermarrying over several generations to create veritable clans.[44] In the countryside around Montauban, patterns of exchange and alliance were usually less explicit, emerging when special circumstances isolated a group of peasant house-

---

[41] Martine Segalen cites numerous proverbs common throughout the south asserting the incompatibility of two women in one house, for example, "When there are two women in the house, one should be in a painting," "Two women in the house, two cats for one rat, two dogs for one bone, make them agree if you can," and "The happiest bride is she with neither mother-in-law nor sister-in-law." Segalen, *Love and Power in the Peasant Family*, pp. 68–69, and "Le Mariage et la femme dans les proverbes," p. 279. See also Collomp, "Conflits familiaux et groupes de résidence," p. 411. Zonabend, in *Enduring Memory*, pp. 115–118, reports that in the twentieth century, hostility between mother and daughter-in-law became more dangerous because not only were communities more fragile but so was marriage. In one instance in the village of Minot, a mother had forced her son to divorce his wife in order to get her out of the household.

[42] AD T-et-G G460 procédures devant l'Official 1780–1789.

[43] AD T-et-G 5E 2133 Latreille-Olivié no. 123 31–1–1806 contrat de mariage Aché-Mouméja; 2136 Latreille-Olivié no. 33 1–10–1809 contrat de mariage Vern-Larroque, no. 185 5–3–1809 contrat de mariage Poujade-Delcros, and no. 873 15–11–1809 contrat de mariage Pujol-Beziat; 2008 Garrigues no. 69 22–1–1788 contrat de mariage Gineste-Bongrat and no. 196 3–3–1788 contrat de mariage Corboué-Aché.

[44] Collomp, "Alliance et filiation en Haute Provence," pp. 445–477, and Lamaison, "Les Stratégies matrimoniales dans un système complexe de parenté," pp. 721–743.

holds. For example, in the village of Peberaye there were few Protestant landowning peasant families in the eighteenth century and they intermarried repeatedly. Fourteen peasants of the Ruelle family married spouses with only five different surnames. Among them were six Larroques, three Ruelles, two Martys, and two Calvets. Double marriages were common including three cases of brothers marrying sisters, two cases of a brother and sister marrying a sister and brother, and two cases of siblings marrying cousins. There were also marriages between first cousins and between second cousins. One of the most direct exchanges was the marriage of Durand Ruelle to his second cousin Jeanne in 1797, followed two years later by the marriage of his sister Marie to his wife's brother Jean. Each bride left her home to join in community with her husband and his parents. Dowries, probably equal in size, were promised but, as is clear from Durand's father's will, they were never paid.[45]

More than a means of connecting households in the present, the pot-and-hearth community was intended to connect households over time. By pooling the members' resources of property and labor, the pot-and-hearth community helped peasants through the two particularly vulnerable points in the family life cycle, the childbearing years and old age. The legal face of the community was egalitarian; this represented not a constant equal sharing of work and authority but a balancing of inequalities achieved in the long-term. The relative dependence of the child's young family compensated the later relative dependence of the aging parents.

The two couples negotiated how much authority and dependence was

---

[45] AD T-et-G E Etat Civil Protestant no. 366 22–3–1788, 25–3–1788, 31–3–1788: 5E 1970 Latreille-Olivié no. 356 6 fructidor Year 7 contrat de mariage Ruelle-Ruelle; 1971 Latreille-Olivié no. 1240 12 fructidor Year 8 testament Ruelle; 1972 Latreille-Olivié no. 934 9 thermidor Year 9 élection Ruelle; 2130 Latreille-Olivié no. 227 7 nivôse Year 12 testament Ruelle; 2132 Latreille-Olivié no. 198 3 nivôse Year 13 échange Ruelle-Ruelle and no. 1144 18 frimaire Year 14 testament Ruelle; 2135 Latreille-Olivié no. 114 5–2–1809 procuration Ruelle à Ruelle et Larroque; 2138 Latreille-Olivié no. 133 6–3–1811 testament Ruelle; 2153 Latreille-Olivié no. 266 19–10–1824 testament Ruelle; 2158 Latreille-Olivié no. 162 23–4–1828 partage Ruelle père et fils; 2159 Latreille-Olivié no. 359 14–12–1829 testament Ruelle; 2161 Latreille-Olivié no. 192 24–4–1831 testament Ruelle. Also see 5E 13176 Deray no. 479 17–9–1781 double marriage contract of Jean Chambart and Marguerite Carbonner, and Pierre Carbonnel and Jeanne Chambart, and 13179 Deray no. 90 26–4–1783 accord among three couples, all siblings, Jean Moulie having married Anne Mulatet in 1756, Geraud Moulie marrying Marie Mulatet in 1761, and Pierre Mulatet marrying Marguerite Moulie in 1767. A double wedding might have to be preceded by a double dispensation. Two petitions for dispensation, both dated January 10, 1757, requested dispensations so that Antoine Belloc, a *laboureur* of Meauzac, could marry his second cousin Marie Belloc and that Jean Belloc, Marie's brother, could marry Catherine, Antoine's sister. Both couples claimed, in identical language, that they had had "carnal commerce" and needed to marry to "repair the honor" of the two women. Sexual intercourse was prima facie grounds for a dispensation. AD T-et-G G 457 procédures devant l'Official 1750–1759.

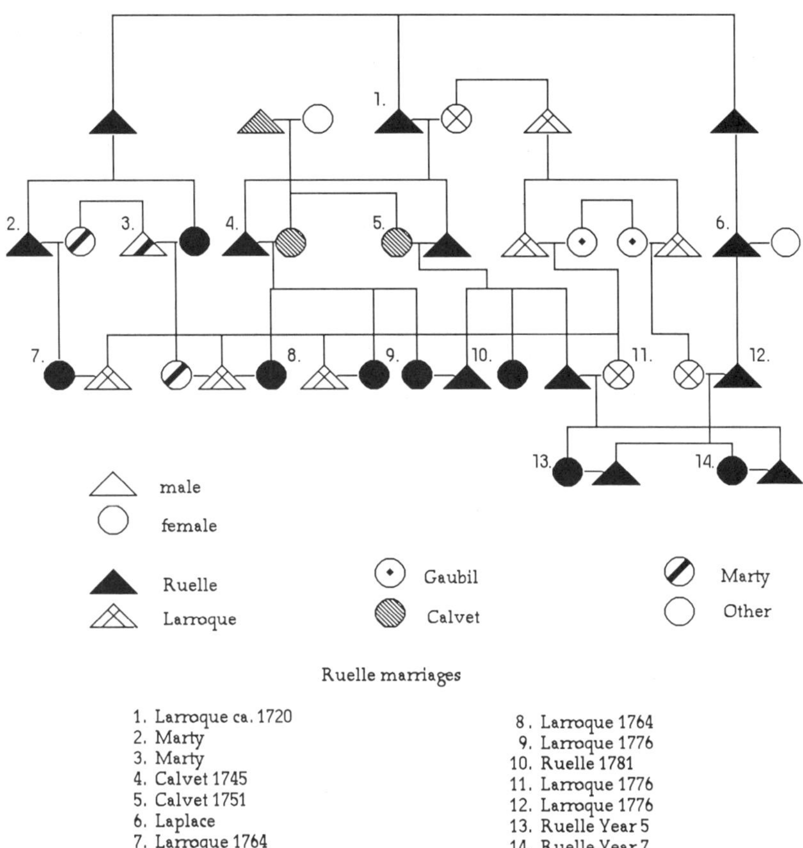

tolerable under the guise of equality. The hidden terms of the equation could suddenly emerge when one party tipped the scales too far. In a lawsuit in 1792 between two brothers over rights to the paternal succession, Jean Baitaillon, the elder brother, claimed that while he had lived in community with his father, he had been, in effect, unemancipated, "under paternal authority," and therefore not competent to make a valid legal act; the act in question was his renunciation of all rights to his father's property. The court agreed, awarding him a portion of his father's estate.[46] A

[46] AD T-et-G L 456 tribunal de famille, Castelsarrasin.

case from 1816 illustrates the other extreme. After having lived and worked in community for nearly fourteen years, winegrower Jacques Garrigues and his son Pierre decided to dissociate. They explained how the community had changed over that time so that it was no longer viable. "At that time, the father could work and had several of his other children [able to work] with him. Today he is alone, unable to work, his other children are married and work on their own behalf and . . . it is not fair that his said son should care for him in his old age while he [the son] remains liable to the claims of his brothers and sisters because of the above-mentioned community."[47] If the distribution of power became too unequal, the partnership could not survive.

Peasants did not expect pot-and-hearth communities to last forever. They were part of a life cycle of households, spanning a decade or so between the son's marriage and the father's death or incapacity.[48] Before the family created a pot-and-hearth community, the son, unmarried and unemancipated, lived as a dependent in his parents' household. At his marriage he and his wife were taken on as junior partners. As time passed, the weight of the work shifted to the younger couple. In some communities, a transfer of authority followed that of responsibility, and the son's legal partnership with his father slowly became reality. But the son did not become head of the household until his father died or retired.

For some men, as was the case for Sanson, retirement meant an abrupt and humiliating loss of authority. When the Garrigues dissolved their community, Pierre promised to "feed, lodge, and care for his father throughout the rest of his life in sickness as in health," and Jacques promised to work for his son to the best of his ability. In other words, he became a dependent in what was now his son's household. He might have ended up like Geraud Alba, aged seventy-two, who lived out the last years

[47] AD T-et-G 5E 12841 Delteil 2 no. 428 11–2–1816 dissolution de société Garrigues. For other examples, see 5E 13184 Deray no. 284 1 ventôse Year 5 dissolution and accord Fabié and 12876 Grelleau no. 495 27–8–1786 donation Coutrasty and B 418 donations no. 2 18–1–1772 Rattier. Gaunt, in "Rural Household Organization," p. 137, describes the moment of transition in a Norwegian peasant household. One day at dinner, the son challenged his father's right to sit at the head of the table. When the rest of the family concurred, the father reluctantly agreed to retire.

[48] Notarial acts dissolving pot-and-hearth communities were not especially common. Informal agreement or death dissolved most communities. However, a small sample of eighteen acts of dissolution recorded by Montauban notaries between 1779 and 1828 shows a mean duration of ten years (the median is ten years and three months). One quarter of the communities lasted less than two years; one quarter lasted more than thirteen years. The majority lasted between five and fourteen years. The shortest duration was three months and the longest thirty-one years. Alain Collomp found that in villages in the Haute-Provence, few communities dissolved during the father's lifetime and those that did had been very short-lived. Collomp, "Conflits familiaux," pp. 412–413. He also argues that ruptures were more common with sons-in-law than with sons. *Maison du père*, pp. 186–187.

of his life in the cow shed on the farm his son rented, "having abandoned all to my children in return for a pension."[49]

The pot-and-hearth community transferred authority in peasant families from father to son; it also served to transfer authority's outward sign and foundation—property. Parents designated their heir in his marriage contract by establishing the community with its gift of property.[50] In the same document, they often set aside portions for their other children, either by making the heir liable for paying a share or by reserving a sum from the community. When Raymond Ruelle took his son Durand into community in 1797, Durand promised, in return for a half-share in his father's land, to pay half of his father's debts including half of his sister's dowry. In 1788, when farm worker Jean Estève married, his father also took him into community. He set aside seventy livres to leave to his other son and fifty livres in furniture to endow his daughter. The rest of his property he gave to Jean, reserving life rights to one half of it.[51]

Property and authority passed between the male members of the community. Although their wives were formally their copartners, in practice women in pot-and-hearth communities may have wielded less power than peasant women in one-couple households.[52] The pot-and-hearth commu-

[49] AD T-et-G L 444 interrogation 17 prairial Year 13 of Geraud Alba. Respect for the elderly, unsupported by material goods, was not part of rural morality. See Lehning, *The Peasants of Marlhes*, p. 96; Collomp, "Tensions, Dissensions, and Ruptures Inside the Family," p. 168, and Zonabend, *Enduring Memory*, pp. 118–119.

[50] A testator could revoke his will unilaterally, but parents could not change the form of the community set up by marriage contract except by negotiation. In 1794 a case came before the family court of Castelsarrasin, which suggests that some peasants believed they could revoke the gifts made to establish a community if the other party broke the agreement. According to the suit of Grégoire Badeur, his son had "abandoned" the community, taking with him several animals and leaving behind considerable debts. Badeur wanted his goods restored and the debts paid, but his son claimed they were less than what was due him by his marriage contract. The court ruled for the son. AD T-et-G L 456 tribunal de famille, Castelsarrasin 1 fructidor Year 2.

[51] AD T-et-G 5E 2008 Garrigues no. 301 6–4–1788 contrat de mariage Estève-Soulie and 2158 Latreille-Olivié no. 162 23–4–1828 partage Ruelle-Ruelle; also see 5E 2008 Garrigues no. 896 3–12–1788 contrat de mariage Caussade-Brousse, 2067 Delmas no. 45 8–1–1788 contrat de mariage Descazoux-Marty and no. 642 25–11–1788 contrat de mariage Mauron-Labruguière.

[52] In *Love and Power in the Peasant Family*, Martine Segalen argues that "the man-wife relationship in peasant society is based not on the absolute authority of one over the other, but on the complementarity of the two" (p. 9). Male authority in the household, she argues, was not taken for granted but was the subject of much discussion and many rituals. Husbands and wives negotiated and struggled over the distribution of power; they did not simply adhere to some hard and fast patriarchal norm (pp. 25–37). Proverbs and charivaris critical of henpecked husbands attest that peasant wives could be very powerful and could dominate their households (pp. 43–44, 155–160). Yet these same proverbs and charivaris also attest that peasants believed it was inappropriate for a woman to dominate the household. It would

nity reinforced male power within peasant households by formalizing it and doubling it. In most communities, the wife was the outsider, moving in and joining the household. As both outsider and female, she was a distinctly subordinate member, subordinate not only to her husband but also to his male partner. Together the men bought and sold property and borrowed and lent money and goods without the intervention or the authorization of their wives, their supposed copartners. In fact, the existence of the community reduced a woman's chance to act as her husband's partner because he already had a ready-made partner in the other male member. When peasants appointed a *procureur*, or legal proxy, for example, 24 percent chose their son or son-in-law; only 3 percent chose their wives.[53]

Although in nuclear households peasant wives may have controlled the larder and the family purse,[54] in pot-and-hearth communities it appears that these rights belonged to the male head of the household. In the Sanson-Bouzeran household, Bouzeran doled out the bread after Sanson's retirement. The Delbert family of landowners, another peasant household that came under police scrutiny due to a murder attempt, was composed of Etienne Delbert, his retired father, his unmarried brother, his wife, and his widowed daughter. According to his wife, Delbert kept the keys to the cash box, doling out only small sums to household members for specific purposes. A monitory notice circulated by the mayor and town council of Castelsarrasin in 1783 gives further evidence of a peasant husband's control within the home. It accused a local sharecropper of keeping a mistress in preference to his wife, "whom he put out the door when he had something good to eat and sat at table with the said concubine while his wife cried on the doorstep." In each case, it was not the man's control over the household that was at issue but how he chose to exercise his rights.[55]

There was less conventional wisdom on the appropriate division of power between the women in the community. Proverbs highlighted the conflict between mother-in-law and daughter-in-law without suggesting which should dominate. However, most assumed that cooperation between them was impossible and that hierarchy was essential for the good of the household.[56] Probably a woman's status in the community was

---

be more accurate to describe the relationship of peasant couples as both complementary and hierarchical. A wife had her own sources of authority, notably her own hard work and her motherhood, but she was expected to exercise her power within the boundaries circumscribed by her husband and patriarchal conventions.

[53] Significance level = .02 contingency coefficient = .314. See Gaudemet, *Les Communautés familiales*, pp. 117, 161–162. Dussourd, *Au même pot et au même feu*, pp. 34–35.

[54] Segalen, *Love and Power in the Peasant Family*, p. 112–121.

[55] AD T-et-G 1 U 137 and 1 U 138 26–6–1827 and AD T-et-G G460 procédures devant l'officialité 1780–1789.

[56] Segalen, *Love and Power in the Peasant Family*, pp. 68–69; Collomp "Conflits familiaux," p. 411.

closely linked to her husband's authority. For example, Jeanne Lisse complained bitterly that since Sanson had retired she had been treated like a servant.[57] If a woman had no man to protect her rights in the community, she could be exceedingly vulnerable. Because there was another woman to do the "woman's work" she might even be expendable, as the sad case of Jeanne Malvides illustrates. Malvides lived in a pot-and-hearth community in Montclar composed of her husband, François Vern; his brother; and the brother's wife, Marie Cazottes. When the brother died, Cazottes moved into François's bed and the two threw Malvides out of the house. Malvides accepted the situation and went to live with her brothers. She brought suit against Vern and Cazottes only after Vern beat her up and Cazottes stole her furniture and linens, that is, her dowry.[58]

If patriarchal convention limited women's authority in the household, formal legal measures limited women's control of the community's property. Through marriage contracts and wills, peasants provided for the maintenance of their wives and daughters but prevented them from owning property. Before the institution of the Napoleonic Code in 1804, most peasants, like most other Montaubaners, contracted marriage according to the Custom of Montauban. The bride or her family set up a dowry, which passed to her husband and his family. If he died without giving her children, she reclaimed her dowry increased by one half. If they had children, she recovered only her dowry. A husband could increase his wife's portion by leaving her a legacy in property or the use of property or by appointing her his heir. Peasants were slightly more likely to follow the Custom of Montauban than were urban couples, and peasants who joined communities were even more likely to follow the strict dowry arrangement. When peasant husbands made wills, they tended to leave their widows legacies in usufruct rather than in ownership, often in pensions in kind and life rights to a room in the house.

These arrangements envisioned two possible futures in the community for a widow. If she was childless, she reclaimed her dowry and supplement—usually furniture, linens, and some cash—and quit the household. Her father-in-law bought her out of the community, not with a share in its property and profits but with a return on her initial investment, her dowry. If she had children, she would remain in the household because her children had an interest in the community as heirs of their father. In this case also her rights in the community were restricted, usually to maintenance at the communal pot and hearth. For example, in his will in 1777 sharecropper Etienne Guyral confirmed his previous gifts to his children and concluded, "Moreover, the testator said he would not make

---

[57] Lisse said nothing explicit about Marie Sanson's behavior during this period, but it is interesting that throughout her testimony she referred to her as Bouzeran's wife rather than "my daughter." AD T-et-G 1 U 137 assises 1827.

[58] AD T-et-G 1 U 3 tribunal correctionnel 1815.

any legacy to his wife, Bernarde Labrignore, but he recommends that his son and heir maintain her." In 1787 landowner Laurent Pecharman left his widow life rights to one half of his estate on condition that she live "at the same pot and hearth" with his heir, his eldest son. And landowner Raymond Vidal, in the will cited in the opening pages of chapter 3, left his wife an annuity in grain, firewood, and lard only if she was *not* living with his heir.[59]

In a society in which property was a synonym for power, peasants generally succeeded in circumscribing women's power. Peasant women in the Old Regime rarely had property they could dispose of as they chose. For example, they rarely acted in property transactions. In a sample of ninety-five land purchases notarized between 1775 and 1794, peasants made 47 percent of the sales by men, whereas their wives and daughters made only 23 percent of the sales made by women. Women in landowning families were even more disadvantaged, making a scant 5 percent of the sales made by women despite the fact that their families sometimes owned substantial property.[60] And peasant women rarely made wills. Although 43 percent of sampled testators between 1775 and 1794 were women, only 24 percent of peasant testators in the sample were women.[61]

Where wives were only second-class citizens in the pot-and-hearth community, noninheriting children, both male and female, composed a third estate, with even fewer rights. In most families, at least one daughter made a match with an heir of another family, moved into her husband's household, and joined her parents-in-law in community. Thus she achieved a position similar to the one she had held in her parents' household.[62] Noninheriting sons often had a more difficult time. The rural hierarchy was double, based first on the rank of the family and then on rank within the family. The youngest son of a small landowner and the heir of a hired worker were in approximately the same position. Families like Mouméja's or Sanson's created an occasional "opening" for a young man to marry an heiress, join her household, and attain the same position in the rural hierarchy as that of his father and older brother. In folktales and popular literature, young men often made their fortune in this way,[63] but in real life, it was only slightly more likely than unearthing a buried treasure.

---

[59] AD T-et-G 5E 2331 Martin no. 281 9–1–1777 testament Guyral; 1943 Caminel no. 354 2–7–1787 testament Pecharman; 2237 Martin no. 326 17–8–1788 testament Vidal.

[60] significance level = .01, contingency coefficient = .354.

[61] significance level = .01, contingency coefficient = .262.

[62] See, for example, the marriage of Antoine Mouméja's younger daughter in AD T-et-G 5E 2141 Latreille-Olivié no. 194 22–3–1813 contrat de mariage Descazaux-Mouméja; 2149 Latreille-Olivié no. 270 9–7–1819 vente et donation Mouméja-Descazaux.

[63] See Le Roy Ladurie, *Love, Death and Money*, and Darnton, *The Great Cat Massacre*, pp. 9–72.

Only 3 percent of farm worker grooms in the sample married the daughters of peasant landowners or tenant farmers and joined their parents-in-law's households.

Some noninheriting children remained unmarried within the household, dependent not only on their parents but also on the inheriting sibling. The position of such a child was made quite clear in an agreement between day worker Jean Dagran and his elder brother. Jean ceded his parental inheritance to his brother in return for the continued use of a room and maintenance at his late parents', now his brother's, pot and hearth. His brother promised "to furnish the giver as if he were a son of the household," in other words, the status quo ante.[64]

In most families noninheriting children left home to become farm servants of other households. From a 1746 list of people confirmed in the Catholic church in Thezels and Saint Sernin, two villages north of Montauban, historian Pierre Valmary determined that at least one quarter of boys between the ages of ten and fourteen were living in a different parish from that of their parents. And it was not only boys who left home to work. Richeprey was shocked to find that in Quercy girls too hired themselves out from a very early age. In the eighteenth century, both young men and women went to Montauban to find work. Teenagers of both sexes, originally from the countryside, were common among the immigrants who wound up in the Hôtel Dieu.[65]

Most children accepted the explicit hierarchy that the community created in the family; there was little they could do to combat it, at least while the father was alive. Occasionally a son sued or threatened to sue his father in order to get his rights. For example, returned veteran Henry Gary took his father to court to make him disgorge the one thousand francs in replacement fees that his father had collected on his behalf.[66] Although suits against parents were not common, suits against brothers were. The death of the father brought the property divisions—and family tensions—into the open. Some excluded children discovered that what they had received was not even the légitime. In 1778 Antoinette Sansot extracted two agreements from her landowning brother, Jean, their father's heir, one in August for a supplement to her dowry to bring it up to the légitime and a second one a month later granting her yet another supplement. She

---

[64] AD T-et-G Q 406 donations no. 24 17–4–1792; similarly, 2136 Latreille-Olivié no. 725 14–9–1809 testament Larroque.

[65] AH de Mont F 4 registre des entrées. Valmary, *Familles paysannes*, p. 50. According to Richeprey, "Young girls, even when they are children, guard the cattle and the flocks. When they grow up a bit, they share all the agricultural work and all the toils of men. If their family is so numerous that they are not needed on the farm, they hire themselves out as servants." Guilhamon, *Richeprey* 1: 50; also see 2: 202.

[66] AD T-et-G 5E 2150 Latreille-Olivié no. 145 20–3–1821 dette Gary père à fils.

had discovered that the property evaluation on which the determination of her rights rested was inaccurate. In the same year Pierre Pimbert, another landowner, agreed to pay his younger brother two hundred livres in coin and eighty-six livres in grain and wine as a supplement to his share in their father's estate. Pierre claimed that this was not because he really owed this to his brother but only "to avoid the cost of a lawsuit." What he was trying to avoid was the misfortune that befell landowner Pierre Pradie in 1790. Repeated suits brought by his two sisters forced him to cede to them part of the family land.[67]

Pot-and-hearth communities shaped rural society in Quercy. Not all peasants lived in such households, nor did they encompass all familial and other interpersonal relationships in the countryside; but pot-and-hearth communities defined many relationships. Nearly everyone at one time or another lived in such a household, was excluded from one, or worked for one. Rural cohesion and conflict often revolved around pot-and-hearth communities.[68]

The investigation of a "murderous attack" on the village clerk of St Nicolas la Grave one night in 1826 by an unidentified gang of men reveals both the complexity of rural society and the central role of the peasant household within it. The victim, Jean Joseph Garrigues, was a local landowner and would-be bourgeois. His recent engagement to peasant Marie Delbert had provoked opposition from a number of groups. A club of Garrigues's friends, which met nightly at a tavern, had held a charivari, ostensibly because Marie was a widow. Despite Garrigues's protests, they proposed to hold another. The Delbert family also opposed the marriage. Marie's father consented only after Marie threatened to enter a convent. Her grandfather, mother, and uncle Pierre continued to object because of Garrigues's bourgeois pretensions. In the tavern where Garrigues and his friends met, Pierre announced belligerently that "the peasants who wear wooden shoes are as good as the *messieurs* who wear frock coats." He also

[67] AD T-et-G 5E 10867 Martin no. 400 21–9–1778 accord Sansot-Sansot ép Rufits; no. 490 22–11–1778 accord Pimbert-Pimbert; 5E 2094 Franceries no. 293 21–3–1790 accord Pradier-Pradier ép Delors and no. 297 21–3–1790 accord et dette Pradie-Pradier v^c Padie. Also see Collomp, "Tensions, Dissensions, and Ruptures Inside the Family," pp. 147, 164, and Caston, *Les Criminels de Languedoc*, pp. 187–190.

[68] In the Quercy countryside, extra-household activities and organizations were many and peasants identified themselves and related to one another on terms other than as members of particular households. Some associations were personal and informal, created by habitually working or socializing together. No reader of police records can help but be struck by the importance of the field, the road, and the tavern as places where peasants met friends and confronted enemies. Other associations were more formal, for example, religious affiliation, parish or village and peer groups. See Roubin, "Espace masculin, espace feminin," pp. 537–560; Arnold van Gennep, *Manuel de Folklore Français Contemporain*, 4 vols. (Paris: A. Picard, 1943), 1: 201–213; Claverie and Lamaison, *L'Impossible mariage*, pp. 248–249; and Darrow, "French Families and the Revolution in Inheritance Law," p. 274.

had private reasons for his opposition; a neighbor to whom he owed money was also courting Marie. This neighbor's father's godson and the Delbert family's tenants were suspected of being members of yet another group, a band of robbers. The police arrested Pierre Delbert, the tenants, the neighbor, and his god-relative but could not prove they were Garrigues's assailants because the Delbert family and servants gave Pierre an alibi.[69]

In this case, as in the Sanson murder, the peasant household was the first arena of the conflict. Unfortunately for us, the Delbert family was quite reticent under police questioning and the records are maddeningly obscure about the organization of the household. These facts are clear: that Marie's father was the elder brother and that Pierre, although forty years old, was unmarried and lived in the household. This suggests a common division between the eldest son, taken into community with his father as his heir, and the younger, excluded from the inheritance and living as a semidependent in his father and brother's household. The breakdown of a pot-and-hearth community led to Sanson's murder by Bouzeran; perhaps it was the tensions inherent within the Delbert community that fueled the attack on Garrigues.

A pot-and-hearth community's longevity and success depended on a regular cycle of younger couples joining and then replacing older couples. Either untimely death or unusual longevity disrupted the intergenerational continuity. The Sanson murder resulted from the problems caused by old people who failed to die on schedule. Early death also broke the rhythm. In communities formed with sons-in-law, the not uncommon death of the daughter in childbirth left her parents owing the son-in-law property yet without any way to force him to remain in the community.[70] In the Vern household, it was the untimely death of one brother that led to adultery, wife beating, and lawsuits.[71]

Even in its ideal, balanced form, the pot-and-hearth community generated tensions within the family and the village. Peasant households, and

[69] AD T-et-G 1 U 138 assises 26–6–1827.

[70] For example, see AD T-et-G 5E 2107 Franceries no. 255 12–1–1811 accord Souloumiac-Malfre and 13517 Martin fils no. 267 5–8–1820 accord Malbreil-Bouye. However, another settlement, 5E 10867 Martin no. 283 21–6–1778 between Gairard and Montaubery, *bordiers* for M. de Ramou in St Hilaire, demonstrates that death did not inevitably break up a community. Gairard's mother, Marguerite Soulié, had married Jean Sirat in 1729, the couple joining her father in community. Sirat died without children but left his share in the community to his nephew, Montaubery. Later, Soulié remarried and her husband joined the community as well. When her father died, he was replaced in the community by her son by her second marriage. Only in 1778, when Soulié herself died, was the community finally dissolved. It had consisted of her son and his family and her first husband's nephew and his family.

[71] AD T-et-G 1 U 3 tribunal correctionnel 1815.

pot-and-hearth communities in particular, made severe psychological demands on their members. Although a peasant's personal status depended on the status of his household, the latter also depended on the former. Ancestral crimes and small lapses—"a son who behaves like a third son when he is only a fourth"—jeopardized a household's reputation. In public, conflict between household members was repressed so that the village saw only a solid front. By preference, peasants directed tensions outside the household, toward their neighbors' misbehaving fourth sons.[72]

Pot-and-hearth communities structured rural society as well as peasant families. They created a privileged group of insiders with an acknowledged stake in the village's resources and a disadvantaged—and sometimes disgruntled—group of outsiders whose claims on the village were limited if not completely denied. According to the clergy, help for the rural poor was not often forthcoming from their neighbors even when, as the curé of Albefeuille-Lagarde reported, there were well-off families in the parish.[73] As in artisan families, a strategy of division and exclusion preserved the patrimony—access to land in this case—which in turn ensured the family's survival and status; it also preserved the stability of the village as a whole. The strategy was predicated upon a scarcity, but not an absence, of resources. A village rarely had enough—enough land, enough food, enough work—to provide for all, but it did have enough to provide for some. Pot-and-hearth communities accomplished the triage by selecting the next generation of villagers, the heirs and their families.

With the pot-and-hearth community, peasants drew a privileged circle within the family, but the size of that circle, the number of people it included, and the nature of the privileges differed from family to family. Although in law pot-and-hearth communities had identical structures, they functioned in a variety of ways, embodied a variety of family strategies, and expressed a variety of goals. Besides structuring the household, the community both organized work and transferred property. The nature of the work and the property determined in some degree the operation of the community. To be a member of—or excluded from—a pot-and-hearth community meant significantly different things to the son of a sharecropper, a landowner, or a rural wage earner. It also meant different things after the revolution in family law than it did in the eighteenth century.

Throughout the late eighteenth and early nineteenth centuries pot-and-hearth communities were most prevalent in the Montauban region among sharecropping families. Here a working partnership and a communal life made good sense to both parents and children. One of the tenant farmer's

[72] Claverie, " 'Honneur:' Une Société de défis au XIXᵉ siècle," p. 750; Gaudemet, *Les Communautés familiales*, pp. 161–162; Caston, *Les Criminels de Languedoc*, p. 180.
[73] A Mont 29 GG 2 and 3 état des pauvres 1778, 1790.

TABLE 7–2
Peasant Pot-and-Hearth Communities, 1775–1824

Occupation of Head of Household	Marriage Contracts Establishing Communities		
	All 1775–1824	*I* 1775–1793	*II* 1794–1824
Tenant (*N* = 51)	57%	65%	53%
Owner (*N* = 65)	28	50	18
Farm worker (*N* = 240)	32	32	32
N	356	154	202

Note: Signficance levels = .02, contingency coefficients = .189 (all), .220 (ɪ), .227 (ɪɪ).

main problems was to field a labor force big enough to work the farm. If he could not supply workers from his own family, he had to employ them at his expense. A pot-and-hearth community solved the problem, not only by keeping adult sons or sons-in-law on the farm but also by lowering expenses and risks. The arrangement was equally attractive to the children, whose only other option was to work for pitifully low wages in an already overcrowded market.[74]

Sharecroppers could expand pot-and-hearth communities as children matured or as larger farms became available. To secure a lease on a large farm, a peasant needed to assemble a team that would impress the landlord or his agent with his ability to work the farm profitably.[75] In the sample of marriage contracts, two thirds of the communities created by tenant farmers were composed of more than two couples. For example, Jean Gasc rented a vineyard in Le Fau owned by the Duc family of magistrates. In 1794, his eldest son married and joined in community with him. Four years later, the younger son married and also joined the community. As the contracting party, Jean retained a half-interest in the farm but each son had only one quarter.[76]

[74] Latouche, *La Vie en Bas-Quercy*, p. 349; Armengaud, *Populations de l'est aquitain*, p. 134.

[75] AD T-et-G 5E 13517 Martin fils no. 68 19–2–1820 société Lafon-Lafon. Individual acts of partnership like this one, which created a community specifically to work a particular *métairie*, were rare. More common were communities created explicitly or tacitly by sharecropping contracts. See, for example, AD T-et-G 5E 2349 Martin no. 295 20 pluviôse Year 9 bail à culture, in which property owner Arnaud Tuffeau leased a farm in La Court St Pierre to Arnaud and Guillaume Gascon, father and son, "conjointly and severally, the two together, one for the other and one between them for all . . . the said Garcon father and son engage themselves with their wives and the other two children of the father" to work the *métairie*. For another example, see 5E 12870 sn Grelleau 1–1–1781 bail à culture Janolz à Meilleurat.

[76] AD T-et-G 5E 12887 Grelleau no. 61 29 nivôse Year 2 contrat de mariage Gasc-Montagne and 12892 Grelleau no. 488 6 frimaire Year 6 contrat de mariage Gasc-Garrigues.

TABLE 7–3
Size of Peasant Pot-and-Hearth Communities, 1775–1824

Marriage contracts that established	Occupation of Head of Household		
	Farm Worker	Tenant Farmer	Landowner
No community	68%	43%	72%
Communities of			
two couples (1/2 interest)	22	18	17
more than two couples			
(1/3 to 1/5 interest)	10	39	11
N	240	51	65

	I = 1775–1793		II = 1794–1824			
	I	II	I	II	I	II
No community	68%	68%	35%	47%	50%	82%
Communities of						
two couples	21	22	12	21	25	13
more than two couples	11	10	53	32	25	5
N	117	123	17	34	20	45

Note: Significance level = .01, contingency coefficients = .279 (all), .335 (I), .357 (II).

For sharecroppers whose only valuable possession was the *métayage* contract, incorporation into the community, rather than leading to inheritance, took the place of inheritance. As a result, daughters who married into pot-and-hearth communities tended to be less well endowed than daughters who did not. The place within the community was their patrimony; to set up independent households required a more substantial outlay. For landowning peasants, by contrast, incorporation into the community signified the future inheritance of the family property. In these families, the dowries of daughters who married into communities were significantly higher than the dowries of daughters who did not. The woman who married into a community married the heir and had to pay a high price to do so.[77]

In the pot-and-hearth communities of property-owning peasants, the family work force was joined to a family homestead and lands. In this form, the family community was very close to the traditional southern

[77] From the sample of marriage contracts, the mean dowry of landowners' daughters who did not join communities was 1,313 livres, whereas the mean dowry of those who did was 2,657 livres (student's $t = -.38$ with a probability level of .02). The mean dowry of tenant farmers' daughters who did not join communities was 570 livres, whereas that of those who did was only 266 livres (student's $t = 3.13$ with a probability level of .01).

ostal.[78] For landowning peasants, the three clauses of the association—shared residence, shared work, and shared property—defined a survival strategy that was cohesive and ruthless. The parents chose one child as the heir. He (for in 94 percent of the communities of farm-owning peasants in the sample it was a son) remained at home, married, joined in community with his parents, and eventually inherited their land. Noninheriting children either remained dependent in the household, working the land that would never belong to them, or left home taking with them a small portion, sometimes less than the légitime. Unlike sharecropper communities, which often included three or four couples, communities in farm-owning families were limited to two couples only, the parents, one son, and his wife. For most landowning peasants before the Revolution, lineage and household came together in the community as eldest sons were joined to the household and became the heir (see table 3–7).[79]

In the years before the Revolution, pot-and-hearth communities were less popular in farm workers' families than they were with tenant farmers or farm owners. This was largely because when contributions to the household were measured in wages rather than in labor, the overall equality necessary to sustain a pot-and-hearth community was difficult to achieve. Although many farm workers also owned or rented some land, their basic resource was the wages that each family member earned.[80] By

[78] See Emmanuel Le Roy Ladurie, *Montaillou: The Promised Land of Error*, trans. Barbara Bray (New York: Vintage Books, 1979), pp. 24–52. The word *ostal* was not used by notaries in Montauban who wrote in French in the eighteenth century; nor did they use the French term, *ménage*. They invariably referred to familial communities as "pot-and-hearth communities" and to the parties as "being in solidarity with one another" and "living and working together," or they simply joined their names as coparties.

[79] In the Gévaudon, it was common practice to "faire un aîné"; by being designated as the heir, a child became "the eldest" regardless of birth order. Claverie and Lamaison, *L'Impossible mariage*, pp. 59–73, 271. This does not seem to have been the practice around Montauban. A random comparison of the birth order recorded in wills with that recorded in birth records (in this case, the Protestant register) found no discrepancies. However Montaubaners may have used the term *l'aîné* in their common speech, in notary records it meant firstborn.

[80] Even children who left the household could continue to contribute to the common pot. See Tilly and Scott, *Women, Work and Family*, pp. 35–36, 109–110, and Ombret et al., *Villes et Campagnes du Bas-Quercy*, B6, for the case of a Montauban merchant paying the wages of his wife's chambermaid to the woman's peasant father. Because servants received their wages in a lump sum, they were among the few working people who sometimes had capital to invest. In a sample of 250 loans recorded by Montauban notaries, only nineteen wage earners were lenders, and thirteen of these were servants. Eight of these lent money—in two cases as much as five hundred livres—to peasant relatives. In 1769 Durand Gasc, a farm worker in St Martial, borrowed 150 livres from his sister Antoinette, who served a Montauban bourgeois. In 1777 he borrowed another 150 livres. AD T-et-G 5E 1996 Garrigues no. 221 12–4–1777 and no. 636 7–12–1778 dette Gasc à Gasc.

Another source of capital for peasant families were military replacement fees, often collected by the recruit's parents. See Schnapper, *Le Remplacement militaire en France*, and A D T-et-G 5E 2128 Garrigues no. 241 15–11–1810 traité militaire; 2360 Martin no. 277 15–3–1813 traité militaire; 13215 Solon no. 306 2–12–1818 traité militaire.

comparing their wages, all members of the household could quickly judge who was contributing more or less than a fair share. When young adult men could earn more than their fathers and when their fathers had little property to throw into the balance, there was nothing to keep sons in the household under paternal authority. For example, when Jacques Crabon married in 1813, his farm worker father took him into a community of shared work and profit with a gift of one quarter of his goods, worth only one hundred francs. The community had lasted less than a year and a half when Jacques Crabon decided he was paying more than his share and pulled out.[81] The same calculations led Sanson to reject the role of dependent which his son-in-law had allotted him. He could earn his living, and therefore he should have retained his authority.

Communities of wage earners tended to be small—limited to two couples—and probably they were more fragile than communities of tenant farmers or landowners. Nonetheless, pot-and-hearth communities did provide essential security to wage-earning families. As part of a nationwide investigation of poverty in 1790, priests from the rural parishes around Montauban supplied lists of destitute families who most needed help. In almost every case, the priests saw the family's poverty as caused by too many young children, by the death, illness, or absence of one of the wage earners, or by old age. These were precisely the weak points in the family life cycle that the pot-and-hearth community buttressed. Only one family in these lists appears to have been a pot-and-hearth community.[82]

During the French Revolution and the early nineteenth century, the popularity of pot-and-hearth communities waned. From 1775 to 1793, half of peasant marriage contracts in the sample established pot-and-hearth communities. Thereafter, the incidence of communities decreased, until in the 1820s they appeared in only 20 percent of peasant marriage contracts. The decline was not smooth, however. After an abrupt drop during the Revolutionary years of mandatory equal inheritance, pot-and-hearth communities made a brief comeback in the early years of the Civil Code, then ebbed once more. The decline was most precipitous among landowning peasants, so much so that after 1800 farm workers and other land-poor peasants were more likely to join a community upon marriage than were landowners (see table 7–2).

[81] AD T-et-G 5E 2142 Latreille Olivié no. 409 2–10–1814 dissolution Crabon père et fils; also see 5E 13184 Deray no. 288 7 ventôse Year 5 dissolution Carnus père et fils. My sample of dissolutions is too small to determine whether communities of *journaliers* broke up more readily than communities of *laboureurs* or *métayers*.

[82] AM de Mont 29 GG 3 état des pauvres, 1790. Parishes of Fonneuve, Léojac, Albefeuille-Lagarde, Le Fau, Verhaguet, St Martial, Gasseras, and Bressols. The one possible pot-and-hearth community was in Bressols: "Pierre Ribayrol, his son-in-law and wife and four young children. They need help for the children."

TABLE 7–4
Peasants' Choice of Heir Before and After the Revolution

	Testator			
	Landowner (N = 85)		*Land-poor (N = 185)*	
Heir Chosen	*1775–1793*	*1800–1824*	*1775–1793*	*1800–1824*
Eldest male	43%	42%	37%	18%
Other heir	43	31	41	39
Spouse	10	8	22	18
Equal division	4	19	0	25

Note: Significance level = .01, 1775–1793 contingency coefficient = .224, 1800–1824 contingency coefficient = .268.

The dwindling popularity of pot-and-hearth communities was directly linked to the changes in family law that took place during the Revolution, especially inheritance law. Among landowning peasants, pot-and-hearth communities accompanied the inheritance of a single heir. The parents took one child, usually the eldest son, into community and gave him one half of their property. Thereafter the community jointly paid off the non-inheriting children with their legal portions, and when the father retired or died, the son succeeded to the rest of the family property. The popularity of the eldest male heir in landowning peasants' wills paralleled the popularity of pot-and-hearth communities in their marriage contracts.[83]

The revolution in inheritance law caused major changes in this pattern. Fewer peasant wills named the eldest son as the favored heir; fewer peasant marriage contracts created pot-and-hearth communities. However, these two changes were not entirely synchronized. Peasant proprietors continued to privilege the eldest male heir, but they abandoned the pot-and-hearth community. Land-poor and landless peasants—farm workers and tenant farmers—opted for equal inheritance while continuing to create communities. What differentiated these two family strategies was land ownership.

For Old Regime peasant proprietors, pot-and-hearth communities had maintained an equilibrium between family labor and family land and tied labor and land together across generations to create families nearly as permanent as the land itself. The egalitarian inheritance law interposed a different bond between family and land, linking land to the rights of the

[83] In the sample of notary documents, 50 percent of farm owners' marriage contracts formed communities and 52 percent of their wills appointed the eldest male heir. The comparable figures for farm workers are 31 percent and 42 percent, respectively; and among tenant farmers, 88 percent formed communities whereas only 55 percent appointed the eldest male heir.

individual. In the eighteenth century, noninheriting children had had no legitimate recourse against the community's monopoly of the family's resources except to decamp. The change in inheritance law placed a weapon in their hands, which the records of the notaries and the courts reveal they were willing to use. In the eighteenth century, sisters and younger brothers frequently had sued to obtain the paltry légitime; now the stakes were much higher.

For a traditional pot-and-hearth community to continue to exist in landowning families under the rule of equal inheritance, all children had to cooperate in a variety of stratagems and legal fictions. Such was the case in the family of Bernard Ruelle, landowning farmers in Peboyer, where convenient reevaluations and divisions of the mother's property allowed the family farm to pass intact to a single grandchild. When Bernard died in 1793, the eldest of his three children was only sixteen, so the estate remained under the direction of his widow. The two eldest children, Pierre and Marie, married a sister and brother, Percide and Pierre Coyne, and joined their mother in community; she remained in control of the third of the estate, which was eventually to go to the youngest child, Marthe. In 1808, Marthe contracted marriage, precipitating a property settlement. First, the mother retired, settling her own succession in a series of gifts. She gave one thousand francs each to Marthe and to Marie's daughter, Marie having died a few years earlier. She gave the rest of her estate, worth four thousand francs including land evaluated at twenty-three hundred francs, to her son Pierre. This division shortchanged each of the female heirs of five hundred francs, giving Pierre one thousand more than was his legal share, but his mother justified this by attaching to Pierre's portion the responsibility to care for her until her death. A week later, Pierre and Marthe agreed to settle their father's estate. Marie was assigned one third of the farm, which she then traded for the land Pierre had just received from their mother. In this agreement, each plot of land was evaluated at five thousand francs, more than double the value assigned to the land only the week before. Apparently, mother, son, and daughter had agreed that Pierre should retain his father's land and that Marthe should be content with a less than equal share in the estate. Fifteen years later, when their mother died, Marthe and Marie's daughter asked Pierre to pay them supplements to their legacies from her. This time, her land was evaluated at three thousand francs. Again, the two women did not require that the land be split up; they wanted a fair share but they did not insist on an equal share. Like Marthe, Marie's daughter "married out," taking her portion in cash, and the farm eventually went to Pierre's only child.[84]

[84] AD T-et-G 5E 2135 Latreille-Olivié no. 880 2–12–1808 donation Ruelle vᵉ Ruelle aux enfants, no. 903 10–12–1808 partage and no. 908 10–12–1808 échange Ruelle frère et soeur, no. 912 10–12–1808 contrat de mariage Girmal-Ruelle; 2142 Latreille-Olivié no. 6

This family's success rested on the willingness of the children who left the household to continue to identify their interests with the family farm and to accept less than their legal rights in order to ensure its survival. Any familial conflict that endangered this solidarity put the pot-and-hearth community in jeopardy. A lawsuit in another of the many peasant families named Ruelle offers an example. Marc Ruelle, a *cultivateur-propriétaire* of Corbarieur, had three children, two sons and one daughter. When the eldest son, Guillaume, married, Marc took him into community, giving him one half of his goods. This gift represented Guillaume's legal inheritance plus the portion disponible, which Marc could leave as he wished. In other words, Marc appointed Guillaume his heir, giving him as much of his property as was legal under the Civil Code. In 1797, when Antoine, the younger son, married and left the household, Marc promised him one quarter of his property, that is, his inheritance. In 1801, Marc and Guillaume supposedly gave Antoine twelve hundred francs in fulfillment of his marriage contract, for which he gave them a receipt. Then relations between the two households deteriorated. In 1805 Antoine took his father and brother to court, not only because they had in fact never paid the twelve hundred francs but also because he suspected that this sum was less than what he was due. The strategy by which a pot-and-hearth community excluded and bought off a legal heir had failed. To pay the debt, Marc and Guillaume had to deed to Antoine part of their house and lands.[85]

Mandatory equal inheritance did not dissolve pot-and-hearth communities; nor did it precipitate a "revolt of cadets." Like Marc Ruelle, some parents undervalued their property to entrust an inflated share to the heir, and in other cases the children agreed to leave the succession undivided to preserve the community. When Jean and Jeanne Ruelle's father died, they left his estate intact for fourteen years. Jean and his wife worked it in community with his mother while Jeanne was living in community with her husband's parents, who were, incidentally, not only her parents' cousins but also the parents of Jean's wife (see figure 7–2). Such arrangements, even with the best will in the world, could not last indefinitely. When Jean died, his widow, mother, and sister decided the time had come to sort out what belonged to whom.[86]

2–1–1814 contrat de mariage Ruelle-Ruelle; 2151 Latreille-Olivié no. 62 18–2–1823 partage et accord Ruelle frères et soeur.

[85] AD T-et-G 5E 12901 Grelleau no. 21 17 vendémiaire Year 13 accord Ruelle père et fils; no. 24 17 vendémiaire Year 13 achât Ruelle; no. 35 23 vendémiaire Year 13 achât Ruelle.

[86] AD T-et-G 5E 2154 Latreille-Olivié sn 13 and 14–9–1824 accords Ruelle. When Le Play observed his model *famille souche*, the Mélougas, in 1856 they had engineered two successions since the onset of equal inheritance without dividing the household's property. However, when his disciple Emile Cheysson carried out later observations he discovered that a suit contesting a succession in 1835 finally led to the division of property in the 1870s. See Assier-Andrieu, "Le Play et la famille-souche," pp. 499–501.

Without such cooperation, the pot-and-hearth community was exceedingly vulnerable. Any familial dispute, regardless of its cause, could wind up in court in the guise of a property suit. For example, consider the suit of Antoinette Meric against her nephew. Her brother had joined their father in a pot-and-hearth community while Antoinette had remained unmarried and dependent within the household. When their father died, her brother had bought her off with, she claimed, a less than legal share, and took his own son, Pierre, into community. After her brother's death, Antoinette sued Pierre for a supplement to her paternal succession. At first glance this appears to be a simple case of the excluded daughter using the new law to pry a larger portion from the family property, but it was much more complicated. In the the preceding six months, Pierre had been involved in two other lawsuits, one relating to his proposed marriage, which his family was trying to stop, and the other to various debts to family members. In this context, Antoinette's claim appears as part of a familial assault on Pierre whose reasons remain obscure.[87] A similar suit by a sister and brother-in-law against Jean Pellet for a new division of the paternal succession also had a long and complex history. Previous suits and agreements had been filed in 1766, 1771, and 1787. Jean was furious at the new maneuvre in 1794. He stated that his relatives' claims were "irregular, erroneous, and pertaining to matters wholly foreign to the said patrimony." However, "wanting to Reestablish in their families the Union and the Peace that this suit had endangered," and, more to the point, because the law now supported their demands, he agreed to a new settlement.[88]

As the investigation of Sanson's murder shows, family quarrels were common knowledge; neighbors' gossip followed every twist of contract and debt, of lawsuit and threat. We can suppose that surrounding households were aware of the circumstances that eventually brought families like the Merics and the Pellets to court and followed these cases with interest. Although the equal-inheritance law directly destroyed only a few pot-and-hearth communities, the instances when it did served notice to the rest that custom and goodwill were poor defenses against the force of the law. Nor had family strategies of the past always been productive of goodwill. Landowning families had only two alternatives: to modify the community to bring it into line with the legal requirements or to abandon it altogether. Most chose to abandon it.[89]

A pot-and-hearth community was legal if it abided by the property division mandated by law. One solution was to reduce the community to

---

[87] AD T-et-G L 456 tribunal de famille, Castelsarrasin, 9–12–1791, 30–3–1792, 17–6–1792.

[88] AD T-et-G 5E 12888 Grelleau no. 303 14 germinal Year 2; similarly, L 456 tribunal de famille, Castelsarrasin, 1 fructidor Year 2 and 3–9–1792.

[89] Dussourd, "Dissolution de communauté," pp. 309–319.

the share the parents could legally leave to the heir. This was practical only when there were few children, as, for example, the cross-cousin communities in the Ruelle family. However, if parents had several children, a community was less likely to be successful. Besides the problem of deciding what constituted one fourth or one sixth of the property, work, and profit, such arrangements were probably not much of an inducement to association. If the child who remained at home, living and working under his father's direction and authority, was to receive no more in the end than the child who "abandoned" the household, the community was likely to dissolve quickly. In fact, few landowners tried this solution. Only one out of seven pot-and-hearth communities formed in landowning families after 1793 involved shares of less than one half.

Another solution was to establish a community of residence and work but to exempt property. This was practical among tenant and farm worker families whose property was in furniture and tools rather than in land. For landowning peasants, once the community was separated from the land it no longer had much to offer, either to the son or to the father, who, by taking a child into community, gave up undivided authority over the farm as well as its ultimate disposition. As James R. Lehning has pointed out, the new inheritance law determined who would inherit how much; the property owner only chose when, whether by gift during his lifetime or by inheritance after his death. Paternal control of children through the control of the family property was largely limited to the timing of the property's transfer.[90]

Deprived of their ability to "make an heir," landowning peasants around Montauban chose to remain in command as long as possible. Farm owner Hughes Mauron of St Martial is a good example. He had four children, two sons and two daughters. To each daughter he assigned a dowry of one thousand francs, considerably less than their legal share in the estate. To each son, at marriage, he gave one quarter of his goods including his land appraised in 1820 at sixteen thousand francs. However, the sons and their wives were to live in his house and work under his direction. There was to be no community here. If either son wanted to leave, he could take only a fraction of the promised property; Mauron reserved the use of the rest for his lifetime.[91]

Increasingly, sons had to wait until their fathers died in order to receive the share of the family property that would allow them to establish themselves and marry. This was a big change from the period before the Revolution, when at least one son—the heir—married while his father was still

---

[90] Lehning, *The Peasants of Marlhes*, pp. 127–128.
[91] AD T-et-G 5E 13517 Martin fils no. 220 25–6–1820 contrat de mariage Mauron-Larroque.

alive and joined him in community. In the Old Regime, fathers of two thirds of the landowning grooms in the sample of marriage contracts had been alive to see their sons married; after 1793, two thirds of the grooms married only after their fathers' deaths. This figure rose to 86 percent during the six-year period of strict equal inheritance during the Revolution.[92]

In the Old Regime, pot-and-hearth communities and inheritance by the eldest son went hand in hand in landowning peasant families, but the Revolutionary and Napoleonic inheritance laws severed that connection. Nonetheless, although fewer and fewer landowners joined in communities at their marriages, they continued to name their eldest sons as their favored heirs by adding the disposable portion to the legal share. In the period from 1775 to 1793, 43 percent of the landowning peasants in the sample of testators left the bulk of their property to the eldest male heir; from 1800 to 1824, 42 percent did so (see table 7–4). No other social group adhered as faithfully after the Revolution to the rule of primogeniture and to the idea of the family as a single line linking father to son and both to property (see table 3–6). Under the new inheritance laws, the pot-and-hearth community no longer served this concept of the family. For property-owning peasants, the ability of the familial community to provide a reliable labor force, to guarantee the transfer of authority, and to cushion the family against the consequences of sickness, accident, and death were secondary to the primary purpose of preserving the family property intact and transmitting it from father to son.[93] When the pot-and-hearth community no longer helped—and sometimes hindered—the preservation of patrimony, Montauban's property-owning peasants stopped forming communities.

Pot-and-hearth communities also declined in popularity in the marriage contracts of tenant farmers. Whereas 65 percent of sharecroppers' marriage contracts set up communities in the period before 1794, only 53 percent did so after this date (see table 7–2). Some of this decline was

[92] Significance level = .02, contingency coefficient = .366. Because marriage contracts rarely gave the ages of the parties, I cannot say whether age at marriage rose, but it certainly seems likely. The ages of grooms given in the Protestant civil register established in 1788 indicate that before the Revolution *laboureurs* married quite young, with a median age of twenty-four and a mode of only twenty-one. Day laborers did not marry until they were several years older, twenty-seven for both the median and the mode. See AD T-et-G E Etat Civil Protestant no. 366.

[93] Smith, in "Family and Class," pp. 74–76, reached the same conclusions about well-to-do peasant families in nineteenth-century Herault. They differ markedly from the patterns found by James Lehning in Marlhes and John Shaffer in the Nivernais, where peasants made little use of the portion disponible and left the ultimate disposition of family property up to the heirs, whether to share it or divide it. Lehning, *The Peasants of Marlhes*, pp. 120–129; Shaffer, *Family and Farm*, pp. 93–100.

probably due to the same reasons as those that influenced landowning peasants. Some sharecroppers and farm workers owned a little land which, like their better-off neighbors, they wanted to leave to a single heir. A few created communities for the purpose of the sharecropping contract only, excluding any sharing of property. When Jacques and Daniel Lafon, *métayers* for Mme de Granol in Verhaguet, formed a community in 1820, they agreed to share residence, work, profit, and loss on the farm they rented but made no mention of Jacques's goods. Specifically excluded from the contract was Daniel's wife's dowry. The contract between *laboureurmétayer* Pierre Flamary and his son Bertrand in 1811 stated that they were to exploit together the farm Pierre had rented from Sr Vidal but that Bertrand had no rights on the land that his father owned. Only if the community were still in existence at Pierre's death would Bertrand receive one half of this property.[94]

But most sharecroppers and farm workers owned little. The Popie family of sharecroppers, who rented a farm from M Hucafol in Bressols in 1805, is a good example. Jean Popie owned about one seventh of an acre of land and farm tools worth less than 200 francs, comprised of a wagon, a plow and harness, a flour sifter, a pail, three sacks, and eight barrels. His wife, Jeanne Anglar, also owned about one seventh of an acre and 251 francs' worth of goods. Besides similar farm implements, her possessions included a bed, a dresser, linens, fire irons and a few pots and pans. The only item of value they owned was their sharecropping contract, which brought them about 300 francs a year.[95]

For the Popie family, as for most sharecroppers, the purpose of a pot-and-hearth community was not to preserve the family property but to share the responsibility and risk of the lease on a farm and to supply the labor to work it. For eleven years Popie and his wife were associated with their two sons to fulfill their sharecropping contract. This kind of association was not endangered by the law of equal inheritance and may even have been encouraged by it. Unable to buy out children cheaply, sharecroppers may have tried to include more of them in the contract.[96] Pot-and-hearth communities of three and four couples remained common in tenant families. Although tenant farmers continued to favor eldest sons and coresidential heirs in their wills, nearly one third left their estates to be divided equally among all their heirs.

---

[94] AD T-et-G 5E 13517 Martin 2 no. 68 19–2–1820 société Lafon-Lafon; 5E 2128 Garrigues no. 98 30–3–1811 société Flamary-Flamary. Also see 5E 2196 Lacaze-Dori no. 398 24–6–1817 contrat de mariage Vabre-Perries and no. 438 9–3–1817 contrat de mariage Bourdarios-Quatre.

[95] AD T-et-G 5E 2352 Martin no. 230 21 pluviôse Year 8 donation Popie à Popie. Jean Popie owned 58 *ares* of land evaluated at 180 francs.

[96] Shaffer, *Family and Farm*, pp. 101–104.

In farm workers' families, pot-and-hearth communities remained as popular as they had been in the Old Regime, declining only slightly in frequency as the nineteenth century advanced. Even more than sharecroppers, farm workers adapted the pot-and-hearth community to the rules of equal inheritance. Like sharecroppers, farm workers had little property, and what they had was mostly in household goods, which were easily divisible. They apportioned the shares in the pot-and-hearth communities to reflect the number of eventual heirs; communities by thirds, fourths, and even fifths were common. Equal inheritance became nearly the most popular testamentary solution.

The revolution in family law affected the distribution of power between the generations in peasant households but did not significantly change the distribution of power between genders. The Napoleonic Code established the marital community as the preferred marital property arrangement. Because the marital community privileged the couple, it did not fit well within the pot-and-hearth community, whose core was the partnership of men. Only 4 percent of peasant marriage contracts in the sample from 1804 through 1824 created marital communities, and not a single marriage contract in the sample that set up a pot-and-hearth community also established a marital community. To do so would have been to give the wife a claim on the profits (*acquêts*) of the community. The marriage contracts of peasant couples who formed pot-and-hearth communities preferred the Napoleonic dowry arrangement, which provided no supplement at all, or a supplement of life rights only.

As testators, peasants followed a similar pattern. Whereas urban husbands increasingly adhered to the notion of a marital community by leaving their widows legacies in property and even appointing them as heirs, peasant husbands continued to restrict their widows to usufruct only. As before the Revolution, few peasant women owned sufficient property to participate in land transactions or to make wills. In fact, after 1800, almost the only peasant women to make wills were brides who made a will in conjunction with their husbands, usually leaving all their disposable property (their dowries) to their husbands.

The Napoleonic Code restricted how much property could be left to nonheirs, such as the widow, and also restricted the amount of the estate that could be left to the widow in usufruct—the entire estate if they had no children, one half of the estate if they had children. This created problems for peasant women who owned little property outright and depended for maintenance on their "use" rights in household. For example, Antoine Mailhes, a *propriétaire-cultivateur* of St Laurens, had willed his widow life "enjoyment" of his entire estate. Jean-Michel Combes-Brassard, a Montauban physician who had treated Mailhes, sued to seize the estate in payment of his bill. The court rejected the provisions of Mailhes's will on the grounds that they exceeded the legal rights of a widow because the couple had children. The judgment allotted the woman the use of one room and one field only. The rest of the property, worth nearly six thousand francs, was sold at a public auction.[97]

In several respects the position of women in farm-owning families resembled that of women in artisan families before the Revolution. Like artisan women, farm wives tended to be illiterate whereas their husbands were often literate (see table 4–2). Like artisan women they rarely acted in property transactions. Like artisan wives, they contracted marriage according to the Custom of Montauban and their husbands rarely supplemented their widows' rights with any legacy of property. The most they could expect was maintenance within the household of the heir.

Whereas artisan women improved their position in the family during and after the Revolution, the position of farm women did not improve. Their husbands did not begin to join them in marital communities or to favor them as heirs. Only 10 percent of farm-owning testators in the period 1800 to 1824 chose their wives as heirs, whereas 32 percent of artisans appointed their wives.[98] The marriage contracts of these two groups also indicate the divergence in their strategies. After 1804, many artisans availed themselves of the new property arrangement, the conjugal community; farmers did not. The weakening of the pot-and-hearth community between two couples did not necessarily strengthen the community of husband and wife, especially in landowning families.

After 1800, fewer peasants in the Montauban region formed pot-and-hearth communities. The law of equal inheritance was largely responsible. Landowning peasants who had used the community structure to appoint an heir apparent and tie him to the family property found that it would no longer accomplish this; instead a pot-and-hearth community could well embroil the family in lawsuits and force the partition of property. So they jettisoned the community and kept control of their property and therefore of their sons as long as possible. But for tenant farmers and farm workers, the pot-and-hearth community remained both viable and popular. In these families, communities were more a means of sharing responsibility and risk than for passing on authority and property. Not only did equal inheritance pose little threat to this strategy, it was incorporated into it. As long as the familial community offered a measure of security not afforded elsewhere, peasant couples continued to join their parents and siblings *au même pot et feu*.

---

[97] *Affiches, Annonces et Avis Diverse de la Ville de Montauban* no. 469, 21–6–1827 and 7–2–1828.

[98] Significance level = .01, contingency coefficient = .367.

Conclusion

WE MAY NOW RETURN to the general question that prompted this study: Did the French Revolution revolutionize French families? In particular, did the laws of equal inheritance create more egalitarian families and, by extension, a more egalitarian society? The investigation of Montaubaners' families during this period argues that the answer is yes, but much qualified and nuanced. It is necessary to specify which families and which family members; as was the case with George Orwell's animals, some families became more equal than others.

The French Revolution disrupted and changed many Montauban families in a variety of ways. Hundreds sent sons, brothers, husbands, fiancés, and fathers to the frontiers and beyond in Revolutionary and Napoleonic armies, some never to return. Politics and religion divided other families, sending some members into exile. Some families lost their livelihood and many more their patrimony when Old Regime institutions were abolished. But not all the changes were for the worse; if some families lost property and prestige, others gained them. The Revolution also brought windfalls of military replacement payments, opportunities to purchase national properties, and a plethora of new public positions available to ambitious men. Changes in the law allowed a few unhappy marriages to dissolve and confirmed Protestant couples' legal right to civil existence. In particular families any one of these changes could have undermined or overthrown established strategies and long-cherished hopes. But most of these occurrences were rather like capricious accidents, like conscription and bankruptcy, or sterility and death, which were common disruptions of any family's best-laid plans. They operated in the realm of conjuncture, not of structure; in other words, they were not revolutionary.

The changes in inheritance law had more revolutionary implications. As conceived by the Revolutionary legislators and by Napoleon's legal experts, the new inheritance laws were to revise the core of family strategies—and southern family strategies in particular—by including within them a new premise, the equal treatment of all heirs. Such a change was meant to affect all families, not just those with unhappy marriages, for example, or those with draft-aged sons. We are now in a position to assess the extent to which this reform succeeded in Montauban and to determine the degree to which the revolution in inheritance law precipitated a revolution in family strategies.

However, inheritance law did not operate on family strategies in a vacuum. Inheritance practices also depended on social, political, and economic considerations so that some of the changes in family strategies resulted as much or more from changes in the latter than from the changes in inheritance law. Take, for example, the behavior of Montauban *négociant* families. During the period of the Revolution and the Empire, most moved out of commerce and into landowning and public office, abandoning strategies that had supported their commercial endeavors. One could attribute this to the change in inheritance law; equal inheritance encouraged merchants to invest in real estate, which was much easier to divide among heirs than was a commercial enterprise. However, powerful social, political, and economic currents swept *négociants* in the same direction. In the classic pattern of upward mobility in preindustrial Europe, families made their fortune in commerce and then transformed it into social and political status through the acquisition of land and office. For Montauban merchants, this route had been blocked at the end of the seventeenth century by religious discrimination. Nonetheless, at the end of the Old Regime some *négociant* families were already taking the first steps up the path. When the Revolution not only removed the religious obstacle but also suddenly facilitated the acquisition of land and civic prestige, virtually the entire group of Montauban's wealthy commercial and manufacturing families swarmed to the top. Montauban's commercial and industrial difficulties during the Revolution only hastened their ascent. The laws of equal inheritance may have been an added reason but were hardly necessary to explain this change in family strategies.

Changes in the definition of property rights impelled other families to revise their strategies. The Revolution eliminated property in privilege, whether venal office, guild membership, commercial monopoly, or seigneurial right. Families in which such privileges had composed the essence of their patrimony found their status reduced and their moral relationship to their property altered. Strategies designed to defend and transmit such patrimony became irrelevant. As these families worked out the nature of their patrimony, they developed new strategies to conserve and transmit it. Again, the revolution in inheritance law added incentives to modify family strategies, but the necessity to do so originated elsewhere.

Montauban's particular economic history during this period also influenced family strategies in important ways. In the 1770s, Montauban was an industrial and commercial city as well as an administrative center and a regional market; by the 1820s, the first two components were on the verge of extinction. The radical change in the city's economic structure changed the nature of the working population. A skilled textile artisan in the 1770s, a fuller, for example, or a dyer, was a prized subcontractor in the city's main export industry and a prestigious member of the working community, a man whose skills and business contacts were a valuable patrimony and whose profits could allow his sons to aspire to be merchant-manufacturers and his daughters to marry into the lower ranks of the literate professions. In the early nineteenth century, as the textile industry shrank to purely local proportions, such artisans were poor workers whose sons were well advised to plan their futures in another trade. Likewise, merchants before the Revolution were wealthy men with contacts in Bordeaux, Amsterdam, and the West Indies, a far different breed from the merchants of the 1820s who supplied local artisans and retailers with shoe leather, buttons, or English cloth. For many families, strategies changed because the nature of their work and property changed. In Montauban, family strategies evolved in a generally egalitarian direction in part because more families found themselves in economic circumstances in which, even before the revolution in inheritance law, egalitarian division had made sense.

In many Montauban families, the laws of equal inheritance did precipitate a change in family strategies, but in ways not foreseen by the legislators who enacted the laws. They had redrawn the grid of inheritance law to promote equality among brothers and between fathers and sons so that civil society would be rooted in egalitarianism. But one of the major consequences of the law in Montauban was to increase expressions of concern and provisions for the material welfare of widows.

Enlightened thought heightened by romantic sentimentality eulogized the unity of the conjugal couple. The marital partnership was to be a mutual but not an equal relationship; the husband was to be the senior partner. The marital community of the Napoleonic Code was the legal formulation of this partnership whereby the pooling of the couple's property paralleled the joining of their persons and individual identities under the legal administration of the husband. This unity dissolved at the death of one of the parties. As the corporeal and personal bond ceased, so did the solidarity of property; the surviving spouse had no claim on the estate of the decedent.

Compared with the Custom of Montauban, the Napoleonic Code severely limited the claims of the surviving spouse, especially for poorer couples for whom the bride's dowry might represent the bulk of their capital. A widower could no longer inherit this property; nor could a widow receive her customary nuptial gains. During the Revolution and under the Napoleonic Code it was a desire to remedy this situation that prompted many Montaubaners to make wills. Thus, an unanticipated result of the laws of equal inheritance was the use of a written testament to replace or augment the wife's nuptial gains, which were now illegal, with the portion disponible or, most commonly, life rights to a major part of the family property. In many poorer families, the notion of the unity of husband and wife as the core of the family survived the husband's death; the marital community was not dissolved until the death of both husband

and wife, at which time the family's property was finally distributed among the legal heirs.

Montaubaners' response to the new inheritance laws' denial of a spouse's rights offset to some degree the restrictions that the Napoleonic Code placed on married women's property. What a Montauban testator left to his wife was not recognized in law as a widow's legal right; it was merely the particular will of her husband. Nonetheless, testamentary provisions for the widow to receive one quarter of the estate in property and another quarter in usufruct or half of the estate in usufruct or even the whole estate in the absence of other heirs were so frequent as to indicate that they had become expected. That a wife was a member of the family and that as a widow she retained a claim to support from the family property had become part of the unwritten principles that governed some Montaubaners' family life.

Thus, some Montauban families were becoming less hierarchical regardless of inheritance law; many became more egalitarian—that is, in recognizing a wife's claim on family property—despite the new laws. Nonetheless, in some Montauban families, the laws of equal inheritance did indeed have the effects intended by the Revolutionary legislators; they provoked a redistribution and a greater equilibrium of family resources between parents and children and especially among siblings. This was the case in families that had employed the faculté de tester in the way the Revolutionary advocates of equal inheritance had imagined, to the advantage of one heir, usually the eldest son, over the others and to reduce noninheriting children to the status of dependents in their brother's household or to exclude them from the household with portions so meager that they suffered a decline in social status and in living standard. Under the rule of equal inheritance, noninheriting children in such families had a material incentive fully backed by law to contest this allocation of resources. In order to prevent dismemberment of the patrimony, such families altered their strategies.

Judging by the imagery and examples in their speeches, Revolutionary legislators thought that elite families and landowning peasants were the main practitioners of such extremely unequal succession in the Old Regime south. The behavior of Montauban testators only partly confirmed their assumptions. First, few Montauban families used the faculté de tester to exclude heirs with no more than the légitime. Most testators desired to provide as well as they thought possible for all of their children. Nonetheless, two groups of families did practice primogeniture by excluding daughters and younger sons with quite small endowments. They were not the elite and the peasants, however, but the peasants, artisans, and retailers. These families had some property but often not enough to establish all of their children on their own socioeconomic level. And almost all the family property was bound up as patrimony, morally even more than materially indivisible. However, although under the faculté de tester, both rural and urban small-property-owning families had developed similar inheritance strategies, the revolution in inheritance law provoked differing responses from them. Moreover, neither group responded in precisely the way intended by the legislators.

The revolution in inheritance law did effect major changes in the strategies of self-sufficient landowning peasants but no revolution in their family values. The goal remained the same: to pass on the patrimony to a single heir, usually the eldest son, even though equal inheritance did pry out a larger share of family resources for distribution to daughters and younger sons. The Revolution strengthened the property rights of peasants, according them private property of their land unencumbered by tithes or seigneurial payments. But the laws of equal inheritance attempted to prevent peasants from treating their new property rights as patrimony. In many testaments, peasants responded to this challenge by defending their patrimony from disintegration with as many weapons as they could devise. While some evaded the requirements of the law, others used what facilities the law provided—in particular, the portion disponible—to approximate their goal. To evade the law successfully required the cooperation of all heirs and of all *their* heirs, and so on; one disgruntled party at any time after an illegal succession could completely wreck the strategy and force the division of the patrimony. The second solution, although it often encumbered the patrimony with enormous debts, proved more successful. It also required the cooperation of all the heirs so that the favored heir could pay off their claims over time in a way that would not imperil the patrimony. However, a patriarch could justifiably hope that with a small measure of good fortune, his heir would be able to pass on the patrimony in his turn. In the meantime, peasant proprietors ceased to appoint an heir in his marriage contract; instead, they retained full power over the patrimony and its final disposition throughout their lives, and through it, greater control over their children whose cooperation had now become essential to the success of their families' strategies.

Artisans and retailers modified both their family strategies and the ends to which they were designed. As the goal shifted from the transmission of the family business to succeeding generations to its economic viability in the present and the immediate future, the core of the family shifted from the dyad of father and son to that of the married couple. The revolution in property rights which strengthened landowning peasants' notions of patrimony undermined the patrimony of master artisans and retailers. The abolition of the corporate system eliminated most of what had been the patrimonial property of a small family business—mastership, membership in a guild, and recognized public status. It left the family with mere possessions and the accoutrements of a livelihood, property that could be divided without moral qualms or social loss. Faced with the reduction of their patrimony, with the economic difficulties of the Revolutionary years, and with the demands of daughters and younger sons for a more equitable share of the family's property, artisans and retailers changed their goals and strategies. Of primary importance became the desire to maintain, and if possible, enlarge, the family business so that it would support the family in the present and eventually provide larger shares for all. To do this, artisans and retailers came to rely more and more explicitly on their wives and their widows as their business partners and trustees.

The revolution in inheritance law was not sufficient in itself to effect a greater equality in the successions of artisans and peasants. For equal inheritance in law to become more equal division of property in practice required the active efforts of disadvantaged heirs. Disgruntled daughters and younger sons had challenged their families' exclusionary strategies even under the faculté de tester whenever they had sufficient grounds to do so. Under the laws of equal inheritance, they would have had grounds far more often. Because artisan and peasant families had never succeeded in obtaining the acquiescence of their noninheriting children to their family strategies, they were forced to modify the strategies to ensure that they were legally defensible. They knew that, given a thin wedge, an ungrateful child could split the patrimony with a few sharp taps of the judicial gavel.

For Montauban families in which all members agreed on the family's strategies or in which to challenge them was too costly to the individual, the revolution in inheritance law produced a flutter of concern but few lasting transformations. For many, inheritance strategies went into temporary abeyance during the six-year reign of strict equal inheritance only to reemerge during the Napoleonic era, slightly modified to conform to the new legal formulas. Such was the case in families of the poor who had rarely used the faculté de tester but left property intestate to be divided equally among the heirs. It was also the case in elite families, who, although they had used the faculté de tester to privilege the eldest male heir, had also established all heirs at an equivalent social level. In both groups, all heirs had acquiesced to the family strategies during the Old Regime and rarely challenged them under the new. The major effect of the revolution in inheritance law was to make the testament rather than the marriage contract the document that would provide for widows. If any revolutionary change occurred in these families, it was not in creating greater equality among siblings but in recognizing the widow's right to support from the family property.

The poor, both urban and rural, had little patrimonial property. Their family possessions—furniture, cooking implements, tools, even a room or a cottage—did not establish or support an *état*, a publicly recognized position in society, but merely provided for daily survival. Few poor people made wills either under the faculté de tester or under the new inheritance laws, not only because the act itself cost money but because they had no patrimony to pass on, no property with moral value even if they did possess goods of material worth. When poor people did make wills, they usually favored the surviving spouse, whose support during their lifetime was often the essential bulwark against destitution.

The elite, on the other hand, owned large amounts of property, both patrimonial and personal. Only a portion of the family property—a public office, a landed estate, a commercial or manufacturing company—established the family's social status. To pass down the patrimony intact did not require the family to entrust all its property to one heir. Instead, families developed strategies to establish each child suitably within the elite. Equality was not the aim, but equity was. As a result and also, perhaps, because unfilial behavior might have severe social repercussions, most children consented to be content with the portion assigned to them.

Once we consider the social groups that most influenced public policy throughout the Revolution and the Empire, we will not be surprised to find that the revolution in inheritance law was hardly revolutionary for many of Montauban's elite families. It embodied goals and encoded strategies they had already developed in the Old Regime. Under the faculté de tester, elite testators had the right to beggar their younger children in order to overprivilege the eldest son, but they rarely did so. Instead, they gave one heir a larger portion, sufficient to ensure the future of the lineage, but not so large as to deprive the other heirs of their social status. The double portion, created by the Napoleonic Code, suited quite well this notion of family equity.

In 1791, when the legislative debate over inheritance law began, Mirabeau had stigmatized the faculté de tester as typical of aristocratic families and of feudal society. Equal inheritance, he claimed, would promote "patriotic" families and underpin an egalitarian society. Although Montauban families who made use of the faculté de tester were not particularly "aristocratic," nor did they become democratic under the sway of equal inheritance, the revolution in inheritance law did correspond to and encourage a shift in attitudes toward family and society, a shift that can perhaps best be characterized as "bourgeois." Encoded in the Declaration of the Rights of Man and Citizen, which included property and security among the "natural and imprescriptible rights,"[1] it was a conception more libertarian than egalitarian, toward individual rights but not to equal things.

---

[1] See Georges Lefebvre, *The Coming of the French Revolution*, trans. R. R. Palmer (Princeton: Princeton University Press, 1947), pp. 169–181.

In Montauban, bourgeois parents hoped to establish an heir but not at the expense of the future socioeconomic status of their other children. They believed that property owners had the right to do as they chose with their property, but also that children (and wives) had a right to an equitable share of the family's resources. In the short-term, individuals might have to make sacrifices in the family's better interest—to delay marriage, for example. But the long-term goal of the family was to secure the happiness and security of its individual family members.

The Revolutionary laws of equal inheritance, as modified by the Napoleonic Code—and further modified by Montaubaners' codicils in favor of their wives—both assumed and supported these attitudes. Together with a host of other legal and attitudinal changes, they privileged individual rights and conceived of both family and society as composed of free individuals with rights. Not equal rights, of course. Law maintained a husband and father in certain controlling rights in the family, just as, for example, it protected a property owner's special rights in civil society. And, of course, women, whether in the family or in civil society, did not have the status of free individuals that men had. Equal rights, conceived as natural, were qualified by equally "natural" prerogatives and disabilities of gender and class. The idea of society as composed of such free and equal individuals was part of the mentality that came to the fore during the French Revolution and that dominated the nineteenth century. By extending this conception from society to family and back again, the laws of equal inheritance emerge as one of the cornerstones of French bourgeois society.

Select Bibliography

ARCHIVAL SOURCES

Archives Municipal de Montauban

OLD REGIME CODES

AA 10–11	Délibérations des officiers municipaux, 1752–1790.
2 BB 13–21	Délibérations du conseil général, 1772–1789.
3 BB 35	Délibérations du conseil de police, 1787–1790.
5 CC 8–9	Capitations, 1731, 1788.
6 FF 46–60	Dossiers et procédures jugés par les jurisdictions consulaires, 1775–1790.
9 FF 1	Déclarations de séjour, 1765–1793.
10 FF 1	Hôtes et cabaretiers, 1783–1785.
29 GG 1–3	Bureau de charité, 1777–1790.
7 HH 1–5	Corporations d'arts et métiers.
8 HH 1–7	Manufactures.
10 HH 1	Dénombrements XVIIIᵉ siècle.

REVOLUTION AND NINETEENTH-CENTURY CODES

1 D 1–2	Délibérations des officiers municipaux, 1790–1817.
3 D 5	Délibérations du conseil général, Years 3–6.
1 F 1	Dénombrement du Carmes, 1791–Year 8.
2 F 6	Subsistances, 1793–Year 3.
4 F 1–3	Manufactures.
1 G 1	Capitation, 1790.
4 i 15–19	Police générale.
5 i 1–2	Passeports.
6 i 1–2	Suspects.
7 i 1–2	Emigrés.
8 i 2–3	Tribunal de police, 1791–Year 3.
8 i 5	Tribunal de famille, 1793–Year 5.
8 i 6–10	Juges de paix, 1793–Year 7.
8 i 20	Procès criminel des officiers municipaux, Year 5.

Archives Hospitalières de Montauban

F 3–6	Entrés et sorties, 1724–1733.

Archives Départementales de Tarn-et-Garonne

B 11	Délibérations de la Cour des Aides, 1774–1788.
B 418–420	Donations entres vifs, 1772–1782.
E Etat Civil Protestant 366–374, 599–600	Registres non-Catholiques, 1788–1792.

5 E	Notaires.
G 149	Administration de l'hospice.
G 457–460	Procédures devant l'officialité, 1750–1789.
Series J	Family papers.
9 J 5	Molières
11 J 284	Selves
11 J 404	Garrisson
11 J 614	Preissac
11 J 616	Dubu, Gironde
12 J 5–7	Lagravere
105 J	Bergis
L 95–97	Suspects et detenus.
L 323–324	Tribunal de commerce, 1792–Year 3
L 407	Club patriotique.
L 442–444	Tribunal civil, Years 3–12.
L 456	Tribunal de famille, Castelsarrasin, 1792–Year 4.
1 U 1–8	Tribunal correctionnel, Year 8–1831.
1 U 91–97, 104, 114, 137, 146, 159, 368–370	Cour d'assises, Year 8–1827.
Q 406–414	Donations entre vifs, 1792–Year 11.

Archives Nationales

F^{10} 227	Mémoires à la Convention.
F^{10} 232	Comité d'agriculture de la Convention.
F^{11} 735	Subsistances, 1817.
F^{12} 559	Manufactures XVIIIe.
F^{12} 776	Corporations des arts et métiers.
F^{12} 1271	Foires et marchés, 1790–1823.
F^{12} 1378	Draperie, 1716–1790.
F^{12} 1586	Etat des fabriques, 1810–1822.
F^{12} 1210–13	Hospices, bureaux de bienfaisances, 1809–1827.
F^{15} 2795	Dépôts de mendicité, 1780–Year 8.
H 1503	Société d'agriculture à Montauban, 1761–1775.

Published Primary Sources

Bloch, Camille, and Alexandre Tuetey, eds. *Procès-verbaux et rapports du Comité de mendicité de la Constituante 1790–1791*. Collection de documents inédits sur l'histoire économique de la Révolution Française. Paris: Imprimerie Nationale, 1911.

Caron, Pierre, ed. *La Comission des subsistances de l'an II: Procès-verbaux et actes*. Collection de documents inédits sur l'histoire économique de la Révolution Française. Paris: Librairie Ernest Leroux, 1925.

———, ed. *Rapports des agents du Ministre de l'intérieur dans les départements 1793–an II*. 2 vols. Paris: Imprimerie Nationale 1913, 1951.

Expilly, Abbé. *Dictionnaire géographique, historique et politique des Gaules et de la*

France. 4 vols. Amsterdam: n.p., 1762–1770; reprint ed., Leichtenstein: Kraus Reprint, 1978.

Ferrière, C. J. de. *Science parfaite des notaires ou le parfait notaire*. 2 vols. Paris: F-B de Visme, 1771.

Gerbaux, Fernand, and Charles Schmidt, eds. *Procès-verbaux des Comités d'agriculture et de commerce de la Constituante, de la Legislative et de la Convention*. 4 vols. Collection de documents inédits sur l'histoire économique de la Révolution Française. Paris: Imprimerie Nationale, 1906–1910.

Guilhamon, Henri. *Journal des voyages en Haute-Guienne de J-F Henry de Richeprey*. 2 vols. Archives historiques du Rouergue nos. 19–20. Rodez: Société de Lettres, Sciences et Arts de l'Aveyron, 1967.

Hugo, Abel. *France pittoresque*. 3 vols. Paris: Chez Delloye, 1835.

Journal de Lot-et-Garonne (Cahors).

Journal de Tarn et Garonne (Montauban).

Malrieu, Victor, ed. *Cahiers de doléances de la sénéchaussée de Montauban et du pays et jugerie de Rivière-Verdun pour les Etats Généraux de 1789*. Montauban: Imprimerie Cooperative, Barrier et cie, 1925.

Ménétra, Jacques-Louis. *Journal of My Life*. Translated by Arthur Goldhammer. Introduction and commentary by Daniel Roche. New York: Columbia University Press, 1986.

Moniteur Universel (Paris).

Ombret, Antoine, Jean-Claude Fau, and René Tournon, eds. *Montauban et les pays de l'actuel Tarn-et-Garonne sous le Premier Empire (1804–1815)*. Montauban: CDDP Archives du Tarn-et-Garonne, 1980.

———. *La Révolution en Bas-Quercy*. 2 vols. Montauban: CDDP Archives du Tarn-et-Garonne, 1978.

———. *Villes et campagnes du Bas-Quercy à la fin de l'ancien régime*. Montauban: CDDP Archives du Tarn-et-Garonne, 1974

Puis, Auguste. *Une famille de parlementaires toulousains à la fin de l'ancien régime: Correspondance du conseiller et de la comtesse d'Albis de Belbeze, 1783–1785*. Paris: Edouard Champion, 1913.

Restif de la Bretonne, Nicolas. *Monsieur Nicolas, ou le coeur humain dévoilé*. 6 vols. Paris: Au Cercle du Livre Précieux, 1959.

Savary, Jacques. *Le Parfait négociant*. Lyon: J. Lyon, 1697.

Young, Arthur. *Travels During the Years 1787, 1788 and 1789*. 2 vols. Dublin: n.p., 1793.

SECONDARY WORKS

Aboucaya, Claude. *Le Testament lyonnais de la fin du XVe siècle au milieu de XVIIIe siècle*. Paris: Sirey, 1961.

Agulhon, Maurice. *La Sociabilité méridionale: Confrèries et associations dans la vie collective en Provence orientale à la fin du XVIIIe siècle*. 2 vols. Publications des Annales de la faculté de lettres Aix-en-Provence, travaux et documents, no. 36. Aix-en-Provence: La Pensée universitaire, 1966.

———. *La Vie sociale en Provence intérieure au lendemain de la révolution*. Bibliothèque d'histoire révolutionnaire, ser. 3, no. 12. Paris: Société des Etudes Robespierristes, 1970.

Arches, P. "Les Débuts de la garde nationale de Montauban." *Actes du 10ᵉ Congrès d'Etudes Régionales de la Fédération des Sociétés Académiques et Savantes Languedoc-Pyrénées-Gascogne* (Montauban, 1954): 303–314.

Aries, Philippe. *Centuries of Childhood: A Social History of Family Life*. Translated by Robert Baldick. New York: Vintage Books, 1962.

Armengaud, André. *Les Populations de l'est-aquitain au début de l'époque contemporaine*. Paris: Mouton et cie, 1961.

Aron, Gustave. "Etude sur les lois successorales de la révolution depuis 1789." *Revue historique du droit français et étranger*, ser. 3, no. 25 (1901): 444–489, 585–620.

Arvisenet, Guy de. "L'Office de conseiller à la cour des aides de Paris au XVIIIᵉ siècle d'après les mémoires inédits de Louis Achille Diones du Séjour." *Revue historique de droit français et étranger*, ser. 4, no. 33 (1955): 537–559.

Assier-Andrieu, Louis. "Le Play et la famille-souche des Pyrénées: Politique, juridisme et science sociale." *Annales. Economies, Sociétés, Civilisations* 39, no. 3 (May–June 1984): 495–512.

Augustin, Jean-Marie. *Les Substitutions fidéicommissaires à Toulouse et en Haut-Languedoc au XVIIIᵉ siècle*. Paris: Presses Universitaires de France, 1980.

Bastier, Jean. *La Féodalité au siècle des lumières dans la région de Toulouse (1730–1790)*. Commission d'histoire économique et sociale de la Révolution Française, Mémoires et documents, no. 30. Paris: Bibliothèque nationale, 1975.

Bergeon, Paul. "La Terre et le paysan dans le Consulat de Montauban (17ᵉ et 18ᵉ siècle)." *Bulletin archéologique, historique et artistique de la Société Archéologique de Tarn et Garonne* 102 (1977): 7–26.

Berkner, Lutz K. "The Stem Family and the Development Cycle of the Peasant Household: An Eighteenth Century Austrian Example." *American Historical Review* 77, no. 2 (April 1972): 398–418.

———. "The Use and Misuse of Census Data for the Historical Analysis of Family Structure." *Journal of Interdisciplinary History* 5, no. 4 (Spring 1975): 721–738.

Berkner, Lutz K., and John W. Shaffer. "The Joint Family in the Nivernais." *Journal of Family History* 3, no. 2 (Summer 1978): 150–162.

Berlanstein, Leonard R. *The Barristers of Toulouse in the Eighteenth Century (1740–1793)*. Baltimore: Johns Hopkins University Press, 1975.

Bien, David D. *The Calas Affair*. Princeton: Princeton University Press, 1960.

———. "Catholic Magistrates and Protestant Marriage in the French Enlightenment." *French Historical Studies* 2, no. 4 (Fall 1962): 409–429.

———. "Les offices, les corps et le crédit d'état: L:Utilisation des privilèges sous l'Ancien Régime." *Annales. Economies, Sociétés, Civilisations* 43, no. 2 (March–April 1988): 379–404.

Bloch, Claudine. "L'Institution d'héritier et le legs universel dans le droit intermédiaire et le code civil." *Revue historique du droit français et étranger*, ser. 4, no. 52 (1974): 30–86.

Bosher, J. F. "Success and Failure in Trade to New France, 1660–1760." *French Historical Studies* 15, no. 3 (Spring 1988): 444–461.

Bossenga, Gail. "Protecting Merchants: Guilds and Commercial Capitalism in

Eighteenth-Century France." *French Historical Studies* 15, no. 3 (Spring 1988): 693–703.

———. "La Revolution française et les corporations: Trois exemples lillois." *Annales. Economies, Sociétés, Civilisations* 43, no. 2 (March–April 1988): 405–426.

Bost, Mlle. "Les Protestants montalbanais après la révocation de l'Edict de Nantes (1685–1790)." *Bulletin archéologique, historique et artistique de la Société Archéologique de Tarn et Garonne* 78 (1951): 42–57.

Boulant, Micheline. "La Famille en miettes: sur un aspect de la démographie du XVIIIe siècle." *Annales. Economies, Sociétés, Civilisations* 27, nos. 4–5 (July–October 1972): 959–968.

Bourchenin, Daniel. *La Géographie du Tarn et Garonne du XVIIIe siècle.* Montauban: Forestié, 1904.

Bourdieu, Pierre. "Les Stratégies matrimoniales dans le système de reproduction." *Annales. Economies, Sociétés, Civilisations* 27, nos. 4–5 (July–October 1972): 1105–1127.

Bourrachot, Lucille, and Jean-Pierre Poussou. "Les Départs de passagers quercynois pour les antilles et le canada au XVIIIe siècle par le port de Bordeaux." *Actes du 23e Congrès d'Etudes Régionales de la Fédération des Sociétés Académiques et Savantes Languedoc-Pyrénées-Gascogne* (Figeac, 1967): 423–438.

Boutier, Jean. "Jacqueries en pays croquant: Les Révoltes paysannes en Aquitaine (décembre 1789–mars 1790)." *Annales. Economies, Sociétés, Civilisations* 34, no. 4 (July–August 1979): 760–786.

Briffaud, Serge. "La Famille, le notaire et le mourant: Testament et mentalités dans la région de Luchon (1650–1790)." *Annales du Midi* 97 (1985): 389–409.

Brinton, Crane. *French Revolutionary Legislation on Illegitimacy, 1789–1804.* Cambridge, Mass.: Harvard University Press, 1936.

Butel, Paul. "Comportements familiaux dans le négoce bordelais au XVIIIe siècle." *Annales du Midi* 88, no. 127 (April–June 1876): 139–157.

———. *Les Négociants bordelais, l'Europe et les îles au XVIIIe siècle.* Paris: Aubier-Montaigne, 1974.

Carrière, Charles. *Négociants marseillais au XVIIIe siècle.* 2 vols. Marseilles: Imprimerie Robert, 1973.

———. "Le Recrutement de la cour des comptes, aides et finances d'Aix-en-Provence à la fin de l'ancien régime." *Actes du 81e Congrès National des Sociétés Savantes* (Rouen-Caen, 1956): 141–159.

Castan, Nicole. "La Criminalité familiale dans le ressort du Parlement de Toulouse, 1690–1730." In *Crimes et criminalité en France, XVIIe–XVIIIe siècles,* pp. 91–107. Edited by André Abbiateci et al. Cahiers des Annales, no. 33. Paris: Armand Colin, 1971.

———. *Les Criminels de Languedoc: Les Exigences d'ordre et les voies du ressentiment dans une société pré-révolutionnaire (1750–1790).* Toulouse: Association des publications de l'université de Toulouse–Le Mirail, 1980.

Castan, Yves. *Honnêteté et relations sociales en Languedoc: 1715–1780.* Paris: Librairie Plon, 1974.

Cavignac, Jean. "Les Négociants, maîtres de Bordeaux, sous la Monarchie de Juillet: Contribution à l'étude de la France des notables." *Actes du 108e Congrès*

National des Sociétés Savantes, Section d'Histoire Moderne et Contemporaine. 2 vols. (Grenoble, 1983) 2: 293–304.

Cayla, Alfred. *Maison du Quercy et du Périgord*. Paris: Librairie Hachette, 1973.

Cerutti, Simona. "Du corps au métier: La Corporation des tailleurs à Turin entre XVIIᵉ et XVIIIᵉ siècle." *Annales. Economies, Sociétés, Civilisations* 43, no. 2 (March–April 1988): 323–352.

Chaline, Jean-Pierre. *Les Bourgeois de Rouen: Une Élite urbaine au XIXᵉ siècle*. Paris: Presses de la Fondation Nationale des Sciences Politiques, 1982.

Chaytor, Miranda. "Household and Kinship: Ryton in the Late Sixteenth and Early Seventeenth Centuries." *History Workshop Journal* 10 (August 1980): 25–60.

Clark, John G. *La Rochelle and the Atlantic Economy During the Eighteenth Century*. Baltimore: Johns Hopkins University Press, 1981.

Claverie, Elisabeth. " 'Honneur': Une Société de défis au XIXᵉ siècle." *Annales. Economies, Sociétés, Civilisations* 34, no. 4 (July–August 1979): 744–759.

Claverie, Elisabeth, and Pierre Lamaison. *L'Impossible mariage: violence et parenté en Gévaudan, XVIIᵉ, XVIIIᵉ et XIXᵉ siècles*. Paris: Hachette, 1982.

Cobb, Richard. *Death in Paris*. Oxford: Oxford University Press, 1978.

———. *The People's Armies: The Armées Révolutionnaires; Instruments of the Terror in the Departments, April 1793 to Floréal Year 2*. Translated by Marianne Elliot. New Haven: Yale University Press, 1987.

Collomp, Alain. "Alliance et filiation en Haute Provence au XVIIIᵉ siècle." *Annales. Economies, Sociétés, Civilisations* 32, no. 3 (May–June 1977): 445–477.

———. "Conflits familiaux et groupes de residence en Haute-Provence." *Annales. Economies, Sociétés, Civilisations* 36, no. 3 (May–June 1981): 408–425.

———. "Famille nucléaire et famille élargie en Haute Provence au XVIIIᵉ siècle (1703–1734)." *Annales. Economies, Sociétés, Civilisations* 27, nos. 4–5 (July–October 1972): 969–975.

———. *La Maison du père: Famille et village en Haute-Provence aux XVIIᵉ et XVIIIᵉ siècles*. Paris: Presses Universitaires de France, 1983.

———. "Maison, manières d'habiter et famille en Haute-Provence aux XVIIᵉ et XVIIIᵉ siècles." *Ethnologie française* 8 (1975): 301–320.

Coornaert, Emile. *Les Compagnonnages en France du moyen âge à nos jours*. Paris: Les Editions Ouvrières, 1966.

———. *Les Corporations en France avant 1789*. 2d ed. Paris: Les Editions Ouvrières, 1968.

Crossick, Geoffrey, and Heinz-Gerhard Haupt, eds. *Shopkeepers and Master Artisans in Nineteenth Century Europe*. London: Methuen, 1984.

Crouzet, François. "Les Origines du sous-developpement économique du Sud-Ouest." *Annales du Midi* 71 (1959): 71–79.

Cuillieron, Monique. *Contributions à l'étude de la rebellion des cours souverains sous le règne de Louis XV: Le Cas de la cour des aides et finances de Montauban*. Paris: Presses universitaires, 1983.

Darnton, Robert. *The Great Cat Massacre and Other Episodes in French Cultural History*. New York: Basic Books, 1984.

Darrow, Margaret H. "French Noblewomen and the New Domesticity, 1750–1850." *Feminist Studies* 5, no. 1 (Spring 1979): 41–65.

———. "Popular Concepts of Marital Choice in Eighteenth Century France." *Journal of Social History* 19, no. 2 (Winter 1985): 261–272.

Daudet, Ernest. *La Terreur Blanche, episodes et souvenirs, 1815.* 3d ed. Paris: Librairie Hachette et cie., 1906.

Daugé, Césaire. *Le Mariage et la famille en Gascogne d'après les proverbes et les chansons.* 2 vols. Bayonne: Editions Harriet, 1982.

Daumard, Adeline, ed. *Les Fortunes françaises au XIXe siècle: Enquête sur la répartition et la composition des capitaux privés à Paris, Lyon, Bordeaux et Toulouse d'après l'enregistrement des declarations de succession.* Ecole Pratique des Hautes Etudes, VIe Section: Civilisations et Sociétés, no. 27. Paris: Mouton, 1973.

Dawson, Philip. *Provincial Magistrates and Revolutionary Politics in France, 1789–1795.* Cambridge, Mass.: Harvard University Press, 1972.

Dejace, André. *Les Règles de la dévolution successorale sous le révolution (1789–1794).* Paris: Librairie générale de droit et de jurisprudence, 1957.

Dellaux, Mlle. "Les Recoltes et la problème des subsistances à Montauban à la veille de la révolution." *Actes du 10e Congrès d'Etudes Régionales de la Fédération des Sociétés Académiques et Savantes Languedoc-Pyrénées-Gascogne* (Montauban, 1954): 315–317.

Delvit, Philippe. "La Cour de la bourse des marchands de Montauban au XVIIIe siècle." *Annales du Midi* 98, no. 174 (April–June 1986): 185–211.

Depauw, Jacques. "Amour illégitime et société à Nantes au XVIIIe siècle." *Annales. Economies, Sociétés, Civilisations* 27, no. 4–5 (July–October 1972): 1155–1182.

Deyon, Pierre. *Amiens, capitale provinciale: Étude sur la société au XVIIe siècle.* Paris: Mouton, 1967.

———. "Le Mouvement de la production textile à Amiens au XVIIIe siècle." *Revue du nord* 44 (1962): 201–211.

Doyle, William. *The Parlement of Bordeaux and the End of the Old Regime, 1771–1799.* London: Ernest Benn, 1974.

———. "The Price of Offices in Pre-Revolutionary France." *The Historical Journal* 27, no. 4 (December 1984): 831–860.

Dupâquier, Jacques, et al. *Marriage and Remarriage in Populations of the Past.* London: Academic Press, 1981.

Dussourd, Henriette. *Au même pot et au même feu . . . étude sur les communautés familiales agricoles du centre de la France.* Moulins: Imprimerie A. Pottier et cie, 1962.

———. "Les Dissolutions de communautés familiales agricoles dans le centre de la France depuis le XVIIIe siècle jusqu'au code civil." *Actes du 89e Congrès National des Sociétés Savantes, Section d'Histoire Moderne et Contemporaine* (Lyon 1964): 309–319.

Elshtain, Jean Bethke, ed. *The Family in Political Thought.* Amherst, Mass.: University of Massachussets Press, 1982.

Fairchilds, Cissie. *Domestic Enemies: Servants and Their Masters in Old Regime France.* Baltimore: Johns Hopkins University Press, 1984.

———. "Female Sexual Attitudes and the Rise of Illegitimacy: A Case Study." *Journal of Interdisciplinary History* 8, no. 4 (Spring 1978): 627–667.

———. *Poverty and Charity in Aix-en-Provence, 1640–1789.* Baltimore: Johns Hopkins University Press, 1976.

Fajn, Max. "La Diffusion de la presse révolutionnaire dans le Lot, le Tarn et l'Aveyron sous la Convention et le Directoire." *Annales du Midi* 83 (1971): 299–314.

Farge, Arlette. *La Vie fragile: Violence, pouvoirs et solidarités à Paris au XVIIIe siècle.* Paris: Hachette, 1986.

Fine-Souriac, Agnes. "La Famille-souche pyrénéene au XIXe siècle." *Annales. Economies, Sociétés, Civilisations* 32, no. 3 (May–June 1977): 478–487.

Fitzsimmons, Michael P. *The Parisian Order of Barristers and the French Revolution.* Cambridge, Mass.: Harvard University Press, 1987.

Flandrin, Jean-Louis. *Families in Former Times: Kinship, Household and Sexuality.* Translated by Richard Southern. Cambridge: Cambridge University Press, 1979.

Ford, Franklin L. *Robe and Sword: The Regrouping of the French Aristocracy After Louis XIV.* New York: Harper and Row, Harper Torchbooks, 1965.

Forestié, Edouard. *Notice historique sur la fabrication des draps à Montauban au XIVe siècle à nos jours.* Montauban: Imprimerie Edouard Forestié, 1883.

Forrest, Alan. *The French Revolution and the Poor.* New York: St. Martin's Press, 1981.

Forster, Robert. *Merchants, Landlords, Magistrates: The Depont Family in Eighteenth Century France.* Baltimore: Johns Hopkins University Press, 1980.

————. *The Nobility of Toulouse in the Eighteenth Century: A Social and Economic Study.* Johns Hopkins University Studies in Historical and Political Science, ser. 78, no. 1. New York: Octagon Books, 1971.

France, Henry de. *Les Montalbanais et le refuge.* Montauban: Imprimerie Edouard Forestié, 1887.

Frêche, Georges. *Toulouse et la région midi-pyrénées au siècle des lumières (vers 1670–1789).* Mayenne: Editions Cujas, 1974.

Furet, François, and Jacques Ozouf. *Reading and Writing: Literacy in France from Calvin to Jules Ferry.* Cambridge: Cambridge University Press, 1982.

Galabert, François. "Le Club jacobin de Montauban, son role politique pendant la Constituante." *Revue de l'histoire moderne et contemporaine* 1 (1899): 124–168, 234–258, 457–474; 10 (1908): 273–317.

Garden, Maurice. *Lyon et les lyonnais au XVIIIe siècle.* Paris: Flammarion, 1975.

Garrioch, David. *Neighbourhood and Community in Paris, 1740–1790.* Cambridge: Cambridge University Press, 1986.

Garrioch, David, and Michael Sonenscher. "Compagnonnages, Confraternities and Associations of Journeymen in Eighteenth-Century Paris." *European History Quarterly* 16, no. 1 (January 1986): 25–45.

Garrisson-Estèbe, Janine, and Marc Ferro, eds. *Une Histoire de la Garonne.* Paris: Editions Ramsay, 1982.

Gaudemet, Jean. *Les Communautés familiales.* Paris: Editions Marcel Rivière et cie, 1963.

Gaunt, David. "Rural Household Organizaiton and Inheritance in Northern Europe." *Journal of Family History* 12, nos. 1–3 (1987): 121–141.

Gausseran, Marcel. "L'Evolution sociale de la bourgeoise montalbanaise, 1700–1789." *Bulletin archéologique, historique et artistique de la Société Archéologique de Tarn et Garonne* 73 (1945): 88–104.

———. "L'Exode des protestants montalbanais au refuge, 1685–1686." *Bulletin archéologique, historique et artistique de la Société Archéologique de Tarn et Garonne* 80 (1953): 35–54.

———. "La Population montalbanaise pendant la periode de 1700 à 1725." *Bulletin archéologique, historique et artistique de la Société Archéologique de Tarn et Garonne* 68 (1940): 60–66.

Giesey, Ralph E. "Rules of Inheritance and Strategies of Mobility in Prerevolutionary France." *American Historical Review* 82, no. 2 (April 1977): 271–289.

Gillis, John R. *For Better, For Worse: British Marriages, 1600 to the Present.* New York: Oxford University Press, 1985.

Godechot, Jacques. *Les Institutions de la France sous la révolution et l'empire.* 2d ed. Paris: Presses Universitaires de France, 1968.

Goody, Jack. *The Development of the Family and Marriage in Europe.* Cambridge: Cambridge University Press, 1983.

Goody, Jack, Joan Thirsk, and E. P. Thompson, eds. *Family and Inheritance: Rural Society in Western Europe, 1200–1800.* Cambridge: Cambridge University Press, 1978.

Goubert, Pierre. *Familles marchandes sous l'ancien régime: Les Danse et les Motte de Beauvais.* Paris: SEVPEN, 1957.

———. "Family and Province: A Contribution to the Knowledge of Family Structures in Early Modern France." *Journal of Family History* 2, no. 3 (Fall 1977): 179–195.

Goujard, Philippe. "Echec d'une sensibilité baroque: Les Testaments rouennais au XVIIIe siècle." *Annales. Economies, Sociétés, Civilisations* 36, no. 1 (January–February 1981): 26–43.

Gullickson, Gay L. *Spinners and Weavers of Auffay: Rural Industry and the Sexual Division of Labor in a French Village, 1750–1850.* Cambridge: Cambridge University Press, 1986.

Gutton, Jean-Pierre. *Domestiques et serviteurs dans la France de l'ancien régime.* Paris: Editions Aubier Montaigne, 1981.

———. *La Société et les pauvres: L'Exemple de la généralité de Lyon, 1534–1789.* Paris: Société d'Edition «Les Belles Lettres», 1970.

Hareven, Tamara K. "Family History at the Crossroads." *Journal of Family History* 12, nos. 1–3 (1987): ix–xxiii.

Harris, Olivia. "Households and Their Boundaries." *History Workshop Journal* 13 (Spring 1982): 143–152.

Hartig, Irmgard A. "Revolution et communautés familiales: Témoignages et représentations." *Annales Historiques de la Révolution française* 54, no. 217 (January–March 1982): 59–70.

Held, Thomas. "Rural Retirement Arrangements in Seventeenth to Nineteenth Century Austria: A Cross Community Analysis." *Journal of Family History* 7, no. 3 (Fall 1982): 227–54.

Higounet, Charles, ed. *Histoire de Bordeaux.* 8 vols. Bordeaux: Fédération historique du Sud-Ouest, 1969.

Hilaire, Jean. "Vie en commun, famille et esprit communautaire." *Revue historique du droit français et étranger*, ser. 4, no. 51 (1973): 8–53

Hood, James N. "Patterns of Popular Protest in the French Revolution: The Conceptual Contribution of the Gard." *Journal of Modern History* 48 (June 1976): 259–293.

______. "Protestant-Catholic Relations and the Roots of the First Popular Counter-revolutionary Movement in France." *Journal of Modern History* 43 (1971): 245–275.

______. "Revival and Mutation of Old Rivalries in Revolutionary France." *Past and Present* 82 (February 1979): 82–115.

Hufton, Olwen H. *Bayeux in the Late Eighteenth Century: A Social Study.* Oxford: Clarendon Press, 1967.

______. "Le Paysan et la loi en France au xviiie siècle." *Annales. Economies, Sociétés, Civilisations* 38, no. 3 (May–June 1983): 679–701.

______. *The Poor of Eighteenth Century France, 1750–1789.* Oxford: Clarendon Press, 1974.

______. "Women and the Family Economy of Eighteenth Century France." *French Historical Studies* 9, no. 1 (Spring 1975): 1–22.

Imbert, Jean. *Histoire du droit privé.* Paris: Presses universitaires de France, "Que Sais-Je?" 1961.

Johnson, Hubert C. *The Midi in Revolution: A Study of Regional Political Diversity, 1789–1793.* Princeton: Princeton University Press, 1986.

Jones, Colin. *Charity and Bienfaisance: The Treatment of the Poor in the Montpellier Region, 1740–1815.* Cambridge: Cambridge University Press, 1982.

Kaplan, Steven Laurence. "The Character and Implications of Strife Among the Masters Inside the Guilds of Eighteenth Century Paris." *Journal of Social History* 19, no. 4 (Summer 1986): 631–647.

______. "Les Corporations, les 'faux ouvriers' et le Faubourg Saint-Antoine au xviiie siècle." *Annales. Economies, Sociétés, Civilisations* 43, no. 2 (March–April 1988): 353–378.

Kaplan, Steven Laurence, and Cynthia J. Koepp, eds. *Work in France: Representations, Meanings, Organization, and Practice.* Ithaca: Cornell University Press, 1986.

Kaplow, Jeffry. *The Names of Kings: The Parisian Laboring Poor in the Eighteenth Century.* New York: Basic Books, 1972

Katz, Stanley N. "Republicanism and the Law of Inheritance in the American Revolutionary Era." *Michigan Law Review* 76, no. 1 (November 1977): 1–29.

Kennedy, Michael L. *The Jacobin Clubs in the French Revolution: The First Years.* Princeton: Princeton University Press, 1982.

Kertzer, David I. *Family Life in Central Italy, 1880–1910: Sharecropping, Wage Labor, and Coresidence.* New Brunswick, N.J.: Rutgers University Press, 1984.

Lacave, Michel, and Mireille Lacave. *Bourgeois et marchands en Provence et en Languedoc.* Avignon: Aubanel, 1977.

Lamaison, Pierre. "Les Stratégies matrimoniales dans un système complexe de parenté: Ribennes en Gévaudan (1650–1830)." *Annales. Economies, Sociétés, Civilisations* 34, no. 4 (July–August 1979): 721–743.

Landau, N., and J-P Landrevie. *De l'Empire à la République: Structure politique et sociale du Tarn et Garonne (1868–1877).* Paris: Hachette Microéditions, 1971.

Lapeyre, Ernest. *Les Insurrections du Lot en 1790*. Cahors: J. Girma, 1892.

Laslet, Peter. *The World We Have Lost*. New York: Charles Scribner's Sons, 1965.

Latouche, Robert. "Etude sur le notariat dans le Bas-Quercy et le Bas-Rouergue." *Revue historique de droit français et étranger*, ser. 4, no. 2 (1923): 5–19.

———. *La Vie en Bas-Quercy du XIVᵉ au XVIIIᵉ siècle*. Toulouse: Edouard Privat, 1923.

Lebret, Henri. *Histoire de Montauban*. 2 vols. Montauban: Chez Rethoré, 1841.

Lebrun, François. *La Vie conjugale sous l'ancien régime*. Paris: Armand Colin, 1975.

Lefebvre, Charles. "Le Droit successoral pendant la révolution." *Académie des Sciences Morales et Politique, Compte Rendu des Séances et Travaux*, n.s., no. 87 (1917): 593–622.

Lefebvre, Georges. *Les Paysans du Nord pendant la révolution française*. Paris: Librairie Armand Colin, 1972.

Lehning, James R. *The Peasants of Marlhes: Economic Development and Family Organization in Nineteenth-Century France*. Chapel Hill, N.C.: University of North Carolina Press, 1980.

Lelièvre, Jacques. *La Practique des contrats de mariage chez les notaires au Châtelet de Paris de 1769 à 1804*. Paris: Editions Cujas, 1959.

Lemaitre, Nicole. "Familles complexes en Bas-Limousin, Ussel au début de xixᵉ siècle." *Annales du Midi* 88, no. 127 (April–June 1976): 219–224.

Le Play, Frédéric. *L'Organisation de la famille*. 3d ed. Tours: Alfred Mame et fils, 1884.

———. *Les Ouvriers européens*. 2d ed. 6 vols. Tours: Alfred Mame et fils, 1877–1879.

Le Roy Ladurie, Emmanuel. *Love, Death and Money in the Pays d'Oc*. Translated by Alan Sheridan. New York: Penguin Books, 1984.

———. *Les Paysans de Languedoc*. Paris: SEVPEN, 1966.

———. "Système de la coutume: Structures familiales et coutume d'heritage en France au xviᵉ siècle." *Annales. Economies, Sociétés, Civilisations* 27, nos. 4–5 (July–October 1972): 825–846.

Levine, David. *Family Formation in the Age of Nascent Capitalism*. New York: Academic Press, 1977.

Ligou, Daniel. "La Cour des aides de Montabuan à la fin du xviiiᵉ siècle." *Annales du Midi* 64 (1952): 297–324.

———. "Etude fonctionnelle de la population de Montauban à la fin de l'ancien régime." *Actes du 86ᵉ Congrès National des Sociétés Savantes, Section d'Histoire Moderne et Contemporaine*. (Montpellier, 1961): 579–602.

———. *Montauban à la fin de l'ancien régime et aux débuts de la révolution, 1787–1794*. Paris: Libraire Marcel Rivière et cie, 1958.

———. "Notes sur la vente des biens nationaux dans le district de Montauban." *Actes du 77ᵉ Congrès National des Sociétés Savantes*. (Grenoble, 1952): 361–387.

———. "Protestants et sans-culottes: La Bourgeoisie reformée de Montauban devant la révolution." *Actes du 10ᵉ Congrès d'Etudes Régionales de la Fédération des Sociétés Académiques et Savantes Languedoc-Pyrénées-Gascogne* (Montauban, 1954): 174–186.

———. "La Structure agraire de la banlieu montalbanaise à la fin du xviiiᵉ siècle. *Bulletin de la Société des Sciences Naturelles de Tarn et Garonne* 1 (1952).

Ligou, Daniel. "Les Suspects dans le district de Montauban." *Actes du 78ᵉ Congrès National des Sociétés Savantes.* (Toulouse, 1953): 209–230.

———, ed. *Histoire de Montauban.* Toulouse: Privat, 1984.

Ligou, Daniel, and Janine Garrisson-Estèbe. "La Bourgeoisie reformée montalbanaise à la fin de l'ancien régime." *Revue d'histoire économique et sociale* 33, no. 4 (1955): 377–404.

Lottin, Alain. "Naissances illégitimes et filles-mères à Lille au XVIIIᵉ siècle." *Revue d'histoire moderne et contemporaine* 17 (April–June 1970): 278–322.

———, ed. *La Desunion du couple sous l'ancien régime: L'Exemple du Nord.* Paris: Editions universitaires, 1975.

Lucas, Colin. "The Problem of the Midi in the French Revolution." *Transactions of the Royal Historical Society*, ser. 5, no. 28 (1978): 1–25.

McFarlane, Alan. *Marriage and Love in England: Modes of Reproduction 1300–1840.* Oxford: Basil Blackwell, 1986.

Magnan, Jean-Louis. *Le Notariat et la révolution française.* Montauban: Imprimerie Forestié, 1952.

Maillet, J. "De l'exclusion coutumière des filles dotées à la renonciation à succession future dans les coutumes de Toulouse et Bordeaux." *Revue historique du droit français et étranger*, ser. 4, no. 30 (1952): 514–545.

Malrieu, Victor. *Les Fêtes civiques à Montauban pendant la révolution.* Montauban: Imprimerie Besson, 1927.

———. "L'Honnête criminel: Deux Incidents au théâtre de Montauban." *Bulletin archéologique, historique et artistique de la Société Archéologique de Tarn et Garonne* 53 (1925): 109–111.

———. *L'Insurrection royaliste de l'an VII dans le Tarn et Garonne.* Montauban: Imprimerie Cooperative, Barrier et cie, 1922.

———. "Notes sur la navigation du Tarn en 1793." *Bulletin archéologique, historique et artistique de la Société Archéologique de Tarn et Garonne* 51 (1923): 75–76.

Mandrou, Robert, ed. *Histoire des protestants en France.* Toulouse: Edouard Privat, 1977.

Maninière, G. "Les Marchands d'étoffes de Toulouse à la fin du XVIIIᵉ siècle." *Annales du Midi* 60 (1958): 251–308.

Markovitch, Tihomir J. *Les Industries lainières de Colbert à la Révolution.* Geneva: Librairie Droz, 1976.

Mauzi, Robert. *L'Idée du bonheur dans la litterature et la pensée française au XVIIIᵉ siècle.* Paris: Armand Colin, 1960.

Maza, Sarah C. *Servants and Masters in Eighteenth-Century France: The Uses of Loyalty.* Princeton: Princeton University Press, 1983.

Medick, Hans, and David Warren Sabean, eds. *Interest and Emotion: Essays in the Study of the Family and Kinship.* Cambridge: Cambridge University Press, 1984.

Mendels, Franklin F. "La Composition du ménage paysan en France au XIXᵉ siècle: Une Analyse économique du mode de production domestique." *Annales. Economies, Sociétés, Civilisations* 33, no. 3 (July–August 1978): 780–802.

Merle, Louis. *La Métairie et l'évolution agraire de la Gâtine poitevine de la fin du moyen âge à la révolution.* Paris: SEVPEN, 1958.

Mitterauer, Michel, and Reinhard Sieder. *The European Family: Patriarchy to Part-*

nership from the Middle Ages to the Present. Trans. by Karla Oosterveen and Manfred Hörzinger. Chicago: University of Chicago Press, 1982.

Moch, Leslie Page, and Gary D. Stark, eds. *Essays on the Family and Historical Change.* College Station, Texas: Texas A & M University Press, University of Texas at Arlington, 1983.

Mousnier, Roland. *Les Institutions de la France sous la monarchie absolue.* Vol. 1: *Société et état.* Paris: Presses Universitaires de France, 1974.

Ombret, Antoine, René Tournon, and Mathieu Meras. *Montauban, cité drapière au XVIIIe siècle.* Montauban: Conseil Général du Tarn et Garonne, 1968.

Ourliac, Paul. "Le Droit privé dans les villes du Midi de la France." *Recueils de la Société Jean Bodin pour l'histoire comparative des institutions: La Ville* 8, no. 3 (1957): 125–134.

Ozment, Steven E. *When Fathers Ruled: Family Life in Reformation Europe.* Cambridge, Mass.: Harvard University Press, 1983.

Petit, Anne-Marie. "Mariages et contrats de mariages à Agen en 1785 et en 1786." *Annales du Midi* 72 (1960): 215–229.

Phillips, Roderick. *Family Breakdown in Late Eighteenth Century France: Divorce in Rouen, 1792–1803.* Oxford: Clarendon Press, 1980.

Pinède, Christiane. "L'Emigration dans le Sud-Ouest vers le milieu du xixe siècle." *Annales du Midi* 69 (1957): 237–251.

———. "Les Migrations temporaires en Quercy." *Revue géographique des Pyrénées et du Sud-Ouest* 27 (1956): 122–134.

———. "La Population du Quercy à la fin du xviiie siècle d'après les documents démographiques de la généralité de Montauban." *Actes du 82e Congrès National des Sociétés Savantes, Section d'Histoire Moderne et Contemporaine* (Bordeaux, 1957): 51–103.

Poisson, Jean-Paul. "La Recherche de l'endogamie dans le notariat. Un Example d'étude de contenue des annonces dans la presse professionnelle." *Actes du 107e Congrès National des Sociétés Savantes, Section d'Histoire Moderne et Contemporaine.* 2 vols. (Brest, 1982) 2: 355–367.

Poland, Burdett C. *French Protestants and the French Revolution: A Study in Church and State, Thought and Religion, 1685–1815.* Princeton: Princeton University Press, 1957.

Poussou, Jean-Pierre. *Bordeaux et le Sud-Ouest au XVIIIe siècle.* Paris: Editions de l'Ecole des Hautes Etudes en Sciences Sociales, 1983.

———. "Recherches sur l'immigration quercynoise à Bordeaux au milieu (1737–1789) et à la fin du xviiie siècle (1782–1786). *Actes du 23e Congrès d'Etudes Régionales de la Fédération des Sociétés Académiques et Savantes Languedoc-Pyrénées-Gascogne* (Figeac, 1967): 405–422.

Reddy, William M. *The Rise of the Market Culture: The Textile Trade and French Society, 1750–1900.* Cambridge: Cambridge University Press, 1984.

———. "The Textile Trade and the Language of the Crowd at Rouen, 1752–1871." *Past and Present* 74 (February 1977): 62–89.

Resnick, Daniel P. *The White Terror and the Political Reaction After Waterloo.* Cambridge, Mass.: Harvard University Press, 1966.

Ricalens, Henry. "Patrimoine et revenus d'un bourgeois de Moissac dans la seconde moitié du xviiie siècle." *Annales du Midi* 96 (1984): 385–399.

Ricalens, Henry. "Statut et revenus de métayers de Moissac au début du XVIIIe siècle." *Annales du Midi* 97 (1985): 39–51.

Richard, Guy. *Noblesse d'affaires au XVIIIe siècle*. Paris: Librairie Armand Colin, 1974.

Richard, Michel. *La Vie quotidienne des protestants sous l'ancien régime*. Paris: Hachette, 1966.

Rivals, Claude. *Midi toulousain et pyrénéen*. Collection Architecture rurale française. Paris: Berger-Levrault, 1979.

Roche, Daniel. *Le Peuple de Paris: Essai sur la culture populaire au XVIIIe siècle*. Paris: Aubier-Montaigne, 1981.

Rochette, Armand des. "Essai sur les preuves de noblesse reconnues dans le Sud-Ouest de la France de 1771 à 1789." *Actes du 10e Congrès d'Etudes Régionales de la Fédération des Sociétés Académiques et Savantes Languedoc-Pyrénées-Gascogne* (Montauban, 1954): 257–286.

______. "'Les Familles montaubanaises (Haut-Languedoc et Bas-Quercy) dans *l'Armorial Général de la France*, 1690–1710." 10 vols. N.d. Microfilm. Mormon Genealogical Library.

Romon, Christian. "Le Monde des pauvres à Paris au XVIIIe siècle." *Annales. Ecomonies, Sociétés, Civilisations* 37, no. 4 (July–August 1982): 729–763.

Root, Hilton Lewis. "Challenging the Seigneurie: Community and Contention on the Eve of the French Revolution." *Journal of Modern History* 57 (December 1985): 652–681.

Ross, Ellen. "Survival Networks: Women's Neighborhood Sharing in London Before World War I." *History Workshop Journal* 15 (Spring 1983): 4–27.

Roubin, Lucienne A. "Espace masculin, espace féminin en communauté provençale." *Annales. Economies, Sociétés, Civilisations* 25, no. 2 (March–April 1970): 537–560.

Schnapper, Bernard. *Le Remplacement militaire en France: Quelques aspects politiques, économiques et sociaux du recrutement au XIXe siècle*. Paris: SEVPEN, 1968.

Scott, William. *Terror and Repression in Revolutionary Marseilles*. New York: Harper and Row, 1973.

Segalen, Martine. "The Family Cycle and Household Structure: Five Generations in a French Village." *Journal of Family History* 2, no. 3 (Fall 1977): 223–236.

______. *Love and Power in the Peasant Family: Rural France in the Nineteenth Century*. Translated by Sarah Matthews. Chicago: Chicago University Press, 1983.

______. "Le Mariage et la femme dans les proverbes du Sud de la France." *Annales du Midi* 87, no. 123 (July–September 1975): 265–288.

Sentou, Jean. *La Fortune immobilière des Toulousains et la révolution française*. Commission d'historie économique et sociale de la révolution française, Mémoires et documents, no. 24. Paris: Bibliothèque Nationale, 1970.

______. *Fortunes et groupes sociaux à Toulouse sous la révolution 1789–1899: Essai d'histoire statistique*. Toulouse: Edouard Privat, 1969.

Sewell, William H., Jr. *Structure and Mobility: The Men and Women of Marseille, 1820–1870*. Cambridge: Cambridge University Press, 1985.

______. *Work and Revolution in France: The Language of Labor from the Old Regime to 1848*. Cambridge: Cambridge University Press, 1980.

Shaffer, John W. *Family and Farm: Agrarian Change and Household Organization in the Loire Valley, 1500–1900*. Albany: State University of New York Press, 1982.

Shammas, Carole, Marylynn Salmon, and Michel Dahlin. *Inheritance in America from Colonial Times to the Present*. New Brunswick: Rutgers University Press, 1987.

Sicard, Germain. "Les Contrats de mariage à Toulouse et dans la campagne toulousaine en 1812 et 1853." *Actes du 93ᵉ Congrès National des Sociétés Savantes, Section d'Histoire Moderne et Contemporaine*. 2 vols. (Toulouse, 1971) 1: 311–320.

Slavin, Morris. *The French Revolution in Miniature: Section Droits-de-l'Homme, 1789–1795*. Princeton: Princeton University Press, 1984.

Smith, Bonnie G. *Ladies of the Leisure Class: The Bourgeoises of Northern France in the Nineteenth Century*. Princeton: Princeton University Press, 1981.

Smith, Harvey. "Family and Class: The Household Economy of Languedoc Wine-growers, 1830–1870." *Journal of Family History* 9, no. 1 (Spring 1984): 64–87.

Smith, Richard M., ed. *Land, Kinship and Life-Cycle*. Cambridge: Cambridge University Press, 1984.

Sol, Eugène. "Les Bureaux de charité en Quercy à la fin de l'ancien régime." *Annales du Midi* 60 (1948): 260–284.

———. *Quercynois de la période révolutionnaire*. Paris: Edouard Champion, 1931.

———. *La Révolution en Quercy*. 4 vols. Paris: Picard, 1929–1932.

Sonenscher, Michael. *The Hatters of Eighteenth Century France*. Berkeley: University of California Press, 1987.

———. "Journeymen, the Courts and French Trade, 1781–1791." *Past and Present*, no. 114 (February 1987): 77–109.

Stone, Lawrence. *The Family, Sex and Marriage in England, 1500–1800*. London: Weidenfeld and Nicolson, 1977.

Strumingher, Laura. "The Artisan Family: Traditions and Transitions in Nineteenth Century Lyon." *Journal of Family History* 2, no. 3 (Fall 1977): 211–222.

Sussman, George D. *Selling Mothers' Milk: The Wet-Nurse Business in France, 1715–1914*. Urbana: University of Illinois Press, 1982.

Tarrade, Jean. *Le Commerce colonial de la France à la fin de l'ancien régime*. 2 vols. Publications de l'université de Poitiers, Lettres et sciences humaines no. 12. Paris: Presses universitaires de France, 1972.

Thomson, J.K.J. *Clermont-de-Lodève, 1633–1789: Fluctuations in the Prosperity of a Languedocian Cloth-Making Town*. Cambridge: Cambridge University Press, 1982.

Tilly, Louise A., and Joan W. Scott. *Women, Work and Family*. New York: Holt, Rinehart and Winston, 1978.

Tilly, Louise A., Joan W. Scott, and Miriam Cohen. "Women's Work and European Fertility Patterns." *Journal of Interdisciplinary History* 6 (Winter 1976): 447–476.

Timbal, Pierre. "La Succession testamentaire dans la coutume de Toulouse." *Annales de la faculté de droit d'Aix* 43 (1950): 283–306.

Toujas, René. "Les Conditions de vie des apprentis dans l'industrie drapière de Montauban au XVIIIᵉ siècle." *Actes du 106ᵉ Congrès National des Sociétés Savantes,*

Section d'Histoire Moderne et Contemporaine. 2 vols. (Perpignan, 1981) 2: 335–345.

Traer, James F. "The French Family Court." *History* 59, no. 196 (June 1974): 211–228.

————. *Marriage and the Family in Eighteenth Century France.* Ithaca: Cornell University Press, 1980.

Trénard, Louis "The Social Crisis in Lyons on the Eve of the French Revolution." Edited and translated by Jeffry Kaplow, *New Perspectives on the French Revolution.* New York: John Wiley, 1965, pp. 68–100.

Trumbach, Randolph. *The Rise of the Egalitarian Family: Aristocratic Kinship and Domestic Relations in Eighteenth-Century England.* New York: Academic Press, 1978.

Valmary, M. "Une Révolution montalbanaise: L'Affaire Sauriac en avril 1848." *Bulletin archéologique, historique et artistique de la Société Archéologique de Tarn et Garonne* 77 (1950): 18–33.

Valmary, Pierre. *Familles paysannes au XVIIIe siècle en Bas-Quercy: Étude Démographique.* Institut National d'Etudes Démographiques, Travaux et documents, cahier no. 45. Paris: Presses universitaires de France, 1965.

Viardi, Liana. "The Abolition of the Guilds During the French Revolution." *French Historical Studies* 15, no. 3 (Spring 1988): 704–717.

Wemyss, Alice. "Les Protestants du Midi pendant la révolution: À Propos d'un livre recent." *Annales du Midi* 69 (1957): 307–322.

Wheaton, Robert, and Tamara K. Hareven, eds. *Family and Sexuality in French History.* Philadelphia: University of Pennsylvania Press, 1980.

Wills, Antoinette. *Crime and Punishment in Revolutionary Paris.* Westport, Conn.: Greenwood Press, 1981.

Yver, Jean. *Egalité entre heritiers et exclusion des enfants dotés, essai de géographie coutumière.* Paris: Sirey, 1966.

Zonabend, Françoise. *The Enduring Memory: Time and History in a French Village.* Trans. Anthony Forster. Manchester: Manchester University Press, 1984.

Index